SERVICE ETIQUETTE

SERVICE
ETIQUETTE

SECOND EDITION

BY

CAPTAIN BROOKS J. HARRAL, U.S.N.

AND

ORETHA D. SWARTZ

REVISED BY

ORETHA D. SWARTZ

UNITED STATES NAVAL INSTITUTE, ANNAPOLIS

Foreword

This is an era of change. Never before in the world's history have changes come with such rapidity, nor with such sweeping finality. Nowhere is there a better understanding of this truth than in the military services, where new methods, new techniques, and new thoughts are commonplace; and, with each new day, there comes the realization that every step into the future takes us farther away from the past.

Yet, there is still the need for an unchanging, well-ordered plan of behavior, based on the experiences of the past, which can guide us in our personal, business, and social relations with our contemporaries as we work toward the future. *Service Etiquette*, first published in 1959, was designed to fill that need by combining the dictates of military tradition with the requirements of correct social usage in a workable, readable text, filled with information covering occasions which one might face during a military career.

Although the first edition of *Service Etiquette* was written primarily for the Navy, it soon gained wide acceptance among military men everywhere. This second edition, therefore, includes much new material concerning social usage unique to the Army, Air Force, Coast Guard, and Merchant Service, as well as to the Navy and Marine Corps. Reflecting a change in military life which is now accepted as a matter of course, the book also deals with the special considerations due to women in military service.

Despite these changes, the purpose of *Service Etiquette* remains unchanged: to encourage careful attention to proper manners and the punctilious courtesy traditional in service life.

WILLIAM R. SMEDBERG, III
Vice Admiral, U. S. Navy
Chief of Naval Personnel

Introduction

What is Etiquette? According to Webster, the word *etiquette* means: "The forms required by good breeding, social conventions, or prescribed by authority, to be observed in social or official life; the rules of decorum." Good manners are the rules of the game of life—the rules which you observe in your daily living with your fellow men. Good manners are more than a way of holding your fork, the proper words spoken in an introduction, or the correct form for going through a receiving line. These tools of etiquette are important, but there is more to being a well-bred person than the mechanics of good manners.

Good manners also mean kindness to others, respect for the other person's feelings, an acknowledgment of right and wrong, an awareness of someone—*anyone*—whom you meet in a hallway, on the street, or at a party. Good manners mean the consideration you grant someone as a person—not because he is important or of high rank, but because he is a human being. George Bernard Shaw expressed it this way, "The great secret . . . is not having bad manners or good manners or any other particular sort of manners, but having the same manner for all human souls . . . ."

And what is Service Etiquette? It is all these aspects of everyday good manners combined with the traditions and customs of the various branches of the Armed Forces. It has been the purpose of the authors to provide this combination of manners and military customs for the use of officers of the Armed Forces of the United States. The question may arise as to the necessity for such a work—a book of good manners and etiquette for an officer and a gentleman. The authors find several valid reasons for compiling such a work. They know that the American service officer is considered not only as a representative of his own service, but also of the United States government; they know he is judged not only by his professional ability, but also by his manners in his social and official life; they know that the American officer must acquire tact in his social and official relations not only when serving at home, but also when serving abroad.

Although this is a book for all officers of the Armed Forces of the United States, it was written especially for the young officers, for the midshipmen and cadets at the Service Academies, and for the young men and women in the various branches of the Reserve Officers Training Corps and the Officer Candidate and Officer Training Schools.

There is a close correlation between the lives of the young men in training at the Service Academies—with the differences mainly those of service regulations and traditions.

During Fourth Class year at the Academies, the "Plebe" at Annapolis and West Point, the "Doolie" at Colorado Springs, and the "Swab" at New London, will have limited social opportunities. This year is an indoctrination period in the highly specialized naval and military training which sets the pattern for his remaining years as an Upperclassman. However, he will be required to attend certain social functions, such as informals, and will be taught such amenities as how to go through a receiving line.

The Third Classman will have increased social opportunities, which will accelerate during his Second Class year. The Ring Dance is the highlight of this year: now he is on the threshold of his ultimate goal, graduation.

A midshipman or cadet comes into his own during First Class year. He is rewarded privileges befitting a junior officer and attends many social functions, frequently of a more formal nature. On air or sea cruises, both at home and in foreign ports, he is "accepted" in Officers' Country. Graduation day is the most important day of his four years at the Academy. Now he is entering a new life in the service of his choice; perhaps he is also entering the wide sea of matrimony. Now, he is on his own.

The midshipman or cadet will find a marked difference in many social customs in the transition from civilian to military life. Upon graduation from the Academies there will be the necessity for blending the civilian and military social customs, as his way of life will be a part of both. The good manners which he should know before, during, and after attending the Academy are fully explained in the following chapters of this book.

To you, the prospective new officer—the midshipmen and cadets of the Service Academies, the ROTC, OCS, and OTS students of each service, the cadets of the Merchant Marine Academies, all students of military schools—it is to you that this book is dedicated.

Preface to the Second Edition

The purpose of revising this book has been to widen the scope of official and social customs to include those for officers of all the Armed Forces, thus making the book of equal value to each service.

In the Acknowledgements to the First Edition, the authors expressed their appreciation for the assistance and cooperation they received when they were compiling information for that edition. I should like to add to that list my sources of information for the Second Edition and to express my gratitude for the interest which was shown and for the aid which I received.

Many official service publications were used as source material, furnished mainly by the Office or Division of Information of the Departments of the Army, Navy, and Air Force, and by the Marine Corps Headquarters, the Marine Corps Schools, and the Coast Guard Headquarters. Thanks are extended to the heads and staff members of these offices (whose rank and duty may have changed in the interval):

Lieut. Colonel L. Gordon Hill, Jr., U. S. Army, Chief, Magazine and Book Branch, Department of the Army; Lieut. Commander F. A. Prehn, U. S. Navy, and Lieut. Commander D. M. Cooney, U. S. Navy, of the Magazine and Book Branch, Office of Information, Department of the Navy; Lieut. Colonel P. N. Pierce, U. S. Marine Corps, Head, Media Branch, Division of Information, Headquarters U. S. Marine Corps; Major James F. Sunderman, U. S. Air Force, Chief, Magazine and Book Branch, Department of the Air Force; Major Gene Guerney, U. S. Air Force, Deputy Chief, Magazine and Book Branch, Department of the Air Force; Captain Joseph A. Skiera, U. S. Air Force, Magazine and Book Branch, Department of the Air Force; and Hyman R. Kaplan, Public Information Division, U. S. Coast Guard.

Sincere appreciation is extended to the Defense Advisory Committee on Women in the Services (DACOWITS) at the Pentagon, of which Lieut. Colonel Kathryn J. Royster, U. S. Army, was director.

Many thanks are given to the directors of the women's services and members of their staffs for their co-operation in the inclusion of material concerning the official and social customs of women in their branches of the services. They include:

Captain Winifred Q. Collins, U. S. Navy, Director of the WAVES, and Commander Rita Lenihan, U. S. Navy, Deputy to Director of the WAVES;

Colonel Margaret M. Henderson, U. S. Marine Corps, Director of Women Marines; Colonel Elizabeth Ray, U. S. Air Force, Director, Women in the Air Force (WAF); Lieut. Colonel Catherine H. Foster, U. S. Army, Director, U. S. Women's Army Corps (WAC).

I express thanks also to Commander Elizabeth S. Harrison, U. S. Navy, and members of the staff of the U. S. Naval School, Officer, Women, U. S. Naval Base, Newport, Rhode Island; Lieut. Commander Martha E. Michaels, U. S. Navy; and Lieutenant Alice V. Bradford, U. S. Navy.

Thanks are particularly extended to Captain William B. Ellis, U. S. Coast Guard, Commandant of Cadets, U. S. Coast Guard Academy; Major Gordon J. Duquemin, U. S. Army, Special Activities Officer, U. S. Military Academy; Major Gordon P. Culver, Special Assistant to the Superintendent, U. S. Air Force Academy; and Captain James W. Kelly, CHC, U. S. Navy, Senior Chaplain, U. S. Naval Academy.

I thank Captain Robert Louis Wetzel, U. S. Army, Aid to the Superintendent, U. S. Military Academy; Major Maurice D. Roush, U. S. Army; Captain Roger W. McLain, U. S. Air Force; Captain Robert W. Clark, U. S. Navy; Commander James K. Jobe, U. S. Navy; Lieut. Colonel J. G. Juett, U. S. Marine Corps, Marine Corps Educational Center, Marine Corps Schools; Major Ben A. Moore, Jr., U. S. Marine Corps; and James R. Foresman, Bureau of Naval Personnel, Department of the Navy.

The warmest thanks go to Mrs. John F. Holland, Cadet Hostess, U. S. Military Academy; Mrs. James G. Marshall, Midshipman Hostess, U. S. Naval Academy; Mrs. William E. Sinton, Cadet Hostess, U. S. Coast Guard Academy; Mrs. Edward O. McComas, Cadet Hostess, U. S. Air Force Academy; and Miss Katharine L. Hill, Social Scretary to the Superintendent, U. S. Naval Academy.

Sincere appreciation is now extended to Rear Admiral Bruce McCandless, U. S. Navy (Ret.), for his very valuable work in reviewing the original manuscript in 1959. As he has been unable to participate in the present revision, he has requested that his name be removed as a co-author of the book.

ORETHA D. SWARTZ

Annapolis, Maryland
6 February 1963

Acknowledgments to the First Edition

Grateful acknowledgments of the authors are extended to those individuals whose kind cooperation has made the preparation of this book possible. Special acknowledgments are also made for valuable aid in compiling the material, to various branches of the Armed Services and to officials of state and civilian organizations.

Much of the material on calling cards, invitations, seating arrangements and toasts has been taken from the Navy's official book on *Social Usage and Protocol*, with the permission of the Director of Naval Intelligence, Rear Admiral Laurence H. Frost. This handbook has been issued for a number of years by the Office of Naval Intelligence for the guidance of naval officers serving at United States Embassies abroad. Miss Ruth Gibson Tarrant, the daughter and granddaughter of well-known flag officers, and herself a commander in the Naval Reserve, has been responsible for compiling this official publication which is used by all admirals' staffs as a protocol reference.

Considerable material on life in the wardroom has been taken from the Navy's guidebook, *The Wardroom*, compiled for officers of the Amphibious Force, U. S. Atlantic Fleet, under the direction of Vice Admiral F. G. Fahrion.

Thanks are particularly extended to the following officers of the Administrative and Executive Departments, U. S. Naval Academy (whose official rank and/or duty may have changed since publication of this book), for assistance in checking the facts:

Captain Allen M. Shinn, Commandant of Midshipmen; Captain James Lloyd Abbot, Jr., Commander David L. G. King, Commander Walter D. McCord, Jr., Commander Isaac C. Kidd, Jr., and Lieut. Commander Alan N. Davidson.

Sincere thanks are rendered to Brigadier General Robert M. Stillman, former Commandant of Cadets, U. S. Air Force Academy; Brigadier General R. D. Salmon, Commandant, U. S. Marine Corps Schools, and Major Young A. Tucker, U. S. Military Academy.

Also to Captain Fred D. Bennett, Senior Chaplain, Naval Academy Chapel; Captain A. C. J. Sabalot (retired), former Naval Attaché to France; Colonel C. W. Harrison, head, Historical Branch, G-3 (Marine Corps); Colonel J. L. Mueller, Lieut. Colonel C. H. Welch and Major John Greenwood (Marine Corps); Major John Schlegl (Air Force), and Commander Winston L. Adair.

Also to Captain Bernard Baruch, Jr., USNR, for facts about the Naval Reserve officer; Mr. Clement E. Conger, Deputy Chief of Protocol, Department of State; Mr. John P. English of the U. S. Golf Association; Mr. R. W. Gieves of Gieves, Ltd.; Mr. H. E. Harding and Mr. Frank Overcarsh of the American Express Company; Mr. Duncan Hines and Mr. Roy L. Park, president of the Duncan Hines Institute; Mr. A. J. Keenan of A. G. Spalding and Brothers; Dean Howard Bagnall Meek, School of Hotel Administration, Cornell University, and Mr. Wesley M. Oler, Director of Public Relations, General Motors Export Corporation.

Our appreciation is extended to the officers and instructors of the Department of English, History, and Government, U. S. Naval Academy; the chairmen and members of the Naval Academy Hop Committees, 1956–58; and the hostesses, Bancroft Hall, U. S. Naval Academy.

In addition, thanks are extended to the following for their advice: Rear Admiral and Mrs. Arthur A. Ageton, Mrs. Harry A. Baldridge, Mrs. Walter F. Boone, Mrs. Charles A. Buchanan, Mrs. Robert B. Carney, Professor Allen Blow Cook, Mrs. Alan N. Davidson, Mrs. John F. Davidson, Admiral and Mrs. Laurence T. DuBose, Mrs. Frank W. Fenno, Mrs. Frank Jack Fletcher, Mrs. Brooks J. Harral, Professor William W. Jeffries, Mrs. Robert T. S. Keith, Mrs. Isaac C. Kidd, Jr., Mrs. Ruthven E. Libby, Mrs. John S. McCain, Jr., Captain John G. McCutcheon, Commander Robert K. Moxon, Medical Corps, Mrs. Albert G. Mumma, Dr. Leone L. Orner, Major General and Mrs. Donald R. Ostrander, Mrs. Henry M. Robert, Jr., Mrs. Allen M. Shinn, Mrs. Morton Sunderland, Associate Professor Raymond H. Swartz, Mrs. Joseph K. Taussig, Jr., Mrs. J. M. P. Wright, and Captain and Mrs. John D. Zimmerman.

CONTENTS

xiii

SECTION VI

EASY CONVERSATION

SECTION VII

ON YOUR OWN

SECTION VIII

STRICTLY SERVICE

SECTION IX

PERSONAL MATTERS IN EVERYDAY LIFE

SERVICE ETIQUETTE

MANNERS AND DRESS

*Good breeding is the result of much good
sense, some good nature, and a little self-denial
for the sake of others, and with view
to obtain the same indulgence from them.*
—Chesterfield

CHAPTERS

CHAPTER 1

Everyday Good Manners— In Uniform and Out

GOOD GROOMING

A good first appearance depends to a great extent upon your personal grooming. A midshipman or cadet is trained during his years at the Academies or in the ROTC units to take care of his gear and his person—and this training should be observed for the rest of his life.

A first appearance may be one of the most important events of your life. It is impossible to foresee which day, which hour, may be that most important event, or what casual meeting may lead to your being accepted—or refused—by a person of value to your career.

It is important that you keep your uniform, cap cover, and gloves in neat and clean condition; your shoes must be shined, and your linens fresh and in good repair. Your civilian clothes should be conservative—not too gaudy or extreme in color and design.

For military women, extreme care in grooming and dress is essential. Eccentricities in hair styling, nail polish, hair ornaments, and jewelry are not acceptable. Boyish haircuts are not worn. Back hair may touch but not fall below the collar, and no hair shall show under the front brim of the uniform hat.

ON TIME!

One of the most valuable habits which you can acquire is that of being on time. All officers are trained to be punctual in their official duties—and this habit should not be laid aside in your daily or social life. It is said that promptness and responsibility go hand in hand—therefore a habitual lack of punctuality must be considered irresponsibility.

At official or state occasions, you are expected to be on time. When royalty, very high ranking officers, or dignitaries of state are guests at a luncheon or dinner, you must arrive before they do; but you will not leave before they do.

While you are not expected to be late at a dinner party, neither should you arrive before the hour named in the invitation and catch your hosts unprepared. It is permissible to arrive up to 10 minutes after the stated time, but no later.

There may be times when you are late through no fault of your own—

when the plane is late, when the car has a flat tire, or when fog closes in and your boat cannot leave the ship.

When you are unavoidably late at a dinner and the guests have already gone into the dining room, you should go directly to the hostess and briefly apologize; then take your seat at the table. For reasons of her own, the hostess may not be able to wait more than 15 to 30 minutes.

When a woman is late, she should also briefly apologize to the hostess; then take her place at the table. If she is your dinner partner, you should rise and assist with her chair. The hostess does not rise; thus, other men guests at the table do not rise—which would further embarrass the late guest and also inconvenience the other seated guests.

While a woman is usually excused for keeping you waiting, you yourself must always be on time and never keep her waiting.

You should never deliberately be late at a party in order not to be the first guest to arrive. This is inconsiderate to the hosts and does *not* show ultra-sophistication on your part.

At an afternoon reception, at-home, or cocktail party, you may arrive at any time after the first hour named in the invitation, but not later than about a half hour before the last hour indicated in the invitation.

When you are a guest at a family dinner, be on time. Older children may join the family group at the table, and they are invariably hungry and impatient to be fed. Most hosts feed small children early and have them squared away before guests arrive. In this case, the dinner hour is a little later than usual.

Of course, a host and hostess are *never* late.

TIME TO GO?

There are no set regulations that will tell you exactly when it's time to leave after a party, but many a weary host and hostess wish there were. The aim of any host is to ensure that guests enjoy the occasion—but sometimes a guest exceeds his host's hospitality.

In the services, officers of high rank are frequently the busiest persons on the base or station. Other than their official responsibilities, senior officers have many social, community, and station obligations. Sometimes, such an officer and his wife make only a token appearance at a reception, tea, or cocktail party.

If you are a junior officer at an official or important social function, you do not leave until after the guest of honor or the high ranking guest departs. This person may leave within 30 minutes after a dinner, and then you may also leave. The ranking lady always makes the first move to leave.

Customarily, the high-ranking guest will stay from 30 to 45 minutes after dinner, and should stay no longer than an hour afterwards. If you are the high-ranking guest, always remember that no one can properly leave until you do—and another guest may have a real reason to leave on time. Altogether, when nothing has been planned afterwards, the time involved at a formal dinner is between three and three and a half hours.

When to leave after an official luncheon is determined by the station duty of the host and his guests, and upon the time schedule and what is planned for the visiting dignitary. Customarily, guests stay about half an hour after luncheon. Altogether, the time involved is about an hour and a half.

At an afternoon reception, at-home, cocktail party, or tea, you should stay no less than 20 minutes, but you should not stay uncomfortably close to the probable dinner hour of your hosts.

At an evening reception, etc., you will probably stay about 45 minutes, but you will possibly stay longer at a smaller reception or cocktail party—say an hour or an hour and a half.

A young couple making a call on a senior couple usually stay 15 to 20 minutes. Although the husband or wife—or single officer—must not be obvious in watching the time, watch it one must. A senior officer and his wife may have other callers, and there are many demands on their time.

Should you, a junior officer, make a call and should a senior officer and his wife also call, you will leave at the proper time. There is no discourtesy in your leaving before the senior officer.

A midshipman or cadet should not form the habit of calling at all hours and staying for hours. If the host invites you to his quarters or home and insists that you stay on for TV, badminton, tennis, etc., you may feel free to do so. When you call unannounced and stay too long, you may be upsetting plans made by your host and hostess. Half an hour is long enough to stay, customarily.

At any party, do *not* be the last person to leave.

RANK TERMINOLOGY

In each service, "junior officer" denotes an officer of less or junior rank. In the Navy, "junior officer" is affixed to others of definite grades, which compare in the other Services to "company grade officer."

In the Navy and Coast Guard, *junior officers* are those of the grades of ensign, lieutenant, junior grade (j.g.), lieutenant, and lieutenant commander; *senior officers* are of the grades of commander, captain, and above; *flag officers* are of the grades of commodore (wartime or retired rank), rear admiral, vice admiral, and admiral.

In the Army, Air Force, and Marine Corps, *company grade officers* are those of the grades of second lieutenant, first lieutenant, and captain; *field grade officers* are those of the grades of major, lieutenant colonel, and colonel; *general officers* are of the grades of brigadier general, major general, lieutenant general, and general.

OFFICIAL MANNERS

As every young officer knows, when a junior reports to the office of a senior, he announces himself either through the orderly or by knocking. He waits until told to enter; then he uncovers, holding his cap in his right hand by the visor, and goes up to the officer or within a few paces of the officer's desk. He precedes his report or request by announcing, "Lieutenant John Doe, Sir." When the business has been terminated, he leaves promptly.

If you are the junior officer, you will call the senior by his title and name, "Colonel Jones," rather than by the impersonal "Sir." On board ship or in any naval organization there is only one "Captain" (the regularly assigned commanding officer) who is addressed as "Captain," regardless of his actual rank, without adding his name.

Juniors reporting to senior women officers announce themselves in the same way as they would to senior male officers.

"Miss" or "Mrs." may be used for junior or company grade officers (lieutenant commander and down in the Naval Service, and captain and down in the Army, Marine Corps, and Air Force). "Ma'am" is used in place of "Sir," and "Yes, Captain," or "Yes, Miss Smith" in lieu of "Yes Ma'am."

You should always be careful not to obtrude your greeting upon your senior. For instance, if the senior is engaged in conversation, working on a chart, or concentrating on some problem, he might be distracted by the necessity of replying to the greeting.

Even though you, the junior, are on a first-name basis with a senior officer, you do not call him or her by the first name during official occasions.

Always remember that a senior sends his *compliments* to a junior; the junior sends his *respects*. In written correspondence the senior may "call" attention, but the junior may only "invite" it.

EVERYDAY MANNERS

By the time you have been a cadet or midshipman, ROTC or OCS student for a few weeks, your practice of showing respect to military seniors will be automatic. Such things as saying "Sir," or "Ma'am" or "Miss," rising when spoken to, removing your hat indoors when you meet an officer— all these and many more fine points become instinctive.

But what about your courtesy to non-military seniors and to your contemporaries? Courtesy and consideration are not to be turned on and off because of rank. Generally speaking, the older the person, the more respect you show him. Therefore, age is an acceptable yardstick, since civilians do not wear such convenient things as insignia of rank.

Undue familiarity from you, a junior, will not be appreciated by a doctor, lawyer, or college president any more than it will be tolerated by an officer of rank considerably higher than your own.

HATS ON—AND OFF

In uniform, it is a custom of the Naval Service that you do not raise your cap when greeting a man or woman in passing out-of-doors. Instead, you give a hand salute. When greeting and passing a woman, a man may accompany the hand salute with a slight bow, but the bow is not necessary. You do not uncover when you are introduced to a woman out-of-doors, and you may salute again when leaving.

In the Army or Air Force, you may salute or raise your hat or cap when introduced to a person out-of-doors. If a lady engages you in conversation, you remove your hat and keep it off while talking with her. If the conversation is prolonged for several minutes, or if it is raining, you replace your hat or cap.

Indoors, you generally take off your hat or cap as you would when in civilian dress. However, although a civilian generally does not remove his hat in an elevator unless leaving his hat on would make him conspicuous, the military man should apply the rule in reverse: he should remove his hat or cap in an elevator unless removing it would make him conspicuous.

Aboard ship, junior officers should uncover when passing through the captain's or admiral's country, except when in evening dress uniform or wearing sword.

Male officers should remove their caps on entering sick bay and when passing through messing compartments while meals are in progress.

In civilian dress, it is easy for an officer to forget to take off his hat as custom demands in civilian life, so make a habit of not forgetting. You take off your hat when you stop to talk, or are introduced, to a woman out-of-doors, and leave it off unless the weather is bad.

You must take off your hat in a place of worship, except in Orthodox Jewish synagogues and in some conservative synagogues; you take it off whenever you pray or witness a religious ceremony, including a burial or outdoor wedding, or a dedication.

You remove your hat indoors except in stores, lobbies, corridors, and in such public buildings as a railroad station, post office, bank, etc. Your hat is safer on your head in a crowded elevator than when held in front of you, but you should take it off in hotel or apartment elevators.

Inside an office building leave your hat on—but take it off when entering an office. If you stop to ask directions of the receptionist, you should touch your hat. Touching your hat means touching the crown of a soft hat or the brim of a stiff one.

Your hat may be lifted momentarily when saying *hello, good-bye, thank you, excuse me,* etc. You grasp the front crown of a soft hat or the brim of a stiff one, then lift it slightly up and forward as you bow your head or smile.

A young man lifts his hat to an older man, and a man of any age lifts his hat in respect to a dignitary or an elderly gentleman. An abbreviated hat tip, something of an informal salute, is always a friendly gesture from one man to another.

You may check your hat before entering a public or club dining room, and it may be checked in a theater or placed in the rack under your seat.

Women in uniform always wear hats or caps out-of-doors; when they are passengers in automobiles, taxis, busses, trains, ferries, and aircraft; and when they are in naval ships.

Indoors, hats are generally worn at luncheons and in church. You remain covered in such public areas as hotels and department stores. You never carry your hat in your hand.

At formal official ceremonies, you cover indoors if military men remain covered, and you uncover if they uncover. However, at some very formal official ceremonies, such as a military graduation, memorial service, or invocation, at which military men uncover during the ceremony, you remain covered.

You uncover in the dining rooms and cocktail lounges of Officers' Clubs. It is optional to uncover when making social calls and when making a long trip in a bus, train, plane, etc. Hats are worn or removed in conformance with local custom when meeting the commanding officer in his office and when visiting in hospitals and other military buildings.

In civilian dress, you comply with customs established by civilian women: at a morning function, such as a coffee or brunch, you do not wear a hat and gloves, unless it is held at an Officers' Club or hotel.

From noon until 6 P.M., you should wear a hat and gloves (unless you are the hostess in you own home) at luncheons, receptions, teas, and cocktail parties.

BOWING

A man should return any bow directed to him—on the street, in a bus, or across the room. When you are being introduced to a woman, you may bow slightly while shaking hands.

A bow is a slight inclination of your body from the waist up, feet together. A deep bow expresses great respect. A too-deep bow is strictly a continental custom and is not customary in the United States.

When you are seated at the table and it is awkward or impossible to arise without disturbing others around you, you may half-rise and give a slight bow. But do not remain seated and bow, unless to someone junior to you. Whenever you bow, do not give the effect of bobbing your head.

SALUTING IN CIVILIAN DRESS

As all servicemen and servicewomen know, in uniform you salute whenever the national anthem is played, the flag is passing in parade or in a review, or the flag is hoisted or lowered.

Out of uniform, you (and any male civilian) will stand at attention, remove your hat with your right hand, place the hat over your heart—but no higher than shoulder level—or if you are uncovered, then you will stand at attention.

When you are with a woman who is in civilian dress, she should stand quietly as she faces the flag and/or the direction of the music.

If wearing a hat or a cap, as you step on the quarterdeck of a ship, you face aft and salute the national ensign and then salute the officer-of-the-deck. On leaving a ship, the procedure is reversed.

Out of uniform, you do not return a salute by a uniformed man or woman, but you will give a verbal greeting. For example, at a base or post gate you would return a guard's salute by saying, "Good morning," etc.

GLOVES

Gloves are worn out-of-doors upon certain occasions whenever a hat is worn. When in uniform, you will wear or carry gloves as prescribed. If you should be introduced outdoors, you may remove your right glove—if you have time. It is better to shake hands with your gloves on than to keep a person waiting—and you need not apologize for leaving them on.

Remove your gloves indoors except when you are ushering at a wedding or funeral, or have official guard duty. When you are introduced to someone during any of these occasions you do not take off your glove.

At an Academy hop or dance, midshipmen and cadets wear white gloves when calling for their young ladies, but remove them with their hats upon arrival at the fete. Ladies in the receiving line, as well as young ladies going through the line, wear long white gloves.

Men wear white gloves at a formal ball, such as a debutante cotillion, and: a, leave them on throughout the receiving line and dance, removing them only when eating or smoking; or b, wear them through the receiving line and then remove them.

Women wear gloves when going through the line at a reception—except when shaking hands with a head of state or a church dignitary, when the right glove is removed. Afterwards, gloves are removed.

Unless in working uniform, military women wear gloves when out-of-doors. In general, gloves should be worn when covered. Exceptions are: when eating or drinking, driving an automobile, visiting an office, traveling in short-haul carriers, or shopping. You wear white gloves when going through a receiving line.

Although a hostess will not wear white gloves when receiving guests at a reception in her own home, she may wear them (without a hat) when in a receiving line at a hotel or Officer's Club.

YOUR HANDS, AND HANDSHAKE

Men will shake hands upon being introduced or saying good-bye to other men—with the senior making the first move. It is unforgivable not to accept a proffered hand. You wait until a woman offers her hand before extending yours. If you are seated, rise to your feet when introduced to anyone, and upon the departure of anyone.

A good handshake is at elbow level. You should avoid a handclasp that crushes or is too limp. Do not hold another's hand too long, or pump it up and down. A slight bow usually accompanies a handshake.

As mentioned elsewhere, you remove your right glove before shaking hands with anyone—if you have time. And of course, when shaking hands, you always look the person you are greeting in the eye.

Kissing a woman's hand is not a customary social gesture in the United States. It is absurd for you to make a practice of it. However, if a continental woman should extend her hand to be kissed, here is the correct technique. You take her hand lightly in yours, then with a slight bow over her hand, merely touch your lips to the back of her hand. It is improper to kiss the hand of an unmarried woman unless she is *of a certain age.*

When women shake hands, a younger woman customarily waits for an older or high ranking woman to extend her hand in greeting first. The younger woman will rise when introduced to the wife of a senior officer or a much older woman, and will remain standing until that woman is seated. A woman need not rise for an introduction to a contemporary.

You hands should be in your lap when you are not eating at the dining table. Avoid awkward positions with your hands at all times—such as locking them behind your head, thrusting them in your suit pockets in unattractive bulges, or standing with clasped hands behind your back or pressed together steeplewise in front.

To stroke your chin, pick at your ears or head, or to drum on a table or chair shows a lack of poise. When you are walking or standing, your hands should be in a relaxed position at your sides.

Midshipmen and cadets do not hold hands or link arms with girls in public; any ostentatious show of affection indicates a lack of tact and proper breeding.

When dancing, your left or leading hand should hold the woman's lightly and naturally. Your right or holding hand should be placed firmly yet easily just above her waist.

When you wish to help a woman down from a bus or train, etc., extend you hand to her, palm up. Don't put your hand under her arm.

Women in uniform conform with military etiquette; in civilian dress, you conform with civilian etiquette on social occasions. Gloves are not removed for handshakes.

YOUR ARMS

A man should offer a woman his arm only to give assistance when needed, or as an escort at a formal dinner, or as an usher at a wedding. You never grasp or take hold of the woman's arm—unless an accident is to be avoided. She will take your arm—you do not take hers.

You do not offer your arm in the daytime unless a woman needs help over rough ground, in a crowd, or when you assist an elderly or invalid man or woman. You do not offer your arm to a woman at luncheon.

When you offer your right arm at a formal dinner, bend your arm slightly at the elbow with your forearm parallel to the floor. Your partner will hold your arm lightly, but not hang onto it. When a guest at a wedding, a woman customarily takes the usher's right arm. A man does not take an usher's arm at a wedding unless he is elderly or an invalid.

Military women, either in uniform or civilian dress, do not hang on a man's proffered arm. Instead, you may touch his arm lightly, and release it immediately after the potential hazard has passed.

ON YOUR FEET

Men should stand whenever a woman enters a room, and should remain standing until she sits down. You again rise to your feet upon her departure from the room.

However, common sense will dictate how long you should remain standing when a woman thoughtlessly continues to stand and keeps all the men on their feet. When a woman prefers to remain standing with a group, you may return to your own group and sit down.

You are not expected to rise to your feet every time a hostess re-enters or leaves a room. And you need not rise to your feet at a business or organization meeting when a woman arrives late and disturbs the business proceedings. You stand when an elderly or high-ranking man enters the room.

You stand up—not jump up—for introductions, greetings, farewells, and whenever a person wants to pass in front of you at the movies, football game—or any place where someone must pass in front of you and you do not want your feet stepped on.

When a woman, senior officer, dignitary, or elderly person comes to your table in a restaurant, you should rise to your feet. When it is very difficult to stand at a crowded table, a half-standing gesture is better than upsetting something on the table or annoying others.

A junior servicewoman will stand when introduced to a senior—male or female—or when the senior enters the room. When in civilian dress at social functions, you conform to civilian etiquette: the junior woman will stand when introduced to an elderly lady or a very prominent personage.

It is not necessary in this modern age of equality among the sexes for a man to offer his seat in a bus or subway to a strange woman, but he may if he chooses to—and a serviceman usually chooses to do so. When a woman, or man, is elderly, disabled, burdened, or obviously tired, you will want to give her, or him, your seat.

When you rise to leave a party, say "good-bye," and then do not continue in conversation or otherwise dawdle and delay. Just—go.

WALKING OUTDOORS

When a man is walking with a woman outdoors, he walks on the curb side or on her left side, if there is no curb. The place of honor is always on the right. When walking with two women, he walks to their left or curb side. He may walk between them only when crossing the street or if both ladies are elderly or are in poor health and need assistance. When abroad, learn the local custom and follow it.

When two men are walking together, the junior always walks on the left of the senior, except when they are pacing to and fro, and then positions are not exchanged. When two or more men in uniform are walking together, they keep in step, with the senior setting the pace.

When passing a senior approaching from the opposite direction, you salute well in advance. When overtaking a senior, you pass to the left if possible (otherwise to the right), salute and say, "By your leave, Sir," just before coming abreast.

A servicewoman will follow these rules and defer to seniors, unless a senior indicates otherwise. The senior may prefer to walk on the left or curb side himself.

OPENING DOORS

When a man is escorting a woman, he will hold any door open; then he will follow her through and close the door. If she gets to the door first and opens it, do not make an issue of it, but hold the door for her to pass through.

You may start a revolving door for a woman or a male senior to pass through. You may precede a woman through any door that opens onto a dark street or leads down steep stairs.

A junior officer, or younger man or woman, opens a door for his or her senior. Junior officers stand aside for seniors to pass through doors, then follow.

To be militarily proper, upon official occasions or in his office, the senior male officer would not hold the door open for the junior woman officer, nor would he follow her through the door.

WHO GOES FIRST?

When you are with a woman, she does—except:

- When your assistance is needed, such as when she is stepping down from a bus or train.
- When there is no waiter to precede you to a table in a restaurant, or no usher at the theater or movies.
- In a crowd, when you will clear the way.
- When going down the White House receiving line. It is the title that takes precedence.
- At official occasions the senior male officer precedes a junior woman officer.

COURTESY IN BOATS, CARS, AND AIRCRAFT

The procedure for getting in and out of a boat, car, or aircraft is similar: normally, the senior officer will enter last, and the junior will enter first. This procedure may be reversed in entering a car at a left-hand curb. Then the senior may enter first, in order that he may sit to the right without stumbling over juniors who are seated to the left. Seniors are always accorded the most desirable seats. When three persons are in the back seat, the junior is in the middle.

In a boat, the junior officer sits forward, with the senior sitting aft. In a car, the junior sits on the left, the senior on the right. In cases of full cars, the senior officers sit in the back seat and the juniors sit in the front.

In getting out of the boat, car, or aircraft, the order is reversed: the senior officer disembarks first, and the junior last. However, if a car draws up to a left-hand curb, it may be more appropriate for the junior to step out first. In an aircraft, if the senior officer is engaged in flying the plane, the disembarkation procedure applies only among the passengers.

When you travel aboard the personal aircraft of a high ranking senior—for example, the aircraft of a flag or general officer—unless instructed otherwise, you should be aboard in a designated seat before the senior arrives at the aircraft. You should also remain in your seat until after he leaves leaves the plane at its destination.

CUSTOMS IN AIRCRAFT

Air Force customs while traveling in military aircraft include:

1. Passengers are subject to the orders of the first pilot or airplane commander, regardless of rank, seniority, or service.

2. Dependents are loaded and unloaded after dignitaries, but before officers, regardless of rank.

3. An aircraft with general and/or flag officers aboard is marked with a detachable plate carrying stars appropriate to the highest rank aboard.

4. Passengers do not enter the flight deck or pilot's compartment unless invited to do so.

5. All safety regulations must be observed, including no smoking on take-off and landing, and during flight, if so announced. Parachute rules must always be observed.

6. Flights are decided by weather conditions; thus, the pilot's decision to fly or not to fly is never questioned.

IN CIVILIAN LIFE

It is customary for a younger man to follow an older man into any vehicle— boat, car, or aircraft—and to sit where you will least inconvenience him.

When accompanying women in a car, you should be the first to get out. You should hold the car door open, assist the woman out, then close the door. You should be the last person to get in the car and you should close the door. On official or formal occasions the woman is customarily seated at your right.

When you are driving the car, you should, if possible, get out, walk around the car and open the door for any women or older person. If it is not possible for you to get out, you may excuse yourself and reach across and open the door for your guest.

When you are the driver and a doorman opens the car door, the woman will get out first. When you are passengers in a car or taxi and not in city traffic, you get out first—even if she is closer to the door than you—and then you walk around the car and open the door for her. In traffic, whoever is closest to the door on the safe side gets out first.

MANNERS AT THE WHEEL

Any serviceman who has not driven for some time—for instance, a naval officer who has been at sea for many months, a midshipman or cadet— should be slow to get behind the wheel of a car and "step on it." Without realizing it, his judgment behind the wheel may be off—regardless of the fact that he is a qualified driver with his driver's license in perfect order.

When driving a car be considerate of others on the road. It is inconsiderate to stop suddenly in the middle of the street to pick up a friend or to talk with him when it is just as easy to pull over to the curb. It is extremely dangerous to make a game of passing other cars at a high rate of speed— even though your are in a hurry to get some place.

On dates, it is good manners to go to the door of your date's house and properly call for the young lady rather than blasting the night or day by blowing the horn. Too-loud and too-long horn blowing is ear-shattering to others as well as conspicuously bad manners on your part.

RIDING IN TAXIS

When escorting a woman, you should give the directions to the driver and pay the taxi fare. If you are not accompanying her to her destination, ask the driver what the amount will be and pay him, not the woman. You also pay the driver's tip along with his charge.

When you share a taxi with a woman member of the Armed Forces or a business woman, she will usually wish to pay for her share of the fare. If she gets out first, she will pay her share to that point, plus her share of the tip. If she shows no inclination to pay for her share, there is nothing for you to do as a gentleman but pay it.

You do not ask a woman unknown to you to share a taxi, but if you have a slight acquaintance and if she is going your way, you may offer to share the taxi. In case of bad weather or at a rush hour, a strange woman may ask if she can share your taxi—and you may accept or refuse as the occasion demands. When you have an important schedule to keep, you should drive there first.

Two or more men (or two or more women) may share a taxi fare. If one person insists upon paying, you may agree and say, "Next time it's mine." Then try to be sure that there is a next time.

Taxi tips vary, but usually they are 10 or 15 per cent of the bill. Do not tip less than 10 cents.

SEATING A WOMAN

A man will assist the woman to his right with her chair when she sits down at the dining table, and when she rises. The chair is pulled back as she steps into place from the left; then, you push the chair under her as she bends to sit down. When she rises from the table, you should draw the chair back without jerking it.

Although it seems easier for a woman to sit down from the left, there is no established rule to this effect. You should be alert to note from which side the ladies nearest you are being seated by their dinner partners, and then, to avoid confusion, seat your own dinner partner accordingly. If you are the host, you will assist the lady at your right; if you are seated at the right of the hostess, you will assist with her chair.

HOLDING COATS

When a man helps a woman with her coat, he holds the coat with the armholes at a comfortable height for her to slip her arms into them. He is careful not to muss her hair.

A woman usually does not check her coat in a restaurant or the theater. The coat may be laid across a vacant chair at the table, or across the back of her chair at the table or in the theater. You should see that the coat does not trail on the floor. A stole may be folded and laid across a chair, or chair back.

You may check your own coat and hat after entering a hotel, but before going into the dining room. These articles may also be checked at the theater, but time may be saved if you take them with you. You generally place your hat on the rack under the seat.

SENDING FLOWERS

When sending flowers to a woman, a man should choose them to fit her type, as well as the occasion at which they will be worn or displayed. Try to find out what she is wearing, and send flowers that are appropriate. You would send chrysanthemums to a woman attending a football game, and gardenias or an orchid when she's attending a dance. Flowers are pinned on a costume as they are grown—heads up.

A very short woman may not care for a very large corsage, but she would like a small corsage or nosegay to pin on her gloves or evening bag. A bouquet of flowers may be sent to a hostess by a guest of honor for the party given for him, or as thanks for a favor received or a special party attended.

It is not advisable to send potted plants to a hostess whose husband has orders as she may be moving. In such a case, the plants and your money may be wasted.

At the Service Academies and college ROTC units, the custom of sending corsages to drags or dates before hops or dances is discouraged, mainly because of the students' lack of spending money. On special occasions, such as the "flower formal" at the Coast Guard Academy and the ring and graduation hops at West Point, cadets send corsages to their young ladies.

CHANCE ENCOUNTERS

A man does not pay for the lunch or dinner at a chance encounter with a woman. If you should happen to run into an acquaintance at a restaurant or lunch counter, you do not need to pay his or her bill—unless you want to. When you chance to meet a man or woman at a bus stop, or decide to share a taxi, you usually pay only your share of the charges.

If you must speak to a woman who is a stranger, or hand her something —such as returning an object she dropped on the sidewalk—you may touch her arm lightly when you catch up with her, to get her attention; then you turn away as soon as you have accomplished your mission.

When you give your seat to a woman in a bus, subway or train, you may touch your hat when you rise to your feet, but you need not say anything. When a man gives his seat to the woman you are escorting, you should touch your hat when acknowledging his courtesy.

You must avoid calling out a woman's name in public in loud tones, even when you are surprised and delighted at the encounter.

SMOKING

Although smoking appears to have become a world-wide habit, there are many people who do not smoke and others who are allergic to smoke in any form. A habitual or chain-smoker frequently is unwittingly offensive to a non-smoker, so you should be careful to observe the following rules:

- Never smoke out-of-doors when in uniform except when seated at an athletic contest or other types of outdoor activities.
- Do not take a lighted cigarette to the dining table, onto a dance floor, or into a church, theater, museum or other public place.
- Always observe the non-smoking regulations in public places.
- Never smoke at, or while taking part in, a formal or official occasion such as a wedding, reception, etc.
- A lady, in or out of uniform, never smokes on the street.
- Abide by the ground rules or desires of the senior officer present concerning smoking while on duty.
- Of course, you never smoke with your gloves on.
- Never use a saucer, dish, or plate at the dining table for an ash tray. Cigarettes are usually offered at the dining table—but when they are not, you must assume that your hostess does not wish any smoking at the table.
- Never smoke cigars during a meal, though you may do so after the women have left the table. Do not smoke cigars in the living room unless you have obtained the hostess's permission first.
- Do not spill ashes on the floor, flip ashes into a wastepaper basket, or lay a lighted cigarette on a table.
- Never take offense when someone asks you not to smoke in his or her presence.
- Smoking in Navy boats and military aircraft is permissible only at specified times and places.

A man always offers a cigarette to a woman, or others nearby, before taking one himself. You strike and hold a match or a lighter for a woman, and also offer the light to others before lighting your own cigarette. Be careful to hold the light high enough so that a person does not have to bend over it. At a party, a man would light his hostess' cigarette before his wife's.

There is no need to cross a room and offer a cigarette to a woman, or to go entirely around a room and offer cigarettes to everyone. Cigarettes are customarily placed in convenient containers throughout a room. You may offer cigarettes to as many as you conveniently can.

When a person does not smoke, you do not need to keep offering him cigarettes. If he does smoke, but does not care for one at the moment, you may offer a cigarette later.

You may smoke during intermissions at the theater. If your woman guest does not care to smoke, she may remain in her seat while you go to the lobby. If she cares for a smoke, and you don't smoke, you should accompany her to the lobby.

CIGARS AND PIPES

There is an old-fashioned rule—now observed only by elderly or very sedate persons—which decreed that a man should never smoke a pipe or cigar in an automobile with a woman. It is customary today for both men and women to smoke cigarettes in automobiles, with men smoking anything they choose. It is important, however, that you do not light up without first asking other persons in the automobile, "Do you mind if I smoke?"

A considerate smoker doesn't blow smoke in another person's face. And you always take your cigarette, cigar, or pipe out of your mouth before lifting your hat, bowing, greeting others, or when you talk.

Men who smoke cigars and pipes should always be sure that an ash tray is large enough to accommodate all the ashes. A chewed cigar or ashes from a pipe should not be left in other persons' homes—and are not attractive in your own.

TELEPHONE COURTESY

You should always be courteous when talking on the telephone. When answering or placing a call, identify yourself. "Hello" may be used in answering when at home, but in an office or upon an official occasion it is discourteous, for the other person must then ask to whom he is talking. Say, "L Two Company orderly room, Cadet Abbott speaking, Sir."

When telephoning a stranger or someone you do not know well, say, "This is Lieutenant Jones. I'm calling about the tryouts for the Navy Relief Show," or whatever your business might be. When you know the person, simply say, "This is John Jones," and so on.

You must always be careful of your calling hours. Unless necessary, do not call a private residence before nine in the morning or after ten o'clock at night. Avoid calling at meal hours.

When you are placing a call and get a wrong number, always apologize to the person who answers—don't maintain a dead silence and then bang up the receiver. Say, "I'm sorry to have distrubed you." Make certain that you have the right number before placing the call again.

After making a long-distance call in another person's home, you should always ask the operator how much the call cost; then pay for it.

When abused, the telephone is a nuisance. Cadets and midshipmen, particularly, should remember that it is inconsiderate to engage in lengthy chitchat when others may urgently need to use the telephone or are trying to call in. Therefore, conduct your business and allow others to do the same.

SOUNDING OFF

There is an old service rule: "Never volunteer information." If you don't give free information about someone or something, you can't be quoted. Gossip is not confined to the feminine sex—a study of military history through the ages forces one to the conclusion that there would be no Mata Haris if servicemen didn't talk.

A young officer should learn early in his or her career not to discuss carelessly military subjects of a classified nature. You should never speak critically of your seniors.

A gentleman does not discuss such subjects as personal business or women at the officers' mess table, or in the wardroom. If you must discuss these, do so elsewhere—and discreetly. Always remember that your business ceases to be personal if made public.

Everyone at sometime in his life has been bored to distraction by the conversationalist who drones on and on. But—are *you* sometimes guilty of being a bore by going overboard on a subject that interests you greatly? When you suspect that you are becoming long-winded—and you may detect this by observing the reactions of those around you—then change the subject and let someone else talk while you listen.

In reverse, there are times when you are exhausted beyond endurance by a monologue, and the only way to break the spell is to interject a remark at the end of a sentence or when the bore needs a fresh breath. A favorite phrase is, "Oh, that reminds me—!"

When you unintentionally interrupt a speaker, you should say, "I'm sorry," or "I'm sorry, but I thought you had finished." You should try not to interrupt a speaker, and you should pay him the attention that you hope he pays you.

EXHIBITIONISM

Exhibitionism means drawing attention to yourself in a public place. This is accomplished by shouting, whistling, clowning, loud laughter, booing, or doing something foolish or unusual. A person of good breeding does not care to make himself, or his friends, conspicuous in a public place—or any place.

You should not make a public display of your emotions or affections. Kissing in public is frowned upon in the services, except in cases of farewell when the separation is expected to be a long one. It is a better custom for men to shake hands in greeting and farewell with women as well as with men, although some women insist upon kissing when meeting—other women as well as men. Kissing and holding hands should be considered a private rather than a public demonstration.

One example of exhibitionism is the couple on the dance floor who execute too-intricate steps or who hold each other in exaggerated positions. No couple should monopolize the dance floor.

Although everyone enjoys talking about friends and acquaintances of high rank or position, with interesting or amusing anecdotes related, you can overdo it.

Another form of showing self-importance is the over-use of foreign words and phrases. Although an occasional foreign expression can be very appropriate in good English conversation, too many such expressions can become tiresome to the average person who does not speak that particular foreign language.

When you use foreign phrases, be sure that you are proficient in their usage and pronunication—you may be among linguists who are really adept!

APOLOGIES

No one likes to apologize, but apologies are in order when:

- You are late at a luncheon or dinner party—or any social occasion such as a reception where the receiving line has already broken up. Then you go directly to the hostess and briefly apologize.
- The host and hostess have waited for your arrival at a luncheon or dinner party, but have not gone into the dining room. Then you apologize and tell them why you were late—and the reason must be excellent!
- You fail to keep an appointment. You should telephone or write a brief note, explaining your failure to keep the appointment—and again, the reason must be a good one.
- You cannot grant a request. In this case you must not only give your regrets, but if possible add some explanation, such as, "I'm sorry, but due to the great sentimental value attached to the object, I can't lend it for the exhibition, etc., etc."
- You break or damage something. You must attempt to replace the article exactly, but if you cannot, then send flowers with your calling card. You should of course, state on the card that you are sorry concerning the mishap.
- You step or pass in front of someone, or bump into them. In such cases you say "Please excuse me," or "I beg your pardon," or "I'm sorry."
- You have caused harm, or have hurt someone needlessly, or through carelessness. In this case you must do more than apologize—you must ask the other person's forgiveness.
- You dial a wrong telephone number—particularly at a late hour.

SOCIAL OBLIGATIONS

A single officer, or a young married couple, cannot be expected to repay the hospitality of an established or older married couple. The young couple may repay their hosts' hospitality in their own way—at a small cocktail party, informal lunch or dinner, or by performing some small act or favor that is sincere and without ostentation.

As a general rule, when you accept someone's hospitality, you are expected to reciprocate in some fashion. The perennial guest will eventually wear out his or her welcome by always being a guest, but never a host or hostess. No one wants the young couple to repay an expensive dinner party with the same kind of party, dollar for dollar. But the genuineness of the juniors' desire to repay, and their attempt to be pleasant and loyal, is all-important. As the younger couple advances in seniority and rank through the years, they in turn will extend hospitality to junior officers and young couples.

A single officer, a widow, or an unmarried woman, frequently repay their hosts by inviting them to the theater, or to lunch or dinner in a club or hotel.

There is no requirement for a junior officer to repay an official social obligation, such as a "calls made and returned" type of party. Junior officers frequently combine their efforts and finances in repaying unofficial social obligations by giving a dinner, luncheon, or cocktail party.

After small parties, a single officer, or any guest, may telephone or write his hosts and say how much he enjoyed their hospitality. If the occasion was a very special one, flowers may be sent to the hostess with a brief and sincere note of thanks written on an enclosed calling card. Flowers are not necessary, but the note, or perhaps a telephone call, is.

However, you do not phone thanks after large parties since innumerable calls would keep the hostess on the telephone by the hour. In such cases, a sincere expression of thanks at the time of leaving the party is generally sufficient.

A cadet or midshipman (or anyone) should write a thank-you note to a hostess after a first occasion—a dinner, lunch, or party—but you do not write a note after each occasion when you are a frequent guest of the same hostess. Fold-over informals may be used.

All social invitations should be answered promptly, preferably within a day or two. Thank-you notes should be written within forty-eight hours after the occasion. A thank-you note will take only a few minutes of your time, but this small courtesy is invaluable in matters of manners and good will.

Persons who have many social engagements should keep a record of them in order not to overlook an obligation. Such a record should include the names of the hosts, with rank, address, and type of occasion—dinner, lunch, cocktails, etc.—as well as any social calls and the date they were made.

MORAL OBLIGATIONS

You must always remember that the word—or signature—of a lady or gentleman is her or his bond. Therefore, think twice before you make promises. Signed to a check your signature means that you stand good for the amount indicated. Signed to the endorsement at the end of an examination it means that you subscribe to the work submitted and that it is your work. Signed to a letter it means that the ideas expressed are your own.

It is of the utmost importance that men and women in the services be honest and direct in all their dealings. Juniors can avoid a great deal of embarrassment by giving a complete but to-the-point answer in replies to questions put by their seniors.

If you are the junior and do not know or cannot give a complete or correct answer, then you should answer *only as much of the question as you can without evasion or giving misinformation.* An honest "I don't know, Sir, but I will find out and let you know," is a better answer than an indirect one that gives misinformation on which your senior may be basing an important decision. An evasive answer might seriously affect your service reputation.

FINANCIAL OBLIGATIONS

It is mandatory that all members of the services discharge their acknowledged and just financial obligations. As a member of a service you remain a citizen and, as such, you have continuing obligations to obey certain civil statutes and to carry out any civil-court orders, decrees, or judgments to which you are a party. You cannot use your Service status as a pretext for evading your financial obligations.

This doesn't mean that you must pay unjust claims just to avoid unpleasant publicity. You are protected by the fact that your commanding officer must make a careful investigation into the justness of any claim you disavow. But be sure you are in the right before you put your commanding officer to that trouble.

However, commanding officers are not supposed to act as agents for claimants in business transactions or claim collections. Usually the CO only makes sure that the claimant's communication reaches the officer or man concerned and that a prompt reply is made. But a commanding officer cannot tolerate actions of irresponsibility, gross carelessness, neglect, or dishonesty in the financial dealings of his personnel. If he is certain that the officer is negligent or careless in regard to his or her personal finances, he will make an entry on the officer's fitness report and, if the circumstances warrant such action, he will necessarily recommend trial by court-martial.

If you are assigned to a job involving the custody of funds—such as mess treasurer—you should make careful check to ensure that you get all that you sign for when you take over. If you should be a member of an auditing board, be sure that what you certify as on hand is actually present. Never be careless in making audits and taking inventories. The fact that someone else may have signed does not mean that you can sign blindly and assume that all is well. Usually, the junior signs first, at the bottom of the page.

Officers should never lend money to, or have any financial dealings with, enlisted personnel. Your Service Regulations are definite in directing you not to make such loans. If someone asks for a loan, you must decline and inform him or her that Regulations prohibit your making the loan. If his case is a deserving one, he should have no trouble in getting a loan from the ship's Welfare Fund or the Navy Relief Society, the Air Force Aid Society, the Army Emergency Relief, or other established welfare societies. While there is no similar regulation prohibiting financial dealings with officers—there should be. It is better to avoid such dealings.

YOUR SERVICE COMMUNITY

The armed services are friendly services. No matter where you go on active duty, there will be a serviceman near you who is in or about your own age group and financial circumstances. It's difficult to be lonely in the service, whether you are at sea or ashore.

Most service communities are also friendly—however, a few service people make themselves undesirable in a town or community due to their lack of consideration for the other fellow's feelings as well as his possessions. Perhaps this lack of responsibility stems from the fact that service people are not in one place very long and thus grow careless in caring for another's property.

You should take care of the other person's property with as much—or more—respect as your own . . . and this is taking for granted that you *do* take care of your own things. When you are in quarters, or rent a house or apartment, you should not abuse it. Don't leave dirt and trash lying around, or generally wreck the place—you will not be welcome back nor will you leave a favorable impression of your service.

It is thoughtless to borrow another person's property and not return it— no matter whether this be a book, a golf club, or a pound of coffee. You must always return what you borrow—and develop the habit of not borrowing.

A wise man will try to fit into a new community rather than attempt to change it. You should always be thoughtful of your neighbors. It is extremely unwise to walk into a commercial house and say, "That can be bought at the Exchange for a third of your price!"

PROSPECTIVE SERVICE WIVES

In order to prepare cadets for one of the major decisions they may make in life—to marry—a course, "Psychology of Family Relations," is taught at the Air Force Academy.

Military instructors in the Department of Psychology teach the course to the Second Class, with emphasis placed on the unique situation of the military—mobility.

A "Bride's Program" is held just before June Week at the Air Force Academy for prospective brides of new graduates. Young ladies will attend a coffee and panel discussion, when officers' wives and Air Force personnel in various departments, such as finance and special services, brief them on the differences in civilian and service life. A question and answer period follows.

Various college and university ROTC units sponsor courses for prospective service wives. For example, the University of Kansas offers the "Navy Co-eds Orientation Course," which provides a basic sketch of military life by a series of lectures, slide programs, and movies. Instructors are active or retired officers of the various Services.

Subjects include ranks and uniforms, pay and allowances, medical and dental care, duty and leave, separation and retirement, household budgeting and insurance, change of duty, household shipment, military courtesy, the military wedding, the Department of Defense, etc.

Classes in social behavior are held at the Academies, with certain courses illustrated—such as table setting and the correct way to use all pieces of flatware.

At West Point, for example, upperclassmen are in charge of a "Courtesy Course for Plebes" which is held during Beast Barracks (summer training program). Cadet hostesses assist with such subjects as table manners, invitations and introductions.

THE SEA OF MATRIMONY

Each man likes to think that he is the head of his house—as he shoud be. However, a man should be a partner in a home—not its dictator. Good manners in marriage mean loyalty to and respect for the other partner—but this loyalty and respect should be earned, not demanded.

A man and his wife should share the responsibility in the management of the family finances, with the wife fully understanding the limitations of a paycheck and the obligations which must be met each month. Since an officer is away from home during much of his career, it is necessary that someone carry on the family's financial obligations and keep an accurate account of the family expenditures during his absence.

A young wife may have had little experience in financial matters before marriage—and a young husband may have had almost as little financial experience himself. It is important that a young couple work together as a team in sharing the household responsibilities—unless one is incompetent. But what appears to be incompetence may only be inexperience.

A partnership in marriage includes a sound evaluation of each other's responsibilities: a man with his busy career and its problems and worries; a woman with a house to clean, food to cook, and children to care for. Sometimes a woman even combines these household activities with a career, or a part-time career, with little or no household help.

A husband often lends a hand—and the wife will do the same—in jobs frequently considered the specific chore of the other. But a man should not be *required* to do a woman's work any more than a woman should be expected to do a man's work or to contribute too much as a bread winner. It is important that neither the husband nor the wife hold their extra work as a mental club over the other.

A partnership in marriage means that both partners say "we" instead of "I" and "our" instead of "my"—with the exception that official business is the husband's concern only. A partnership, however, does not mean that one or the other cannot have any liberty of thought or action. Partnership and domination do not go hand-in-hand.

A happy household is one where both the man and woman have a certain money allowance for their own personal use—with no strings attached whatsoever.

A happier household and a stronger partnership may be worked out when:

A husband does not:

- Give orders (you should confine orders to your professional career).
- Drop ashes from cigarettes, cigars, or a pipe on the floor or furniture.
- Bring someone home for a meal or overnight without advance notice.
- Interrupt his wife's story—or anyone else's.
- Forget to compliment his wife when she merits it.
- Criticize his wife's appearance, or anything else about her, in front of others.
- Compare his wife's cooking unfavorably with another's.
- Toss a hat or coat on the chair or sofa, or forget to hang up his gear.
- Leave a razor lying around uncleaned, drop a wet towel on the bathroom floor, or leave the toothpaste uncapped.
- Forget anniversaries.

A wife does not:

- Act "bossy" or nag.
- Gossip or tell personal, official, or business affairs to others.
- Make a practice of being late.
- Dress slovenly—such as wearing a robe instead of a housedress, or hair curlers or face cream during hours when these can be avoided.
- Interrupt her husband's story.
- Forget to compliment him when he deserves it.
- Talk *too* much about the baby, at parties or elsewhere.
- Visit her mother too often, or have too many in-laws as houseguests (a woman old enough to marry is old enough to maintain her own home).
- Become jealous of her husband's time, classmates, or long-time friends. (He should not be jealous of her friends, either.)
- Decide abruptly when to leave a party or any social function (she should consult her husband first).
- Say "our orders" for "my husband's orders." Unless a servicewoman herself, a wife is not in the Armed Forces.
- Overdress or dress carelessly at parades and reviews.

As partners, a man and wife should never belittle each other. Any family dissension should be discussed in private—but *not* before the children or a servant. It should be a matter of personal pride for both a man and his wife to be as neat and attractive, and as mentally stimulating, after marriage as before.

CHAPTER 2

Service and Civilian Dress

The brief uniform charts which appear on the following pages have been compiled for the convenience of men and women officers. These charts show the type of uniforms, with prescribed medals or ribbons, which are worn to formal afternoon functions, as well as to semiformal and formal evening functions.

The uniforms in the charts are the equivalent of the civilian formal afternoon dress and of the evening "Black tie" and "White tie." However, the distinctions between "Black tie" and "White tie," and when each is worn, have necessitated further description of civilian dress. There is also a more general description of the civilian clothes needed by officers for everyday living out of uniform.

Decorations, medals, and ribbon bars are worn on the left breast pocket of the uniform coat or jacket, and are pinned or sewed from the wearer's right to the left in the order of precedence as listed in the *Awards Manual.* Insignia, such as aviator's wings, are worn above the pocket.

In general, *regular size medals* are worn with semiformal dress; *miniature medals* are worn with mess dress, formal evening, and dress white uniforms; *unit award emblems* are worn with service, semiformal dress, and dress whites; *ribbons* are worn with service, semiformal dress, mess dress, evening dress, and dress whites. Decorations and service medals, regular size are worn with semiformal dress uniforms in lieu of ribbons.

Insignia of speciality, grade, and branch of service, are worn according to regulations, and aiguillettes are worn when authorized.

NOTE: The local uniform regulations differ in various parts of the country, according to climate and locale. The change from one uniform to another differs in various sections, according to the season. Details of all uniforms will be found in the *Uniform Regulations* of each Service.

UNIFORM CHARTS
ARMY (Men)

Uniform	Coat	Trousers	Cap	Shirt	Necktie	Shoes	Socks	Gloves
ARMY BLUE AND ARMY WHITE UNIFORMS:[1] Wear at general official/social occasions.								
• Army Blue	Dark blue, general officers; dark blue, others	Dark blue; Sky blue	Dark blue	White	Black bow,[2] or four-in-hand[3]	Black	Black	White
• Army White	White	White	White	White	Black bow,[2] or four-in-hand[3]	Black	Black dress	White

1. Wear ribbons, or miniature or regular medals.
Cape optional with taupe overcoat; white scarf.

2. Constitutes "Black Tie."
3. Constitutes semidress.

Uniform	Coat	Trousers	Cap	Shirt	Necktie	Shoes	Socks	Gloves
ARMY GREEN UNIFORM: General duty wear; acceptable for informal social functions after retreat.								
• Army Green	Green	Green	Green	Tan	Black four-in-hand	Black	Black	Black
ARMY BLUE MESS AND WHITE MESS UNIFORMS:[1] "Black Tie."								
• Blue Mess	Dark blue jacket, general officers; dark blue, others	Dark blue; Sky blue	Blue	Evening dress or full dress, white; wing collar	Black bow	Black	Black dress	White
• White Mess	White jacket	Black	White	Evening dress or full dress, white; wing collar	Black bow	Black	Black dress	White

1. Wear miniature medals.
Optional, white vest or black cummerbund. Dark blue cape or outercoat.

Uniform	Coat	Trousers	Cap	Shirt	Necktie	Shoes	Socks	Gloves
ARMY EVENING DRESS:[1] "White Tie."								
• Evening Dress	Blue-black or black evening dress	Blue-black or black evening dress	Army blue	Full dress, white; wing collar	White bow	Black	Black dress	White

1. Wear miniature medals.
Cape, optional; white studs and links; white vest.

ARMY (Women)

Uniform	Coat/Jacket	Skirt	Shirtwaist	Necktab	Hat/Cap	Shoes	Stockings	Gloves
ARMY BLUE AND ARMY WHITE UNIFORMS:[1] General social/official occasions.								
• Army Blue[2]	Blue	Blue	White	Black	Blue hat	Black	Beige	White
• Army White[3]	White	White	White	Black	White	White	Beige	White

1. Wear ribbons, or regular miniature medals.
2. Wear tan scarf with taupe outercoat. Black handbag.
3. White handbag.

Uniform	Coat/Jacket	Skirt	Shirtwaist	Necktab	Hat/Cap	Shoes	Stockings	Gloves
ARMY MESS AND EVENING DRESS UNIFORMS:[1] Equivalent to **"Black Tie"** or **"White Tie."**								
Army Mess[2,6]	Black	Black	White	Black		Black	To complement uniform	White
Army White Mess[2,6]	White	Black	White	Black		Black	Beige	White
Army All White Mess[3,5]	White	White	White	Black		White	Beige	White
Army Evening Dress[2,4,6]	Black	Black	White	Black		Black	Beige	White
Army White Evening Dress[2,4,6]	White	Black	White	Black		Black	Beige	White

1. Wear miniature medals.
2. Wear black cummerbund.
3. White cummerbund.
4. Full length skirt.
5. White handbag.
6. Black handbag.

Note: The Army Green Uniform is for general year round wear. The Army Green Cord Uniform is for summer wear.

NAVY (Men)

Uniform	Coat	Trousers	Cap Cover	Shirt	Necktie	Shoes	Socks	Gloves
SERVICE DRESS UNIFORMS: General duty wear.								
Service Dress:[1]								
Blue	Blue	Blue	White	White	Black	Black	Black	
White	White	White	White	White	.....	White	White	Gray
Khaki	Khaki	Khaki	Khaki	Khaki	Black	Brown	Khaki	
1. Wear with ribbons.								
FULL DRESS UNIFORMS:[1] Wear at official/social functions.								
Full dress:								
•*Blue*	Blue	Blue	White	White	Black	Black	Black	White
•*White*	White	White	White	.....	.....	White	White	White
1. Wear large medals; sword.								
DINNER DRESS UNIFORMS: Equivalent to "Black Tie."								
Dinner Dress:								
•*Blue*[2,6]	Blue	Blue	White	White dress[5]	Black bow	Black	Black	White or gray
•*Blue Jacket*[1,2]	Blue mess jacket	Blue evening[3]	White	White dress[5]	Black bow	Black	Black	White
•*White*[2,6]	White	White	White			White	White	White
•*White Jacket*[1,2]	White mess jacket	Blue evening[4]	White	White dress[5]	Black bow	Black	Black	White

1. Optional for Lieutenants (jg) and below.
2. Wear miniature medals.
3. With gold cummerbund.
4. With black cummerbund.
5. Stiff turndown collar.
6. Primarily for Lieutenants (jg) and below not possessing the jacket uniforms.

NAVY (Men) Continued

Uniform	Coat	Trousers	Cap Cover	Shirt	Necktie	Shoes	Socks	Gloves
EVENING DRESS UNIFORMS: Equivalent to "White Tie."								
Evening Dress								
• Blue[1,2]	Blue evening	Blue evening	White	White dress	White bow	Black	Black	White
• White[1]	White	White	White			White	White	White

1. Wear miniature medals.
2. Wear white waistcoat; wing collar.

COAST GUARD (Men)

UNIFORMS: Men in the Coast Guard wear the same uniforms as prescribed for men in the U. S. Navy, except for identifying insignia. The hat/cap device is the Coast Guard emblem, and the Coast Guard shield is worn by officers above the stripes on the uniform coat sleeves. Buttons have the Coast Guard design.

MERCHANT MARINE

UNIFORMS: Officers of the Merchant Marine who are officers of the U. S. Naval Reserve wear the Naval Reserve Merchant Marine insignia on their Merchant Marine uniforms. Members of the Naval Reserve who are serving as officers under licenses issued by the U. S. Coast Guard in ships under contract with the Federal Maritime Administration, or those serving as staff officers on certificates of registry issued by the Coast Guard, wear the USNR Merchant Marine insignia. Other members of the Naval Reserve serving in merchant ships in positions which require them to wear a uniform appropriate to an officer, wear the insignia on their uniforms.

NAVY (Women)

Uniform	Coat/Jacket	Skirt	Shirt	Necktie	Hat/Cap	Shoes	Stockings	Gloves
SERVICE DRESS UNIFORMS:[1] Regular official/social occasions.								
• *Service Dress*								
Blue, A[2]	Blue	Blue	White	Black	Blue cover	Black dress	Beige	White
White[3]	White	White	White	Black	White	White dress	Beige	White
Light blue	Light blue	Light blue			Light blue	Black dress	Beige	

1. Worn with ribbons.
2. Black handbag.
3. White handbag.

NOTE: Service Dress Blue and White Uniforms, worn with large medals, are referred to as *Full Dress (Blue/White) Uniforms*.

Uniform	Coat/Jacket	Skirt	Shirt	Necktie	Hat/Cap	Shoes	Stockings	Gloves
DINNER DRESS UNIFORMS:[1] (worn in lieu of Evening Dress Uniform).								
• *Dinner Dress Blue*:								
Blue A[2]	Blue	Blue	White	Black	Blue	Black dress	Beige	White
Blue B[2]	Blue	Blue	White	Black	White	Black dress	Beige	White
Blue C[2]	Blue	White	White	Black	White	White dress	Beige	White
White[3]	White	White	White	Black	White	White dress	Beige	White

1. Wear with ribbons.
2. Wear with black handbag.
3. Wear with white handbag.

NAVY (Women) Continued

Uniform	Coat	Skirt	Shirt	Necktie	Hat/Cap	Shoes	Stockings	Gloves
EVENING DRESS UNIFORMS:[1] Equivalent to "Black Tie" or "White Tie" occasions.								
• Evening Dress Blue[2]	Blue jacket	Blue evening dress[2]	White evening dress	Black	Blue headdress	Black evening dress	Beige	White
White	White	White	White	Black	White	White dress	Beige	White

1. Worn with miniature medals.
2. With blue cummerbund. Blue or white evening handbag.

COAST GUARD (Women)

UNIFORMS: Women in the Coast Guard wear the same uniforms as prescribed for women in the U. S. Navy, except for identifying insignia. The hat/cap device is the Coast Guard emblem, and the Coast Guard shield is worn by officers above the stripes on the uniform coat sleeves. Buttons have the Coast Guard design.

MARINE CORPS (Men)

Uniform	Jacket Coat & Belt	Trousers	Cap	Shirt	Necktie	Shoes	Socks	Gloves
BLUE DRESS A, B, C, AND WHITE DRESS UNIFORMS:[1] Wear at general/official occasions.								
• Blue Dress A[2]	Blue	Blue	Dress	White		Black	Black	White
• Blue Dress B[3]	Same as "A"—except with ribbons.							
• Blue Dress C[3]	Blue	Blue	Dress	Khaki		Black	Black	Black
• White Dress A[2]	White	White	Dress			White	White	White
• White Dress B[3]	Same as "A"—except with ribbons.							
Blue/White Dress A[2]	Blue	White	Dress	White		White	White	White

MARINE CORPS (Men) Continued

Uniform	Jacket Coat & Belt	Trousers	Cap	Shirt	Necktie	Shoes	Socks	Gloves
Blue/White Dress B[3]	Same as "A"—except with ribbons.							

1. Wear badges; sword.
2. Wear large medals.
3. Wear ribbons.
Black leather gloves with outercoat.

MESS DRESS UNIFORMS:[1] **"Black Tie."**

Uniform	Jacket Coat & Belt	Trousers	Cap	Shirt	Necktie	Shoes	Socks	Gloves
Mess Dress	White mess scarlet cummerbund	Black mess	Dress	White	Black bow square ends	Black	Black	White

1. Wear miniature medals.

EVENING DRESS A AND B UNIFORMS:[1] **"White Tie."**

Uniform	Jacket Coat & Belt	Trousers	Cap	Shirt	Necktie	Shoes	Socks	Gloves
•*Evening Dress A*	Dark blue evening waistcoat	Dark blue evening	Dress	White, strip collar		Black	Black	White
•*Evening Dress B*	Same as "A"—except with cummerbund.							

1. Wear miniature medals.

MARINE CORPS (Women)

Uniform	Coat/Jacket	Skirt	Shirtwaist	Necktie	Hat/Cap	Shoes	Stockings	Gloves
BLUE DRESS UNIFORMS: General official/social occasions.								
• Blue Dress A[1]	Blue	Blue	White	Blue	Blue	Black	Beige	White
• Blue Dress B	Same as Blue Dress A—except ribbons are worn.							
1. Wear large medals. Black gloves are worn with outercoat. Black handbag.								
WHITE DRESS UNIFORMS: Summer official/social occasions.								
• White Dress[1]	White	White	White		Summer service cap	White	Beige	White
• White Dress B	Same as White Dress A—except ribbons are worn.							
1. Wear large medals. Clutch purse with green cover.								
EVENING DRESS UNIFORM: Equivalent to "Black Tie" or "White Tie" occasions.								
• Evening Dress A[1]	Evening	Long black	White		Tiara	Black	Dark	White
• Evening Dress B[2]	Same as Evening Dress A—except short black evening skirt is worn.							
1. Wear miniature medals. 2. With cummerbund. Wear boat cloak (optional) Clutch purse with black cover.								

AIR FORCE (Men)

Uniform	Coat	Trousers	Cap	Shirt	Necktie	Shoes	Socks	Gloves
ALL-SEASON AND SUMMER SERVICE UNIFORMS: Wear on informal occasions.								
• *All-Season Service*	Blue (heavyweight or lightweight)[1]	Blue (same material as coat)	Blue service or flight	Blue	Dark blue four-in-hand	Black	Black	Gray
• *Black Informal*	Black[3]	Black (same material as coat)	Black	White	Black four-in-hand	Black	Black	White
• *White Informal*	White[1]	White (same material as coat)[2]	Service with white cover	White	Black four-in-hand	White	White	White

1. Wear ribbons.
2. To be worn with white belt or white suspenders.
3. Wear miniature medals.

Uniform	Coat	Trousers	Cap	Shirt	Necktie	Shoes	Socks	Gloves
MESS DRESS AND SEMIFORMAL UNIFORMS:								
• *All-Season Semiformal*	Blue (heavyweight or lightweight)[1]	Blue (same material as coat)	Blue service	White	Black bow	Black	Black	Gray
• *Winter Mess Dress*	Black Mess Jacket[2]	Black (same material as jacket)[4]	Black dress	White dress	Black bow	Black	Black	White
• *Summer Mess Dress*	White Mess Jacket[2]	Black (same material as winter jacket)[4]	White dress[3]	White dress	Black bow	Black	Black	White

1. Wear ribbons.
2. Wear miniature medals.
3. When overcoat, topcoat, or raincoat is worn, service cap and gray gloves will be worn.
   NOTE: Black evening cape optional (to be worn with dress cap and white gloves).
4. Black silk cummerbund.

AIR FORCE (Men) Continued

FORMAL EVENING DRESS: "White Tie."

Uniform	Coat	Trousers	Cap	Shirt	Necktie	Shoes	Socks	Gloves
	Black or Blue-black[1]	Black or Blue-black (same material as coat)	Black dress	White full dress	White bow	Black	Black	White[2]

1. Wear miniature medals, white commercial evening dress vest.
2. When overcoat, topcoat, or raincoat is worn, service cap and gray gloves will be worn.

NOTE: Black evening cape optional (to be worn with dress cap and white gloves).

AIR FORCE (Women)

ALL-SEASON AND SUMMER SERVICE UNIFORMS: Wear on informal occasions.

Uniform	Coat	Skirt	Shirt-waist	Undertabs	Hat/Cap	Shoes	Stockings	Gloves
• All-Season Service	Blue (heavyweight or lightweight)[1]	Blue (same material as coat)	Blue	Dark blue	Blue service w/gray cover or Blue flight	Black	Beige[4]	Gray or Black leather
• Black Informal	Black[2]	Black (same material)	White	Black	Black service, w/white vinyl cover	Black	Beige[4]	White
• White Informal	White[1], wool, wool polyester or polyester viscare	White (same material)	White	Blue	Blue service with white vinyl hat cover	White	Beige[4]	White
• Summer Service 2-piece dress[3]	Blue and white cotton/Polyester	Blue and white (same material as coat)			Blue service with white vinyl hat cover or Blue flight	Black	Beige[4]	White

1. Wear ribbons.

NOTE: Black handbag with above uniforms except white handbag with white informal.

2. Wear miniature medals and shoulder boards.
3. Ribbons optional.
4. Or to compliment uniform.

AIR FORCE (Women) Continued

MESS DRESS AND SEMIFORMAL DRESS UNIFORM:

Uniform	Coat	Skirt	Shirt-waist	Undertabs	Hat/Cap	Shoes	Stockings	Gloves
• All-Season Semiformal	Blue (heavyweight or lightweight)[1,2]	Blue (same material as coat)	White	Dark blue	Blue service, white vinyl cover	Black	Beige[4]	White

1. Wear ribbons.
2. Black handbag.

NOTE: Overcoat and raincoat may be worn as necessary; white scarf optional if these items are worn.

Uniform	Coat	Skirt	Shirt-waist	Undertabs	Hat/Cap	Shoes	Stockings	Gloves
• Winter Mess Dress[2]	Black Mess Jacket[3]	Black (same material as coat)	White dress	Black crescent		Black	Beige[4]	White
• Summer Mess Dress[2]	White Mess Jacket[3]	White (same material as coat)	White dress	Black crescent		Black	Beige[4]	White

1. Wear ribbons.
2. Wear silver or black cummerbund. Black handbag.
3. Wear miniature medals.
4. Wear stockings to complement uniform.

NOTE: Overcoat and raincoat may be worn as necessary with white covered service hat.

AWARDS

Awards is an all-inclusive term covering any decoration, medal, ribbon, badge, or an attachment thereto which is bestowed on an individual.

A *decoration* is an award conferred on a person for an act of gallantry or for meritorious service, or given to units distinguished for gallantry in action against the enemy. Certain decorations carry the word "medal," for example the Medal of Honor and the Distinguished Service Medal. The Medal of Honor is worn from the neckband ribbon.

A *miniature medal* is one-half the size of the original large medal, with the exception of the Medal of Honor which is not in miniature. A *ribbon* is a part of the suspension ribbon of a medal which is worn in lieu of the medal. The dimensions of all ribbons are $1\frac{3}{8}$ inches by $\frac{3}{8}$ inch. A *badge* is an award to an individual for some special proficiency and consists of a medallion hung from a bar or bars.

Miniature medals are worn by men and women officers with formal and semiformal winter and summer uniforms. The holding bar is no longer than $4\frac{1}{8}$ inches in length. When six or less medals are worn, they are attached in a single row, fully exposed. When the number exceeds six, each medal may overlap the medal to its left, but not more than 50 percent. Thus, the maximum number worn in a single row is 11. If more than this number are worn, they are arranged in two rows; if more than 22, in three rows evenly divided. If this cannot be done, the top row will contain the lesser number of medals with the center of the row placed over the center of the row below it.

When ribbons are worn, badges, such as the Navy command insignia, are worn immediately below the bottom row of ribbons. When large medals are worn, badges are placed directly below the bottom row of medals so that the medallion of each badge may be seen.

MEDALS ON CIVILIAN DRESS

The Medal of Honor may be worn with civilian evening dress (White tie). Likewise, miniature medals may be worn with "White tie" in the same manner as prescribed for formal service evening dress uniforms.

Miniature replicas of ribbons made in the form of lapel buttons, or rosettes, may also be worn on the left lapel of civilian clothes, with the exception of civilian evening dress (White tie). Honorable discharge and service buttons may be worn on the left lapel of civilian clothes, except on evening dress.

RETIRED OFFICER'S DRESS

Although most officers retired from the services wear civilian dress at various official and social occasions, there are occasions when the uniform may be worn—such as a military wedding or an official reception when all other officers will be in uniform.

SERVICE

ARMY	AIR FORCE	MARINE CORPS	NAVY	COAST GUARD
GOLD / BROWN — GOLD / BROWN W-1 WARRANT OFFICER — W-2 CHIEF WARRANT OFFICER	GOLD / SKY BLUE — GOLD / SKY BLUE W-1 WARRANT OFFICER — W-2 CHIEF WARRANT OFFICER	GOLD / SCARLET — GOLD / SCARLET W-1 WARRANT OFFICER — W-2 CHIEF WARRANT OFFICER	W-1 WARRANT OFFICER — W-2 CHIEF WARRANT OFFICER	W-1 WARRANT OFFICER — W-2 CHIEF WARRANT OFFICER
SILVER / BROWN — SILVER / BROWN W-3 CHIEF WARRANT OFFICER — W-4 CHIEF WARRANT OFFICER	SILVER / SKY BLUE — SILVER / SKY BLUE W-3 CHIEF WARRANT OFFICER — W-4 CHIEF WARRANT OFFICER	SILVER / SCARLET — SILVER / SCARLET W-3 CHIEF WARRANT OFFICER — W-4 CHIEF WARRANT OFFICER	W-3 CHIEF WARRANT OFFICER — W-4 CHIEF WARRANT OFFICER	W-3 CHIEF WARRANT OFFICER — W-4 CHIEF WARRANT OFFICER
(GOLD) SECOND LIEUTENANT	(GOLD) SECOND LIEUTENANT	(GOLD) SECOND LIEUTENANT	ENSIGN	ENSIGN
(SILVER) FIRST LIEUTENANT	(SILVER) FIRST LIEUTENANT	(SILVER) FIRST LIEUTENANT	LIEUTENANT JUNIOR GRADE	LIEUTENANT JUNIOR GRADE
(SILVER) CAPTAIN	(SILVER) CAPTAIN	(SILVER) CAPTAIN	LIEUTENANT	LIEUTENANT
(GOLD) MAJOR	(GOLD) MAJOR	(GOLD) MAJOR	LIEUTENANT COMMANDER	LIEUTENANT COMMANDER
(SILVER) LIEUTENANT COLONEL	(SILVER) LIEUTENANT COLONEL	(SILVER) LIEUTENANT COLONEL	COMMANDER	COMMANDER

SERVICE				
ARMY	**AIR FORCE**	**MARINE CORPS**	**NAVY**	**COAST GUARD**
COLONEL	COLONEL	COLONEL	CAPTAIN	CAPTAIN
BRIGADIER GENERAL	BRIGADIER GENERAL	BRIGADIER GENERAL	COMMODORE	COMMODORE
MAJOR GENERAL	MAJOR GENERAL	MAJOR GENERAL	REAR ADMIRAL	REAR ADMIRAL
LIEUTENANT GENERAL	LIEUTENANT GENERAL	LIEUTENANT GENERAL	VICE ADMIRAL	VICE ADMIRAL
GENERAL	GENERAL	GENERAL	ADMIRAL	ADMIRAL
GENERAL OF THE ARMY	GENERAL OF THE AIR FORCE	NONE	FLEET ADMIRAL	NONE
AS PRESCRIBED BY INCUMBENT GENERAL OF THE ARMIES	NONE	NONE	NONE	NONE

The number of years of retirement has nothing to do with the retired officer's decision to wear—or not to wear—his uniform: the elements of good taste and propriety are the key to his decision.

Retired officers on active duty wear the same uniforms prescribed for officers on active duty.

When not on active duty, you may wear the uniform corresponding to the grade at the time of retirement, or as authorized, upon the following occasions:

- At military ceremonies.
- Military weddings or funerals.
- Memorial services, inaugurals, patriotic parades on national holidays.
- Other military parades or ceremonies in which any active or Reserve United States military unit is taking part.
- At educational institutions when giving military instruction or when responsible for military discipline.

It is optional to wear civilian clothing or the uniform when you are riding in military aircraft.

The uniform is *not* worn when you are visiting or living in a foreign country, except when attending by formal invitation a ceremony or social function at which the wearing of the uniform is required. Under these circumstances, authority to wear the uniform may be granted by the service secretary and/or the nearest military attaché.

RESERVE OFFICERS

Reserve officers on active duty (other than on training duty in the Navy) have the same minimum outfit of uniforms and insignia, as well as accessories, as prescribed for the regular service, except that the sword, sword accessories, and formal evening dress uniform are not required.

When not on active duty, Reserve officers wear the uniforms upon the same general occasions as listed for the retired officers.

SEPARATED PERSONNEL

Any person who has served in the Army (including personnel assigned to the air components prior to the establishment of the Department of the Air Force), Navy, Air Force, or Marine Corps, during wartime, and whose most recent service was terminated honorably, is entitled to wear the uniform of the highest grade held during his or her war service, upon the following ceremonial occasions:

- Military funerals or weddings, memorial services, inaugurals.
- Patriotic parades on national holidays, or other military parades

or ceremonies in which any active or Reserve United States military unit is taking part.

The uniform worn may be the one authorized at the time of separation, or it may be that prescribed by authorization at the time of the ceremony.

CIVILIAN DRESS (MEN): FORMAL

BLACK TIE (AFTER 6 P.M.)

"Black tie" means your dinner jacket or tuxedo. The term "tuxedo" came about in the 1890's when the dinner jacket was introduced into the United States from England and was first worn at the Tuxedo Club.

This is the favorite form of men's evening dress and is worn at almost any formal occasion—receptions, weddings, theater or opera, dances, dinners, etc. Guests may wear dinner jackets at a formal evening church wedding, although members of the wedding party wear full dress. "Black tie" is not properly worn on Sundays or before six o'clock in the evening. The following items of dress may be worn:

Jacket—Of black, or dark blue tropical-weight material of good quality, usually single-breasted; in summer, white linen or tropical-weight, dacron, etc. The dark jacket may be worn in the summer time—but it is hot. Nowadays, the plaid dinner jacket is worn for cruise or less formal occasions.

Trousers—Material matches the coat, with single stripe of matching colored braid or satin. Trousers are without cuffs. (Black trousers are worn with white jacket.)

Waistcoat—Is not worn with a double-breasted jacket; with a single-breasted jacket, the waistcoat will be of white piqué or black plain, ribbed, or self-figured silk. Instead of a waistcoat, a *cummerbund* is worn, usually black, maroon, or midnight blue.

Shirt—The popular (and comfortable) attached fold collar with pleated or plain soft bosom. White is customary.

Tie—Black bow.

Socks—Black or dark blue to match trousers.

Shoes—Black patent leather.

Hat—Not necessary, but a black or dark blue Homburg or black soft-brimmed fedora in winter, a gray felt snapped brim hat in the spring or summer, and a straw in the summer—if any is worn.

Gloves—Gray mocha, nylon, chamois, or buck.

Topcoat—Black, Oxford gray, or dark blue Chesterfield, with or without velvet collar.

Accessories—White linen handerchief; white silk scarf; studs and cuff links.

Boutonniere—Red or white carnation. (See "White tie.")

WHITE TIE (AFTER 6 P.M.)

"White tie" means full dress evening wear, or "tailcoat." Tails are not worn often except by men in the diplomatic service, senior officers, or at a very formal wedding, dinner, etc. When you need civilian tails for a special occasion, a good rental service will furnish them for the occasion.

Like dinner jackets, tails should never be worn before six o'clock, or on Sunday. Also, tails are not worn in the summer. Properly, the tailcoat should hang just below the knee in back. Here are the necessary items:

Tailcoat—Black worsted; peaked lapels, faced in satin or grosgrain.

Waistcoat—White pique, single or double-breasted, with self-covered buttons, or fastened with separate studs which should match shirt studs.

Trousers—To match the coat. Stripes of black faille or braid; without cuffs.

Shirt—White with detachable wing collar, and stiff, single cuffs; starched white piqué bosom or plain linen.

Tie—White piqué bow, butterfly, or straight club shape.

Socks—Black.

Shoes—Black patent leather pumps or oxfords.

Hat—Black opera hat or, more frequently, the black Homburg or black soft-brimmed fedora—if a hat is worn at all.

Topcoat—Same as for Black tie.

Gloves—White mocha, nylon, chamois, or doeskin; gray doeskin are worn on the street.

Boutonniere—White carnation for left buttonhole, for full dress; or a small white gardenia, lily-of-the-valley, rosebud or miniature rose. At a wedding, the bridegroom usually wears a white carnation, with the ushers wearing a white flower which differs from those of the best man and groom. You do not wear a boutonniere when wearing decorations or when you are in uniform tails—or in any uniform.

Accessories—White suspenders; white linen handerchief; white silk scarf; studs and matching cuff links.

FORMAL DAYTIME CLOTHES (*Before 6 P.M.*)

Formal daytime clothes—the *cutaway* or *sack coat*—are mainly worn at diplomatic or governmental affairs. A man taking part in a formal daytime wedding party, or a pallbearer at a large funeral, also wears such dress. When taking part in any formal function before six o'clock, you wear:

Cutaway—Worn less frequently than the tailcoat, may also be rented. It is of black or Oxford gray worsted, cashmere, or cheviot, with peaked lapels with plain edges; bone or self-covered buttons.

Waistcoat—Single or double-breasted, will match the coat, or may be of pearl gray or buff doeskin; in summer, white or tan linen.

Trousers—Black and gray stripes, or black and white striped worsted or cheviot, cuffless.

Shirt—White, with plain or pleated bosom. You may have a fold collar and double cuffs, or wing collar and stiff cuffs.

Socks—Black or gray.

Shoes—Black calf oxfords.

Tie—Gray, black, or silver-gray silk; plain, figured, or striped. An ascot is usually worn with wing collar at weddings; at funerals, the tie is a black four-in-hand with fold collar. For other occasions, either a four-in-hand or bow may be worn with either a wing or fold collar.

Hat—Black silk, black Homburg or black soft felt.

Topcoat—Black, dark blue, gray, or any conservative color.

Gloves—Gray mocha, or any good material.

Accessories—White or gray scarf; white linen handkerchief; gray or black and white suspenders; white or red carnation (no boutonnieres are worn at funerals or with officer's uniform); matching studs and cuff links. Boutonnieres are the same as for "White tie."

The sack coat is interchangeable with the cutaway, but is slightly less formal. When it is needed, it can be obtained from a good rental service.

Sack Coat—Single-breasted, of black or Oxford gray worsted.

Waistcoat—Matches the sack coat.

Trousers—Same as for cutaway.

Shirt—White, with fold collar, stiff cuffs.

Tie—Four-in-hand, of black or black-and-gray silk. Sometimes a bow tie is worn.

Hat—Black Homburg.

Shoes, *socks*, *gloves*, *topcoat* and *accessories* are the same as with a cutaway.

Concerning certain accessories, boutonnieres other than white or red carnations may be worn at various occasions. Cornflowers and small white gardenias are sometimes used, and a groom at a wedding occasionally wears an orange blossom or a small sprig of lily-of-the-valley. Such flowers are always worn in the left buttonhole of a suit but are *never* worn when you are in uniform.

A handkerchief placed in the breast pocket of your suit is entirely for show. It must, of course, be clean and folded, and only an inch or two shows. When you use a colored handkerchief in your breast pocket, it must blend with the colors in your tie.

A dress handkerchief is white linen and can be initialed with a single letter or with all your initials. For evening use, the initials are white, gray, or black, but other colors are correct for daytime use.

CIVILIAN DRESS FOR SERVICEMEN

Any officer faces a distinct problem in the matter of his clothes. This is because he must possess two wardrobes—service and civilian. Since uniforms are a necessity, they are purchased first.

When an officer of average financial circumstances purchases his uniform wardrobe and maintains it in the high state of excellence in which it should be kept, usually there is only a modest amount left over in the clothes budget. It is important that he purchase a conservative civilian wardrobe which can be worn for many occasions and seasons.

The best clothes are always those of good quality, subdued color, and the best possible tailoring. Such colors as gray, blue-gray, dark blue, or tans and browns, are best. Tweed sports jackets in moderate-toned greens, browns, blues, and gray mixtures are always in good taste. The same conservative overtone is important in all other items of dress—such as socks, ties, shirts, etc.

However, if you must display a flamboyant streak, it should be confined to such items as sports shirts, bathing trunks, pajamas, and even then it is possible to go too far. Although it is true that more color is used in men's clothing today than ever before, it is wise to purchase shirts and ties, particularly, with care.

In the long run, cheap clothes are the most expensive because they do not last as long and must be replaced earlier than expected. It is wise, therefore, that when you buy your first civilian wardrobe after graduating from the Academy, or when you first start out "on your own," you don't succumb to the extremes in color and style, "gambler fashion."

It is well to remember that what is good taste in one part of the country may be poor taste in other parts. The bright and unusual sports shirts and slacks which are so familiar in Hawaii or southern and western states, may not look the same in more conservative—and cooler—northern and New England states—or vice versa.

Although it is difficult to state any rule for wearing or buying clothes—particularly when you are transferred from one coast to another—appropriate dress is usually the conservative type of clothes which are good taste any place. Dress in foreign countries is generally on the conservative side, and a "loudly" dressed American is not a good representative of the service.

The question often arises as to the clothes needed for a young officer's civilian wardrobe. The following suggestions are based on the consensus of a cross-section of officers who have learned through actual experience.

MINIMUM CLOTHING LIST

1. *A conservative suit.* One such suit will be adequate at first, but you should plan on getting two as soon as the financial situation permits. One or both suits should be suitable for wearing after six o'clock when semi-formal conditions are to be met. The dark blue business suit is traditional, is worn at daytime and less formal evening weddings and receptions.

2. *A sports jacket.* This jacket will probably be the most useful and the most worn item in your wardrobe. You should be sure to get a good one

that will not shrink despite many cleanings; choose one that can be worn with almost any color slacks.

3. *Slacks.* At least two pairs of slacks are necessary, preferably of solid colors and of good quality. Gray flannel slacks are standard anywhere in the world and if of good material will wear very well.

4. *Topcoat.* If you find that you cannot afford a topcoat in the early stages, you can always use your officer's raincoat without the insignia. But making the raincoat "double in brass" reduces its longevity, and you should plan on getting a topcoat in the near future. Unless you expect to be stationed in very cold climates the topcoat that has a zipper lining is practical.

5. *Summer clothes.* It may develop that you will need summer suits and slacks immediately. Therefore, you will have to use your own discretion as to how many you should buy. Eventually you will need one or two summer suits—or odd jackets and trousers—but don't be blinded initially into sinking too much money into this type of clothes. Duties involving winter clothes will surely turn up.

6. *Dinner jacket.* This should be the last item on your list, for you may have the least use for it. (This dinner jacket is a good item to put on your Christmas list for your parents to give you!) Actually, the need for a dinner jacket is increasing each year. If you know that you are going to be the only military person at a particular affair, you may develop a reluctance to being dressed differently from all the others.

7. *Hat.* A gray felt snap-brimmed hat may be worn with a business suit and a dinner jacket. (A derby is worn with a business suit only.)

Your list should also include drip-dry sports and dress shirts, both colored and white, striped or checked, depending on your taste. And neckties, suitable socks (but watch out for the too-gay variety), walking shorts, etc. A pair of loafers is always a good buy. Frequently, such items are received as gifts.

CIVILIAN DRESS FOR SERVICEWOMEN

The types of civilian clothes which are needed by women in the services must be determined by the climate and season, the size and location of your base, post or station, and your specific needs. The rapid changes in women's fashions make it impractical to give a detailed list of clothing for a civilian wardrobe.

In an area where civilian clothes are worn at work, the woman officer should select her wardrobe with care. She should dress as her civilian counterpart—the executive woman. Appropriate clothes—suits, tailored dresses, and street dresses—in subdued colors and of excellent quality and tailoring are always in good taste for daytime wear.

Since the junior officer may be able to acquire only a limited civilian wardrobe, she will be wise to select fashions of such quality that they can be worn frequently and can be expected to remain in style for more than one season. Large and/or bright designs soon become tiresome, and such a dress may seem old after being worn only once or twice. On the other hand, an older dress of dark or subdued shade and design may seem new when worn with different accessories.

Appropriate outfits and accessories for "after five" should be included in a woman officer's wardrobe. However, the number and kind of social affairs you attend will dictate your needs. In such areas as Pearl Harbor or Cape Kennedy, you may need more sports or casual clothes; in Washington, D.C., you may have more need for cocktail and evening dresses.

In selecting your civilian clothes, you should always pay attention to good workmanship and quality of fabrics, and choose styles which are becoming to your individual figure.

In general your *civilian wardrobe* should include the following:

- Raincoat or all-weather coat.
- Topcoat for cold weather, preferably a solid color which can be used for both dress and informal wear.
- Casual suit, to be worn with sweaters or blouses.
- Cocktail dress, of conservative style.
- Basic black or white afternoon-type dress, silk, linen, or woolen, according to the season.
- Three hats: one for dress, chapel services, etc.; one (casual) for sports and informal wear; one (usually small) for cocktails, the theater, etc.
- Three handbags: one for dress, one for casual wear, one for evening dress.
- Gloves, stockings, and shoes appropriate to the above outfits.

GOOD GROOMING

It is, of course, important that military women exercise great care in grooming and dress. When civilian clothes are worn at work, appropriate executive-type clothing should be the style of dress.

Nail polish is considered appropriate.

No pencils, pens, pins, handkerchiefs, or jewelry shall be worn or carried exposed upon the uniform. Earrings, hair ribbons, and other hair ornaments are not worn. Wrist watches, identification bracelets, and rings should be in good taste.

The frames of spectacles and sunglasses should be conservative in style and color, but some coloring, or gold or silver ornamentation, may be used.

WHEN TO WEAR WHAT

The clothes discussed here mainly pertain to those localities where conservative dress is preferred for all functions except the most casual. Although there seems to be a trend toward more informality in men's dress, there are only certain times when sports jackets should be worn.

The latitude that exists today permits almost anything to be worn until six P.M. Sports jackets and sports shirts are often worn to such afternoon affairs as cocktail parties—particularly if the section of the country in which you are stationed condones this practice. However, a good rule to follow is: if you are going to an afternoon affair that you know is not formal and your date or wife is not wearing a cocktail dress, you are correct in wearing your sports jacket, preferably with a white shirt.

At most cocktail parties, you will find a varied assortment of dress among the men, but the predominant dress will usually be that of a conservative suit for the practical reason that you may want to take your date or your wife out to dinner afterwards. A couple's attire should conform to the formality of the occasion: for a man to wear a sports jacket to a party when his date of wife is in formal or semiformal attire would be as poor taste as a woman wearing a cocktail dress to a football game.

If you are asked for dinner and the dress is not specified, you should assume that you will wear a conservative suit. When the dress is specified in the invitation—such as "Black tie"—you are expected to wear a dinner jacket or the corresponding uniform—after six P.M.

Extremely formal affairs, such as debutante balls and embassy receptions, customarily call for full dress. This fact will be spelled out for you by the hour of the affair or else on the invitation itself. For debutante balls starting after nine P.M., you are expected to wear full dress—that is, "White tie," or your full dress midshipman or cadet uniform, or evening dress officer uniform.

The type of uniform worn by servicewomen is generally the same as that worn by servicemen attending the same occasion. At a non-official occasion, such as a cocktail party, civilian dress may be worn.

Out of uniform, servicewomen wear civilian dress in accordance with local custom. You may, or may not, wear uniform when making social calls. At a luncheon or tea, women officers leave on their hats in accordance with the custom of civilian ladies.

In various public places, such as a chapel or church, hotel or restaurant, theater, etc., women in uniform leave on their hats or caps.

A practical rule to remember is: if you have any doubt about what to wear you may call the house of your hostess and ask. It is much better to do this than to be sorry when you get there.

TRAVEL TIPS

Travel light! The basic travel wardrobe for a 2 to 4-week trip can be packed in one suitcase—and take you anyplace in this country or abroad. The wash-and-wear fabrics are best for shirts, pajamas, underwear, blouses and some dresses, with cleaning services usually slow and expensive abroad. Unless you know that you will need formal attire, a dark suit for a man and basic dark or neutral attire for a woman will take you almost anywhere in the evening. You should check the climate of the country to be visited before selecting your wardrobe; charts showing the average temperatures day and night throughout the year abroad and at home are available at most airports and travel agencies.

Small purse or wallet-size currency, language and menu converters are also available at airports and these with your Traveler's checks, passport, ballpoint pen and writing pad, cigarettes and lighter, if used, may be carried in your pocket or wallet or handbag. An overnight bag can be placed under your airplane seat, or be folded and placed in your suitcase for later use.

Men need a waterproof utility kit for shaving soap, lotion, razors, plugs and adapters. Laundry soap granules come in handy. Women need a zippered plastic cosmetic bag for shampoo, nail polish and remover, hair curlers, face powder, and such. But *remember:* when you fly overseas you are allowed 66 pounds on a first class ticket, 44 pounds for the economy fare. A coat, umbrella, books, camera, may be carried into the cabin. Within the U.S. luggage weighing in excess of 70 pounds is shipped as air freight. Remember too, that many beautiful accessories such as leather goods, jewelry, perfume, gloves can be purchased abroad—so take few of these.

HIS CHECK LIST

1 Topcoat (rainproof) cool weather or folding raincoat, warm weather
1 Hat (wear)
2 Suits: one dark for evening, one for practical wear
1 Sports jacket, 1 pair slacks, for travel
2 Pairs shoes (one dark)
6 Pairs socks (4 quick-drying)
6 Cotton or quick-drying undershirts
6 Ties (or fewer if you buy some)
6 Handkerchiefs, and facial tissues
1 Pair pajamas, quick-drying
1 Lightweight robe, optional; folding slippers
1 Cuff links, tie clasp, collar pin
For winter travel—gloves and scarf, heavy sweater
For summer, bathing trunks, shorts, sports shirts, extra slacks in lieu of one suit
When packing place shoes, shaving kit (if not in overnight bag), along bottom of suitcase with shirts on top to avoid wrinkling.

HER CHECK LIST

1 Basic color coat (weight according to season)
1 Folding raincoat/umbrella
1 Travel suit, with comfortable skirt
1 Dress suit or 2 or 3-piece costume suit
1 Afternoon dress or a jacket-dress
1 Late-day or dinner dress
2 Casual daytime dresses
3 Pairs shoes: dressy pumps, low-heeled, comfortable walking; 3 pairs per two weeks nylon stockings
3 Blouses (washable), one dressy
1 Cardigan, basic color
2 Pairs gloves, one basic color, one white
2 Sets nylon underwear
1 Pair nylon or dacron pajamas or nightgown
1 Travel Robe, lightweight; folding slippers
2 Handbags, one large travel bag with zippered inside pocket, secure clasp, with handle or over the shoulder; a flat envelope bag for evening
1 Four-cornered scarf, hair protection.
1 Hat, wear or packable.

THE SOCIAL SIDE OF LIFE

CHAPTER 3

Hops and Dances

Young men in training at the Service Academies, ROTC units, or Officer Candidate Schools—or, for that matter, any young officer anywhere—will find that the etiquette observed at the Academy hops* and the college dances will generally be the same at any dance or ball. The earlier the correct etiquette at a dance is learned, the easier it will be for you to attend with complete poise and confidence any debutante ball or embassy dance.

The new Fourth Classmen at the Academies each year are young men from all walks of life. Many have had previous college or preparatory school training, and have escorted young ladies to fraternity or class dances.

Others, directly out of high school, may not have had the opportunity of learning what to do at formal dances, or how to greet those in the receiving line.

A midshipman or cadet, or any student, should be well versed in such courtesies before being graduated and receiving an assignment in a Service that may take him all over the world and into various social situations.

THE ACADEMY HOPS

There are three kinds of hops: *informal*, *semiformal*, and *formal*. The distinction between them is mainly in dress.

Informal hops are held for Fourth Classmen, as well as for upperclassmen, on Saturday or Sunday afternoons. Young ladies wear afternoon-style dresses and gloves, but no hats. Cocktail-style dresses and gloves are worn at the semiformal hops.

The uniform is prescribed for all hops—with evening dress uniform worn at the formals. A "drag"† will also wear evening dress, either long or

* Hop is a Service Academy word for dance.
† "Drag" is a Service Academy word for the young lady guest or "date" or a midshipman or cadet.

53

short, with long white gloves. But at any hop, the important thing for a young lady to remember is to dress in accordance with the formality—or informality—of the occasion.

Cadets and midshipmen will wear white gloves to the formal hop or dance, but will remove them along with their hats. Therefore, you do not wear gloves when going through the receiving line or on the dance floor.

A hostess will always be on hand at the hop to receive, or assist in receiving, guests. She will always be ready to help the couples in any way possible. At Annapolis, the hostess is escorted to and from the hop by a member of the Hop Committee.

HOP TIME

Formal hops at the Service Academies are usually held from 9 or 9:30 P.M. to 12 P.M. Upper Classmen attend on a voluntary basis, but must return to their barracks or quarters by 1 A.M., or by a designated time after the hop is over.

When you arrive at the hop, you will wait while your young lady takes her coat to the coatroom. Maids are available at all hops to assist with coats. They will have needles, thread, etc., for any emergency.

When the hop is over, the National Anthem is played. You will stand at attention, while your drag stands quietly at your side.

At the Plebe informals, Fourth Classmen arrive and leave by designated times.

RECEIVING LINES AT HOPS

It is a courtesy—and therefore mandatory—that you go through the receiving line at all hops. This is good training for future events and is similar to receiving lines at dances, balls, receptions, etc., any place.

The receiving line customarily forms near the entrance to the ballroom, and standing first in line is the hop manager or chairman, or the escort of the receiving lady. The wife of an officer on active duty in the yard or station will be invited to receive the guests.

The hop manager (chairman or escort) always keeps his hands at his sides, or at his back, so that guests will not shake hands with him. It is his duty to announce the names of guests to the receiving lady at his side. She will offer her hand to each guest, and greet everyone in a gracious and friendly manner. She will wear long, white gloves when in the receiving line, and girls being received leave their gloves on.

At Naval Academy hops, the husband of the lady receiving does not stand in the receiving line, but he usually attends later in the evening. The line is kept short due to the large number of guests attending. At the other Academies—the Military, Air Force, and Coast Guard—he will stand in the line.

At a formal hop at West Point, the officer will stand to the right of the hop manager, with the officer's wife to his right, then the cadet hostess. At less formal hops, the receiving line may be as follows:

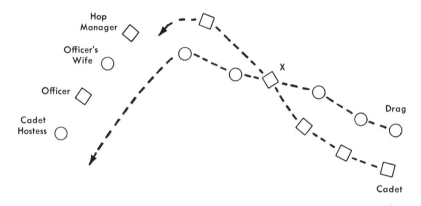

The Receiving Line at a West Point Hop

The young lady is on the right of the cadet as they enter the ballroom. At point "x," the cadet has passed behind the young lady and is now on her right.

PROCEDURE

The steps in going through the receiving line are:

1. The hop manager (chairman or escort) stands first in line, in order to present the guests to the receiving lady at his side. He does *not* shake hands with the guests, but she does—and she offers her hand first.

2. When the midshipman or cadet and his young lady approach the line, she will be on his right. She does *not* hold his arm.

3. Nearing the line, the young lady steps ahead and the cadet or midshipman is now behind and to her right, in position to give their names to the hop manager.

4. The midshipman or cadet gives the girl's *last* name only: "Miss Smith."

5. When the girl steps ahead of the midshipman or cadet, the hop manager turns to the receiving lady and says the *receiving lady's name first:* "Mrs. Brown, Miss Smith."

6. The receiving lady will shake hands with the young lady and say something similar to, "Good evening, it's so nice to see you." The girl may answer, "Good evening, Mrs. Brown," or "Good evening, it's nice to be here."

7. After the escort presents the girl to the receiving lady, he turns to

you (a midshipman or cadet), and you give your last name: "Cadet Jones."*
You do not fail to give your name, regardless of how well you know the
escort. If a guest does not state his name, the escort may say, "Your name,
please?"

8. The escort will then present you to the receiving lady: "Mrs. Brown,
Cadet Jones." She will probably greet you in a manner similar to her greeting to your young lady, and you may answer in the same way or say, "How
do you do, Mrs. Brown?" or simply, "How do you do?"

9. When the husband of the lady receiving stands in the line, you would
greet him in this manner: "Good evening, Sir," or "Good evening, General Davis." It is always correct to say, "How do you do, Sir?"

10. You may bow slightly when you shake hands, you should look at
the person addressed—escort, receiving lady, etc.—and not attempt a conversation.

11. The line does not form again at the end of the hop. It is always courteous, however, to thank the lady (and officer) receiving, and the hostess, and
to say "good-bye."

INTERMISSIONS

Fruit punch and cakes are served during intermission, and smoking is
permitted, but in authorized areas only. You may have the minor problem
of finding your young lady if she was dancing with someone else when intermission was called.

If you should pass her, you may extend your arm and tell her partner
that you will take over, which will release him to find his own young lady.
If something unexpected happens to the escort of the lady with whom you
have had that dance and he has not reclaimed her, *then it is your duty*—
and your date's—to stand by until he appears.

CONDUCT AT HOPS

Midshipmen and cadets are expected to conduct themselves as gentlemen at all times—on or off the dance floor. Displays of affection on the
dance floor are not tolerated, and Hop Committee members will ask those
who violate courtesies to leave the hop. Members of the Hop Committee
at the Coast Guard and Naval Academies are distinguished by their gold
aiguillettes; at the Air Force Academy by silver aiguillettes; at West Point by
red sashes. They have the authority to enforce regulations.

You will never leave your drag sitting alone, or embarrass her with

---

* A midshipman, or West Point or Coast Guard cadet, is introduced or addressed as "Mister"
at social or official occasions, except at certain military, state, or social occasions when he is
introduced or addressed by title for purposes of identification or designation. At the Air Force
Academy, cadets are introduced (or will give their names) as "Cadet Doe," but are addressed
thereafter as "Mr. Doe."

boisterous conduct. Never leave her in mid-floor. If an occasion arises when you must leave, you should leave her with a group before excusing yourself. If you are not adept at certain steps, such as in the more intricate dances, you may suggest "waiting this one out."

However, since it is the gentleman who invites the lady to dance, it is up to her to suggest that you stop. She might say, "Shall we rest a moment?" or "Please, let's have some punch." Otherwise, you should dance indefinitely (perhaps this is the origin of the term "dragging!").

When you complete a dance with a girl who is not your guest, take her back to her escort or to her party, and thank her.

Since the general tone of the hop is formal, rather formal dancing is expected. A contemporary dance is permitted, but not in the too-strenuous form that demands a wide area for the performance.

It is inconsiderate to remain talking in groups on the dance floor. If you want to talk, rather than dance, you should move to the side of the floor.

OBLIGATIONS

The *first* obligation of a midshipman or cadet—or any man—is to the young lady whom you are escorting. She should be shown every consideration, and in turn, it is her duty to you to make this the most memorable of occasions.

You should dance with your drag frequently, but not exclusively. You should introduce her to other couples and offer her refreshments. You must see to it that she is never neglected, even though this is a blind date and she is not "Miss America." Using the hop card is a good way to ensure an exchange of dances.

Your *second* obligation is to the others in your party or at your table. You must join in the general conversation, bring your drag or others into the conversation, help get refreshments during intermission, and dance with other ladies in the group.

Your *third* obligation is to the midshipman or cadet hostess, the receiving couple, and any other senior person or guests present.

Each cadet or midshipman in the host company for that evening has this particular obligation; he must make it a point to talk briefly to the receiving officer and to any senior male guests, and to dance with their ladies and with the midshipman or cadet hostess. These ladies are well aware of your desire to dance with others of your own age, so don't be afraid of being "stuck."

In asking an officer's wife for a dance, you would first approach Colonel and Mrs. Rank, greet them, and introduce your young lady, if she has not already met them in the receiving line.

After a brief exchange of small talk, you ask Mrs. Rank if she would care to dance. Colonel Rank will then talk or dance with your date.

At the end of the number—or earlier, if indicated by Mrs. Rank—you will both return to the place from which you started. You will thank her for the dance, as you would thank any partner, before you and your young lady move away.

DUTIES OF HOP ESCORT

At a Naval Academy hop, the escort (midshipman hop chairman or member of the First Class hop committee) will call for the receiving lady, since her husband does not stand in the receiving line. Usually he appears at the hop later in the evening; but if he does not, the escort will take her home.

It is a tradition that the Superintendent's wife receives at the Christmas Hop, when she is escorted by the chairman of the hop committee. Members of the First Class hop committee, and their drags, are invited as dinner guests in the Superintendent's house before going on to the dance.

First Classmen do not act as escorts during June Week. Second Classmen will escort the receiving lady and members of the Third Class will escort the hostesses.

While on escort duty, you do not invite a young lady to be your own guest.

CARD OR PROGRAM HOPS

The advantage of the card or program dance is that you and your young lady will have the opportunity of meeting and dancing with others. Before the hop, you place the names of friends on your young lady's program— and in turn, they place her name on theirs.

A blank card at a program hop might be embarrassing to your date unless it is mutually understood that you are retaining all the dances for yourself—which is not the purpose of program hops.

You must always remember that when you have allowed your name to be placed in a girl's dance program, you *must* fulfill your commitments.

CUTTING IN

During any hop, program or otherwise, unless the tune being played has been designated a "no break," you may cut in on another couple if you are already acquainted with the young lady, or are such a close personal friend of her partner that you can expect to be introduced. You accomplish this operation by tapping the man on his shoulder and saying, "May I cut in?" or just, "Cut, please." However, it is customary that cutting in is not permitted during the first number of each dance.

When someone cuts in on you, it is improper to cut right back. If you want to dance with the girl again, wait until someone else cuts in on him— or arrange for it if you're in a hurry!

When you are the one who cuts in, you must return the young lady to her escort after the end of that one dance. Since hops are usually very large affairs, it is wise for couples to have a pre-arranged place of meeting following a cut-in.

If one of your classmates has not drawn "Miss America" as a blind date, the gentlemanly thing to do is cut in on him. This will not only "spell" him a bit, but will give him the opportunity to line up somebody to cut in on you—which he is absolutely obligated to do.

It should be pointed out that the Fourth Class, or "Plebe," informal dances at the Naval Academy operate on a different set of rules. At Plebe dances, the young ladies have been invited as guests of the entire class. Thus, any Plebe, as a host, is expected to cut in and to introduce himself to any young lady present.

DANCING INSTRUCTION

It is required of all midshipmen and cadets at the Academies that they learn to dance, and classes for Fourth Classmen are held at scheduled times with a professional instructor in charge. Advanced classes are available for all midshipmen and cadets.

At the Military Academy, Plebes are given instruction in basic steps and ballroom etiquette during Beast Barracks, and optional dancing classes are held during the fall. Optional dancing classes are sometimes available to the Third Class during their summer training at Camp Buckner.

Instruction covers problems of etiquette, in addition to dance steps. You are taught the way your left or leading hand should hold your partner's hand lightly and naturally, with your right or holding arm placed firmly yet loosely just above her waist. Exaggerated positions make for bad manners, as well as bad dancers.

Courtesy classes are held at the Academies, when Fourth Classmen are taught how to conduct themselves and how to ask for a dance: "May I have this dance?" or "Will you dance with me?"

SPECIAL HOPS AND DANCES

JUNE WEEK

The hops and balls held during June Week at the Service Academies are considered the most important of all. They mark the first formals for many Fourth Classmen and are the final dances for the First Classmen.

First, Second, and Third Class hops and dances, and many others are held throughout the Week.

The Ring Dance is the highlight for the Second Class (except at West Point) with couples passing through a replica of the class ring, and each young lady receiving a kiss.

At the Naval Academy, class rings are received at a formal dinner in the Mess Hall, with young ladies attending, after which they go on to the dance.

At the Air Force Academy the Ring Presentation and Banquet is a formal stag affair, with a guest speaker. Following the banquet the cadets call for their dates and escort them to the dance.

The formal Ring Banquet and Hop are held in Washington Hall at West Point the first Saturday in September. At this time, the First Classmen wear their new rings. The chairman of the Ring and Crest Committee is the host, and there is always a speaker at the banquet.

The Farewell Ball and the Graduation Balls held on the eve of graduation traditionally bring to a close the Week's social activities.

SERVICE DANCES

Among the numerous service dances held throughout the country is the Army-Navy-Air Force Cotillion in Washington, D.C., which is open to Service Juniors who are sons or daughters of active, retired, or deceased officers of the Army, Navy, Air Force, Marine Corps, and Coast Guard. Members must be at least 16 years old.

Commanders of various posts, bases and stations, and service organizations such as Alumni Association chapters, invite cadets and midshipmen to attend dances held during Christmas and spring leave.

Hops for midshipmen and for cadets are held after the Army-Navy football game in Philadelphia and in cities following other Service Academy games. Dress is informal.

SPECIAL BALLS

Members of the First, Second, and Third Classes at the Air Force Academy attend the formal Military Ball held at Loretto Heights College, Denver. The fete is held each spring.

These three classes also attend the Superintendent's Ball, the first formal of the academic year; the Commandant's Ball held in February, and the Dean's Ball in the spring. Fourth Classmen at the Air Force Academy attend the spring formal held at Temple Buell College, Denver.

One of the largest hops at the Naval Academy is the Christmas Hop, when each midshipman and his drag bring a toy to be placed under the Christmas tree. Later, the toys are distributed to underprivileged children.

FOURTH CLASS HOPS

The informal Fourth Class hops and tea dances at the Service Academies serve as instructional periods, as well as afternoons of dancing. The cadets and midshipmen gain experience in going through the receiving line, in getting acquainted with young ladies they have never met before, and in the perfecting of dance steps.

NAVAL ACADEMY INFORMALS

The Plebe Informals at Annapolis are a means of introducing approximately fourteen hundred Fourth Classmen to young ladies in the community and from nearby colleges.

Since the duties of the social director do not include obtaining dates for the midshipmen, this is considered the most correct way for Plebes to meet future drags.

The majority of the young ladies arrive unescorted. They are met at the entrance of Dahlgren Hall by members of the Hop Committee. After disposing of their wraps, the girls are taken onto the dance floor and introduced to the young men: "Miss Smith, Mr. Jones." The couple will go through the receiving line—then they are on their own.

Plebes are encouraged to cut in and introduce themselves. Fruit punch is served during intermission, and this time presents further opportunities to become better acquainted.

Plebes are required to attend the informals which are held throughout the academic year. There are always more Plebes than girls, and the stag line is longer than at other hops. For the Plebe learning to dance, the stag line serves as an observation post—but you cannot remain there throughout the hop.

Young ladies must be between 16 and 21 years of age to have their names placed on the invitation list. The invitation card is non-transferable and must be presented at the door.

Plebes drag during June Week.

MILITARY ACADEMY PLEBE HOPS

Plebes at the Military Academy go home for the Christmas holidays. They must, however, remain at West Point during Plebe Parents' Weekend which is held at the same time as spring leave for upperclassmen. At this time, activities are planned for their parents and their drags, and a formal hop is held on Saturday night.

During the academic year, Plebes are permitted to drag on weekends, and Plebe hops are held on Saturday nights. They also attend mixers at nearby womens' colleges once a month.

Plebes do not drag during June Week of their first year at West Point— except the night before the graduation of the First Classmen, when they may attend their Recognition Hop with the girl of their choice.

AIR FORCE ACADEMY MIXERS

Informal dances called "Mixers" are held for the Fourth Classmen, or "Doolies," at Colorado Springs prior to the Christmas season. Young ladies in the area, as well as from nearby colleges, are invited to the mixers. Doolies have a Christmas Ball, Valentine's Ball, and Recognition Ball in early May. Doolies date during June Week, when they attend the All Class Ball.

COAST GUARD ACADEMY TEA DANCES

The Fourth Class cadets, or "Swabs," are entertained by the Superintendent and his wife at a tea dance on a Sunday afternoon in October. Young ladies in the New London area, and from nearby colleges, are invited to attend.

Swabs are required to attend a designated number of the formal dances held throughout the academic year for all classes. They drag during June Week.

MARINE CORPS BIRTHDAY BALL

The Birthday of the Marine Corps—10 November 1775—is observed throughout the world, aboard ship and at all posts and stations. At a Marine Corps post commanded by a general officer, the celebration usually includes a troop formation, holiday rations, maximum liberty and minimum work, a memorial service, and a Birthday Ball with cake-cutting ceremony.

Distinguished guests from other services and from civilian life are invited to attend the formal ball, with officers wearing evening dress or blues with large medals. Civilian guests will wear full evening dress or dinner jackets, and ladies will be dressed in formal attire.

The cake-cutting ceremony follows a time-honored procedure which includes the playing of the "Foreign Legion March," followed by a band or orchestra playing "Semper Fidelis." A rectangle is formed by escorts who enter the room in pairs, followed by officers of high rank and the Color Guard.

"The Marines' Hymn" is played; the cake escorts bring in the birthday cake and a Mameluke sword on a serving cart. The commanding general makes a brief talk and introduces the guest of honor. The senior cake escort then takes the sword, passes it over his left forearm, grip forward, and hands it to the commanding general who cuts the first piece of cake. After everyone is served, the floor is cleared for dancing.

COLLEGE DANCE

A college man will wear "Black tie"—his tuxedo, or a white dinner jacket in the summer—to a formal college dance.

A midshipman or cadet, ROTC student, OCS, OTS—or any officer—may wear his service uniform which is the equivalent of "Black tie," or he may wear civilian dress.

When a dinner precedes a dance at a women's college, the girl usually pays for the dinner—in advance, so no one will be embarrassed. But if you invite her out for dinner, you will pay for the meal. You will pay for all taxi fares during the weekend and for any flowers, movies, etc.

After you return to your Academy, college, or station, you should write a thank-you note to the girl and also to the hostess in the house where you stayed, if she was a family friend or relative of the girl. In turn, you should try to repay the hospitality of the girl by inviting her to the Academy, college, or station, for a hop or dance.

DEBUTANTE BALLS

In metropolitan cities throughout the country, debutantes make their bows to society in large groups at cotillions and assemblies. Such balls are usually held for the benefit of various charity organizations, with the young ladies' fathers making contributions to charities in lieu of the greater expense of private debuts.

Dinners honoring individual debutantes are customarily held before the balls. Daughters, or daughters of close friends and relatives, will be honored by their parents or sponsors at afternoon tea dances, which are usually held in exclusive clubs or hotel ballrooms.

Each girl attending a formal debutante ball will subscribe for two or three partners—or many more. Debutantes wear long white dresses and white gloves for their presentation. Midshipmen, cadets, and young bachelor officers are often invited to become dancing partners at a ball, or to attend as "stags." Officers will wear evening dress uniform or "White tie." Midshipmen and cadets wear evening dress uniform. Civilian gentlemen wear "White tie."

Partners of the debutante, as well as her close relatives and friends, will send flowers to the girl before the ball, with one corsage or bouquet selected to be worn. The other flowers will be used as a background at the place the debutante will be presented.

A buffet supper is served after midnight, and the ball is over in the early morning hours. No line is formed at the conclusion of the affair, but guests are expected to thank the debutante's parents or sponsors. If a dinner, at which you were a guest, was held before the ball, then you will thank the host and hostess of that dinner, also.

Since each cotillion has various customs and traditions, it is important that you learn the ground rules in advance, from the person who sent you the invitation.

THE FORMAL DANCE

A formal dance may be held in a large room or club, usually starting about ten o'clock, with dancing getting underway an hour later. For a very formal affair, a carpet may run from the curb to the front entrance, with an awning overhead. Guests are announced at formal and semiformal dances.

The hostess and the guest of honor—say, a debutante—will be standing near the entrance to the ballroom, where they greet guests. The host usually stands in the receiving line during the early part of the evening, but will leave the line before the hostess and the guest of honor do, so that he can mix with the guests. The receiving line usually breaks up after three-quarters of an hour.

There will be a stag line, with an extra man for each nine or ten girls. If you are invited as a "stag," your duty is to see that the girls receive the proper attention and never lack for dancing partners.

A buffet supper is served after midnight, with no announcement made concerning its serving. The hostess usually initiates the movement of a few guests toward the buffet table, and other guests follow.

When you attend as a "stag," you may ask any unattached woman to have supper with you. You may fill both your plates, and sit wherever you like. Usually, small tables are arranged for a few guests to sit at each. At a large dance, the food may be served directly to guests seated at small tables.

DUTY DANCES

"Duty" dances are those that good manners require you to have with certain ladies at a private dance, or dinner dance. Such duty dances are those with your hostess, the guest of honor, and any feminine member of the hostess's family.

If you attended a dinner before the dance or ball, then you will also dance with the hostess and the guest of honor at that occasion. You have a certain duty (but it is not required) to dance also with the two women who sat at your left and right at the dinner. If the woman at your right was your assigned dinner partner, then you are obligated to dance with her.

When you are the guest of a woman at a party, or are the guest of a subscription party member, you will dance several times with her, and you should invite her to have supper with you.

At a service dance, you will dance—or sit and talk for a few minutes—with the wife of the senior officer present, whether she is the hostess or not.

A HOP WEEKEND

When you invite a girl to your Service Academy for the first time, write the letter in a simple but sincere manner. If she has never been to the Academy before, you should include a brief but general idea of any plans for the weekend. You should write her three or four weeks in advance of the hop.

After the girl accepts your invitation, then write a more specific letter in return. She will not want to arrive either unprepared or overloaded with luggage. If she has not been in the Academy town before, she will want to know the best way to come—by bus, train, plane, or car.

When she is to arrive by bus, the bus schedule must be checked beforehand. You will want to tell her the time that you can—or cannot—meet her, owing to drills, classes, etc. If you know that other girls from her area or college will be arriving that weekend, you might mention their names so that she may have company on the trip.

When a person is not arriving by private car, a bus is the most convenient method of transportation. For a person coming from a distance, a train or plane to the nearest large city would save time, then a bus or taxi to the Academy. There is no train service directly to West Point or Annapolis.

There are regular bus schedules out of New York City for West Point, New York, and New London, Connecticut. And there are regular schedules out of Washington, D.C., and Baltimore, Maryland, for Annapolis, as well as out of Denver and Colorado Springs for the Air Force Academy, which is located about 12 miles north of Colorado Springs.

DRESS FOR "DRAGS"

Your "drag" will be anxious to know what clothes to bring on her hop weekend, so tell her of the events that you plan to attend. A formal hop means her prettiest formal dress, either long or short—but not a cocktail-style dress—evening shoes, and long, white gloves.

The informal or afternoon hop means an afternoon-style dress, but the extreme cocktail-type dress is not desirable. White gloves are usually worn. Semiformal hops are occasionally held on Saturday evenings in place of formal hops, when midshipmen and cadets wear the uniform of the day, and drags wear cocktail-style dresses and white gloves.

Sunday morning chapel services may be attended by the young lady. She should wear a suit, hat, and gloves, or a plain afternoon dress with a coat or jacket in season, hat, and gloves.

High heels are fine for dress occasions, but not for walking—and considerable walking is accomplished over a hop weekend. Therefore, comfortable walking shoes are a "must" for the weekend.

A football game, or any sports event, means sports clothes. The suit worn on the trip may be worn at such a contest, or a skirt and sweater. Although shorts may be worn for sailing, tennis, or other sports, brief shorts are frowned upon, and bathing suits are never paraded away from the beach or swimming pool. Your young lady should be advised that soft-soled shoes should always be worn for sailing or tennis, and hiking gear is necessary for a mountain climb.

A lightweight, packable raincoat, or all-purpose coat, is indispensable. And for the late season football games at Michie Stadium or Falcon Stadium, for instance, a wise drag will bring along a blanket to help keep her warm.

"DRAGGING" EXPENSES

When a girl comes to the Service Academies for a hop weekend, or during June Week, she can expect to pay for her transportation to and from the Academy. She will pay for her meals en route and for any during the visit which have not been arranged for by you, her host, or by friends. She will also pay for her room during the visit (even though you made the reservation), unless she has been invited by friends to be a guest in their quarters or home.

At the U.S. Hotel Thayer on the grounds of the Military Academy, dormitory rooms are available for drags at about two dollars a night. When the hotel is filled, the cadet hostess will assist in getting a room in an accredited "drag house" in Highland Falls (which will cost more). Such accredited rooms are available near all Academies, and a list is kept in the office of each hostess.

As a midshipman, cadet, or ROTC student, you can expect to pay for anything to which you invite your guest, or guests, such as meals, movies, etc. You pay for flowers for your drag, which you order in advance, and for taxis—when you are permitted to ride in them. However, sending a corsage to your young lady is the exception nowadays, rather than the rule.

As almost everyone knows, an Underclassman receives only a small amount each month for spending money, with a First Classman receiving a little more. For those who have little or no financial assistance from home, this amount does not go far.

REGULATIONS FOR CARS

When a drag—or any person—is to arrive in your Academy town by car, that person should know who can, and cannot, ride in cars. Regulations governing the riding in cars by midshipmen and cadets are authorized by the superintendent of each institution, and are modified or changed whenever necessary.

Each Academy has a radius within which cadets and midshipmen can, or cannot, ride, with First Classmen having certain privileges within the radius. First Classmen are permitted to purchase cars and leave them in a designated area, at an authorized time.

CHAPTER 4

Receptions and Cocktail Parties

RECEPTIONS

According to Webster's dictionary, a reception is a "ceremony of receiving guests." There are many kinds of receptions—afternoon or evening, formal or informal. They are of a limited duration of time, and a few or many people may be invited.

Receptions are usually held in honor of someone—a dignitary, a bride and groom, a debutante, or a newcomer. They are also held to mark a special occasion, such as the christening or commissioning of a ship, a golden wedding anniversary, or the baptism of an infant. But no matter what the occasion may be, the routine of holding a reception is basically the same.

The purpose of a reception given in honor of someone is to have as many friends and acquaintances of the hosts as possible meet the guest (or guests) of honor. In the services, one type of reception is an "at-home"— when, for example, the senior officer of a large command designates a certain day for "calls made and returned."

When this type of reception is held, it means that the senior officer of a very large command cannot possibly receive and return individual calls made by all the officers and station personnel and their families. Thus the at-homes are held as often as necessary, ranging from one or two a year, to one every month or so.

It is no longer customary for guests to leave cards, and their call is considered repaid. (See Chapter 5, *Calls and Calling Cards*.)

TIME

The hours of the reception are indicated on the invitation and usually span a two-hour interval. They are held at various hours, according to their nature, with less formal receptions frequently held from six to eight o'clock in the evening. Afternoon, receptions and at-homes are often held from five to seven o'clock. An informal reception may be held in mid-afternoon or early evening; a formal debutante reception may be at five o'clock, or at half past ten or eleven o'clock at night.

An official or formal reception usually starts at nine o'clock in the evening, and a very formal reception and dance may be held at ten or half past ten o'clock at night.

DRESS

At *informal daytime receptions*, men wear the uniform of the day or dark business suits. Women wear afternoon dresses or suits, hats, and gloves. Ladies in the receiving line do not wear gloves. Such words as "Informal," or "Service Dress White" and "Civilian Informal," would be written or engraved in the lower right-hand corner of the invitation.

At *formal daytime receptions*, a man will wear the uniform of the day or the prescribed civilian dress for the very formal occasion—the cutaway —which is worn at an inaugural reception, or any formal State or public function. Such dress is also worn at a very formal wedding when you are a member of the bridal party. Women wear an afternoon dress, a more elaborate hat, and white gloves. The gloves are not removed until after you have gone through the receiving line, with the exception of shaking hands with a head of state or a dignitary of the church; then, the right glove is removed.

At *formal evening receptions*, the formality of the occasion is indicated by the words "Black tie" written or engraved in the lower right-hand corner of the invitation. "White tie" indicates a very formal occasion. "Decorations" always indicate full evening dress.

A reception is usually "Black tie," unless specified otherwise. Women wear evening dress and long gloves, and men wear mess or dinner dress uniforms, or the prescribed uniform according to the season. (See Chapter 2, *Service and Civilian Dress*.)

At *semiformal receptions* "Black tie" or "Civilian Informal" (your best dark business suit) with corresponding uniform designation, would indicate the type of dress to be worn.

At large official receptions, or at a large reception somewhat of a public nature, "Dress Optional" is frequently engraved or written on the lower right-hand corner of the invitation.

Small cards stating the type of uniform to be worn are usually enclosed with naval and military invitations of official occasions.

WHITE HOUSE RECEPTIONS

Dress for an afternoon reception at the White House is the same as at any afternoon reception.

As a guest, you must be on time. You should arrive at the White House gate no less than 10 minutes before the hour of invitation, which will give you time to be checked at the gate and to leave your hat and coat in the designated room.

You will be directed to the place of reception, where a military aide will announce guests' names. Since it is the title that takes precedence at an official occasion, the men precede the women they are escorting through the receiving line. Before shaking hands with the President, a woman would have removed her right glove. You will say, "Good evening, Mr. President," and "Good evening, Mrs. ——," and move on—unless the host or hostess stops you briefly to say a few words. Otherwise, you do not open a conversation with either the President or the First Lady while going through the line. You do not leave cards, and you do not leave the reception until after the President and his wife have left the room.

ARRIVAL AND DEPARTURE

There is no particular time limit on how long you will stay at a reception. You may arrive at any time between the hours indicated on the invitation, but guests are expected to arrive before the receiving line disbands. It is imperative that you first pay your respects to your host and hostess. You may stay a little longer at small receptions than at large ones.

Usually, you stay about 45 minutes at a reception, but you may stay until the closing hours at a formal reception and dance. You should not arrive uncomfortably near the closing hour of the reception—unless you have been asked to stay on for supper by the hosts. A guest who arrives late at an afternoon reception and lingers on through the dinner hour can be a problem to the hosts, who may have other social obligations.

RECEIVING LINE

There are differences in the way receiving lines are formed at various official, formal, and informal receptions. Customarily, the host stands first in line at *official* receptions, with his wife at his side. The hostess stands first in line at social, *non-official* functions, with her husband at her side.

At *official* receptions, an aide will stand either at the head of the line or facing the host and he will announce the names of guests as they arrive. The protocol established by the State Department, not counting the aide, is:

1. The official host
2. The guest of honor
3. The guest of honor's wife
4. The official host's wife
5. Extra man, if possible, to avoid leaving a woman at the end of the line.

When the guest of honor is the President of any country, a reigning

King and/or Queen, or a dignitary of the Church, the host and hostess will relinquish their positions in favor of their guest. The line would be:

1. President, King (or reigning Queen)
2. The honored guest's wife (or husband of Queen)
3. The official host
4. The official host's wife.

At many Washington receptions, when the honor guests are of high rank or position (for example, when the Secretary of Defense gives a reception in honor of a Service Secretary), the receiving line is frequently arranged in the following manner:

1. The host
2. The hostess
3. The guest of honor
4. The guest of honor's wife.

Some hosts invite a man appropriately connected to the occasion to stand at the end of the line, in order that a woman need not be in this position. Other hosts feel that this is incorrect, since a reception is to honor certain individuals only.

At formal non-military receptions, a butler will announce the names of guests as they arrive. At some formal—and at most less formal receptions —guests are received in the same way as at a formal dinner. The hostess greets each guest and presents him or her to the guests of honor; then the guest is greeted by the host, who is near the hostess but is mixing among the guests and introducing newcomers into groups.

The receiving line at receptions should be kept as small as possible. Usually, those in the line are the host, hostess, and guest or guests of honor. No one likes to go down a long line—which generally means that a guest's name is mixed up midway in the line. Names are not announced at small and informal receptions.

The receiving lines at wedding receptions, at-homes, and formal dances, are discussed in chapters pertaining to those subjects.

When a President, King, Queen, or dignitary of the Church, or a person of very high rank, attends a reception, all other guests should arrive before they do. In the case of a King, President, or dignitary of the Church, women are presented to them, rather than the customary rule of presenting men to women.

RECEPTIONS FOR GRADUATES

It is customary each year for the superintendents and presidents of the various Service Academies and Colleges, and their wives, to entertain at an afternoon or evening reception in honor of the graduates, their parents and other members of their families, and their young ladies.

This custom prevails not only at the Academies, but also at the Officer Candidate and Officer Training Schools, Marine Corps Schools, ROTC units, etc.

When the reception is held in the evening, after 6 P.M., and is followed by a formal hop, officers wear evening dress uniform and ladies wear long or short formal dresses and gloves.

GARDEN PARTY

The procedure for guests going through the receiving line at a large reception may be illustrated by the Superintendent's Garden Party, which is held at the Naval Academy each spring during June Week for the parents and guests of the First Classmen. In recent years two parties have been held, due to the size of the graduating class.

The Superintendent and his wife receive guests inside the Superintendent's house. The guests greet their hosts; then they go into the garden where punch and small cakes are served.

At an evening party, guests go on to a dance after the reception, which will continue until midnight. In case of rain, the receiving line forms inside Dahlgren Hall. Staff officers and their wives assist in hospitalities throughout the evening.

Although the majority of parents and other relatives of the midshipmen will wear evening dress—the men in dinner jackets and the women in evening attire—many persons coming from a distance may not be able to bring formal clothes. In this case, women are properly attired when they wear their prettiest afternoon dress, with white or pastel-colored gloves— but no hat. Men wear a dark or conservative business suit, with white shirt.

Customarily, the Superintendent is first in the line—due to his official position—with his wife at his side. The aide will announce the names of guests as they arrive, and he will stand nearer the entrance to the reception room, either at the head of the line or facing the host—whichever way names are more clearly heard. As the guests approach the line, the aide will turn and face them. Guests do not shake hands with the aide, and last names only are given.

The midshipman will step forward and clearly state the name of each person in his party, starting with his parents: "Mrs. Jones"—then "Dr. Jones"—and his drag, "Miss Smith."

If there are other members of his family, they would be presented in this order: his mother, father, grandmother, grandfather, aunt, uncle, sister, brother, and lastly his drag.

After each person in the midshipman's party has been presented, the aide will turn to the midshipman, who will give his name: "Mr. Jones." The aide turns to the Superintendent and says, "Admiral Blank, Mr. Jones," or simply, "Mr. Jones." The Superintendent and his wife will shake hands with each guest as they greet her or him.

The midshipman may say, "Good evening, Sir," or "Good evening, Admiral Blank," or "How do you do, Sir."

Midshipmen and naval officers, as well as Coast Guard cadets and officers, up to and including the rank of lieutenant commander, give their titles as "Mister" at official and social occasions at the base or station, unless it is desirable that identification of the officer be made. Officers of the rank of commander and above state their rank, with admirals of all grades stating their rank as "Admiral." Officers of the Marine Corps, Army, and Air Force, regardless of rank, use their titles, rather than "Mister."

You will remember to shake hands lightly—but with a degree of firmness. Your hosts have many hands to shake during the evening, and a pressure grip is to be avoided. Guests may arrive at any time between the hours stated in the invitation, but it is customary at this reception that the midshipmen attend by battalions at certain designated hours. When the line is very long, guests may dance first, then later go through the line—but all guests *must* go through the line.

Upon leaving, you do not look up your hosts and say good-bye. This is a very large reception, and it is not expected or desired that guests again shake hands.

DEPARTURE

At receptions other than the Superintendent's Garden Party, the receiving line may form again at the end of the evening, and once again you will go down the line. You will thank your hosts as you shake hands, express pleasure for the evening, and say good-bye.

At a reception to meet a newcomer, the line is usually broken up after the first hour, but the hosts and guests of honor usually stay near the door, mingling with other guests. At a large affair, you do not look them up; at a small reception, you do. In the latter case, you thank them—and leave.

COCKTAIL PARTIES

Cocktail parties vary in size from a handful to many people. They are, perhaps, the easiest means of entertaining a large number of guests—who may arrive at any time within the customary two hours stated in the invitation.

The main difference between cocktail parties and receptions is that cocktail parties usually are informal, with no formal receiving line, cards are not left, and alcoholic drinks are always served. (However, alcoholic beverages are forbidden aboard ships of the Naval Service.) Cocktail parties are customarily held during or near the close of daylight hours, an hour before dinner, and less frequently before luncheons. Receptions may have fruit punch and/or alcoholic punch served, they may be held in the evening as well as in the daytime, and usually they are of a formal nature, with a receiving line.

Hosts frequently give cocktail parties for a special guest or guests, or "to meet," newcomers to the station or neighborhood. The guest or guests will be standing near their hosts, in order to be introduced to other guests as they arrive.

A host and hostess will be near the door when guests arrive, and guests are always greeted in an informal manner. If you are a stranger, your host or hostess will probably introduce you to someone nearby—but after this, you are on your own. You may talk with stranger or friend, and you may stay as long as the invitation specifies.

Customarily, a choice of two drinks (three at most) is offered at cocktail parties, as well as whiskey and soda, ginger ale, and perhaps sherry. Fruit juice or tomato juice or soft drinks should be available for non-drinkers. A host will never insist that a guest take a drink when he does not want one. If you do not drink, say so; you don't have to drink. When a drink is offered to you, simply say, "No, thank you," without any explanation of why you don't want it. In case of a toast, however, you go through the motions of drinking.

Some cocktail parties may be small affairs, for perhaps a dozen friends, with the host mixing and serving drinks from a tray placed at a convenient spot in the room. Cocktail food may consist of a bowl of nuts or potato chips with a dip, with guests serving themselves or assisting in passing the food around the room.

At the average party, a host should figure on three cocktails per person. Drinks are frequently served from a bar which has been set up in a designated room, with a waiter in attendance. Guests are expected to order their choice. When you arrive, the host may say, "Won't you go over to the bar and have a drink?" You will ask your date—or anyone whom you have brought—what she would like to drink; then you get both drinks. Do not set a damp or cold glass on a table without something underneath it—a coaster, napkin, magazine, or anything convenient when coasters are not provided.

Some hosts prefer that drinks be served on a tray by a waiter. If your host, or the waiter, should ask if you prefer a drink not offered, you may state your preference; otherwise you do not request a drink not offered, other than non-alcoholic beverages. If you must request anything at a party —such as a glass of ginger ale or water, etc.—you make your request of the servant, not of your busy host or hostess. If you want a non-alcoholic drink, it is proper to ask for it. You may say, "I'd like a ginger ale or a Coke, if you have some," etc.

At small cocktail parties, the host usually acts as bartender. If he does not limit or state what he has to drink, you may ask, "What are you serving?" However, a wise host will first state what is on hand, and then ask each guest which he prefers. Most hosts mix drinks beforehand; frequently drinks are stored in the refrigerator, "deep freeze" fashion, with ice added when needed.

ORGANIZED PARTIES

The organized group party—for officers in a unit, headquarters, division, wing, group, squadron, department, etc., and their wives or dates is a popular type of party.

A committee will be appointed to make arrangements for the party, which is frequently held in an officers' club at a designated time. Notices may be telephoned or posted, stating the proper dress, and the estimated cost for each couple.

Such parties are usually informal, with their purpose the opportunity for the officers of each unit, etc., and their wives, to become better acquainted. Or they may be of a more formal nature, with an evening of cocktails, dinner, and dancing.

Junior officers will remember to greet the senior officers and their wives upon arrival.

COCKTAILS-BUFFET

A popular type of cocktail party, which originated in Washington, D.C., is called "Cocktails-Buffet." As a guest, you would know that you are expected to partake of the buffet-style food which would be more elaborate than the usual cocktail fare.

The main purpose of the hosts in extending an invitation to this type of cocktail party is to inform the guests that they need not make other plans for supper. The time is usually 6:30 P.M. (See Chapter 18, *Invitations and Replies*.)

CANAPES (COCKTAIL FOOD)

Canapes (or cocktail food) are growing progressively more substantial, but a guest invited to a cocktail party, not cocktails-buffet, should eventually move away from the table or tray of food. Roast ham, turkey, or beef, with hot and cold breads, seafood, elaborate dips, broiled olives wrapped in bacon, bite-size biscuits filled with hot mixtures, miniature hamburgers on toothpicks—any or all of these, and more, may be served at a large party, and several are often served at small affairs.

Frequently, the hosts invite several guests to stay on for supper, but without such an invitation in advance, no guest should linger so long after the hours of the party that he forces himself to be invited.

Most cocktail food is eaten with the fingers, except that some food, such as shrimp, is served on or with toothpicks. Food, however, is not offered until after a guest has been served a drink. Napkins are either handed to guests or are available on a buffet table nearby.

At large parties, a staff of waiters is necessary to serve drinks. Not counting servants in the kitchen who mix drinks, prepare food, wash glasses, etc., two waiters are needed to serve each fifty guests. In this case, guests will serve themselves at the buffet table. When food is not served buffet style but is to be passed around by the waiters, extra help is necessary.

CHAPTER 5

Calls and Calling Cards

In times of war or national emergency the social life in the services is relatively informal. Many social customs were held in abeyance during World War II and the Korean conflict; some have been slow to come back, and others may never return, due to the changing times.

One of the customs which has changed since the days of the more recent wars is that of making formal calls. Formerly, there was a rigid system of etiquette observed in making official and social calls. The system of official calls is unchanged, but that of making and returning social calls is greatly simplified.

In many parts of the country, social calls are extinct; in others, they are being re-established. Many old hands in the services desire the return of such calls as a gracious way of living. The more formal system of calling in the pre-war services had its merits—mainly in the promotion of friendships between senior officers, and their wives, and junior families.

However, there are problems involved in today's living that did not affect the old services particularly. With few servants in the modern household, there is far less time to make calls; junior officers and their wives frequently have no one with whom to leave their children when making calls. There are many more officers serving at larger bases than ever before—thus more officers' families on whom to call.

The commanding officer of a large station cannot possibly take the time today to receive and return all the calls that were required to be made in the pre-war days. In order to extend hospitality to the officers in his command, and their wives, and to become better acquainted with them, the commanding officer and his wife will hold one or more receptions which are considered "calls made and returned."

76

CHAIN OF COMMAND

There are two types of calls which are made in the services: *official calls* and *social calls*. The chain of command determines those upon whom you must call.

Flag and general officers pay official calls upon seniors; commanding officers and unit commanders call only on seniors in the type of ship or command to which they are assigned; juniors call on their immediate superiors.

It is customary for flag and general officers to leave cards on the Chief of Naval Operations, the Chiefs of Staff of the U.S. Army and U.S. Air Force, and the Commandants of the U.S. Marine Corps and U.S. Coast Guard, respectively, and their wives. Other officers should inquire whether their immediate chiefs wish to receive callers.

Reporting officers will call on the family of the commanding officer first; then, the executive officer, the head of the department, and so on.

It is courteous for officers returning from foreign duty to call at the embassies of countries in which they have served.

It is no longer customary for officers in the Washington, D.C., area to leave cards at the White House.

OFFICIAL CALLS

Official calls are those made by newly arrived officers on their commanding officers in their office ashore or aboard ship. The call is of no less than 10 minutes duration and of no more than 15, unless the caller is requested to say longer.

In the *Naval Service*, a junior officer is expected to call on his or her Commanding Officer, Executive Officer, Head of Department, etc., on the *first day after arrival*, if possible—but always within 48 hours.

In the *Army* and *Air Force*, custom decrees that you pay your office call *within the first three days* of your arrival. An Army lieutenant who is joining an infantry company, for example, would call on his Company Commander and his Battle Group Commander. In the Air Force, you call on the Base Commander and/or Wing Commander, Group Commander, and so on.

Before making the call, you should first ask the aide or adjutant the time which is most convenient for calling.

SOCIAL CALLS

Social or "first" calls are those you make on your immediate senior or commanding officers, and their wives, in their quarters. Such a call should be about 20 minutes in duration—never less than 15 or more than 30. An informal visit among friends is considerably longer, but you should avoid staying too long and wearing out your welcome.

At bases and posts where social calls are customary, some commanding officers designate times on certain days or evenings when they will receive calls, and these days or evenings are considered to be "at-home." You will ask the aide or adjutant about any such calling days. Otherwise, it is considerate for a junior family to telephone the senior family beforehand and ask when it will be convenient for them to make a social call.

CALLS MADE AND RETURNED

At any large activity, such as the Service Academies or Marine Corps Schools—or any very large base, post, or station—the complement of officers is so great that the senior officer is unable to receive many individual calls, or to return them.

It is a widespread and popular custom for the senior officer and his wife to entertain at one or a series of receptions or at-homes, to which the officers in the activity, and their wives, are invited. It is announced in advance that attendance serves as "All calls made and returned."

At the Service Academies, the Superintendent and his wife will receive guests at one or more receptions held during the early part of the academic year. The hours are usually 5 to 7 P.M.

In a very large area, such as Marine Corps Headquarters, Washington, D.C., the Commandant of the Marine Corps will entertain at a series of receptions in his quarters at Marine Barracks. All Marine officers and their wives in the area, including Quantico, will be invited at least once during their tour of duty.

Usually, cards are not left at such receptions, at-homes, etc., but at a command where this is done, guests will leave them in a tray or receptacle placed on a table, usually in the entrance hall.

PROCEDURE

An aide will be standing near the entrance to the reception room to announce the name of each guest to the Superintendent or Commandant, whose wife will be at his side. You will give the name of your lady to the aide, giving the last name only, "Mrs. Jones." The aide will announce her; then he will turn to you, and you will say, "Captain Jones." The Superintendent or Commandant, and his wife, will greet and shake hands with each guest.

Staff officers and their wives do not stand in line, but they will assist in greeting guests and in directing them to the punch bowls placed in the various rooms. You will stay about 45 minutes.

The line does not form again at the end of the reception, but if your host and hostess are nearby and not busy with other guests, you may thank them and say good-bye.

CALLING TIME

In the *Naval Service*, the customary time for making social calls is between 4 and 6 P.M.

In the *Army* and *Air Force*, the calling time is between 7:30 and 9 P.M., with the exception of Saturday evenings. Calls may be made on Sunday afternoons between 4 and 6 P.M., as well as in the evening.

In tropical climates, the social calling hours might be later because of the afternoon heat; the hours may be earlier in the north where daylight hours are short. Working hours and the distances from stations may necessitate changes in the usual calling hours at some stations.

DRESS

You will wear your uniform when making official calls. In the *Naval Service*, you may wear your uniform when making a social call, but you usually wear civilian dress. Men wear a conservative business suit and women wear an afternoon dress or a suit, with hat and gloves.

At less formal calls, men may wear sports jackets, but this depends upon the hour of the call and the day. A sports shirt with no tie or jacket is not correct dress for any type of call. Women do not wear hat and gloves.

In the *Army* and *Air Force*, officers wear the prescribed uniform when making their evening calls. Women wear the type of dress conforming to the custom of the post or base, with this information determined through the aide or adjutant.

A woman officer may wear her uniform when making a social call, and remove her hat upon arrival. Or she may prefer to wear civilian dress—an afternoon dress or suit, with hat and gloves according to the occasion.

GENERAL CALLING PROCEDURES

At bases and stations where calls are still being made, particularly on foreign stations, you will leave cards when making "first" calls. A card tray is usually placed on a table in the entrance hall, or in the living room. Cards should be left on the tray at a convenient moment either upon your arrival or departure, but you never hand them to the host or hostess.

The number of cards that you leave depends on the number of adults in the family you are calling on, and the type of card which you use. A man will call upon each adult member of the family, man or woman, therefore you leave a card for each. If you are married, your wife leaves a card for each adult woman only; she never calls on a man, not even the President.

In contrast, the woman officer does call on and leave a card for the man who is the official for whom a call is required. Otherwise, and in addition, she leaves calling cards upon the same occasions as a civilian woman, one for each adult woman in the household.

When a steward or maid opens the door of the house where you are calling, you may hand the cards to him or her. When you wish to be received, but the family is not at home, you leave the cards and the call is considered made. Otherwise, do not leave your cards but return at another time. If you want to leave cards without being received, you will say to the steward or maid, "Will you please give these to Mrs. Smith?"

When a member of the household opens the door, you may introduce yourself—but do not give him or her your card. If admitted, you leave your card on the table; when your host is not in, you may ask if you may leave your card, then you step inside and lay the card on the table yourself.

Upon occasions when you call at a home or quarters and are told by a maid or steward that your would-be hosts are not at home (and you know they are), do *not* take offense. The maid or steward means no more than that the officer and is wife are not receiving guests for reasons of their own. This is correct procedure, and is completely within the privileges granted a senior officer who has many obligations—or any host and hostess, for that matter.

Junior officers and officers of intermediate rank are always received whenever practicable, so do not consider failure to receive you a rebuff. You should just leave your card, and you will receive credit for the call anyway.

Wives of senior officers at some stations have regular days to receive callers. When a senior officer insists that you stay longer than the customary length of a first call—twenty minutes—you may do so, but it is better not to stay much more than the prescribed length of time, or more than thirty minutes. If you have known the family previously, or have served with the officer at another station, your call will probably be a little longer than the usual time.

It is customary in the services for the host to offer refreshments to callers—tea, coffee, soft drinks, or alcoholic beverages. Some hosts feel, however, that offering a drink to "first" callers is an invitation to extend the call, and therefore, it is optional for a host to offer drinks. When they are offered, a guest should never accept more than one.

Since the purpose of a call is to become acquainted, a host can be defeated in this purpose by having to act as bartender instead of talking with the guests. Also, many younger service families are finding that the prevailing custom of serving drinks during calls is a financial burden. When guests do not accept drinks, there is no problem involved.

In terminating a call, it is the wife who will rise, with her husband following her lead.

RETURN CALLS

All calls should be promptly returned. In this country the usual interval for returning a call is within two weeks, but there are variations depending on the size of the station and the number of calls to be made. The procedure for returning calls is the same as when making them.

Should the family not be at home when you return a call, you may leave cards and the call is considered as having been returned. If you want to visit with the family, do not leave your card but return at a later date.

When cards are left, all calls must be returned, whether the callers were received or not—with the exception of certain bachelor calls.

A woman may make or return a call and leave cards for her husband when he cannot accompany her. A man cannot leave cards for his wife when she does not accompany him.

CALLING CARDS

At no time does any individual leave more than *three cards*. (For example, a husband and wife may leave a total of six cards at one call.) You will remember that a man calls on adults, man or woman, but that a civilian woman only calls on another woman.

A military woman *calls as an officer* and therefore calls on the officials for whom a call is regularly required.

The following rules apply to the individual cards a husband and wife leave:

- When calling on a senior officer and his wife—2 officer cards and 1 "Mrs." card.
- When calling on a senior officer and his wife, and his mother—3 officer cards and 2 "Mrs." cards.
- When calling on a senior officer, his wife, his mother, and his father—3 officer cards and 2 "Mrs." cards.
- When calling on a senior officer, his wife, his mother, his mother-in-law, and adult daughter—3 officer cards and 3 "Mrs." cards.

When a husband and wife use "joint" calling cards (Lieutenant and Mrs. John Smith Jones), these rules apply:

- When calling on a senior officer and his wife, leave—1 officer card and 1 joint card.
- Cards in addition to joint cards are left in accordance with the general rules given for individual cards.

SEPARATE ARRIVALS

Upon occasions when an officer's wife precedes him to a new station where formal calls are customary, she is not expected to make such calls until after he arrives and can accompany her.

Should you precede your wife to the station, formal calls should be delayed until she arrives, but this must be explained to the aide or Executive Officer in order that you do not seem remiss in your social obligations.

If your wife will not arrive for several months, you should make your required and formal calls as usual; then later it would be courteous for you both to call together informally.

When you are reporting to a new duty station and learn that a senior officer or his wife will be absent for some time, you may discuss with the aide or executive officer the problem of calling on one, or waiting to call on both.

LEAVE-TAKING CALLS

Leave-taking calls are those you make, prior to your detachment, on the officers constituting the required call list. However, most calls made at detachment time seem to be made *on* the officer and his wife being detached rather than *by* them. This change from former custom arises from the fact that packing and making preparations for the move are exhausting, and that detachment may come earlier than expected. Since the departing couple is usually entertained at parties before detachment, it does not seem necessary for them to call on the families whom they saw only a night or so before.

In former years, when leaving cards, it was customary to write "p.p.c." in the lower left-hand corner of the card to indicate that the call was *pour prendre congé*—"to take leave." Most Americans, however, prefer simply to write the word "good-bye."

Leave-taking calls are not made at large stations where the commanding officer and his wife are contacted infrequently. Instead, telephone calls are usually made to friends before you leave, and notes of appreciation are written at your new station and then sent back to those who entertained you.

Such leave-taking calls are not to be confused with the official calls that are made by officers on the commanding officer and executive officer in their offices prior to detachment.

SINGLE OFFICERS' CALLS

Single officers have as much responsibility in making social calls as married officers. The return of the single officer's call is not required, however, mainly because of the inadequacy of his or her quarters for receiving visitors.

The single officer's social call is usually repaid by his or her later being invited to dinner or some other occasion by the family on whom the call was made.

When a senior single officer has a home of his (or her) own, his call will be returned. Although both a husband and wife will make or return the call, only the husband will leave a card since a civilian woman never calls on a man.

Women officers make the same official calls as male officers. Single and married women officers make formal social calls on married male officers.

DESIRABLE CALLS

It is desirable that you make calls on your contemporaries in their department or on the station, as well as on seniors. A call on a newly married couple means a welcome of the couple into the service community—and the bride into the service.

Calls made upon the occasion of a new baby show a sincere interest in the family of a fellow officer.

It is the accepted custom all over the country to telephone first before making a call.

ACADEMY, OCS, OTS, ROTC CALLS

Whenever time permits, it is desirable that midshipmen, cadets, OCS, OTS, and ROTC students make social calls on senior officers and professors. This will give you experience in making calls and the opportunity for you to become better acquainted with your seniors. Fourth Classmen are welcome to make calls whenever they can.

You may ask the senior officer beforehand if it is convenient for you to call on a certain day and hour, although a Sunday afternoon between three and five o'clock is the best time for calling. If the officer asks you to come for Sunday dinner, or to stay on for badminton, TV, etc., you should feel free to do so.

Otherwise, *you should not stay over thirty minutes*—unless your hosts specifically ask you to do so. A senior officer may be very busy, and he may have other callers and obligations. Students do not leave cards since they are not required to have official cards.

CALLS ON FOREIGN STATIONS

It is mandatory that officers on foreign stations pay official calls within their own embassy group, on officials of the host government, and on diplomatic representatives of other governments.

Upon the arrival of a new member of an Embassy, such as a Service attaché at a foreign capital, introductory calls are arranged by his predecessor and made promptly upon the civilian heads of the foreign military establishments which correspond to the Secretary of Defense and/or the Secretary of the Army, Navy, and Air Force. Calls are also made upon the military chiefs of these activities, and any other person, according to local custom. These office calls are made in uniform and usually cards are left.

The Chief of Mission (Ambassador or Minister) is the highest ranking American on the diplomatic staff in a foreign embassay or legation. The attaché and his wife should call on the wife of the Chief of Mission at the Residence within 24 hours after their arrival. You should first inquire of the protocol officer or her secretary if she would like to receive you in person, or if you should leave cards instead. When received, you will stay no longer than 15 minutes.

Then you should call on the wife of the Counselor of Embassy, who will advise you concerning any additional calls necessary to make. However, some foreign officials do not wish to be called upon at home, and this information can be determined in advance by asking the Secretary of Embassy.

The custom of bending the upper right-hand corner of the card, to indicate that the cards were left in person, is infrequently observed today. The address of the new attaché is written *in pencil* in the lower right-hand corner of the card.

It is customary in diplomatic circles that the new arrival calls first on those of equal rank and above; those of junior rank call first on the newcomer. Such calls should be made within one week of your arrival.

In addressing high officials, you will say "Mr. Ambassador" or "Mr. Minister," but his wife is "Mrs. Doe." If married, you will refer to your wife as "my wife," *not* "Mrs. Jones." And she will refer to you as "my husband," or by your first name.

When leaving a country, cards are left on the Ambassador and his wife, or the Minister and his wife, and the Economic Minister and his wife, with the top right-hand corner of each card bent forward and "p.p.c." (to take leave) written in pencil in the lower left-hand corner of the top card.

Cards for Counselors, Army, Navy, and Air Attachés (and any others whom you wish to know that you are leaving) may be mailed. When mailing cards, write "p.p.c.," but do *not* bend the corner.

When an officer and his family are going on home leave, no cards need be left. When returing from home leave, single officers and wives of officers should again leave cards and sign the book at the Residence. You should write in pencil "returned from home leave" in the lower left-hand corner of the top card.

Should a Minister, Counselor, Army, Navy, or Air Attaché, or the officer's Section Chief have arrived during your home leave, cards should be left on him and his family.

Upon detachment, an official should make official and courtesy calls in the chain of command. When detached on short notice, cards marked "p.p.c." may be mailed when you do not have time to leave them.

All calls must be returned; first calls within a week.

OFFICER'S CARDS

An officer's personal (calling) card is narrow and may vary slightly in size, according to the length of his name and title, and the type of engraving selected. The length and width of the cards are approximately:

Male officer (or civilian): $3\frac{1}{8}$ inches by $1\frac{5}{8}$ inches.

Single woman officer: $2\frac{7}{8}$ inches by 2 inches.

Married woman officer (or civilian): $3\frac{1}{8}$ inches by $2\frac{1}{4}$ inches.

Attaché: $3\frac{1}{2}$ inches by 2 inches.

Joint cards (man and wife): $3\frac{1}{2}$ inches by $2\frac{1}{2}$ inches.

RANK AND TITLE

The placement on the card of rank (or title), name, and service, is in one of three ways:

- The rank precedes the name in the center of the card, with service designation in the lower right-hand corner.
- The rank precedes the name in the center, with service designation directly underneath.
- The name only is in the center of the card with rank and service designation in the lower right-hand corner. It is now correct for officers of all services and of all ranks to use this placement.

In the *Navy* and *Coast Guard*, an officer's rank of commander and above may precede his or her name in the center of the card, with the service in the lower right-hand corner. Junior officers (lieutenant commander and below) place rank and service in the lower right-hand corner.

In the *Army*, *Air Force*, and *Marine Corps*, the rank of major and above may precede the name in the center of the card with the service in the lower right-hand corner. Company grade officers (second and first lieutenants and captain) place their name in the center of the card with rank and service in the lower right-hand corner. All Air Force officers usually place rank and service in the lower right-hand corner. First and second lieutenants are designated "lieutenant in the Army."

Retired officers in all services use the word "Retired" centered beneath the service designation in the lower right-hand corner of the card.

A Cabinet officer is entitled to use only his title on his card, but his wife will use their surname. The Service Secretaries and the Under Secretaries are also entitled to use only their rank or title on their cards.

Senior flag officers and department officials are entitled to use their rank or title and surname on their cards. However, many officials prefer to use their full name, for purposes of identification.

When a man's name is the same as that of his living father, you will add "junior" written out in full—unless the line is too long, and "junior" may then be written "Jr." The Roman numeral II is used to identify a younger man who has the same name as an older living relative, such as a grandfather, uncle, etc. Other numerals, III, IV, and so on, would be used accordingly.

You do not put a home address on a personal card. Matching envelopes should be ordered with the cards, since they have many usages. But you *never* place a card in an envelope when making a social call. When the cards are used for informal invitations, remember that Postal Regulations require mailing envelopes to be at least 3 by 4¼ inches. It is proper to write only the name, "Miss Smith," on the envelope of the card and to enclose this in a larger envelope for mailing, similar to wedding invitations.

MIDSHIPMAN OR CADET CARDS

A midshipman or cadet, or ROTC student, is not required to have personal cards. If you do want them, however, you should have your full name engraved in the center of the card and your rank in the lower right-hand corner. The rank may be stated as follows:

CADET

UNITED STATES MILITARY ACADEMY

SELECTION OF CARDS

Your choice of calling cards will reflect your good taste. Only engraved cards are correct. According to American usage, your name, rank, and service should be engraved in full, without abbreviations or initials.

Clear lettering should be chosen rather than a heavy or unusual type. Popular letterings for junior officers are Saint James Script, English Script, and Roman. Senior officers frequently use Old English or Gothic (which are somewhat more expensive), as well as Roman. Go to the very best engraver and take his advice in the matter. Your Service Exchange will advise you.

Cards should be of excellent quality paper; this is customarily white, but may be a very light cream color. The lettering is always black. The engraver will give you the engraving plate, and you can have additional cards made up at any time thereafter. However, you should order only the number that you anticipate using; when you advance in rank, the old cards may never be used.

ATTACHÉ'S CARDS

On the cards of all officers attached to a diplomatic office, two sizes of lettering are used, with the larger for the name and the smaller for the title. Such officers sometimes have two sets of calling cards; one engraved in the language of their own country, the other engraved in the language of the country to which they are assigned. It is customary for such an officer serving in the Orient to have his name and title in the characters of the Oriental language on the back of his cards.

The official card of an attaché is larger than the regular card since it will carry some five or six lines of engraving. The customary size is about 3½ inches long and 2 inches wide, corresponding in size to official cards of State Department representatives.

Official Cards

Admiral John Paul Smith
United States Navy

Chief of Naval Operations

General Randolph Henderson

Commandant
United States Marine Corps

General George Washington Jones

Chief of Staff
United States Army

Flag or General Officers' Personal Cards

Vice Admiral Jones

United States Navy

Robert Edward Decatur

Major General
United States Air Force

Flag or General Officer's Joint Card

GENERAL AND MRS. SMITH

Including and below the rank of rear admiral or
brigadier general, full names are used.

Brigadier General and Mrs. Robert Edwards

Personal Cards, Senior Officers

Captain Stephen Sidney Preble

United States Coast Guard

COLONEL PAUL JOHN O'BANNON

UNITED STATES ARMY

Commander James Richard Briggs

United States Maritime Service

John Carl Brown

Lieutenant Colonel
United States Air Force

Married Woman Officer's Card

Major Mary Ames Smith

United States Marine Corps

Single Woman Officer's Card

Eleanor Sarah Harris

Lieutenant Commander
United States Navy

Personal Cards, Retired Officers

Albert Edward Dewey

Captain
United States Army
Retired

or

Rear Admiral Willard Arthur Saunders

United States Coast Guard
Retired

Junior Officer's Joint Card

Lieutenant and Mrs. Peter Winston

Midshipman's or Cadet's Personal Card

William Orrmond Paul

**Cadet
United States Military Academy**

Reserve Officer's Card

Joan Doris Puller

Ensign, Medical Service Corps
United States Naval Reserve

Air Force Attaché

Colonel Albert Paul Truxton
United States Air Force
Air Attaché
Embassy of the United States of America

Athens

Marine Attaché

Richard Brinton Butler
First Lieutenant, United States Marine Corps
Assistant Naval Attaché
Assistant Naval Attaché for Air
Embassy of the United States of America

Tehran

Staff Corps Attaché

Commander Dan Murray Hill
Supply Corps, United States Navy
Assistant Naval Attaché
Embassy of the United States of America

Paris

WOMEN'S CARDS

A woman's calling card is about the same length as a man's card, but is wider. The customary size is about $3\frac{1}{8}$ inches long by $2\frac{1}{4}$ inches wide, but the size varies slightly according to the length of the name. It is desirable that a wife's card match her husband's in color, style, and type of engraving.

Mrs. Henry George Dickinson

A married woman officer in the services uses a similar card with the same type of information engraved in the same way as a male officer's personal card. A single woman officer's card is narrower, about $2\frac{7}{8}$ by 2 inches in size.

JOINT CARDS

The *joint card* that married couples frequently use is about $2\frac{1}{2}$ by $3\frac{1}{2}$ inches in size. When used in making formal calls, one such card may be used along with any additional individual cards as needed, or two joint cards are used in accordance with the number of adults in the family. The officer's branch of service is never indicated on the card, but his individual card will provide this information.

A senior flag or general officer's joint card may have only the rank and surname engraved in the center of the card; a brigadier general or rear admiral and officers of less rank will use their full names. It is now customary for junior officers to have their rank precede their names on joint cards.

The joint card is also useful for extending and replying to invitations, and is frequently enclosed with gifts. Notes of thanks, condolence, etc., are written across them; an address is sometimes engraved in the lower right-hand corner of the card. Matching envelopes should be ordered with the cards.

As no envelope smaller than 3 by $4\frac{1}{4}$ inches may be placed in the mail, write only the addressee's name on the envelope for the card and enclose it in a larger one for mailing.

INFORMALS

The fold-over cards, known as *informals*, are widely used for informal invitations and brief notes, but they are *not* used for calling cards. The name is engraved on the outside, and the message or invitation is written on the inside of the card. They are about 3 by $4\frac{1}{4}$ inches in size.

Another style of informal is the *message card*, a single flat card about $3\frac{1}{2}$ by $4\frac{1}{2}$ inches in size. The address is engraved above and to the right of the name, with the name engraved in the center or near the top center of the card. Message cards are not used for calling cards.

ABBREVIATIONS ON CARDS

There are a number of conventional abbreviations on calling cards. Although some of these abbreviations are not often used in this country, you should be aware of their meaning. Such abbreviations are customarily written by hand:

p.p.c. (*Pour prendre congé*)—"To take leave." This indicates that one is leaving town. The initials are written in the lower left-hand corner of the card.

p.c. (*Pour condolénce*)—"To condole"; to extend sympathy.

p.f. (*Pour féliciter*)—"To congratulate"; to extend congratulations; to felicitate.

p.p. (*Pour presenter*)—"To introduce." This means that the friend who left the card is introducing a stranger to whom the receiver should send cards, phone, or call on.

p.r. (*Pour remercier*)—"To thank"; to reply to a "p.f." card (above) or instead of a dinner call.

n.b. (*Nota bene*)—"Note well"; this calls attention to any words or messages written on the card.

R.s.v.p. or R.S.V.P. (*Répondez s'il vous plaît*)—"Please reply." These initials are customarily written on invitations when an answer is requested.

The old-world custom of bending the upper right-hand corner of the card toward the name is rarely observed in this country, but the custom is still prevalent in foreign countries. It is done to denote that a call was made in person, or upon all members of the household.

YOUR TABLE MANNERS

CHAPTER 6

Manners at the Table

Good table manners in the services are good table manners anywhere. Customs may vary abroad and in various parts of the United States, but good fundamentals in eating are generally the same. The proper use of table silver should be as easy and as familiar to you as the proper use of any mechanical device you consider important to your career.

Mealtime is the time for enjoyment, not only of foods but also the company of others. Pleasant conversation, coupled with the relaxation that comes with knowing what to do, will mean pleasure in dining any place— in a luxurious hotel, in a home, or at an embassy.

Good manners are not turned on or off, in accordance with the importance of the occasion or the individual, yet neither do they mean rigid formality. The desirable attitude at even the most formal occasion is *relaxed politeness*, plus the ability to make interesting "small talk."

But it takes everyday practice before manners at the table become easy and automatic. Poor manners at home will invariably mean poor manners in the wardroom or the commandant's quarters.

TABLE TRADITIONS

The modern day use of table silver goes back to A.D. 1100, when the wife of an Italian nobleman introduced the two-tined fork into table usage in Venice, because she did not like to pick up meat with her fingers.

The use of forks was not entirely satisfactory, and their use spread but slowly, even in Italy where they had the blessing of the nobility. Complete acceptance of the fork came only with the Renaissance, which also ushered in the use of the table knife to displace the common hunting knife which every freeman carried at all times on his belt and used at the table for cutting.

France and England were slower in accepting these customs, and it was not until the mid-1600's that English craftsmen commenced the manufacture of table knives and forks, and then spoons. These utensils were made of silver, and were considered a rarity.

As a result of the scarcity of table silver, it fell to the lot of the English gentry to formulate the table manners of the land. It is from them that Americans inherit their table manners, modified somewhat by native American thought and customs.

The first table napkins made their appearance in Reims, France, in the court of Charles VII. They were used exclusively in the palaces of kings and princes, and from the early part of the fifteenth century, they were lace trimmed and intricately embroidered.

Later, in the seventeenth century, napkins were an important decorative part in table setting. They were folded and pleated to represent flowers, birds, fans, etc. Ornate foldings are still used occasionally in Europe, and it is claimed that there are 400 ways of folding napkins. In this country, however, a few simple foldings are preferred.

MEALS

Dinner is the main meal of the day in the United States, when it is the evening meal except for Sundays and holidays. Luncheon is everyday noon meal, and a light or informal evening meal is usually called supper. (In certain sections of this country, dinner is the noon meal and supper the evening meal.)

Suppers are also held after formal occasions, such as weddings, dances, receptions, etc., and may be served very late. Buffet meals served in the evening are referred to as suppers, never dinners—even when guests are in evening attire. Luncheons and dinners are the only completely served meals.

EATING CUSTOMS

You may use the American or Continental way of eating, but the favored American custom is to hold the dinner fork in your left hand to pin down the food for cutting, and then to transfer the fork, tines up, to the right hand for the purpose of eating. The Continental, or European, custom of eating is to transfer the food to the mouth from the fork while it is still held in the left hand, tines down. Either fashion is correct.

CUSTOMS AT THE TABLE

The simplest silver service at any meal is the knife, fork, and spoon. The fork is placed at the left of the plate, and the knife and spoon at the right, with the knife closer to the plate.

In the United States, the *knife* is always held in the right hand, with the handle in your palm and your index finger along the back of the blade. After using the knife, never lay it down on the table. You place the knife across the upper half of the plate, or on the right side of the plate, with the blade facing in.

The *fork* is held in the left hand while being used with the knife to cut food. The handle of the fork will rest in your palm, with your index finger extending along the back.

Courtesy Florists' Telegraph Delivery Association

At all other times, the fork is preferably held in the right hand, tines up, with the handle controlled by your thumb and first two fingers in a manner similar to holding a pencil. The end of the handle should extend out between your thumb and index finger.

After the fork is used, lay it on the plate below the knife, or at the left, and parallel to the knife, with the handle at the right, and the tines up.

The *spoon* is held in the right hand in the same manner as the fork. Correctly, the only spoon to appear on the table at the beginning of a meal is a soup spoon—except at breakfast. However, a modern hostess frequently places the teaspoon or place spoon at the right of the knife at an informal or family meal.

The most commonly used spoon is the teaspoon. It is used at informal meals for tasting soup served in handled soup cups, desserts, tea, coffee, cereals, grapefruit, etc. The multi-purpose *place spoon* is slightly larger than the teaspoon and is used for desserts and cereals as well as for soups.

ADDITIONAL SILVER

In settings other than the simplest, you will also find other table silver, such as a butter knife, salad and/or dessert fork, a seafood fork, dessert spoon, iced beverage spoon, soup spoon, coffee or demitasse spoon, etc.

The individual *butter knife* (sometimes called a *butter spreader*) is usually laid across the top of the butter plate, with the handle at the right, the blade facing the edge of the table. The individual butter knife is used only to spread butter on a piece of bread. It is not used to take butter from the butter plate. A knife to be used for the purpose of taking butter from a butter plate will be placed on the butter plate—when such a plate is used. The individual butter knife is much smaller than a dinner knife.

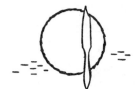

Courtesy Florists' Telegraph Delivery Association

The *salad fork* is shorter than the luncheon or dinner fork, and may be used for either a salad or dessert course. The placing of the fork depends upon the time the salad course will be served. When the salad is served after the main course—as is customary—the fork will be placed next to the plate on the left-hand side, and inside the luncheon or dinner fork. When served as a first course at family or informal meals, the salad fork will be placed outside the luncheon or dinner fork. When there is no separate salad course and the fork is to be used for dessert, the fork is usually placed on the dessert plate.

A *seafood fork*, usually called an oyster fork, is much shorter and slimmer than the salad fork, and is placed at the right or outside of the spoon. Sometimes the tines of the seafood fork rest in the bowl of the spoon, with the handle of the fork placed even with the handle of the spoon.

The *dessert spoon* is longer than a teaspoon and is placed on the dessert plate at formal meals as well as at most informal meals. But the dessert spoon, and/or fork, may be placed on the table at the beginning of an informal meal. (See *illustration* next page.)

The *iced beverage spoon* (called iced tea spoon) is a long-handled spoon, and after being used is laid on the small service plate or coaster which should be placed under the iced beverage glass. However, when no such plate or coaster has been provided, there is nothing to do but to leave the spoon in the glass and to drink with the handle held against the far side with your first and second fingers. You will then leave the spoon in the glass. This is awkward—but correct.

Soup spoons are longer than the dessert spoon or teaspoon, and are oval-bowled. In using a soup spoon, dip the spoon *away* from you and avoid scraping the bottom of the soup bowl. After the spoon is used, it is placed on the soup plate on the right-hand side.

Demitasse (*Coffee*) *spoons* are used with small cups of after-dinner, or after-luncheon, coffee. They are usually about four inches long, and are customarily placed on the saucer when coffee is served.

The *serving fork and spoon* are placed on the platter or in the vegetable dish. These pieces are larger than the regular fork and spoon. In serving

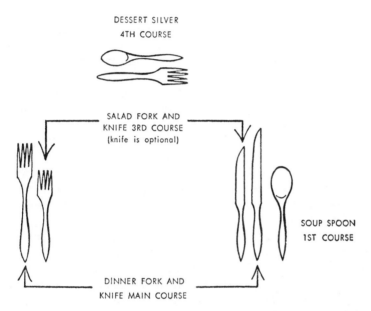

DESSERT SILVER
4TH COURSE

SALAD FORK AND
KNIFE 3RD COURSE
(knife is optional)

SOUP SPOON
1ST COURSE

DINNER FORK AND
KNIFE MAIN COURSE

*Courtesy Florists' Telegraph
Delivery Association*

yourself, you hold these like other forks and spoons, with the fork in your left hand, the spoon in your right hand. You will slip the spoon under a portion of food, and, while holding the food in place with the fork, you transfer the food to your plate. Meats are usually portioned before serving, but if not, you will cut the food with the spoon and transfer it to your plate with the fork. A pierced serving spoon, which permits liquids to drain from such vegetables as peas and corn, is available in many patterns.

Table silver, or *flatware*, as it is called, is always placed on the table in the order of use, beginning from the outside and working in toward the plate. There will never be more than three knives and three forks placed on the most formal table at any time. If more silver is needed, it will be brought in with the courses they accompany.

TABLE CHINA AND GLASSWARE

There are three main types of *plates* used daily: breakfast, luncheon, and dinner. In setting the table, the plate is placed an inch from the edge of the table, and the silver and napkin are also placed an inch from the table's edge.

At a formal luncheon or dinner, there will be a *place plate* (sometimes called a *service plate*) on the table when you sit down. The first course, in its own plate, will be set in the place plate.

The *butter plate*, which is much smaller than the regular plate, is placed above the forks at informal and semiformal dinners and formal or informal luncheons. Although they were never used at a formal dinner in former years, they are frequently used today. The individual butter knife is laid across the top of the butter plate. When butter is passed in a butter plate at an informal meal—never at a formal dinner—you place your butter directly on the butter plate and not on the luncheon or dinner plate. You also place bread, jams, etc., on the butter plate.

The *salad plate* is larger than the butter plate, and usually is flat and round. There are also crescent-shaped salad plates to be used when meat and salad are served in the same course at less formal meals. Although salad is usually served as a separate course, at informal or family meals it may accompany the main course, with the filled plate placed to the left of the forks.

The *dessert plate* is about eight or nine inches in diameter, and is interchangeable with place plates.

Soup plates are used at formal dinners, and although they are called "plates" they really are a broad bowl about an inch deep and usually have a broad flat rim—but also many be rimless. The soup plate sets in an underplate, with the rim of the underplate showing about half an inch.

Soup cups are used at luncheons, with the standard soup cup looking like a two-handled teacup—only larger. There is always a matching saucer.

A *cup and saucer* are set at the right of the knife and/or spoon. No cup or bowl is set on the table without a saucer or plate under it. Soup, cereal, or dessert bowls are always placed in a plate or served with their own plates under them. A coffee cup is always in its saucer. When you hold a coffee cup, avoid curling your little finger.

Demitasse cups and saucers are much smaller than coffee cups and saucers. Demitasse coffee is served after informal as well as formal dinners.

The *water goblet* is placed above the knives, and is usually filled before guests sit down.

Wine glasses are placed in the order of their use at the right of the water goblet, but nearer the table's edge. Wines are poured with the courses they accompany. It is correct to hold long-stemmed water goblets or wine glasses with the thumb and first two fingers at the base of the bowl, but not around the bowl itself. Small-stemmed glasses are held by the stems, and tumblers are held near the base.

NAPKINS

Napkins are placed at the left of the forks at luncheons and informal meals, and in the place plate at formal meals. After you sit down at the table—and after grace has been said—you will place your napkin, half unfolded, in your lap as soon as your hostess takes up her napkin. To lay the napkin smoothly, pick it up by the right top corners and unspread in one motion across your lap.

At the end of the meal, replace the napkin *unfolded* at the left of your plate. At formal dinners, the napkin may be laid at the right of the plate. When paper napkins are used at informal meals, these are laid at the left of the plate, and when you are through with them, you never crush them or roll them into a ball.

HOW TO EAT:

Artichokes are eaten by pulling off each leaf, with the base of the leaf dipped in a sauce and eaten. When down to the heart, you scrape or cut off the fuzz with a knife, then cut and eat the heart. Leaves are piled on the plate or butter plate.

Avocados, when halved, are eaten with a spoon. When peeled and served in a salad, they are eaten with a fork.

Bacon is eaten with a fork unless very crisp, then it is eaten with the fingers.

Cake is eaten with a fork when served as dessert.

Caviar is served on small pieces of toast with cocktails, or in a bowl before dinner or at buffet suppers.

Cheese is frequently served at the table with the salad course. Cheese, fruit, and coffee are frequently served together as the final course, instead of dessert.

Chicken, broiled or fried, is held with the fork in the plate, while you strip the meat off the bones with your knife. Or, if not greasy, you may hold the chicken in your left hand against the plate, while you strip the meat off with the fork. At informal occasions, such as picnics, family meals, etc., fried chicken is eaten held in the hand.

Corn on the Cob is usually served only at informal meals, and may be held with the hands or by small spears inserted in each end. Salt, pepper, and butter are sometimes mixed in small pats or balls before the meal, or you can mix them yourself on the dinner plate before eating. Butter only a few rows of kernels at a time. Kernels may also be cut off the ear with the dinner knife.

Cream Puffs or Eclairs are eaten with a fork when served at the table.

Fish, unless served in pieces, is held in the plate with the fork while you slit it with the tip of the knife from head to tail. Insert the tip of the knife under the end of the backbone and lift out the skeleton. Lay the skeleton and bones on the side of the plate out of the way, or on plates provided by the host.

Frog Legs are eaten in the same manner as chicken.

Fresh Fruits (except citrus fruit) served at the table may be eaten either the American or Continental way. Continental fashion is to skin the fruit, halve and stone it, then cut it into small pieces and eat these with the fork. The American way is to halve, quarter, and stone the fruit with the knife and fork, but not skin it (except peaches); then you eat the quarters with your fingers or a fork. At a formal dinner, such fruit is always eaten with a fruit knife and fork. Fresh grapes and cherries are eaten whole. The pits are removed with the fingers and placed on the side of the plate.

Grapefruit, or Oranges, are usually served in halves, and eaten with a fruit spoon or a teaspoon. Do no squeeze the fruit after eating.

Honey is taken by the spoonful. With a twisting motion of the serving spoon, catch any drops, then transfer the spoonful to the butter plate.

Ice Cream is served with a fork and/or spoon; the fork is for the solid part, the spoon for the softer. Ice cream is always eaten with a spoon when it is served in a sherbet glass.

Olives are held in the fingers while the flesh is eaten, and the stones are then placed on a butter plate. Small stuffed olives are eaten whole.

Oranges and Tangerines, served other than at the table, are peeled and held in the fingers, and segments eaten by hand; served at the table, they are of course eaten with a spoon.

Onion Rings are eaten with a fork.

Pâté de Foie Gras, an imported paste made of goose livers, is frequently served on toast at cocktail parties, or with cocktails before dinner. Or you may find it placed in its own earthenware crock on a tray with a knife, and served at a buffet supper.

Pickles are held with the fingers and eaten when served with a sandwich, but are eaten with a fork when served with meat at a table.

Potato Chips are eaten with the fingers.

Potatoes, French fried, are eaten with the fork after being cut in shorter lengths, if necessary. Do not spear the potatoes with the fork, and then bite off pieces of them.

Radishes are placed on the side of the plate, or on the butter plate until you eat them.

Roast Beef may be carved at the table by the host, but is sometimes partially carved in the kitchen before bringing into the dining room. The carving of a three-rib roast is illustrated:

Salad is cut and eaten with a fork. When iceberg lettuce is served, it may be cut with a knife and fork, then eaten with the fork.

Sandwiches are eaten by hand. The large or double-decker sandwiches may first be cut in half, then in quarter pieces, with a knife.They are then eaten by hand.

Seafoods are often eaten both with the fingers and with table silver, but usually with the latter.

  Clams are usually served steamed, until the shell has opened. If not fully open, bend the shell back with the fingers, then hold it in the left hand just over the dish and lift out the clam by its neck with your right hand. Pull the body of the clam out and discard the neck sheath. Hold the clam in your right hand, dip it whole in melted butter or broth, or both, and eat in one bite. You place the empty shells on the butter plate or on a dish especially provided for that purpose. Fried clams are eaten with a fork, since they are too greasy to hold. Clam broth is drunk in a separate bouillon cup or small bowl.

  Lobster and Hard-Shelled Crabs, boiled or broiled, demand dexterity. The major part of the meat is in the stomach cavity and the tail or claws. The claws of both the lobster and crabs demand careful— but similar—handling. (See following page.)

  For crabs, etc., the general objective is the same as that for lobsters. The best meat is in the large claws and the main body of the crab.

  Oysters and Clams on the half shell are eaten raw, with an oyster fork. They are lifted whole from the shell, sprinkled with lemon juice or dipped in cocktail sauce, and eaten in a single mouthful. When served as a first course, the half shells come to the table imbedded in cracked ice. Regardless of size, do not cut oysters or clams with your fork before eating them.

  Shrimp, Oysters, Scallops, when fried, are eaten with a fork. When shrimp are French fried, they may be held in the fingers by the tail, dipped in sauce, and eaten to the tail. Unshelled shrimp, which are never served with heads on, are held in the fingers, shelled, and eaten whole except for the very tail.

Spaghetti is twisted around the fork, cocoon fashion, and eaten from

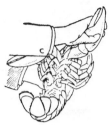

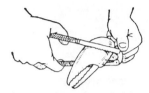

1. Twist off the claws.

2. Crack each claw with a nutcracker, pliers, knife, hammer, rock or what have you.

3. Separate the tail-piece from the body by arching the back until it cracks.

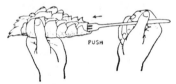

PUSH

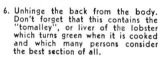

4. Bend back and break the flippers off the tail-piece.

5. Insert a fork where the flippers broke off and push.

6. Unhinge the back from the body. Don't forget that this contains the "tomalley", or liver of the lobster which turns green when it is cooked and which many persons consider the best section of all.

7. Open the remaining part of the body by cracking apart sideways. There is some good meat in this section.

8. The small claws are excellent eating and may be placed in the mouth and the meat sucked out like sipping cider with a straw.

Courtesy State of Maine Department of Economic Development

the fork tip. It is sometimes cut with the side of the fork before winding, but it is never bitten off.

Tortillas (thin Mexican corncakes) are laid flat on the left hand, or plate, and are filled with frijoles (kidney beans) or special sauce, as provided, then rolled and eaten from the end with the fingers.

Turkey (or poultry) is usually carved at the table by the host, and is eaten like chicken. There is an art in carving:

Midshipmen, cadets, and other junior officers should make every effort to become adept at carving. It is quite customary at the Service Academies when a midshipman or cadet is invited to the home of an officer for Thanksgiving or Christmas dinner, to have the host request one of the invited midshipmen or cadets to carve. This is considered part of his training.

CHAPTER 7

Eating Habits

There are many simple rules in eating that may seem elementary, but they are the rules by which you are judged. The difference between good or crude manners is the way you observe the following rules:

Do *not* talk with food in your mouth, make noises while eating or swallowing, chew food with your mouth open, or blow on hot liquids to cool them.

You will avoid such unattractive eating habits as smacking your lips or taking too-large mouthfuls from food piled high on your fork. Use your napkin before drinking from a glass of water in order not to leave traces of food on the glass. Never lick your fingers after they have been in contact with food—use your napkin.

If something is out of reach at the table, do not rise out of your seat to obtain it, but ask for it to be passed. However, you may reach for anything you conveniently can without bothering your dinner partner.

You will avoid curling your little finger on a cup handle—and be sure to remove the spoon from the cup after stirring and before drinking. Remember to place the spoon in the saucer, at the right of the cup handle, and not on the tablecloth. If the liquid seems hot, test it by sipping a spoonful—but do not continue drinking by spoonfuls.

You may tilt a soup bowl away from you when almost empty, and you must remember to dip the spoon in the bowl *away* from you. Clear soup served in a cup or bowl with handles may be drunk. You must not place the bowl on the spoon in your mouth, but should sip somewhat from the side. Leave the spoon in the soup plate, *never* in the cup or bowl.

Bread and rolls are broken in half, and then into smaller pieces with the fingers. Do not cut breads with a knife. If butter is served, you butter each piece of bread before eating.

Jams and condiments go directly onto the butter plate, not onto the bread. You must never place your elbows on the table while eating. Between courses, you may momentarily place your forearms on the table—if you do not turn your back on your dinner partner.

You should keep your elbows at your sides when cutting food; they move as easily up and down as sideways, and if held in, cannot hit your partner.

Do not slump at the table, but do not sit too rigidly or "at attention," either. Avoid twisting your feet around the chair legs or extending your legs under the table.

Loud talk and laughter at the table are disturbing to others. The monopolized or too-intimate conversation between partners, to the exclusion of others, is equally ill-bred.

Be careful of controversial or unpleasant subjects, such as politics, religion, or death. Be careful of talking "shop." Carry your share of the conversation; do not make it a burden for others. But always remember not to discuss personal affairs or the opposite sex at the table, or before groups anywhere. Also, never criticize a senior in wardroom talk or in a group.

Olives, celery, etc., may be placed on the butter plate or dinner plate, and cranberry sauce may be placed alongside the turkey, or mint jelly alongside the leg of lamb. Gravies and liquid sauces go directly over the foods they accompany.

Usually, what goes into the mouth may be taken out in the same way—when necessary, and only then. A cherry stone in a pie would be removed on the fork, and olive pits are removed with the fingers. But fish bones should be removed with the first finger and the thumb, rather than a fork, and placed at the side of the plate or on the butter plate. You will remember not to call attention to these little embarrassments at the table.

Common sense will dictate what to do in unexpected situations, such as uncontrolled coughing, choking, sneezing, blowing your nose, or when a foreign object is taken into your mouth.

When a sip of water does not help a fit of coughing, or when you are choking, you will necessarily leave the table. If it is your dinner partner who is choking, you may assist her or him on leaving the table and going to another room. If you have to sneeze, use your handkerchief, or your napkin.

Although it is better not to attend a dinner when you have a cold, sometimes it is necessary that you attend unless quite ill, particularly at an official or state occasion. If you must use a handkerchief at the table, do so as unobtrusively as possible. If your cold is a serious one, it may be better to be excused from the table than to disturb the other guests.

Upon returning to the table, you should not apologize profusely, if at all. A murmured "sorry" may be said to the hostess, or in the general direction of the hostess at a long table. By apologizing or acting embarrassed over such a situation, you only draw attention to an incident that is best ignored.

When you drop a piece of silver at the table, do not pick it up. When you have used the wrong piece of silver and obviously need another piece, ask the waiter for it. Do not apologize for the mistake. The less the incident is noticed, the better. You will make fewer mistakes at the table if you will remember always to start from the *outside* of the array of silver, and work in toward your plate.

WHEN WOMEN ARE GUESTS

When women are guests before and at a meal, there are certain rules customarily observed: you rise to your feet when women enter the room and remain standing until they are seated. An exception is when women prefer to remain standing in conversational groups other than your own. In that case, you may return to your own seated group and sit down.

Women are seated at the table as soon as they enter the dining room. You will not take your seat at the table until after all women have been seated. You do not rise from the table until your hostess rises. At a formal occasion, you may remain standing at your place until the women have left the room and entered the living room, and then you may remain at the table with the host and other male guests for coffee and cigarettes. You normally rejoin the women in the living room after half an hour or so. Frequently, demitasse (a small cup of black coffee), cigarettes, and liqueur, are served to both men and women in the living room or library.

The following rules are customarily observed with women guests:

- You will assist the lady at your right with her chair by stepping behind the chair and drawing it back. You will move the chair forward as she starts to sit down from the left. You will assist with her chair when the meal is over.
- At a small luncheon or dinner you start eating only after all guests have been served and after the hostess starts eating.
- At a large luncheon or dinner you may start eating after a few near you have been served.
- At formal dinners your host and the ranking woman guest will enter the dining room first, with the ranking woman seated at the right of the host. Other guests will enter in pairs, with no order of precedence. The hostess and ranking male guest will enter the dining room last. He will be seated at her right.

When a very high ranking officer, or a dignitary of state, is a guest, the hostess and the high ranking officer or dignitary will enter the dining room first, and the host and ranking woman guest will be next to enter.

When a lady is late and arrives after all other guests are seated, the man at her right will rise and assist with her chair. The hostess does not rise; if she did all other men would have to rise, which would cause inconvenience to the other guests at the table.

- At luncheons, there are *no partners* when entering the dining room. You will enter the room with whomever you were most recently talking.
- At informal or less formal meals, such as buffet suppers, the hostess and women guests usually enter the dining room first, with the men following.
- You may assist your partner with her plate at buffet meals, or she may prefer to fill her own plate. She does not fill your plate, but the hostess may ask a guest to assist in serving at the table.
- The hostess will rise at the conclusion of the dinner, which is the signal for others to leave the table.
- The ranking woman guest, or the woman at the right of the host, should be the first person to leave the host's house or quarters at the end of the dinner or other occasion. So wait until the high ranking guest, or guests, leave before taking your own departure.
- It is the woman who suggests that it is time for a couple to leave.
- Upon your departure, you should tell your dinner partner at your right, the woman at your left, and as many guests at a small party as you can, that you enjoyed the pleasure of their company at dinner, or for the evening. You will express pleasure for the evening, and thank your host and hostess for their hospitality. After saying good-bye—*leave*.
- It is thoughtful of hosts to make arrangements for unescorted ladies to have a way to come to the dinner—or any party—as well as a way for their safe return home. This may be accomplished before-hand by the hosts asking other guests if it would be convenient for them to stop by for the unescorted lady or ladies. If a lady prefers to drive her own car, or to leave by taxi, the host should see her safely to the car or taxi.

CHAPTER 8

Dining in Public Places

Restaurants in the United States vary in as many ways as American ingenuity can express itself. They range from the milkshake-and-hamburger spots to expensive supper clubs. Hotel dining rooms and coffee shops cater to the most particular gourmet as well as the man who eats and runs.

There is an adage to the effect that experience is the best teacher. For the average man, it is good that experience has a few foundation stones on which to build. Mainly, you should remember that the more elaborate or formal the restaurant, the higher the bill and the slower the service.

SELECTING A RESTAURANT

Three basic principles should be followed in choosing a restaurant: (a) the quality of food you desire; (b) the amount of money you can spend; (c) the length of time you can stay.

You should learn something about the restaurant before entering its doors. In a strange city or in a foreign country, guide books will give such information. You can always ask a bell captain in a reputable hotel— regardless of whether you are staying there—about a good place to eat, and the approximate cost. You can mention the type of place you have in mind, inquire if there is music and dancing, and state that you like seafood or Italian food, etc. When money is an important consideration, you had better find out in advance whether or not a supper club has a cover charge. In order to ensure your getting a table as a well-patronized eating place, it is advisable that you make a reservation in advance.

When making a cross-country trip, quick information concerning good eating places can be found in excellent and inexpensive books or pamphlets which may be purchased in almost any drug store, or in travel guides put out by chain hotels or motels.

ENTERING THE RESTAURANT

You may check your coat and hat at a restaurant, hotel, or supper club, and your lady guest may check her coat or any bundle she may be carrying-ing. Usually, women prefer to wear their coats into the dining room and lay them back across their chairs. You wait at the entrance of the dining room until the headwaiter comes up, and then you may say, "Have you a table for two?"—or any desired number. You may tell the headwaiter where you would like to be seated, but when there is a crowd you may not get what you want.

Women will precede the men and follow the headwaiter to the table. When there is no headwaiter or hostess, you go first to find a table. In a mixed group of several couples, the women are given the desirable seats, which usually are those facing the room at large or any view that is offered. Usually, the preferable seats are away from the aisle. At tables in an open space, women sit opposite each other; at banquettes or wall tables, they will have the wall or inboard seats. At a small table for two, the man sits across from the woman, or by her at a banquette.

A man should help a woman with her coat by laying it over the chair back, or stand by while the waiter does this.

ORDERING

In most restaurants there are two methods of ordering a dinner: *table d'hôte* (pronounced "tahble doat") and *à la carte*. The first method means paying a single price for the complete meal as outlined on the menu. The second method involves paying a specific price for *each* item ordered. If a complete dinner is desired, it is more economical to order *table d'hôte*. Ordering *à la carte* is always more expensive, but also more selective; you get what you want.

The host will perhaps make suggestions to his guest or guests concerning the ordering of the dinner, such as "I understand that the chicken tetrazzini is excellent here. Do you care to try it?" or "Seafood is their specialty. Do you care for lobster?" Regardless of suggestions, the host always asks his guests, "What would you like?"

When you take a lady out to lunch or dinner, she will tell you what she wants even though the waiter asks her directly, and then you will place both orders. When you are host to a group, your guests will tell you what they want, and sometimes how they wish certain dishes prepared—steaks well done, rare, etc. The waiter takes the individual orders from you after the guests tell you what they want. Dessert is usually ordered following the main course, when the waiter again brings menus for everyone to study.

Depending upon the part of the country you are in, the size of the city, and the type of restaurant involved, many different menus are encountered which may list local dishes, or menus entirely in French, or foods which are completely disguised. When you do not know what the dish may be, ask the waiter.

Most menus for a complete dinner include soup and/or an entrée, such as tomato or fruit juice, shrimp or fruit cocktail; a main course of meat and two vegetables, plus salad, dessert, and coffee. When young ladies accompany junior officers, it is to be hoped that they are aware of his financial status, but a young man should not ask someone to have dinner with him in an unknown restaurant *unless he is solvent.*

When you are host to a large group at dinner or luncheon, it is best to order the menu in advance. You may always telephone, but when you have time it is wise to talk with the headwaiter personally and make all plans in advance. The guests will accept what is placed before them at such a dinner or luncheon, and there will be little effort for a host and/or hostess.

WAITERS

A good waiter or waitress will give a couple or a group time to study the menu and determine what they care to order. But you should always remember that every waiter or waitress is a human being, and a little consideration toward them may prove the difference between good or indifferent service.

You address a waiter as *"Waiter,"* not *"Hey, you!"* or *"Boy,"* and a waitress as *"Waitress,"* not *"Miss."* In speaking to the waiter, you refer to your guest as "the lady." When the waiter or waitress is busy, you do not attract their attention by clapping your hands, drumming on the table with silverware, or hissing. When a waiter passes nearby, within hearing distance, but fails to notice you, you may call "Waiter!" in a clear tone—but don't bark an order for attention.

The host will make any complaints concerning improperly prepared or served food, or when a mistake of any consequence has been made in the order. A very small error is not worth mentioning, but when anything of importance needs correcting, you do so quietly, but with firmness. Mistakes do happen, but they may not be the fault of the waiter who serves the food but does not prepare it.

If the waiter assigned to your table disappears continuously, or takes too long to serve you, this may be mentioned to the headwaiter. But do not lose your temper and shout or create a scene.

PAYING THE BILL

When it is time to leave, you quietly say to the waiter. "The check, please." The waiter may bring the check on a small tray, with the check face down, and set the tray by the host or whoever did the ordering. In a small eating place, the check may be laid on the table, face down. The host will look at the bill long enough to see if it is correct, and then place the money on the tray.

The waiter will take the tray to the cashier and return any change; you usually leave this for the tip, deducting or adding to the sum, if necessary. Or, in small eating places where the bill says. "Please pay the cashier," the host takes the check directly to the cashier and pays there. In this case. be sure you leave a suitable tip on the table for your waiter or waitress.

Tips customarily are *fifteen per cent* of the entire check. Pennies should not be left unless they add to an even amount, but it is better not to leave them at all.

If you should find an error in the check (other than a few cents), you call this to the attention of your waiter. If he should insist that the bill is correct—when you are certain that it is not—you may discuss this matter with the headwaiter, the cashier, or the manager. After all, it is your money that is involved.

When a stag or mixed group goes "Dutch treat," one person may be designated beforehand to pay the check, with others in the party settling up later. This avoids the clutter of paying at the dinner table, but it is inexcusable for anyone to forget to settle accounts immediately afterward with the one who had paid.

If you are a guest at a dinner held in a hotel or restaurant, you should not offer to help your host pay the bill. You should repay his hospitality later with a dinner, or similar social occasion, of your own.

RESTAURANT MANNERS

Although a man should rise to his feet when a woman stops to chat at his table, this can be awkward to do, as well as inconsiderate of others, at a crowded table. You need not rise completely to your feet under such crowded conditions, even when introductions are underway. A half-rise, or a brief attempt to rise, is acceptable. Ladies seated at the table may give a slight inclination of their heads, accompanied by a smile.

It is thoughtless of anyone to stop and talk at a table when hot or very cold food is before those eating. It is better just to nod or speak and then go on your way; later you can talk briefly with your friends during a lull in the service, or over coffee. When someone stops at your table, you need not ask him to sit down unless you and your guest so desire.

You do not rise when the restaurant hostess stops at your table to inquire about the service and the quality of your food. This is a courteous, business gesture—not social.

In any public eating place, you should never wipe the silver with your napkin; if it appears unclean, ask the waiter for fresh silver. When you drop a piece of silver or a napkin, leave it alone and ask for another. Do not write or chart a course on the tablecloth, and avoid cluttering up the floor space with your feet or bundles.

CHAPTER 9

Toasts

Toasts are given upon various occasions—after weddings, or at bachelor dinners, birthday parties, christenings, engagement parties, dinners, anniversaries, or at a "wetting down" party, etc. A "wetting down" party is one held in celebration of an advancement in rank in the services.

Champagne is the favorite wine for toasts, but dessert wines, sherry, port, angelica, or marsala, are suitable. Liqueurs and soft drinks are not suitable. At a table, the person receiving the toast remains seated; all others stand.

When you are the one receiving the toast, you will remain seated and not even sip the drink—or you will be drinking to yourself. After everyone else sits down, you may rise and thank them or offer a toast in return.

At an informal *engagement party*, given by the parents of the engaged girl (or a close member of her family if her parents are not living), the father will propose a toast to his daughter after all guests have arrived and have been served champagne or another wine. He would call for attention and raise his glass, saying words to this effect: "To my daughter, Susan, and my future son-in-law William Smith. Let's drink to their happiness." Or, "I would like to have you join me in welcoming a new member to our family. To Susan and her fiancé, William Smith." The couple would smile and, if seated, remain seated. Then the future bridegroom would propose a toast to his fiancée's family: "To Susan and her very wonderful parents."

At a *wedding reception*, the first toast is always offered by the best man and is always a toast to the bride and groom. For example: "I propose a toast to the bride and groom. Congratulations and best wishes." The couple usually accept the toast by smiling and remaining seated. At a reception where all guests are seated at tables, the second toast at the bride's

118

table may be proposed by the groom to the bride's mother, with other toasts to the bridesmaids.

At a reception where everyone stands, the bride cuts the cake with the bride and groom eating the first piece; then everybody else has a piece of cake, and the toasts begin. A toast in champagne is frequently drained at one drink.

At a *bachelor dinner* given by a groom for his ushers (See Chapter 33, *The Military Wedding*), the groom's toast to the bride traditionally is, "To the bride." He will rise to his feet when giving the toast, and all others at the table will also rise to their feet.

At a *small dinner* a toast may be proposed by anyone as soon as the first wine has been served, and guests stand only if the person giving the toast stands. More than one toast may be drunk with the same glass of wine, and you may informally say, "To your health," or "Your health." You might say "Many happy returns" at a birthday party.

You will remember that it is an insult to refuse to participate in a toast; if you are averse to alcoholic drinks, you may simply lift your glass and go through the semblance of drinking.

It is customary for the *toastmaster or master of ceremonies* at a luncheon or dinner to give his toast after the dessert. The toast should always express the personal sentiment of the toastmaster or master of ceremonies (M.C.), and it should be brief and appropriate to the occasion.

A very high ranking officer or a dignitary does not always return a toast. At a service organization dinner, a dinner chairman would propose the first toast to the president of the organization. The organization president may bow in recognition of the honor and remain seated while others stand.

At a *child's baptism*, the toast to the child's health and prosperity would be given during the reception, luncheon, or tea which usually follows the baptismal ceremony. The toast would be proposed by the child's godfather.

CEREMONIAL TOASTS

All American officers should be familiar with the international customs observed when toasts are exchanged on board foreign ships or in foreign messes ashore, or at official dinners or luncheons given in honor of visiting dignitaries.

On these occasions, toward the end of the meal, the host—or the highest official of his country present—proposes a standing toast to the head of state (Sovereign or President) of the guest's country. This toast is customarily followed by the national anthem of the country concerned. The highest ranking guest then responds with a toast to the ruler of the host country, followed by its national anthem.

The preliminary ceremonial toasts may be succeeded by toasts to the countries or services represented. The order and subjects of all toasts should be previously agreed upon so that the host and guests will know what is expected of them. All present drink to a ruler or country, but they do not drink toasts proposed to themselves or to their own services.

When the guests represent more than one nation, the host proposes a collective toast to the heads of their several states, naming them in the order of the seniority of the representatives present.

To this collective toast the highest ranking foreign officer present will respond on behalf of all the guests by proposing the health of the head of state of the host.

Occasions and toasts typical of certain countries are given in the next few paragraphs.

BRITISH CUSTOMS

At an official dinner given by a British officer to an American officer, the British officer rises during or after dessert to toast the President of the United States, and then the orchestra plays "The Star-Spangled Banner." After the guests are seated, the American officer rises to toast "Her Majesty, Queen Elizabeth II," and the orchestra plays "God Save the Queen." These toasts are sometimes followed by short speeches and toasts to the services represented.

At regular mess dinners in the Royal Services, the senior member of the mess proposes the toast, "The Queen," and all members in a low voice repeat "The Queen," and sip the toast. If an American officer should be a personal dinner guest in a mess where a toast to the Queen is drunk every night, the mess president might propose a toast to the corresponding U. S. Service after the usual toast to the Queen.

The proper reply by the American officer then would be a toast to the corresponding Royal Service. At official dinners, the Britisher would toast "The President of the United States," and the senior American would reply with a toast "To Her Majesty, Queen Elizabeth II."

Officers of the Royal Navy have the unique and traditional privilege of remaining seated when toasting their sovereign at mess, although those serving in the Royal Yacht choose to rise.

FRENCH AND ITALIAN CUSTOMS

Officers of these services are more likely to begin a toast with the phrase, "I have the honor, etc." At a dinner for a senior American officer, the French host would probably say, "I have the honor to propose a toast to the President of the United States," and the American officer might reply with the toast, "It is my great honor to propose a toast to the President of the Republic of France."

SCANDINAVIAN CUSTOMS

In the Scandinavian countries ceremonial toasts are not customary, but instead the host "skoals" (toasts) each individual guest. No one drinks any wine at the table until after the host has made a general skoal welcoming all the guests. Then skoaling proceeds all during the meal, and women in particular must be on the alert to respond to individual skoals from the men.

Each man is supposed to skoal the woman sitting at his right at least once. The procedure is for him to raise his glass slightly from the table, and looking straight into his partner's eyes draw the glass down and toward his body, bow slightly, say "Skoal" and drink—not forgetting to salute again with his glass before putting it down. This skoal must be returned a few minutes later.

During the dinner the host and hostess are supposed to skoal everyone around the table, but it is incorrect for guests to toast them immediately. At the end of the meal, the guest of honor (seated at the left of the hostess in Scandinavian countries) makes a little speech of thanks, and skoals the host and hostess on behalf of all the guests, who join in this skoal.

JAPANESE CUSTOMS

At a Japanese dinner the customary procedure is all but reversed. The host, before dinner is begun, welcomes and toasts the guests from a seated position. The senior guest replies and thanks the host. Throughout the dinner, individual toasts are given. One person will pick up his cup, catch the eye of the one he is toasting, and both will drink but remain seated.

Toasts may be drunk with soft drinks, tea, sake, beer, etc. The important thing is to return the toast.

CHAPTER 10

Tipping

IN AMERICA

It's easy to trip over tips, particularly since tipping varies in certain sections of this country, as well as abroad. Like death, poverty, and taxes, tipping is always with us.

Originally, tips were given to individuals for services better or beyond those expected. Nowadays, tips are expected for almost any kind of service, but you should never tip a person for inefficient or discourteous service; neither should you allow yourself to be bullied into too large a tip by a scornful attendant.

Never over-tip; that is considered to be flashy. But neither should you be cheap and under-tip. Learn at the start what a fair tip is—and then stick to your system.

If a crafty waiter brings you only large coins or folding money, don't allow yourself to be intimidated; just ask him courteously to bring you some smaller change.

When you do tip, be pleasant about it. You should glance at the person you are tipping, and for good service you should say, "Thank you."

It is a wise man who always carries a quantity of small change for small tips.

WHEN NOT TO TIP

While it is important to know when to tip, it is equally important to know when not to tip. If you make a mistake and offer a tip to someone who should not be tipped, you will discover your error when your tip is waved away. In such a case you simply re-pocket your money.

You do not tip professional people, including nurses, ship's officers, government employees, lawyers, doctors, stenographers, department store

122

workers, or owners or managers of places of business.

You do not tip ushers in theaters. You may give presents at Christmas time to any delivery person, such as your postman, a newspaper boy, garage attendant, or garbage collector. They may prefer to present of folding money—a dollar or two—or a carton of cigarettes, cigars, a tie, candy or fruit.

You do not tip nurses or doctors, but you may tip maids and attendants at a hospital. In a private or semi-private room, you may give a dollar to each attendant; you do not tip in wards. If you would like to give something to your nurse, fruit, candy, or cigarettes are acceptable.

Tipping Chart
(Minimum)

Wine and Dine

In a Restaurant:

WAITER—15% of the bill; over $15, 10% of check.

HEADWAITER (maitre d'hotel or captain)—no tip unless he made advance arrangements, then $2 to $5.

WINE STEWARD—when he serves, 10% to 15% of the wine bill.

CHECKROOM ATTENDANT—25¢.

DOORMAN—25¢ for getting a cab; a little more when he parks your car; 50¢ when he both parks and gets your car.

BUSBOY—no tip.

AT A COUNTER—10% of your check, or follow "No Tipping" sign.

CAFETERIA—no tip.

In a Nightclub: (Generally the same as in a restaurant; but—)

ENTERTAINERS—do not tip; you may buy the star a drink.

CIGARETTE GIRL—10¢ or 15¢ on pack of cigarettes.

HAT CHECK GIRL—25¢.

AT A BAR—bartender 15% of check (do not tip manager or owner).

Hotels and Motels

At a Hotel:

BELLBOYS—25¢ to 50¢ a bag depending on size and weight.
25¢ for room deliveries.

DOORMAN—25¢ for each service, such as hailing a taxi.

ROOM WAITERS—10% to 15% of bill; 25¢ to 50¢ for each service.

CHAMBERMAIDS—no tip for brief stay; for longer stay, $1 up, depending on service.

VALETS—no tip, since they are concessionaires and not employees.

ROOM CLERKS, MANAGERS, STAFF—no tips.

At a Motel: Customarily, no tips. Bellboys, same as at hotel.

At a Resort: (Generally the same as for hotels, plus)

HEADWAITER—usually tipped at the end of your stay, or every two weeks.

BOATMEN, GUIDES—$1 to $5, according to service, for a one- or two-week stay at a resort. (This is in addition to their regular wages.)

CADDIE—25¢ for a fee of $2 or less; 50¢ for a fee over $2.

Transportation

In a Taxi:

DRIVER—15% of bill; 50¢ or under, 15¢.

On a Train:

PULLMAN PORTER (day trip)—25¢ to 50¢ a day, depending on service; 50¢ to $1 a night.

CONDUCTOR—no tips except for special services, $1 and up.

DINING CAR STEWARD—same as for waiters and headwaiters in restaurants.

STATION REDCAPS—rates differ, usually 25¢ to 50¢ a bag.

On a Plane: (No tipping of stewards, stewardesses, pilots, reservation clerks, limousine drivers, or anyone in airline uniform.)

AIRCAP (not employed by the airlines)—25¢ a bag.

On a Ship (Non-Service):

SHIP'S OFFICERS (including doctor and chief steward) not tipped. 10% to 20% of the cost of your passage is distributed to:

CABIN STEWARD, TABLE STEWARD AND HEADWAITER—each $7.50 to $10.

WINE STEWARD—15% of bill.

DECK STEWARD—$2 to $5.

(Remaining amount is for others who give good services.)

Grooming

Barbershop:

BARBER—25¢ for one service. 35¢ for two or more services. (Do not tip owner.)

SHOESHINE BOY—25¢ for shine and tip.

MANICURIST—25¢.

At a Hospital

NURSES AND DOCTORS are never tipped.

ATTENDANTS—$1 each after a week. $3 to $4 after a stay of a month or longer.

Private Clubs   (No tips to any employee at a private or country club or Officers' Club, but Christmas presents are given to employees by members who chip in.)

CADDIE—25¢ for a fee under $2. 50¢ for a fee over $2. (In tournaments, the fee is higher.)

GOLF PRO—no tip.

LOCKER ROOM ATTENDANT—$1, by a guest; $1 to $2 a month by a member.

GROOM—50¢ for hired horse. $1 to stable boy of host's stable.

WAITERS—15% of drink bill.

Special Sports

SKIING PRO—no tip. (Tips are usually included in the cost of the lodge; otherwise, tip as you would in a hotel.)

SHOOTING—$2 for general helper. $4 to $5 for guide for the day. This is in addition to the guide's wages. (Take your own ammunition when you are a guest at a lodge.)

FISHING—Prices vary in all sorts of fishing, including charter boat fishing. Dutch treat is customary in group fishing, and the tips above fees may be:

CAPTAIN—frequently the catch but no tip.

MATES—$2 to $5 each.

GUIDES—$2 a day (in addition to their wages).

House Guest   (You usually do not tip servants unless you have spent several nights in a home. You tip just before your departure, preferably not in front of your hosts. You may give presents instead of tips—cigars, or a carton of cigarettes, or candy.

ABROAD

No matter where you go, when abroad you do not tip in American money. Make certain that you have sufficient quantities of small foreign change for tips. Before leaving the U.S. you should obtain about ten dollars worth of the currencies for each of the countries on your itinerary. Large banks and money exchanges can obtain the monies for you; then cash Travelers checks as needed.

It is helpful to carry a currency converter with you until you become familiar with the currency of the country. Then, you can tell at a glance that 100 lire is about 16 cents, 15 pesetas is 21 cents, and 1 mark equals a quarter.

Wallet or purse-size booklets are available at airport newstands or at travel agencies.

In the better hotels throughout Europe, and in countries such as Japan, there will be a 15 per cent service charge which is prorated and added to your bill instead of tipping. Extra tips are for such services as shoe shining and the carrying of luggage. When there is no service charge you prorate the customary 15 per cent among those who help you, in accordance with custom and services rendered.

Some working people depend on tips to make ends meet; they receive little or no wages and must rely on tips. The washroom attendant, for example, counts on the 10 cents, or equivalent, that you will pay. And remember that in Europe and the British Isles, "W.C." means water closest—the lavatory—with signs posted in public places on signs or on doors. You will tip the attendant at bath houses in the Orient and at the saunas in the Scandinavian countries. You bathe in private or public bath houses or saunas in these countries.

Guides are always tipped in Europe. If there is no fixed fee for the guide, then tip the equivalent of 25 cents or more, depending on the length of the tour. If there is a fixed fee, tip 10 per cent of that amount. The gas station attendant—especially in Germany, Italy, and France—should receive a small tip when he does more than fill the gas tank. And the porter who shines the shoes which you leave outside the door of your hotel room should receive a small tip, equvalent to about 15 cents.

A Guide to Tipping Abroad*

	Waiters	Chambermaids	Bellhops & Baggage Porters	Doorman
GREAT BRITAIN	10% to 15% of check.	1 shilling (12¢) a day, or 7-10 shillings (84¢-$1.20) a week.	1 shilling (12¢) a bag, but not less than 2 shillings.	1 shilling (12¢) for calling a cab.
FRANCE	12% to 15% service charge usually included on check.	1 franc (20¢) a day, 4-6 (82¢-$1.22) a week.	2-3 francs (41¢-61¢) for a load of luggage, 1 franc (20¢) a bag or a service.	1 franc (20¢) for calling a cab.
GERMANY	5% of check over usual service charge.	50 pfennige (13¢) for 1 night's stay, 3 marks (75¢) a week.	50 pfennige (13¢) a bag or a service.	20-50 pfennige (6¢-13¢) for calling a cab.
ITALY	10% of check over service charge.	100 lire (16¢) a day, 500 lire (80¢) a week.	25-125 lire (8¢-20¢) a bag or a service.	100 lire (16¢) for calling a cab.
SWITZERLAND	15% to 15% of check. If service charge, leave small change in addition.	Included in hotel service charge. Tip 2 Sw. Fr. (46¢) for a special service.	Not included in hotel service charge. 50 centimes (12¢) per bag or minimum or 1 Sw. Fr.	50 centimes (12¢) for calling a cab.
SPAIN	10 pesetas minimum (14¢) over 15% service charge; 5% to 10% over check.	10 pesetas (14¢) a day 50 pesetas (71¢) a week.	25 pesetas (36¢) a bag, or a service in room; 5 pesetas to bellhops.	5 pesetas (7¢) for calling a cab.
PORTUGAL	10% to 15% service included on check; leave 5% more.	50 escudos ($1.74) a week.	5 escudos (17¢) a bag, 2$50 escudos (9¢) a service.	2$50 escudos (9¢) for calling a cab.
GREECE	15% service charge is made; add 5% to 10%.	15 drachmas (50¢) for day; 50 drachmas ($1.67) for a week,	5 drachmas (17¢); for a lot of luggage, 15 drachmas (50¢).	3 drachmas (10¢) for calling a cab.
EGYPT	5% of check over 10% service charge, or 15%.	50 piastres ($1.15) per week.	5 piastres (11¢) a bag or a service.	5 piastres (11¢) for calling a cab.

* Chart courtesy of Mary Gordon, Travel Advisor, TWA.

Concierge	Taxicab Driver	Station Porter	Ladies' Room Attendant	Hairdresser	Theatre Usher
3-7 shillings (36¢-84¢) for special service.	Nine pence (9¢) if fare is less than 5 shillings; 1 shilling if more; 15% if fare is over 10 shillings.	1 shilling (12¢) a bag, but not less than 2 shillings.	Six pence (6¢)	15% to 20% of the bill.	Nothing.
1 franc (20¢) a service, 5-6 francs ($1.02:$1.22) a week even if no services are performed.	10% to 15% of the meter.	Railroad Station, 1 franc (20¢) a bag, Airport ½ franc (10¢) a bag.	½ franc (10¢).	15% to 20% of the bill, if not included.	1 franc (20¢) at a cinema, up to 2 francs (41¢) for orchestra seats at a play or concert.
1-2 marks (25¢-50¢) a special service.	10% of the meter.	Fixed rates.	20 pfennige (6¢).	50 pfennige-3 marks (13¢-75¢).	Nothing.
10% of his bill for cables, phone calls, etc.	10% of the meter. Average, 50 to 100 lire. (8¢-16¢)	100 lire (16¢) a bag.	50 to 100 lire (8¢-16¢)	300 lire (48¢)	50 lire (8¢).
Sw. Frs. 2-5 (46¢-$1.16) for special service, given on departure.	12% to 15% of the meter.	Local tariff plus 10%.	50 centimes (12¢)	15% of the bill.	Nothing.
No tip if not much service; 25 pesetas (36¢) a day or more, depending on service performed, if by hotel.	2-5 pesetas (3¢-7¢).	5-10 pesetas (7¢-14¢) a bag.	2-5 pesetas (3¢-7¢).	10 pesetas (14¢).	2 pesetas (3¢) per person (bullfights, football matches, etc.).
10 escudos (35¢) a service.	15% of the price registered.	5 escudos (17¢) a bag.	2$50 escudos (9¢).	5-10 escudos (17¢-35¢).	2$50 escudos (9¢).
20 drachmas for special service. (67¢)	4 drachmas (14¢). or less.	10 drachmas (33¢) for a load of luggage.	2 drachmas (7¢).	20 drachmas. (67¢).	5 drachmas (17¢).
25 piastres (58¢) at end of stay.	5 piastres (11¢)	5 piastres (11¢) per bag.	2 piastres (5¢).	20% of the bill.	3 piastres (7¢).

ENTERTAINING

CHAPTER 11

Entertaining at Dinner

Today's service family is the forerunner in the new American custom of adapting the best of old European traditions to present-day needs on a modest income. With the modern service family living briefly in many states and various countries all over the world, it is only natural that the best of American as well as Continental or Far Eastern customs are modified into everyday living.

The goal of any host and hostess is to serve the best food in the most pleasant surroundings to congenial guests. The service family combines the French tradition of good food with a Yankee minimum of time and expense. With the general lack of servants in the average household today, it is essential that modern entertaining fits today's needs—not yesterday's.

A young officer's household will probably have little, if any, help. A higher ranking officer's family may have a part-time maid—but household help is almost a vanished profession. Stewards are assigned to the quarters of high ranking officers, such as the Chief of Naval Operations, the Chiefs of Staff of the Army and Air Force, the Commandant of the Marine Corps, and the superintendents and presidents of the various academies and colleges.

When the occasion demands, waiters are available from a catering service or from an officers' club. Maids frequently serve at today's formal luncheon or dinner—a procedure which once was considered incorrect.

In keeping with the times, less formal dinners are the order of the day, with the semiformal dinner or sit-down buffet the most favored. Buffet meals, with guests helping themselves, are favored from coast to coast.

The modern service family entertains more often, more casually, and has more fun by entertaining all over the house, then ever before. The dining table may be in the dining room, in a corner of the all-purpose living

131

room, or on the patio. It is characteristic of this family that men and women often exchange household duties that once were considered the duty of only one or the other. A man often enjoys selecting furnishings or decorations for his home, and the opportunity to find interesting and useful objects while serving in distant parts of this country or abroad is limitless.

It is gratifying to any host to know that friends come to his quarters because they want to—not have to. But it is not by chance that a luncheon or dinner, large or small, is successful. The part that seems so easy is that way because it was planned to the last detail, long in advance.

However, officers and members of their families will attend many formal occasions through the years. As an officer, you will attend official, public, and state occasions, starting as a midshipman or cadet, and will comtinue to do so throughout your service career—and on into retired life.

But formal or informal, you will want to know exactly what to do as the guest—or the host—at any type of dinner or luncheon.

CLASSIFICATIONS OF ENTERTAINING

There are three general classifications of entertaining:

Informal: There may be no servants, therefore no service at the table. The host and hostess will serve two or three courses, probably buffet style.

Semiformal: There will be service at the table, with the host and hostess helping somewhat (mostly before the meal); from three to five courses may be served, but three or four are customary.

Formal: There will be full service at the table, with no assistance from the host and hostess; stewards or waiters will serve four or five courses.

INFORMAL DINNERS

THE FAMILY DINNER

The family dinner is one that you will attend the most often as a guest, or will most often give as the host. Since a dinner with a family is an intimate occasion, guests should consider it an honor to be invited into a home. It is customary for the hostess to extend the invitation. (See Chapter 18, *Invitations and Replies.*)

As a guest, you will be invited by telephone or in person, or perhaps by a brief note. As the host, you may extend the invitation in the name of the hostess: "Mary would like you to have supper with us on Saturday, at seven." If you are the only guest, and if there are children in the family, the dinner hour may be as early as six o'clock. You will wear a conservative suit, or sports coat, if indicated, and women will wear daytime dress.

If you are a guest, the hostess will precede you into the dining room and will tell you where to sit. And if you are the ranking or oldest male guest, you will be seated at the right of the hostess.

When a blessing, or grace, is said at the table, it is said before anything is touched—including the napkin. You may be asked to say the blessing. A blessing that is acceptable to all faiths is:

> For what we are about to receive,
> Lord, make us truly thankful.   Amen

The food may already be on the table when you sit down, with the meat placed in front of the host to serve and the vegetables in front of the hostess. When soup is the first course, the soup cup or bowl will be in the place plate, and the main course of meat and vegetables will not be brought in until after the soup plates have been removed. When there is no servant, the hostess (sometimes the host) will remove the soup plates.

The table may be simply set, with mats or a cloth, and a small bowl of flowers will be the centerpiece. Two or three courses are customarily served:

Two courses:

        Main course (meat and vegetables), and dessert,
- or   Casserole with, or without, salad; dessert (cool weather menu),
- or   Seafood, chicken or turkey salad, etc., and dessert (summer menu),
- or   Main course, salad and cheese (no dessert).

Three courses:

        Soup, main course, and dessert,
- or   Main course, salad, and dessert,
- or   Entrée (seafood, melon, etc.), main course, and dessert,
- or   Casserole, salad, and dessert.

When the host and hostess serve the meal without the help of a maid, the host usually serves the meat. The stack of plates is placed directly in front of the host, with the meat placed in front of the plates, along with carving knife and fork. A portion of meat is placed by the host on each plate, which is then passed to the hostess for vegetables. The hostess usually indicates who is to receive the plate, with the first plate going to the woman at the right of the host.

Should the hostess not say to whom the plate will go, a male guest should pass it to the woman nearest him. All persons at the table will be served in this manner, with the next to the last plate for the hostess, and the last plate for the host. If the hostess prefers, the platters and dishes of food may be passed in one direction around the table, with each guest serving himself. If you are a guest at such a meal, you may hold the dish for the woman at your right to serve herself before you take your portion; then the dish would be passed on around the table. The bread tray is also passed to each guest. The water glasses would have been filled before the family sits down, and each filled salad plate would have been placed to the left of the forks.

Dessert may be served directly from the kitchen, after all plates and dishes have been removed from the table. When the dessert is to be served from the kitchen, the dessert silver will be in place on the dessert plate.

When dessert is served at the table, the stack of plates, along with the dessert, serving fork, and/or spoon, are placed directly in front of the hostess. The dessert silver may be in place on the table, parallel above each plate. The spoon will be above the fork, with the handle of the spoon at the right, and the handle of the fork at the left. If the hostess prefers, she may place the dessert silver on the plate before it is passed down the table.

Coffee is frequently served throughout the family dinner, in medium size cups (teacups), or it may be served with or after dessert. The coffee service may be placed on the sideboard or nearby table, with cups and saucers, sugar and cream. The coffee may be poured from the sideboard or table and placed at the right of each person at the table, with cream and sugar passed down the table.

Or, after the table has been cleared, the coffee service may be placed there, and the hostess will pour. She will ask each person his preference for cream and sugar; then she will pass each cup with the spoon in place on the saucer.

At a family dinner, you may take second helpings when offered—or even a third, if your hostess insists and if you really want the food. It is flattering to your host and hostess that you enjoy the meal, and you should say so. But if you do not care for a second helping, you need not feel any obligation to take it. When passing your plate for a second helping, leave your knife and fork on your plate, the knife above and parallel across the top or at the right of the plate, the fork placed below with tines up.

You will wait for the hostess to begin eating before beginning yourself (unless she especially asks you not to wait for her). And you will wait until she rises from the table before doing so yourself. She will precede everyone from the room, probably walking with the guests. When something needs to be done during the meal, or afterwards, you may offer to assist—such as bringing in the coffee service, stack of plates, etc.—but most hostesses prefer that guests do not help at a small or family meal. If nothing has been planned after dinner, you may leave within an hour.

DINNER WITH NO MAID

A small two- or three-course dinner for several guests may be served at the table by the hostess, or by the host and hostess, with everything arranged for convenience in serving. The dining table should be set early in the day with cloth or mats, and as much food preparation as possible must be completed in advance of the dinner.

Soup, dessert, and various foods may be prepared the day before (a

Place arrangement when the hostess serves.

frozen food compartment will permit other dishes to be prepared and stored days in advance of the dinner).

A menu should be planned which requires little last-minute preparation. A hostess may plan as a main dish something that can be placed in the oven before the arrival of the first guests and that will finish cooking during the cocktail hour. Casseroles and roasts are favorite foods of the sort that can be prepared early.

The host and hostess will not attempt to carry out the same type of service as would be done by a maid. The host will place ingredients and glasses for cocktails on a tray which is placed on a convenient but out-of-the-way table in the living room. Cocktail food is set out as soon as the first guests arrive, and tomato or fruit juice will be brought on a separate tray.

The dinner may be served by the host and hostess in the same manner as the family dinner. However, many hostesses prefer not to crowd the table with dishes and platters of food, and will place them, instead, on the sideboard or on a sturdy card table, along with the stack of plates.

Frequently, the host will carve and portion the meat, and will place each portion on a plate which is handed to the hostess for vegetables. She will place the plate before each guest at the table, serving from the left.

Guest's place arrangement when the hostess serves.

After the plates are removed by the hostess, she will serve the dessert directly from the kitchen, or she may remove the dishes and platter from the sideboard or card table and serve the dessert and coffee from there.

The hostess may prefer to serve coffee to guests in the living room, with the coffee service placed on a low table. The hostess would ask each person his preference for cream and sugar, and the cup would be handed to each guest—who would come forward—or the host or another guest would hand the cups to the guests. The cream and sugar may be passed on a small tray, with each guest helping himself.

INFORMAL DINNER, WITH MAID

When a maid serves 8 or 10 guests at a three-course dinner, where all the guests are seated, the hostess will assist in serving at the table while the maid is busy in the kitchen. The first course of soup or an entrée may be in place on the table when guests sit down. Upon the removal of the first course, the main course will be brought in by the maid and placed in front of the hostess for serving.

The warmed plates will be set directly in front of the hostess, and the hostess will fill each plate. The maid will set the plate in front of each guest, serving from the left. The woman at the right of the host will be served first, then the woman at the left of the host and on around the table. The hostess is served next to the last and the host last.

The hostess may prefer to pass each plate directly down the table, designating the plate for the woman at the right of the host, etc. This would leave the maid free to pour the water, pass the rolls, or work in the kitchen.

The maid may serve the main course on a platter, with the vegetables placed by the meat. The maid would offer the platter at the left of each guest.

After the main course is eaten, the maid will remove the plates, the bread

Dessert silver placed above the plate at informal dinner or luncheon, Continental fashion.

and butter plates, the relish dishes, salt and pepper shakers, bread tray, and serving platters, and then she will brush the table. The dessert may be served from the kitchen, or the maid may place the dessert in front of the hostess for serving.

Coffee may be served at the table with the dessert, but it is usually served in the living room for all guests. It is served in the same manner as at the "no-maid" dinner with the maid removing the used cups.

Ashtrays are usually on the informal table, either individual or one larger tray for each two guests, which is placed between the guests' plates. Smoking usually starts just before the serving of dessert.

When no entertainment has been planned following the dinner, you should leave about ten-thirty o'clock.

BUFFET SUPPERS

The buffet (pronounced "boo-fay") supper or luncheon is the favorite form of serving a large number of guests in a small space with, or without, a maid. A buffet supper, luncheon, or late supper is the best type of get-acquainted party.

At such a meal the table is placed in a space convenient for guests to move around it and serve themselves. The table is usually covered with a cloth, placed over a silence pad. There will be a centerpiece, not too large, and several sets of salt and pepper.

The stacks of plates, napkins, rows of silver, platters, and bowls of food will be placed in sequence around the table. Serving forks and spoons will be near the dishes they accompany. Dinner forks may be the only silver on the table, since a wise hostess will not serve foods difficult to cut, but knives will be placed on the table if needed.

When there is no maid, everything will be placed in the dining room, for convenience in serving. A water pitcher and glasses, coffee service, and wine decanter and glasses may be on a sideboard or convenient table, if not on the dining table. Dessert and dessert plates and silver may also be on the sideboard, or they may be placed on the table or sideboard after the dishes for the main course have been taken away.

As a guest, you will fill your plate and carry it into the living room, or any other room designated by the hostess. Small tables or folding tables are frequently provided by the hostess, but if not, you will sit any place and balance your plate on your knees. At very large buffet meals, you will probably eat while standing up.

When you are through eating, you may place your plate on the sideboard or dining table, leaving the host or hostess, or the maid to carry them into the kitchen. Or the maid may take the plates personally from before each guest, removing two at a time. Guests may serve themselves dessert from the table or sideboard, and the maid will serve coffee from a tray.

At buffet suppers, two or three courses are usually served, as well as hot buttered rolls or biscuits. The buffet luncheon food will be lighter, but with similar service. Although soup may be a first course, this is inconvenient to serve and is usually avoided by a busy hostess.

Buffet menus are varied, but may include:

>   Roast beef, turkey, or ham; salad, and dessert. All three roasts may be served at very large occasions.

or   Main course of meat and vegetables, with or without salad, and dessert. The meat dish, such as chicken à la king, can usually be prepared well in advance.

or   Any of the curries that are favored in the service set, with innumerable side dishes, plus salad, and dessert.

or   A casserole, salad, and dessert.

SIT-DOWN BUFFET

The sit-down buffet is a more comfortable form of entertaining than is the stand-up buffet. The table is set as it would be for dinner—with the exceptions of the plates and the main course, which are placed on the sideboard for guests to serve themselves. The napkins, silver, glasses, salt and pepper, and butter plates are all in place on the table.

Place mats are frequently used on the table, and there will be a centerpiece. Small tables—usually card tables—are often arranged in the same manner as the larger table, except that the centerpiece on such tables is usually very small, to save space. The inexpensive circular card table

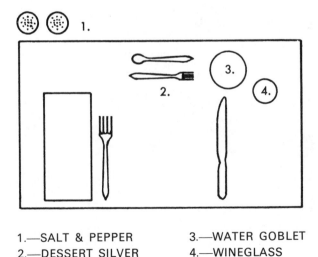

1.—SALT & PEPPER   3.—WATER GOBLET
2.—DESSERT SILVER   4.—WINEGLASS

The sit-down buffet.

covers, which may be purchased at most department stores, are a great convenience since five or six persons can be seated at the table for any type of meal. Attractive and inexpensive circular table cloths are also available.

The dessert silver may be in place above the space for the plate, and butter plates are used as a matter of convenience. When dessert is served from the kitchen, the dessert silver will be brought on the dessert plate.

When there is a maid, soup is frequently the first course, and this may be in place on the place plate when the guests sit down. The maid will remove used plates while guests serve themselves at the sideboard. Coffee is usually served at the table.

At very large buffet parties, the coffee service, water, wine, and glasses may be placed on trays, with guests helping themselves.

SEMIFORMAL DINNERS

The main difference between the semiformal and the formal dinner is in the service. Fewer waiters will serve fewer courses to the same number of people. The semiformal dinner (particularly the sit-down buffet) is a favorite form of entertaining, because the very nicest appointments may be used. Table decorations may be as elaborate as any at the most formal table.

Place arrangement for a semiformal dinner or formal luncheon.

Men usually wear "Black tie" or the equivalent uniform, and ladies wear long or short formal dresses.

A table cloth of linen or damask or lace may be used, or mats of the same materials. The silver will be sterling, the glassware may be clear or jewel toned, and butter plates and ashtrays are used. The first course of soup or seafood may be in place on the table when guests sit down, but it is preferable that soup be served after guests are seated in order that it does not get cold.

Three or four courses are customarily served. A good sample for such a meal is:

First course: soup, usually clear, or oysters or clams on the half shell, melon, etc.
Second course: main course of meat and vegetables.
Third course: salad.
Fourth course: dessert.

You may smoke just before dessert, unless ashtrays are not provided— from which you may assume that your hostess does not wish you to smoke at the table.

After-dinner coffee may be served to the women in the living room and to the men at the dining table, or to both men and women in the living room. The ranking woman guest will make the first gesture toward going home about ten-thirty o'clock, when dancing or other entertainment has not been provided.

FORMAL DINNERS

A formal dinner is always a dignified occasion, but it should not be a cold and formidable affair. Although most very formal entertaining has disappeared in the services, there are still many official and state functions which high ranking officers must give and attend.

At such dinners the most delicious food is served, with the utmost efficiency, at a table set with the most beautiful and correct appointments. Full service, preferably by men servants, is required at the truly formal table.

Tradition rules that all guests sit at one table. Men will wear "Black tie," unless "White tie" is indicated on the invitation, and ladies will wear formal attire. Place cards are used, and the hostess will plan the seating arrangement, with due regard for the service rank of those present, for congeniality of guests, and the number to be invited. When an equal number of men and women are at the table, care must be taken that men do not sit by other men or women by other women.

The formal table is customarily set with sterling silver, a damask, linen, or lace cloth, or mats, fine china, and crystal glassware. There will be a centerpiece of flowers flanked by silver candlesticks or candelabra. Customs have changed in recent years concerning the number of courses served, with four or five the usual number, but as many as seven or as few as three are occasionally served.

Although guests are seated according to protocol at an official or state dinner, they are seated according to congeniality in most homes, as well as with due regard for the rank of service officers attending.

The high ranking man is customarily seated at the right of the hostess, and the high ranking woman will be at the right of the host. The host and hostess may be seated at opposite ends of the table, or they may sit opposite each other at the center of a very long or round table.

If you are a guest, you should arrive at the designated time—usually eight or half-past eight of an evening. You should be on time. In quarters, a steward will open the door for you, say "Good evening, Sir (or Madam)," and direct you to the coatroom. In homes of civilians with considerable means, a butler usually is at the door.

The service for a very formal dinner.

In the center, upright in a holder, is the menu card. From left to right, at the edge of the table are: fish fork, meat fork, salad fork, plate with napkin and place card, salad knife, meat knife, fish knife, soup spoon, and oyster fork. In the upper right are the glasses. Starting at the top, from left to right, they are: water, sherry, red wine, and champagne glasses. Each glass is removed with the course it accompanies, with the exception of the dessert wine glass which stays throughout the serving of demitasse to the gentlemen at the table. The salad and fish knives may not be needed, and only two wines, sherry and champagne, may be served.

You will find a small envelope in a tray on a hall table, with the name of your dinner partner enclosed. A table diagram will be conveniently displayed to enable you to check the seating arrangement. At large dinners, a small folded card with the man's name on the outside and his partner's name on the inside on a small diagram, will show the seating positions at the table. Such cards are frequently used instead of the usual card and envelope.

Your hostess will be standing just inside the living room door to greet guests, and the host will be nearby. Guests will greet the hostess first, and then the host, before greeting other guests. A guest, or guests, of honor will be with the host and hostess. It is customary that when the guest of honor is a dignitary, an aide to the host will meet the guest at the gate of the station or base and will escort the guest to the host's quarters. The host will be waiting in the hall to greet the honored guest, and to present other guests to him.

It is the duty of the host to see that each guest meets his dinner partner before going into the dining room. At large official dinners, aides will introduce dinner partners when necessary; at other dinners, the host may ask a friend to make necessary introductions.

Your host, or an aide, will introduce you into a group, then it is up to you to meet and talk with many other guests. A choice of one or two cocktails, as well as sherry and fruit or vegetable juice, will be offered before dinner. You usually take one, but no more than two cocktails before dinner.

When dinner is announced, the hostess will turn to the ranking male guest and say, "Shall we go in to dinner?" *But it is the host and the high ranking woman guest who lead the way into the dining room.* When a guest is late—not counting the honor guest or guests—the general rule is to wait from 15 to 30 minutes before going in to dinner.

When the guest of honor is a man of very high position, or a dignitary of note, the hostess and guest of honor will enter the dining room first, with the host and ranking woman following. All other guests follow in pairs, in no order of precedence.

Place cards are usually laid flat on the napkin in the place plate, or they will be standing at the head of each plate. Names are handwritten, with titles and last names only: "Mrs. Smith," "Captain Jones," "The Ambassador of Thailand," or "The Secretary of the Navy." The last two are addressed as "Mr. Ambassador" and "Mr. Secretary." (See Chapter 14, *Seating Plans and Precedence.*)

Women are usually seated as soon as they enter the dining room, not always waiting for the hostess to enter and be seated. Stewards may assist with some of the ranking women's chairs, but you will probably seat your dinner partner at your right. You will step behind her chair, draw it back carefully, then as she starts to sit down from the left, you will push the chair forward.

The number one steward will be standing behind the hostess's chair, directing the service. As soon as all guests are seated, the first course is placed in the place plate, which is on the table when guests sit down. There will always be a plate before you until dessert is served.

The service customarily begins with the woman at the right of the host. (See Chapter 15, *Table Service*.) The number one steward will pour wine as soon as the first course is served, and will serve other wines with the courses they accompany. If you do not care for wine, you may lightly touch the rim of the glass with your fingertips before the server starts to pour, or you may simply say, "No, thank you."

At dinners held in homes, and at small formal dinners anywhere, you start eating as soon as the hostess begins (or the host, at a stag luncheon or dinner). At large formal dinners or banquets, you start eating as soon as those near you have been served. Menus for formal dinners are varied.

The following courses, with the wines that accompany each course, may be changed to three-, four-, or five-course menus by omitting certain courses. In this country, soup is traditionally the first course, although it may be preceded by seafood, such as oysters.

Sequence of Courses

COURSE	ACCOMPANYING WINE
Shrimp cocktail, oysters or clams on the half shell, or	white Burgundy
Soup (usually clear)	sherry
Fish, hot or cold	white Rhine
Main course of meat and vegetables, or	claret
Main course of game and vegetables	Burgundy
Salad	no new wine
Dessert (ice cream, sherbert, etc.)	champagne
Fruit (pears, grapes, etc.)	champagne

A *five-course dinner* could be: soup, fish, main course, salad, dessert.

A *four-course* dinner could be: soup, main course, salad, dessert.

A *three-course* dinner could be: soup, main course (with asparagus instead of salad), and dessert.

Rolls, condiments, and after-dinner coffee are always served. Candy is frequently served after the final course, but is not necessarily offered.

Although the use of butter plates is now condoned on the formal dinner table, their use depends upon the amount of space at the table since crowding is always to be avoided.

Cigarettes are offered at most formal dinners, but some hostesses prefer that there be no smoking at the table. Individual ashtrays may be placed above the plate, or between each two guests at the table. Urns or other containers of cigarettes may be placed on the table, and individual ashtrays offered each guest. Cigars and cigarettes may be served to the men after the women leave the table.

Demitasse and liqueurs may be served in the living room to the women, and at the table or in the library to the men. Or they may be served in the living room or library to both men and women.

When the hostess rises, you will stand and again assist your partner with her chair. You will remain standing while the hostess leads the ladies from the room, then you may move toward the host's end of the table—or the host may move toward the dignitary—or you will go with your host and other men into the library. You rejoin the women in about half an hour.

If dancing or games have not been planned for the evening, and if you are not going on to the theater or some function, the guests will form in conversational groups. The high ranking woman guest will make the first move to leave when the time for departure comes—which usually is within an hour after the dinner is over.

Upon departure, you will shake hands with your host and hostess and thank them for their hospitality. The hostess will rise when guests rise to leave, but she will not leave the living room. The host, however, accompanies all guests to the door of the living room, and may even walk to the front door or into the hall with high ranking guests.

Although it is impossible to tell each guest good-bye at a large dinner, you should speak to your own dinner partner before leaving, as well as with others with whom you were just talking. The steward or butler will open the door for you and will say, "Good night, Sir (or Madam)." You will answer, "Good night and thank you."

THE LATE GUEST

When a guest is late, a hostess may wait from 15 to 30 minutes, if possible. If she must proceed, the latecomer will go to his or her place upon arrival; the hostess remains seated—otherwise all gentlemen at the table would also have to rise. Only the man at the right of a late lady guest rises to seat her. The latecomer should briefly say, "I am very sorry to be late, it was unavoidable." Then later she should give an explanation to the hostess.

RÉSUMÉ

INFORMAL DINNER RULES TO REMEMBER:

- Invitations may be extended by telephone, in person, by note or by calling card. You may answer in the same manner.
- The time is anywhere from 6 to 8 P.M., with 7 P.M. customary.
- A man will wear informal dress—usually a dark or light business suit, in season, or sports attire if indicated. Women will wear afternoon, cocktail, or sports attire, as indicated. The hostess may desig-

nate what to wear when the invitation is given, or a guest should feel free to ask.

- There will be two or three courses served, with the host and hostess serving, or with a servant assisting in serving.
- The hostess is not served first by a servant unless she is the only lady at the table. When other ladies are at the table and the hostess serves, she is served next to last and her husband last.
- The table will be set simply but attractively, with a table cloth or mats, and a centerpiece.
- One or two wines may be served, if desired. The bottle or decanter may be placed on the table, with guests serving themselves.
- When nothing has been planned afterwards, such as bridge, you may leave within an hour after the dinner's conclusion.
- Write a "Thank you" note to your hostess after being entertained, or telephone her. Regardless of the informality of the luncheon or dinner, it's the hospitality of your hosts that you are thanking them for—not the expense.

SEMIFORMAL DINNER RULES:

- Invitations may be extended by telephone, by letter, or by the semi-engraved card. You will answer promptly and in the same manner, except that the semi-engraved invitation is answered by handwritten note, third person.
- The time is usually 8 P.M., and gentlemen wear "Black tie." Women will be in long or short evening dress.
- Three or four courses are customarily served.
- The dinner may be buffet style, or sit-down buffet.
- Butter plates and ashtrays are usually on the table.
- Small tables seating four, six, or eight, are frequently used for seated dinners; tables for eight are popular, since they offer wider conversational range for guests.
- Elaborate appointments, place mats or tablecloth, are customary at semiformal as well as at formal dinners.
- Guests may leave at about 10:30 P.M. when nothing is planned after dinner.
- Remember to write a "Thank you" note, or telephone your hostess.

FORMAL DINNER RULES:

- Invitations will be handwritten, engraved, or semi-engraved, in the third person, and you must reply in the third person on white or cream-colored note paper. You will answer promptly. Invitations are also issued and replied to by telephone.
- The time is usually 8 or 8:30 P.M., and you must be on time.

- Men will wear "Black tie" or "White tie" as indicated on the invitation. In telephone invitations, the hostess, aide, or secretary will indicate which to wear. Women wear long or short evening dress.
- A guest at any type of dinner greets the hostess first, the host next, and then the other guests.
- There will be full service at the table, with from three to seven courses served—customarily, four or five.
- Butter plates are now used on the formal table. Nothing is passed at a formal table; everything is served.
- "Turning the table" means co-operating with your hostess midway of the meal by talking with the person at your left.
- You will not leave until after the high ranking guests leave, which may be 30 minutes after the dinner is over, or usually within an hour. When there is no guest of honor, the lady who sat at the right of the host is the first to leave.
- The ranking lady will make the first move to leave—even when a man present outranks her.
- Courtesy requires that you write your hostess a note of thanks within two or three days after being entertained. Or you may telephone.

CHAPTER 12

Luncheons and Lighter Repasts

LUNCHEONS

Most luncheons that you will attend will be official occasions, frequently held in honor of a high ranking officer or dignitary who may be a visitor to your base or station. These luncheons are often "stag," but when the guest of honor's wife is in attendance, other women will be invited.

The service for formal luncheon is like that for a semiformal dinner. Three courses are customary, or four at the most. An informal luncheon may have two courses, since the food served at noon time is lighter than that served at evening meals.

The high ranking guest will be seated at the right of the host at a stag luncheon, or at the right of the hostess when women are present. Place cards are used for eight or more guests, and the table may be covered with a lace or linen cloth, but not damask. Mats are frequently used, and there will be a centerpiece but no candles.

Butter plates are used at formal as well as informal luncheons, and ashtrays are usually in place on the table. The first course will be in place on the table when guests sit down, and each course is served at the formal table by waiters or maids. The hostess serves or assists in serving at the less formal table.

Tomato juice and sherry are usually offered about 30 minutes before luncheon, and cocktails may also be served. Coffee is served to both men and women in the living room after formal meals, and at the informal table with, or following, dessert.

When speaking of the noon meal, you will say "lunch." The steward announces, "Luncheon is served." But you will say, "Shall we go in to lunch?" or "Yesterday I lunched with your classmate."

TIME

Luncheons usually start at noon or 1 P.M., depending upon duty hours. You should stay about half an hour, or 45 minutes after luncheon, unless you must return to your ship or station. You will wear the uniform of the day at official luncheons. Non-military women will wear afternoon dress or suits, hats and gloves. Luncheons may be longer when women attend. The high ranking woman will properly start to leave no later than three o'clock.

INVITATIONS

Luncheon invitations may be given in person, by telephone, letter, "informals," calling cards, or the engraved or partially engraved cards. You may answer in the same manner—except you always reply by handwritten note in answer to the formally written or engraved card.

GUEST OF HONOR

At a stag luncheon, the guest of honor or highest ranking guest will be seated at the right of the host, with the second ranking guest at his left.

At a mixed luncheon, the guests are seated in the same way as at a dinner— the ranking lady at the right of the host and the ranking man at the right of the hostess.

At a women's luncheon, such as an officers' wives luncheon, the senior officer's wife will be at the right of the hostess. When there is a guest of honor, such as a prominent speaker, the honored guest will be at the right of the hostess and the wife of the high ranking officer will be at the left of the hostess.

MENUS

The menu for any luncheon is varied. A two-course summer luncheon could be: fruit or seafood salad, and dessert. A two-course winter luncheon could be: casserole with, or without, salad and dessert.

The customary three-course luncheon could be:

      Soup, main course, dessert,
or   Main course, salad, dessert,
or   Fruit (melon or grapefruit), main course, dessert,
or   Casserole, salad, dessert,
or   Soufflé, salad, dessert.

A formal luncheon will consist of no more than four courses. For example: Soup, main course, salad, dessert.

Soup is usually in place on the table when guests sit down. A two-handled cup or bowl, with matching plate, is customarily used. These cups are sometimes called "bouillon" cups, and a wide bowl would be called a "cream-soup" cup or bowl. When soup is served at the informal table, the hostess may serve from a tureen placed in front of her.

Sherry is often served with the soup course, and may be the only wine served at luncheons. A white or red wine may be served, or both may be served at formal meals. Iced tea is frequently in place on the summer table when guests sit down. The iced tea spoon may be at the right of the knives, or above the plate at an informal meal; it may also be placed on a coaster or small serving plate holding the iced tea glass. Hot tea may be served at the table, with the service the same as for coffee—except that the hostess always pours.

Second portions are not offered at a formal luncheon.

BREAKFAST

Breakfast is usually a simple meal, served informally except for such occasions as wedding breakfasts, hunt breakfasts, etc. A small bowl of flowers or fruit may be on the table, and the table is frequently bare. Mats of almost any gay material may be used. As a rule the early morning hours are an undesirable time to entertain.

The silver at each place is usually a fork, knife, and cereal spoon. A butter knife will be in place on the butter plate at a more formally set table. The coffee cup will be at the right of the knife, and the coffee spoon will be in place on the saucer at the right of the cup handle.

Jam is served in a dish set on a small plate, with the spoon in the plate. Fruit or fruit juice is usually in place on the breakfast plate, or the juice glass may be set at the right of the water glass—when water is on the table.

Plates may be arranged in the kitchen and brought in individually, or the food may be placed in dishes set on the table and passed around the table. Food is frequently kept hot on the sideboard, along with the coffee and toast, with everyone serving himself.

At a family breakfast, the food is placed on the table for convenience in serving. When guests are present and time is not important, a leisurely breakfast may be served by the hostess or a maid. Then, fruit or fruit juice will be in place on the breakfast plate, with dry cereal placed above the plate on the table. The butter plate and knife will be set above the fork, and hot cereal and food will be served from the kitchen or from the sideboard.

WEDDING BREAKFAST (OR SUPPER)

Following a formal morning wedding, a breakfast is usually served for the guests. Wedding breakfast etiquette is discussed fully in Chapter 33, *The Military Wedding.*

OTHER LIGHTER REPASTS

COFFEE

A "coffee" is an informal type of entertaining that is popular for wives of a unit or ship, and usually is held on a weekday between 10 and 11:30 A.M. When held in a home, guests do not wear hats; in a club, hats and gloves may be worn, with a simple, but attractive daytime dress.

The menu is similar to that of a breakfast and usually consists of coffee, sweet rolls, biscuits, small sausages, etc.

BRUNCH

A brunch starts a little later than a "coffee," and is usually held between 11 A.M. and 1 P.M. It has a more elaborate menu than a "coffee," with hot muffins, scones, ham, sweet rolls, pastries, and fruit juice, as well as coffee.

The brunch may be held in a home, on the patio or terrace, or in a club. Men as well as women are invited. Women do not wear hats.

Invitations to coffees and brunches are usually extended by telephone or in person a few days in advance of the occasion. You reply in the same manner.

TEA

Teas, for a few or many guests, usually start at 4 or 5 P.M., and frequently are given in honor of someone or to meet someone—a houseguest or a very special person. Guests should arrive no later than half an hour before the last hour indicated in the invitation. Your nicest afternoon dress, hat, and gloves are worn.

In a home, a tea is usually held in the dining room and the table is always covered with a lace or elaborate cloth. The platters of food, the stacks of little plates, the napkins, cups and saucers, are arranged in a balanced pattern in relation to the floral centerpiece and to the two trays—one for the tea service and one for the coffee service—which are placed at opposite ends of the table.

The food served at a tea is varied, but always includes thin sandwiches and small cakes. The menu may include small rolls or biscuits filled with marmalade or hot creamed chicken, small doughnuts, tarts, pastries, cake, nuts, and mints, as well as tea and coffee, with lemon and cream. The serving of tea may start as soon as the first guests arrive, with the hostess greeting each guest upon arrival.

Invitations are extended by telephone, note, calling card, or informals, and replies are made in the same way.

When guests depart, the conventional remark is, "I must be going; thank you so much." The hostess may answer, "Good-bye, I'm so pleased you were able to come." The hostess may accompany a guest to the door of the living room, or a high ranking guest or a much older guest, to the front door.

Junior officers' wives, with limited budgets, frequently repay luncheon or dinner obligations with invitations to such brunches or teas. In the services, obligations are repaid in keeping with one's budget.

RÉSUMÉ

LUNCHEON RULES TO REMEMBER

- Invitations are extended by telephone, in person, by informal notes or calling cards, or by the partially or fully engraved cards for formal occasions. You will answer in the same manner, but always by a handwritten note in answer to the partially engraved card.
- The time is usually noon or 1 P.M. You are expected to be on time.
- There are *no* luncheon partners when entering the dining room. You will walk in the room with whomever you were talking when luncheon was announced. You do *not* offer your arm to a woman when entering the dining room.
- Butter plates and ashtrays are placed on the formal as well as the informal table.
- Men and women usually have coffee together in the living room after the more formal luncheon. Coffee or hot tea may be served at the less formal table.
- One wine is customarily served at the luncheon table, but two may be offered. Lighter wines are served at luncheons.

CHAPTER 13

Setting the Table

The basic rule in setting any table, formal or informal, is that crowding must be avoided—there should be at least 24 inches of table space for each person—and everything on the table must balance. The centerpiece is in the middle of the table and is balanced by any other decorations placed around it—unless the table is placed against a wall, such as at a large buffet when space is needed; in that case, the centerpiece would be placed closer to the wall.

The traditional table arrangements for six, eight, or eighteen guests shown here may be adapted for various numbers of guests:

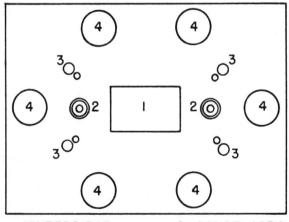

1-CENTERPIECE   2-CANDELABRA
3-SALT & PEPPERS   4-PLATES

A table set for six.

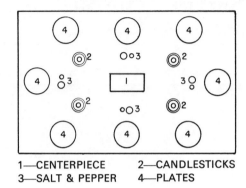

1—CENTERPIECE   2—CANDLESTICKS
3—SALT & PEPPER   4—PLATES

A table set for eight.

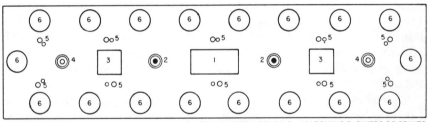

1—CENTERPIECE   2—TALL CANDELABRUM 3—MATCHING FLOWERS OR FRUITS
4—CANDLESTICK OR SMALL CANDELABRUM 5—SALT AND PEPPERS 6—PLATES

A table set for eighteen.

THE MODERN TABLE

Although such things as table decorations—china, linens, and sterling silver patterns—are usually confined to a "woman's world," it is a sharp young man who will take time to learn something about the furnishings of a household, since sooner or later most men get married. For instance, informal tables are now set with stainless steel because it is attractive and easy to polish. However, sterling silver flatware is essential for more formal entertaining.

In the present-day world of the midshipman, cadet, OCS, OTS, or bachelor officer (who may have no immediate thoughts of marriage), it is well to know what is correct in furnishings for the home since you will have the opportunity to buy excellent articles at prices usually much lower than at home, when you are on the midshipman practice cruise or overseas air cruise, and when you have duty abroad. Furthermore, such articles make excellent Christmas, wedding, birthday (or any anniversary) gifts, as well as gifts for a hostess when you have been an overnight guest in a home.

Today's modern table is one of utility as well as beauty. Mats have replaced the tablecloth on most tables—even the more formal table. Harmony in color and design, and balance of table appointments and decorations, are the main rules in setting any table, formal or informal.

The type of entertaining to be enjoyed usually determines the formality of the silver and china service. Table linens may be in every color of the artist's palette and in a wide range of fabrics.

Fine bone china, or any of the serviceable potteries or earthenwares, may be the choice of the hostess; glassware may be crystal—clear or colored, plain or etched. Silver flatware will be sterling, with another set of silver plate or stainless steel for breakfast and informal use. But sterling or silver plate, porcelain or pottery, fine table service is never mixed with coarse accessories any more than fine evening accessories would be mixed with sports attire.

There are a number of rules that are followed in setting the table:

TABLE LINEN

- The formal dinner table may be covered with a white or ivory-colored damask tablecloth. However, the modern pastel-colored damask cloth, lace, or fine embroidered linen cloth is more frequently used, as well as place mats of linen or lace.
- The tablecloth never overhangs the table by more than 18 inches, and no less than 12 inches. A silence pad should fit the top of the table, with the tablecloth placed over the pad.
- Matching damask napkins should be between 18 and 22 inches square—or 24 inches square for the very formal table.
- A lace or linen tablecloth for the formal luncheon or semiformal dinner table must not overhang the table. Elaborate mats are frequently used.
- Luncheon napkins are from 14 to 16 inches square. They may be of linen, plain or with matching lace, or damask.

HOW TO FOLD NAPKINS

Large formal napkins are used at formal dinners or banquets when the service is quite formal. There are three customary ways of folding napkins: (1.) Fold the napkin once in each direction, then fold the square into thirds.

Place on the place plate. (2.) Fold the napkin into a square, then fold opposite corners together to form a three-sided shape. Place on place plate. (3.) A standing napkin—which is frequently used on European tables but rarely on American tables—has a roll placed inside the fold. Make a square, then a triangle, tuck one point of the triangle inside the other and fold the points

Formal napkin folds.

down so that one lies a little above the other, and until the top one is left pointing straight up. Place on place plate. (When formal napkins are monogrammed with three initials of equal size, their order is the order of the hostess's name: Mary Senn Fisher would read: "MSF" or "mFs." A single initial is: "F.")

Informal napkins are from 14 to 16 inches square, and are used for breakfast, luncheon, tea, or informal dinners, or buffet suppers. They are usually placed at the left of the forks. The open edges may be placed toward the plate and the table edge, or toward the left as illustrated.

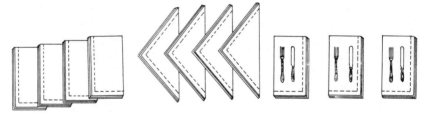

Informal napkin folds.

Napkins are customarily placed one inch from the edge of the table, on a line with the place plate and table silver. There are several ways to fold napkins at the informal table: (1.) Fold the napkin into a square, then fold it in half again. (2.) Fold a smaller napkin from corner to opposite corner to form a triangle, and place beside the plate with the triangle pointing *out* from the plate. (3.) Napkins for buffet suppers are folded in triangles or rectangles, and are placed near the stack of plates. Napkins may be placed in folded rectangles on the buffet table, with silver for each guest laid on each napkin. (4.) Napkins may be placed on the place plate when a first course is not on the plate.

FLATWARE

Silver flatware is always placed on the table in the order of its use, starting from the outside and working in toward the plate. There are rules that are followed in placing table silver. Below is a résumé of those rules:

- The silver, napkins and plate are lined up *one inch* from the edge of the table.
- Forks are placed at the left of the plate—with the exception of the seafood fork, which is placed at the right of the spoon, tines up.
- There are never more than three forks in place on the table at any one time. If more forks are needed, they will be brought in with the course they accompany.
- Knives and spoons are at the right of the plate, with the blade of the knife facing in toward the plate.
- Teaspoons or place spoons are placed on the informal luncheon or dinner table, and are used for soup served in cups or for fruit. Teaspoons are placed on the breakfast table and are used for grapefruits, cereals, etc.
- Spoons for tea and coffee are placed on the saucers, at the right of the handles, before service.
- Dessert spoons and/or forks are usually brought in on the dessert plate, with the fork at the left, the spoon at the right of the plate.
- At informal meals, dessert spoons and/or forks may be placed on the table above the plate. The spoon will be above, with the handle at the right, and the fork will be directly below the spoon, with its handle at the left. This is a European, not American, custom.
- The iced beverage spoon, used mainly at luncheons, may be placed on the table at the right of the soup spoon, or it may be laid above the plate, with the handle of the spoon at the right.
- The individual butter knife is customarily placed across the top of the butter plate, parallel with the edge of the table. The handle of the knife is at the right, the blade facing toward the edge of the table. The knife may be placed on the right side of the plate, parallel to the other table silver. (See *illustration* page 102.)
- The steak knife is placed on the table in lieu of the regular knife.

CHINA

A china service is composed of plates for breakfast, luncheon, and dinner; coffee and tea cups, serving dishes, as well as various size plates for various uses.

There are large flat plates (usually called "dinner plates") for the main course, a slightly smaller plate for luncheon, and a plate that may be used for dessert or salad. Various size plates are needed for the soup cup or bowl, butter, oysters, fruit, fish, etc.

Place plates are the plates that are on the formal or semiformal table when guests sit down.

Although all china used throughout the meal need not match, it is a rule that all plates used together at the same time *must match;* that is, all dinner plates used in the main course must be alike, all dessert plates alike, etc.

There are three sizes of cups most customarily used: the demitasse or small coffee cup used after formal and semiformal meals; the teacup or medium size coffee cup at luncheons and less formal meals; and the large coffee cup for breakfasts and informal meals.

The sizes of the main types of plates are:

- The plate for the main course (the dinner plate): about 10 inches in diameter.
- The luncheon plate: 9 inches.
- The flat dessert or salad plate: about 8 inches.
- The butter plate—a small flat plate for bread and butter—between 4 and 6 inches.
- The soup plate, between 9 and 10 inches across, is a broad bowl about an inch deep with a broad flat rim; it is used only at formal dinners. The handled soup cup or "bouillon cups" are used at luncheons.

SERVING DISHES

A complete set of serving dishes is required to serve each six or eight guests. At a meal for 12 to 16 guests, a second set of serving dishes would be required. Serving dishes may match the china service, or they may be silver. They should blend with the china service if they do not match exactly. There are many shapes and sizes, with oblong or oval dishes having broad flat bottoms and deep sides the most useful.

Two pairs of vegetable dishes are necessary, if you entertain often, with a smaller pair for everyday use and a larger pair for the serving of many persons. The customary sizes are:

- Vegetable dishes, 12 to 14 inches, one or two pairs.
- A bowl 5 or 6 inches deep, for soft foods, etc.
- A shallow bowl, about 10 inches in diameter and 2 or 3 inches deep, for serving fruits, desserts, etc., or used as a centerpiece.
- Bread tray or basket, of various sizes and materials. A silver tray may be used for serving asparagus, celery, carrot sticks, radishes, etc.
- Sauceboat or gravy boat.

PLATTERS:

- A small oval platter, 15 inches long, for meat or fish for a few persons.
- A large oval platter, 18 inches long, for large roasts and cold meats; it is particularly useful at buffet meals.
- A round platter, 12 inches in diameter, for serving pies, cakes, canapes, cookies, etc.

WATER AND WINE GLASSES

The stemmed water goblet is used on the luncheon or dinner table, and is customarily placed above the knives. The goblets are usually filled with water before the guests sit down. Stemless water glasses are used at the less formal table, and after or between meals. Goblets and glasses come in a variety of sizes, shapes, and quality of crystal or glass.

The smaller wine glasses are placed on the table in several ways—customarily at the right and forward of the water goblet. Wine glasses are placed in the order of their use, and are filled immediately after the course they accompany has been served. Sherry glasses are filled almost to the top, but wine glasses are filled no more than two-thirds.

The basic triangle at a *formal luncheon* or *semiformal dinner*, with two wines served, is:

Wine glasses are held by the thumb and first two fingers at the base of the bowl. Small stemmed glasses are held by the stems, and the tumblers are held near the base. Brandy snifters are held in the palms of both hands to warm the brandy.

When you hold a glass of chilled wine, hold it by the stem so that your fingers do not warm the glass, and thus the wine.

TABLE DECORATIONS

The center of interest on the luncheon or dinner table is the centerpiece. The size of the centerpiece depends upon the size and shape of the table, but it should not be so tall or large that guests cannot see over it. When candles are used, the flame must either be above or below eye level.

The basic formal table decoration is a centerpiece of matching china or porcelain bowl or tureen, filled with white flowers, flanked by silver candelabra or four candlesticks. A long table will have matching replicas of the centerpiece placed midway down each side of the table—and both sides of the table must be alike.

In addition to the candelabra on the long table, four or more candlesticks with white or cream-colored candles, may be placed in rectangular fashion around the centerpiece. When two candlesticks are shorter than the others, they are placed at the ends of the table.

A single candelabrum, or a small bowl of flowers artistically arranged, may be used on the small formal or semiformal table. Flowers are customarily used, but modern table settings include the use of almost any material or container in good taste—fruit, vegetables, figurines, or driftwood. Modern or antique containers may be of silver, china, porcelain, or crystal for the most formal table, and wood, pewter, glass, or pottery for the less formal table.

ASHTRAYS

Ashtrays are customarily placed on the most formal table today, but until recent years smoking was not permitted at the table. Individual ashtrays of sterling, china, or porcelain may be placed above the place plate, with two cigarettes laid across the top of the tray, and a small book or box of matches laid in the lower part of the ashtray.

Larger urns or containers of china or porcelain, or of sterling, may be placed on the table, with individual ashtrays. At formal dinners, the guests may be offered cigarettes in silver boxes placed on a tray and served by a waiter just before dessert.

Ashtrays, either individual or for every two guests, are usually in place on the semiformal and informal table when the guests sit down.

CANDY DISHES

Candy is served at the table less frequently now than in former years. Candy dishes are considered a part of the table decorations, however, and may be placed between the candelabra and the place plates at each end of the formal table.

At a long table, the candy dishes would be spaced, equal distance, midway down the sides. The candy may be passed by the hostess or served on a tray by a waiter.

FINGER BOWLS

Finger bowls may match the glass at the table, but not usually so. The finger bowl is brought to the table in one of two ways:

- On the dessert plate, with the dessert spoon at the right and the dessert fork at the left of the plate. The bowl is taken off the plate by the guest, who sets it on the table above and to the left of the plate. The guest places the dessert silver on the table, with the fork at the left and the spoon at the right of the plate. When a lace doily is under the finger bowl, this is also removed from the plate and is placed on the table under the finger bowl.

- Or the finger bowl may be brought on the fruit plate, when fruit is the final course served. The finger bowl and fruit knife and fork are removed from the plate by the guest, and are placed on the table in the same manner as described above. When the finger bowl is brought in with no silver, the guest will know that no other course will be served.

Finger bowls may be brought in at any meal, but are most frequently offered at formal meals, or after the serving of lobsters or clams or any food that is greasy or that must be handled. The finger bowl is three-quarters filled with cool water—or with warm water, when foods have been greasy to handle.

SALTS AND PEPPERS

One salt and pepper set may be placed on the informal table and passed around the table when needed. Antique condiment sets are frequently used on the informal table, and unusual or antique sets can add interest to a table.

On the formal table, individual sets may be placed directly above the place plate, or one set may be placed to the right of the line of glasses of a guest and used by the guest next to him as well as by himself. Sets are customarily placed in a rectangle around the centerpiece, with the pepper above and the salt below.

Open salts and peppers require a very small sterling or glass spoon.

TABLE LISTS

A young couple just starting out may begin the table service with a "starter set" for two. "Open-stock" china or silver or glassware means that extra pieces or sets may be purchased at most stores at most any time. Established patterns are advisable, since replacements may be purchased whenever needed.

Sets of 4 or 8 are preferable for a young couple, with service for 12 the average in most households. When purchasing a service for 6, it is well to know that when the number of *dinner plates* and *coffee cups* is doubled, the same list will take care of 12 guests at a two-course luncheon or dinner.

The average sizes in plates most frequently used are: dinner, 10 inches; luncheon, 9 inches; dessert or salad, 8 inches. The place plates used at formal meals are approximately 9 or 10 inches in diameter.

In the average household, the medium-sized cup, or teacup, is used more often than any other cup; and the new *place spoon* may be used for dessert, cereal, or soup—but not for cream soup.

A place setting includes the dinner plate, salad plate, butter plate, teacup, and saucer. A service for 6 persons would include:

CHINA

- 6 Dinner plates
- 6 Butter plates
- 6 Salad or dessert plates (12 preferable)
- 6 Teacups and saucers
- 2 Large coffee cups, family use
- 1 Sugar bowl
- 1 Cream pitcher
- 6 Soup bowls
- 6 Soup plates

Extra pieces:
   6 Demitasse (after dinner) cups and saucers
   6 Luncheon plates
Serving dishes:
   Platters, small, medium, or large
   Platter, round buffet
   Vegetable, open or closed
   Sauceboat
Useful pieces:
   Casserole
   Water pitcher of silver, glass, or pottery
   Salad bowl, wooden (preferable)
   Individual salad bowls
   Cereal bowls
   Butter dish, of china or silver
   Tea, coffee service:
   Silver or china

Most table service sets can be purchased or ordered at your nearest PX or Service Exchange at considerable savings.

GLASSWARE

Thin crystal, plain or etched, is used for formal and semiformal occasions. Modern glassware comes in all qualities, colors, and designs, and is used instead of crystal at less formal occasions. Water goblets and wine glasses may match, but not necessarily so. Glasses should harmonize in color, quality, and design for various occasions. A desirable list is:

   6 Water goblets, stemmed, holding about 10 ounces (formal)
   6 Water glasses for informal occasions
   6 Wine glasses, stemmed, holding from 3 to 5 ounces
   6 Sherry glasses, stemmed, 2 ounces
 12 Cocktail glasses, 3 to 4 ounces (the cocktail and wine glasses may be interchanged if the wine glass is not too large; a large sherry glass may be used for cocktails)
 12 Highball glasses, also used for iced fruit juices, soft drinks, etc., 12 to 14 ounces, no stems
   6 Fruit or vegetable juice glasses, no stems, 4 to 5 ounces
   6 Liqueur glasses, stemmed
   6 Finger bowls (usually for formal entertaining)

SILVER

The sterling silver pattern selected should be for a lifetime. Service families frequently use stainless steel for informal occasions. A minimum place setting includes the knife, fork, teaspoon, salad fork, soup spoon (or the new place spoon) and butter spreader.

The place spoon doubles for soup, cereal, and dessert. The salad fork serves for dessert. There are also new place knives and forks that can be used for breakfast, lunch, or dinner.

For a complete place setting, it will be necessary to eventually add coffee spoons, oyster forks, iced beverage spoons, and individual steak knives. Serving spoons and forks are essential in table service. Service lists for 4, 8, and 12 persons are:

Starter Set (Service for 4)

8 Teaspoons	2 Table or serving spoons
4 Knives	1 Sugar spoon
4 Forks	1 Butter serving knife
4 Salad or pastry forks	1 Gravy ladle
4 Soup or place spoons	1 Cold meat or buffet fork
4 Butter spreaders	

Medium Set (Service for 8)

16 Teaspoons	1 Butter serving knife
8 Knives	1 Gravy ladle
8 Forks	1 Sugar spoon
8 Salad or pastry forks	1 Cheese serving knife
8 Soup or place spoons	1 2-pc. salad set
8 Butter spreaders	1 Pie server
8 Cocktail or oyster forks	1 Lemon fork
8 Iced beverage spoons	1 Jelly server
3 Table or serving spoons	1 Tomato or flat server
1 Cold meat fork	1 2-pc. steak set

Regular Set (Service for 12)

24 Teaspoons	12 Forks
12 Knives	12 Salad or pastry forks
12 Soup or place spoons	1 Tomato or flat server
12 Butter spreaders	1 Cheese serving knife
12 Coffee or cocktail spoons	1 2-pc. Steak set
12 Cocktail or oyster forks	1 3-pc. Roast set
12 Iced beverage spoons	1 2-pc. Salad set
12 Steak knives, individual	1 Cream or sauce ladle
4 Table or serving spoons	1 Olive or pickle fork
2 Sugar spoons	1 Pie server
2 Table or serving forks	1 Cake slicer
2 Cold meat forks	1 Bonbon or nut spoon

1 Butter serving knife
1 Gravy ladle
1 Jelly server

1 Lemon fork
1 Sugar tongs
1 Punch ladle

TEA AND COFFEE SERVICE

A tea set includes a teakettle (usually with an alcohol burner and stand), a cream pitcher, a sugar bowl, a tea caddy, and a bowl into which dregs of the teacups may be emptied. Sugar tongs or a spoon, a fork for serving lemon, and a strainer are needed, and all these should be placed on a tray.

A coffee set includes a coffeepot, a cream pitcher, and a sugar bowl, with sugar spoon, and all these should be placed on a tray. The tray should be large enough so that there is no crowding.

A tea and coffee set are usually combined, with the same sugar bowl and cream pitcher, sugar tongs, spoon, and tray useful for either service. There are three sizes of trays most useful in a household:

1. Eight-inch tray, used for serving one or two glasses of water or drinks; may be placed in the hall for calling cards, etc.

2. Medium size 13-inch tray, for serving iced beverages, cocktails at small dinners and luncheons, or liqueurs at larger dinners, etc.

3. Large tray approximately 16 to 24 inches, for tea and coffee service. Useful for serving sandwiches, cakes, or at informal parties to place in a room with decanter and glasses or food for guests to serve themselves, etc.

CHAPTER 14

Seating Plans and Precedence

SEATING ARRANGEMENTS

It is customary at mixed dinners and luncheons that the high ranking man sits at the right of the hostess, and his wife is seated at the right of the host. But at occasions governed by protocol, the high ranking man is seated at the right of the hostess and the *high ranking woman* is seated at the right of the host.

The high ranking woman may be a Congresswoman or Senator and not the wife of the high ranking man. The second ranking man is then seated at the left of the hostess and the second ranking woman is at the host's left. The third ranking woman sits at the right of the man of highest rank, the fourth woman is at the left of the man of second rank. Under this arrangement a hostess may find that a man would be seated alongside his wife, and since this is not done, it is the wife who is moved.

It is also customary for the host and hostess to sit opposite each other at the ends of the table, or they may sit across from each other at the center of a long or round table. However, an equal number of men and women could result in women sitting at the outside places on one of the sides, and this should be avoided. In this case, two places may be set at each end of the table—though this usually results in crowding.

Plans 1A and *1B* will show the customary arrangements, with *Plan 1A* the usual dinner or luncheon plan, and *Plan 1B* usually used at large official dinners.

Small dinners for six or 10, 14 or 18, etc., are easily arranged, with the hosts sitting opposite each other and with married couples sitting by other guests. Women will not be sitting at the outside places, when such numbers of guests are at the table.

However, any *multiple of four*—such as tables of eight, 12, 16, etc.—

166

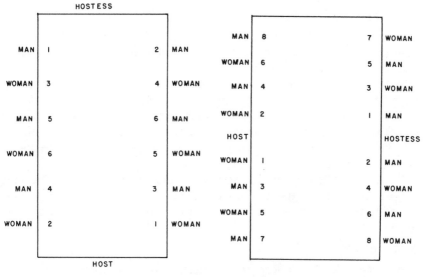

Plan 1A.   Plan 1B.

mean that the host and hostess cannot sit opposite each other without having to place two men or two women together when there is an equal number of each sex present. When this happens, the hostess may relinquish her position at the end of the oblong table and move one seat to the left, which places the male guest of honor opposite the host. When one couple is not married they will sit side by side as in *Plan 2A*. When all couples are married, follow *Plan 2B*.

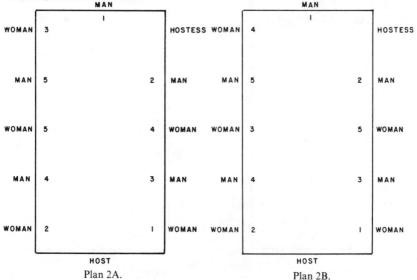

Plan 2A.   Plan 2B.

SEATING IN-LAWS

When the parents of a man or those of his wife are guests in their home, your (a man's) mother or mother-in-law is seated at your right at the table, and your father or father-in-law is at the right of your wife.

When both sets of in-laws are on hand, your wife's mother is seated at your right, and your mother is seated at your left. Your father is seated at your wife's right and her father is at her left. If many in-laws should be gathered in your home, such as at a holiday dinner, then the rule of seniority may be followed. When children are present, alternate them and the grand-parents. Teen-agers may prefer to have a separate table.

If special guests have been invited to a dinner when both sets of parents are present, then the guests of honor take precedence—unless the parents are considered the guests of honor with the other guests invited to meet them.

BACHELOR HOST

A *bachelor host,* or a host who is entertaining in the absence of his wife, may choose from several seating arrangements, depending upon the number of guests, their rank, etc. The high ranking guest will be seated at the right of the host.

At a mixed luncheon or dinner, the host may ask a woman guest to act as hostess to balance the table when the number is not divided by four. In this case, *Plan 1A* may be followed, with the ranking male guest seated at the right of the guest-hostess.

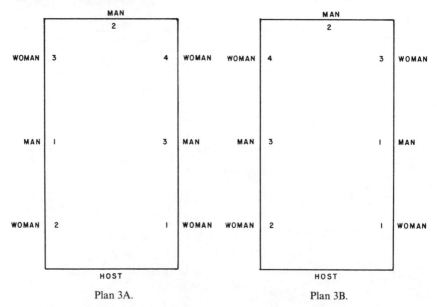

Plan 3A.   Plan 3B.

The host may prefer to ask the ranking male guest to sit opposite him, when *Plan 3A* may be used. *Plan 3B* may be used when the ranking man and woman are not married to each other and the bachelor host does not want a hostess or co-host at a dinner divisible by four.

UNMARRIED WOMEN GUESTS

When a bachelor asks a young unmarried woman to be hostess or to assist at a luncheon or dinner party at his home or club, he should remember that this might be interpreted as a sign of intimacy of relationship when none is intended. When one particular young lady is asked to act as hostess at this special occasion, other guests may hear the sound of wedding bells—when none are planned. In such a case, the bachelor should make certain that the young woman leaves the party at the same time the other guests leave.

A bachelor officer will want to know that the buffet style of entertaining is not only the easiest to plan and serve, but it also eliminates the necessity for seating a hostess at the table.

For the sake of propriety, a bachelor host at a house party should have a married couple or an older lady—preferably a relative—in his home when unmarried women are guests.

STAG DINNERS AND LUNCHEONS

A co-host is frequently appointed to assist the official host at a large stag dinner or luncheon. This is usually done in order to balance the rank at the official table.

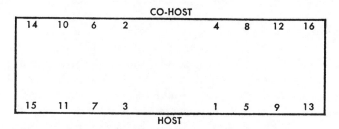

(*Above*) The co-host may be the next ranking guest after the guest of honor. If there are guests from foreign countries, as well as from the United States, the ranking United States guest could be appointed co-host. Foreign guests should be seated between guests of the host country.

Usually, the host and co-host sit opposite each other at the center of a long table. When there is no co-host, or when the dinner or luncheon is small, the host will sit at the head of the table and the juniors at the foot.

SPEAKERS' TABLE

Tact and diplomacy are required in seating toastmaster and speakers at a banquet. The host or chairman will be seated at the center of the long or main table, with the guest of honor at his right and the second ranking guest at his left. The toastmaster is customarily at the left of the second ranking guest.

5	
3	
1	Guest of Honor
	HOST OR CHAIRMAN
2	Second Ranking Guest
4	Toastmaster
6	

The customary banquet table.

7	Air Force General
5	U. S. Representative to U.N.
3	Civic Leader
1	Ex-President
	HOST
2	Foreign Ambassador
4	Red Cross Official
6	Congressman
8	Protestant Bishop

The seating of distinguished guests.

When dignitaries of state or official or very important unofficial guests are present, these distinguished persons may be seated in between the guests of official rank after the guest of honor and second official guest are seated.

When ladies are seated at the table, the most distinguished lady would be seated at the right of the host or chairman, with the second ranking lady at his left. If the speaker is a lady, she would be seated at the right of the host or chairman, with the distinguished lady at his left. Thereafter alternate ladies and gentlemen would be seated accordingly, with the junior (or younger) couples at the extremities of the table.

At the Academies, when the cadets or midshipmen are the official hosts and high-ranking officers and their ladies are guests, there may be variations in seating arrangements. For example, at the formal ring banquet at West Point, where there always is a guest speaker, the chairman of the ring and crest committee (cadet) is host. To his right may be seated the superintendent's wife (1); the speaker (3); the dean's wife (5); the commandant (7). To his left are his drag (2); the superintendent (4); the speaker's wife (6); the dean (8); the commandant's wife (10), and so on.

HORSESHOE TABLE

When horseshoe tables are used at large official banquets, the host and hostess will sit with their honor guests on the outside of the curving center. The other guests will sit down the sides.

When places are set both inside and outside the curving ends, the inside seats begin at X, with the seats inside but nearer the host ranking those farther away on the outside. When the horseshoe has a prong, the junior guests are seated on each side of it.

Plan 4A—Simple horseshoe.

Plan 4B—Horseshoe with prong.

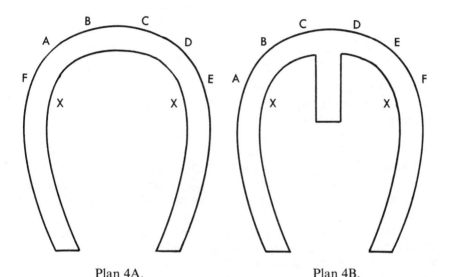

Plan 4A.   Plan 4B.

A. Wife of guest of honor
B. Host
C. Wife of second ranking guest
D. Guest of honor
E. Hostess
F. Second ranking guest

FORFEITURE OF POSITIONS

The only time that a host and hostess, excepting the President of the United States and the First Lady, relinquish their positions at the head and the end of their luncheon or dinner table is when their guest is a president or head of any country, a king or a queen.

Then, the reigning king or queen will sit at the head of the table, and the wife or husband, respectively, will sit at the other end of the table.

In order that they do not "give honor to themselves," the host and hostess will sit at the *left* of the president or royalty, and their wives, re-

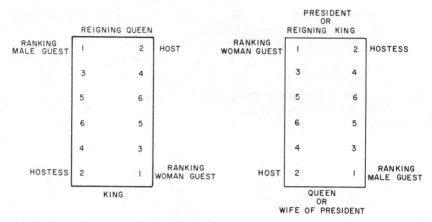

spectively, with the high ranking man and woman guests sitting at the *right* of the honored guests. This will place the high ranking guests in the traditional guests of honor position.

PLACE CARDS

Place cards are used at the luncheon or dinner table, formal or informal, mainly as a matter of convenience in seating guests without confusion or according to protocol. Cards are of heavy plain white or cream-colored paper, with plain, or gold or silver beveled edges.

The cards are about $1\frac{1}{2}$ by 2 inches, or 2 by 3 inches in size. The flag of an admiral or general, the seal of a ship or an embassy, or a family crest may be embossed or stamped in the top center or the upper left corner of the card.

The cards are customarily placed on top of the napkin in the place plate, or laid flat on the table above the plate.

Folded place cards are about 3 by $3\frac{1}{4}$ inches in size, and are folded in half, with the name written across the lower half of the card. They usually stand directly above the place plate.

Names are written by hand on place cards, in black or dark blue ink. At formal occasions, names are usually written in script, such as "Mrs. Jones," "Colonel Smith," "The Ambassador of Norway," "The Secretary of the

Flat place card.   Standing or folded place card.

Army." At informal occasions, names may be written in the same manner, but at more intimate occasions first names are often used: "Marion," "Allan," etc.

MENU CARDS

Menu cards may be used at official dinners, at state and public occasions, and occasionally in a home—such as for an anniversary dinner. A crest or coat of arms may be embossed at the top center of the card, which is of heavy white or cream-colored paper. An admiral's or general's flag, or the seal of a ship are customarily used.

The card is about 4 by $5\frac{1}{2}$ or 6 inches, with a gilded or silvered beveled edge. It is usually placed in a stand, or laid on the table. In homes, the cards may be placed in front of the host and hostess, and one for each three guests down each side of the formal table. They are placed about 6 inches above the plate.

The word "Menu" is written by hand in black ink beneath the crest, and one dish is written on each line centered directly underneath. The first letter on each line is capitalized and each course is separated by a space or asterisks.

Appetizers, bread, relishes, jellies, candy and coffee are not written on the menu as they are on hotel menus. Menus for formal dinners are usually engraved in French, but on naval ships—for instance at formal dinners in flag messes—they are printed, embossed, or handwritten in English.

Menus are frequently considered as souvenirs, such as those at the inaugural luncheon or at the Christmas dinners given annually at the Academies.

PRECEDENCE IN OFFICIAL ENTERTAINING

An officer of high rank, or one who serves with high-ranking officials, such as a service attaché, must be well versed in local customs both at home and abroad. When serving abroad, you will consult the Protocol Section of the American Embassy. In Washington, you will be advised on problems of protocol by the Foreign Liaison Section of the office of your service.

At non-official occasions, precedence at a dinner or luncheon is determined by the prominence of the guests, their age, and degree of friendship. In civilian life, age receives deference, as do professional and scholastic achievement. In one's personal life, married women take precedence over widows, widows over divorced women, divorced women over unmarried ladies.

In official life, strict protocol governs governmental, ecclesiastical, and diplomatic precedence, which has been established by international agreement. A younger official will precede an older official—if the office of the former is in a higher echelon. A younger military officer precedes an older military officer if the former's rank is higher. The seniority of the governmental office, or of the military officer when the rank is the same, is determined according to the date of founding of the office, or of the commission or promotion of the officer.

When a person is asked to be a guest of honor at a dinner or luncheon, he may not be seated in the ranking position at the table—unless his rank justifies it, or if the higher ranking guest concedes his position. When ambassadors and very high-ranking guests are present, guests are seated according to precedence—even though the guest of honor is seated down the table.

When non-ranking guests are present at an official dinner or luncheon, their places at the table are determined by age, prominence, linguistic ability when foreigners are present, and congeniality. After the guests of honor and top officials have been seated, these non-ranking guests are placed between those of official rank in the most congenial way for all concerned.

There are various ways in which a host and hostess may determine the equal seating of a number of high-ranking guests. For example, at a state dinner at the White House, three tables were arranged side by side with the President the host at one table, with the Chief Justice seated across from him; the First Lady was hostess at the second table, with the Speaker of the House beside her; and the Vice President was host at the third table. This was the first time that the heads of the legislative and judicial branches of the United States government had been invited to dinner on the same night with the head of the executive branch.

MILITARY PRECEDENCE

Rules of military precedence have been established whereby military, naval, and air attachés take precedence next in succession after the counselors of embassy or legation, or at a post where the Department of State has considered it unnecessary to assign a counselor, after the senior secretary.

Military, naval, and air attachés take precedence among themselves according to their respective grades and seniority of service—with the U.S. Army the oldest of the services.

Assistant military, naval, and air attachés take precedence next after the lowest ranking second secretary. At a post to which the latter is not assigned, these assistant attachés take precedence as a group among the officers of the Foreign Service of rank equivalent to second secretaries as the Chief of Mission may direct. They also take precedence among themselves according to their respective grades and seniority of service.

CHAPTER 15

Table Service

Due to the general lack of servants in the modern household, the semi-formal dinner is usual and the formal seated dinner of former years is less customary. According to national statistics, less than *one per cent* of the families in America have a full-time servant and only about *four per cent* have servants of any kind—most of whom are part-time. The percentage of families with servants of any kind has dropped from six to four per cent in 15 years.

Today, four or five courses are served at the most formal dinner. Occasionally, when guests are going on to an official or social occasion such as a reception, lecture, or a service ball, only three courses are served.

For a formal dinner of five courses, two or three waiters or stewards are needed to serve 10 to 12 guests, not counting the cook in the kitchen. Two complete services (sets of serving dishes) are necessary. At a very formal dinner, one waiter will serve each four guests.

In the services, most entertaining is done at home—and done often. Fewer courses, thus fewer waiters, are needed for the semiformal dinner of three or four courses. Two waiters and a cook may serve 14 guests at a seated three-course dinner, and, if very efficient, may serve 16 guests.

Almost twice this number of guests may be served with the same amount of help at a semiformal buffet supper or sit-down buffet, when the very nicest table appointments are used and guests will serve themselves.

A waiter or steward, or maid, can serve eight guests at a seated dinner of three courses in a home. But a hostess will assist in serving at the table for a luncheon or dinner for 10 or 12, when there is help in the kitchen.

Many a versatile hostess serves a buffet supper for twelve guests with no maid or cook, but this takes advance planning and food preparation. No guest wants to see his hosts in a frenzied, exhausted condition—and no host wants to appear in such a condition. The hosts, too, should enjoy the party.

ESSENTIALS OF SERVICE

The service at the table must be efficient, quiet, and unobtrusive. Guests should not be rushed in eating, and there should be no long waits between courses.

In a modern household, the hostess is never served first except at family meals or informal meals when no other ladies are guests. When the hostess serves at the table, she may designate to whom the first plate will go— usually the woman at the right of the host.

Second helpings may be offered at informal and semiformal meals, but not at formal meals. Small side dishes of vegetables or fruit are not placed on the formal or semiformal table.

Fruit and vegetable juice are not offered as a first course or placed on the more formal table, but they may be offered in the living room before the meal to non-alcoholic drinkers.

When there is service at the table:

- Nothing is ever taken directly from the waiter's (or steward's) hand, or vice versa. Whatever it is, must be brought on a tray—a glass of water, etc.—with the tray held in the waiter's left hand, his right hand at his side.
- Stewards, waiters, or a maid will address the host and male guests as "Sir" and the hostess and women guests as "Madam."
- The steward or waiter will be in white coat, the maid will be in dark or conservative colored uniform with apron.
- The woman at the right of the host is always served first and is always offered an untouched dish.
- Everything is served at the formal luncheon or dinner. Nothing is ever passed by the guest at the formal table.

RULES OF SERVICE

The rule of *informal* service is: Serve left, remove from the right. (An exception is the removal of the butter plate—from the left.)

The rule of *formal* service is: Serve left, remove from the left.

There are a number of rules of service which should be observed:

- A waiter (or steward) will place one plate at a time at a formal luncheon or dinner. He will place the plate in front of the guest, serving from the left, and he will never reach in front of a guest.
- A waiter (or steward) will place two plates at a time at an informal dinner. He will place one plate with his left hand to the left of the guest, then will place the other plate with the right hand to the left of the next guest.
- The serving dish is offered at the left of each guest at a comfortable

level for serving. Dishes are offered with the servant's left hand, with the right hand held close at his side or slightly behind his back. If the dish is very heavy it may be held with both hands.

- The dish or platter will rest on a folded napkin placed on the flat of the servant's hand. At no time will he grasp the dish or platter by its rim.

- A large serving spoon and fork are placed in each serving dish, face down, with the handles toward the guest.

- At semiformal or informal meals, a waiter (steward or maid) may carry a serving dish in each hand, offering first the vegetable dish in his left hand, then the other vegetable dish in his right hand. The matching vegetable dishes may be placed on a tray and served to each guest, with the tray held on the left hand of the servant. A vegetable (usually potatoes) may be placed on the meat platter.

- Plates are removed after each course at luncheons or dinners when *all* guests have finished eating. Plates are removed at very large dinners or banquets after each guest has finished eating.

- At a formal luncheon or dinner, the waiter will hold the fresh filled plate in his *right* hand while removing the used plate from the left of the guest with his left hand. The fresh plate is set down at the left of the guest.

- At informal meals, to speed service, the waiter will remove two plates at a time. After removing a used plate and a butter plate (or two used plates if butter plates are not used), he will then bring back two fresh plates placing one with the right hand to the left of a guest and the other plate placed with the left hand to the left of the next guest.

- Two waiters (or stewards) may work as a team in removing used plates, with the first waiter removing the used plate from the left, and placing it on the large tray carried by the second waiter. The first waiter will take up a fresh plate from the tray, and place it before the guest, from the left side.

- The table is cleared of crumbs before dessert, with the waiter (or steward) holding a tray below the edge of the table, at the left of the guest. Crumbs, place cards, etc., are brushed into the tray with a folded napkin or table brush.

- The order of removal at an informal luncheon or dinner is: plates, butter plates, serving dishes and platter, pepper, salt, bread tray, and crumbs.

ORDER OF SERVICE

At a dinner with *one service* (complete set of serving dishes) for six or eight guests, the woman at the right of the host is served first, then the host, then the woman at his left, and on clockwise around the table.

According to the placing of the table, the location of the kitchen, etc., the service may be counter-clockwise, always starting with the woman at the right of the host, then around the table, with the host served last.

At a dinner with *two services*, and from 12 to 16 guests, the *first* service will start with the woman at the right of the host and the *second* service will start with the woman seated to the right of the man at the right of the hostess.

When a very important man is guest of honor at the dinner, the second service may be started with the guest of honor at the right of the hostess.

When there are *three services*, and 18 to 22 guests, the *first* service goes to the woman at the right of the host, then clockwise; the *second* will start where the first would leave off (or after six servings), then the *third* will take up where the second would leave off. However, all services must be synchronized so that food is offered at about the same time.

At times it may be better to start one of the services (never the *first*) with a man. When there are 14 people, the man at the right of the hostess may be the first to be served at that end of the table, and when there are 20 persons, a service may start with the man at the left of the hostess.

A custom that is not practiced very often in this country, but that is observed in many foreign countries, including Latin America, is the serving of all women before the men. This is customary at very formal dinners and in most service messes. In this case, the woman on the right of the host is served first, then the woman on his left, and so on, ending with the hostess. Then the men are served in the same way, ending with the host. Men and women frequently leave the table together and go into the living room for demitasse.

COFFEE SERVICE

INFORMAL SERVICE

Coffee is served in several ways at informal luncheons and dinners. There are three main sizes of coffee cups: demitasse, or small cups used mainly after formal or semiformal meals (but also after informal dinners); medium or teacup size for less formal meals; and large cups for breakfast or family meals.

Coffee is frequently served at the informal table with, or following, dessert. At a family meal, with or without guests, coffee may be served throughout the meal. The coffee tray is usually prepared in advance, ready to be served by the hostess whenever needed. The tray may be placed on the sideboard, or the hostess may place the service on the table at her place, and serve each person. The cups may be passed down the table, after they are prepared with cream and sugar, or the cream and sugar may be passed around the table, with each person helping himself.

At informal luncheons or dinners, when there is a maid or steward, they may place the coffee service before the hostess, who will pour and prepare each cup with cream and sugar. The cup may be passed around the table, or the maid or steward may place it at each person's right.

The servant may place the coffeepot on a small tray, with an empty cup, sugar, and cream. He will stand at each guest's right and ask his preference concerning sugar and cream, then place the cup at the right of the plate. Or the servant may stand at the left of each guest, with the guest helping himself to sugar and cream and placing the cup on the table himself. Additional cups will be on the sideboard convenient for serving.

The hostess may pour coffee in the living room, from a tray placed on a low table in front of her. She will ask each guest his preference concerning cream and sugar, and will hand each cup to the guests. The host may assist in handling the cups to the guests, or another woman guest may assist.

Before the coffee is served, the spoon is always placed on the saucer to the right of the cup handle.

FORMAL SERVICE

Demitasse is usually served in the living room to both men and women after formal luncheons, and frequently after formal, semiformal, or informal dinners.

Demitasse may be served in the living room to the women and at the dining table or in the library to the men, after formal and semiformal dinners. There are a number of ways of serving:

- Two waiters (or stewards) will work as a team, with the first waiter holding a small tray with a coffeepot, sugar and cream, and one cup. The second waiter (or steward) will follow with a large tray filled with cups and saucers. The first waiter will ask each guest his preference for cream and sugar, then will offer the cup on his small tray. Or the guest may help himself to cream and sugar.
- The waiter will have several cups on a tray, with cream and sugar, and, holding the tray on one hand, will stand before each guest and pour the coffee. Each guest helps himself to cream and sugar.
- At large occasions, the tray may be brought in with filled cups, cream, and sugar, with each guest helping himself.
- The favored form of pouring coffee is by the hostess. The coffee service will be placed in front of her on a low table, the hostess will ask each guest his preference concerning cream and sugar, and the cup will be handed to the guests, or the guests will come to the table for their cups. The spoon is placed on the saucer, at the right of the cup handle, before handing to the guest.
- The men will be served coffee at the dining table before the women are served in the living room. The service is the same, except that the host does not pour coffee at the table.

TEA SERVICE

The serving of hot tea at the luncheon or informal table is similar to the service of coffee—except that the hostess invariably will pour the tea. Although coffee is customarily served after luncheons and dinners, tea should be served to those who prefer it.

The maid (or steward) may place the tea service in front of the hostess, or the hostess will place the service on the table herself when there is no maid. The hostess will ask each guest his preference for lemon, cream, or sugar, then will pass the cup down the table. The first cup will go to the woman at the right of the host.

When only one or two guests care for tea, the teapot, lemon, cream, and sugar would be placed on a tray and offered by a maid at the left of the guest, with the cup placed on the table at the guest's right.

When there is no maid, the hostess may arrange a small tray and have the water hot before the meal, then quickly prepare the tea and serve it when needed.

Teaspoons are always placed on the saucer to the right of the cup handle before the tea is served.

COCKTAILS BEFORE MEALS

Cocktails may be offered before luncheons, and are customarily offered before dinner parties. Sherry, fruit juice or tomato juice are usually offered on separate trays, the juice being for those who do not care for alcoholic drinks. The juice glasses are filled before bringing into the living room.

There are several ways to serve cocktails before meals:

- At formal or semiformal occasions, the waiter (or steward) may bring a large tray into the living room, with filled shakers and unfilled glasses. He will stand in front of each guest and ask if he wants a cocktail, then pour it. The guest takes the glass from the tray.
- At more formal occasions, two waiters (or stewards) work as a team. The first waiter will hold a tray with one or two shakers, and a second waiter will follow with a tray with glasses for all drinks, and perhaps another shaker. The first waiter will ask each guest what he wants, etc., and offer the drink on the small tray.
- At large dinners, the tray of filled glasses is brought from the kitchen by the waiter, and offered to each guest.
- When there is no servant, the host may mix the cocktails in advance and place the tray with shakers and glasses in a convenient place in the living room before the guests arrive. The ice and the canapes (cocktail food) are brought in after the arrival of the first guests.
- The host may prefer to place all ingredients on a large tray, and mix each drink upon the arrival of the guests.

SERVICE FOR WINES AND LIQUEURS

Wines are served at meals with the courses they accompany, with the first wine (usually sherry) poured after all guests have been seated and after some have been served. One wine is customary at the less formal meal, but two may be offered. As many as four or five wines may be served at the very formal dinner, but two or three wines are customary. After the serving of sherry, champagne may be the only wine served throughout the formal dinner.

The waiter (or steward) stands to the right of each person at the table, and pours the wineglass half or two-thirds full, according to the type of wine. An old custom is that a tablespoonful is poured first in the host's glass, in order that he determine the quality and clearness of the wine. Then the woman at the right of the host is served first, then the woman at the left of the host, and clockwise around the table. The glass of the host is filled last.

Wineglasses may remain on the table throughout the meal, except when three or four wines are to be served. In that case, the sherry glass is removed after the salad course. Wineglasses are refilled whenever empty.

Wines served at luncheons are lighter than those served at dinners. Sherry may be the only wine served at luncheons, or a white or red wine— sometimes both. Usually, red wines are decanted and the white wines are left in the bottle.

At informal meals, one bottle or decanter will serve each five or six guests, and a bottle or decanter may be placed at each end of the table for 10 or 12 guests. The host may fill the glass for the woman at his right, and at his left; then the bottle is passed around the table to his left.

Champagne may be served in the living room after a very formal dinner, or at a home wedding reception or dance. The bottles and empty glasses will be placed on a tray, with a waiter pouring and serving each guest.

LIQUEURS

Liqueurs are customarily served after dinners, *not* luncheons. They are offered after formal and semiformal meals, and frequently after informal suppers and dinners.

At a formal dinner, liqueurs are served to the men at the table following the service of coffee and cigars and cigarettes. The service for liqueurs is similar to that for cocktails. Two waiters (or stewards) will work as a team, with the first waiter holding a small tray and taking the liqueur and glass from a tray held by the second waiter, etc.

Liqueurs are served to the women in the living room after coffee has been offered, but before the cups have been removed.

At informal meals, the host or hostess will serve liqueurs from a tray arranged beforehand with bottles and glasses.

CHAPTER 16

Duties of the Host and Hostess

The "rule of thumb" at any party, formal or informal, is: good food, good conversation, and good company. The prime responsibility of the host and hostess is that guests enjoy the occasion. Not only must the food excel, but the guests must be congenial. An air of cold formality is to be avoided—even though the occasion is formal.

When incompatible personalities are brought together, a pleasant evening is frequently ruined. If it is unavoidable to have two such personalities at the same party, place them as far apart at the luncheon or dinner table as possible.

When a high-ranking person or dignitary is your guest, he must not be lionized to the extent that other guests feel neglected. Special respect is due guests in high position, but each guest must feel equally welcome.

As the host, you must talk with all guests during the course of the evening. You will move from group to group and make a special effort to introduce newcomers or a shy individual into small groups. You will bring persons of less rank or position to meet the person of high rank, or the guest of honor.

A good host will "hear all and see all." You will notice when a guest is left out of a group, or when he seems bored. You will come to the assistance of a guest who cannot gracefully move away from a bore. You will be careful of interrupting a group that is obviously congenial and enjoying themselves—but you will interrupt a group when the conversation has turned to an unwise discussion, particularly if the discussion is to the discredit of another guest or person.

Although you will do everything within reason to make your guests comfortable, your hospitality should not be taken advantage of by a rude or unthinking guest. It is always difficult for the host to handle a situation where one guest makes himself undesirable by coarse conversation or by over-drinking, or by becoming insulting to another guest. However, you may tactfully introduce another subject of conversation, and you may suggest to the insulting guest that you show him something in another room, and thus draw him away from the group where he is not desired.

If necessary, you may have to assist the unwise drinker into another room, or you may ask a trusted friend to assist you in this task. But while guests often assist the host and hostess, they can not assume the duties of either. Since you are responsible for whatever happens within your home, no guest should be permitted to feel embarrassed about anything—whether he was awkward and broke something of value, or made an untimely remark. A thoughtful host will minimize the damage and will adroitly change the topic of conversation.

A good host will try to anticipate his guest's needs, but should never be either over-anxious, or over-casual. A host should not insist that a guest have another drink or more food when he refuses. You may offer again, but allow 10 or 15 minutes to elapse. Never urge a guest to have "just one more drink." And if a guest does not drink at all, never make a joke of it or a point it out to other guests. Instead, offer any soft drinks that you have without comment.

When something goes wrong—when the food is burned, for instance, or when you run out of ginger ale—do not apologize profusely. Never apologize for what you have—or do not have. If your quarters are small and the food not elaborate, do not discredit your hospitality by continually mentioning it. Guests should not feel forced to reassure their host that the evening *is* wonderful and the food *is* superb.

The host and hostess should be in the living room at least five minutes before the luncheon or dinner hour, relaxed and ready to greet the guests. Each guest should be greeted warmly, but not in a superfluous manner.

The hostess will speak to and offer her hand to each guest, and will make every effort to put the guest at his ease. The host greets each guest, shakes hands with him, the introduces him into a conversational group. When drinks are served, it is the duty of the host to ask each person what he cares for (after first stating what he is offering), and then make certain that he gets it.

The host and hostess must decide how long to wait for a late guest. When something is being served that may be spoiled by waiting, the hostess may not be able to wait. Also, sometimes the hosts may be planning a theater party later, or to attend a lecture or dance, and thus it would be impossible to wait for the late guest.

Before the party, the host and hostess have planned what guests will do following the luncheon or dinner. Bridge or canasta, charades or dancing, are frequently enjoyed, but many hosts prefer that guests continue in conversational groups.

At a buffet meal, when plates must be balanced in guests' laps, a wise hostess never serves food that must be cut. The hostess should not finish eating before the last guest, and she should always have a little food on her plate so that she can keep pace with the slowest eater.

As host, you may have to speed on his way a guest who overstays your hospitality. You can sometimes accomplish this by mentioning an early morning golf game, the next day's duty, or an important conference. And again you may also have to disentangle yourself from the guest who opens a new—and lengthy—conversation at the door after he has already said good-bye.

Concerning the friend who habitually "drops in" around mealtime, the host and hostess should feel no obligation to ask him to stay for the meal at times when this would be inconvenient. The hostess, or host, may say, "We have already made plans for the evening or I'd ask you to join us. . . . Perhaps some other time." When the guest is a parasite, you will excuse yourself—but you must never be rude.

DUTIES OF THE GUEST

As a guest, you owe it to your host and hostess to be congenial and to mix and talk with other guests at the luncheon or dinner party. Upon arrival and departure, you will shake hands with your host and hostess.

At sometime during the party, large or small, you will talk with your host and hostess for a short time, but you will not monopolize their time. A congenial guest will move from group to group, conversing with as many other guests as possible.

When your luncheon or dinner partner is a stranger to you, there are many agreeable subjects with which to start and maintain a conversation —current plays, a best seller, a TV program. If your partner is a service wife, you can always discuss the merits of a recent duty station. However, each guest must carry his share of the conversation, and "small talk"— which does not include business or "shop."

If it is your misfortune to be seated at the table alongside someone whom you do not particularly care for, you must conceal your personal feelings. You are expected to talk with your partner at your right, but you must not forget the person at your left, either.

It is wise to refrain from mentioning the foods you do not care for— *that very dish may be on the menu!*

A thoughtful guest will offer assistance to the host or hostess when assistance seems needed in a servantless house, but he will never insist. If your offer in such a case is accepted, go about it quietly but efficiently. You must never "do the honors" in another man's house.

You must not point out an error in the service, or an oversight on the part of the host. If you can correct something unobtrusively, do so. If the dinner was not up to your expectations, do not discuss it with other guests —or with anyone else.

You should not take a lighted cigarette to the dining table, and should *never* use a saucer or plate as an ashtray. Although it is customary to have cigarettes and ashtrays on the most formal dinner table today, a hostess may prefer that there be no smoking at the table, and hence smoking is not appropriate until after dinner.

A guest should accept no more than one or two cocktails before dinner, and no more than one or two liqueurs after dinner. The guest who over-indulges in drink is a problem to a host—and a nuisance to everyone else.

Although no one wants to make an error in the use of silver at the table, do not worry about it if you do. And when you spill something, do *not* over-apologize and make everyone else uncomfortable.

But if you break something of value, you should replace it if possible. If you cannot exactly match a coffee cup, do not buy another pattern—it will be of little use to the hostess and just a waste of your money. You may, instead, send flowers and a note of apology to the hostess. The note should be brief but sincere, with an expression of regret concerning the mishap.

A thoughtless guest is one who asks his hostess at the last minute if he may bring a friend along—thus upsetting the seating plan at a more formal table. Also, it is very thoughtless to arrive late at a luncheon or dinner, and keep everyone else waiting. And a guest will soon wear out his welcome if he continually drops in at a friend's home at meal time, and then stays on to dinner.

A guest should not break an engagement for a formal luncheon or dinner, unless an emergency arises. This means at least a serious illness, a sudden transfer, an accident or death in the family, etc. But a sudden whim not to go because "you don't want to," or because a better invitation has been received, is no excuse at all after an invitation has been accepted.

An acceptance or refusal of an invitation should be made as soon as you can—usually within 24 hours after your receive the invitation. This gives you ample time to check your calendar and to make certain you have no other commitments on that date. When you refuse an invitation, you should give the reason for the refusal.

If you are a young single officer, a midshipman or cadet, you are not expected to return the hospitality of your host and hostess. But you are expected to write a "thank you" note to your hostess, expressing your appreciation of the luncheon or dinner and the hospitality of the hosts.

The note should be written within a day or two after the party. It is not necessary to send flowers or candy to the hostess, but if the occasion was a very special one—such as Christmas dinner, or your birthday—the gift of candy or flowers would not be out of order. A small card would be enclosed with the gift—perhaps your calling card—with a few words of "thanks" written on it.

Other guests, however, will repay the hospitality of their host and hostess by later extending an invitation to them for a similar occasion. An invitation is not extended by saying, "You must come to dinner with us *sometime* . . ." but it *is* extended by setting the *date*.

GENERAL CORRESPONDENCE AND INVITATIONS

CHAPTER 17

Correspondence

As an officer in the services, you will probably be writing or dictating letters for the rest of your life, and whereas in conversation you are judged by what you say, in correspondence you are judged by how you write. Plain words and phrases are preferable in letter writing, just as they are in conversation. A letter difficult to compose is handled with more ease when written as though you were speaking to the person addressed.

When you choose your stationery, consider its use: whether for official* or business correspondence, or social or personal. White paper is customarily used for all types of correspondence, but personal stationery may also be cream color, gray, blue-gray, or a light tan.

Black and dark blue engraved or printed letterheads are used for business or personal stationery, but personal paper may also be engraved or printed in shades of dark green, gray, maroon, or brown. Initials, crests, and monograms are also used on some personal stationery. A man's stationery should look masculine, however, and feminine colors are to be avoided.

All engraving is more expensive than printing, and rag paper is more costly than wood-pulp. Wood paper is used for general correspondence, and rag paper for more personal or important correspondence. There are various textures of paper: *bond*, the one most customarily used, is firm but fairly transparent; *laid* means a paper with striations in the body; *granite* has shredded threads in the paper; and *lawn* has almost invisible lines drawn horizontally across the surface.

---

* Since the official correspondence for the various services is a part of the Regulations for each service, it is not considered necessary to add such information in this chapter.

BUSINESS PAPER

Official or business stationery is white, with black or dark blue engraving or printing. The official letterhead is usually at the top center of the sheet, but may also be placed at the top left-hand side.

There are various sizes of business paper most frequently used:

The traditional white bond paper, single sheet, 8 by 10 inches, with standard matching envelope of oblong shape and plain flap.

A slightly larger sheet, with or without telephone number in the letterhead, $8\frac{1}{2}$ by 11 inches.

A slightly narrower sheet for business-personal use, $7\frac{1}{4}$ by $10\frac{1}{4}$ inches, used for both longhand and typewriter.

A smaller business-personal sheet, 7 by $8\frac{1}{2}$ inches, used for business invitations.

BUSINESS LETTERS

Business letters are frequently typed in the *block style*, with all lines flush with the left-hand margin and the date flush right, with double spacing to separate single-spaced paragraphs. The complimentary close and signature start at the center of the page.

A semiblocked form with indented paragraphs (about 10 indentions) is also used. The dates in business letters, civilian form, are written, "May 7, 1969," but the official service form is usually "7 May 1969." No letter should be dated "5/7/69."

Customarily, there is a colon after the salutation, and a comma after the complimentary closing of a letter.

The *inside address* is written in the same way as on the envelope, with no punctuation at the end of the lines. The title may be abbreviated when it precedes the name, as "Dr. John B. Jones," but it is written in full in the salutation, as "Dear Doctor Jones." In official service correspondence, the order of address usually is: (a) administrative position; (b) station; (c) city, zone, and state. Sometimes, rank and name are "(a)."

In business, the order usually is: (a) title and name; (b) administrative position; (c) company name; (d) company address; (e) city, zone, and state.

The *salutation* is "Dear Mr. Jones:" or "Dear Captain Jones:". When names are unknown, "Dear Sir:" or "Gentlemen:" is used. A business woman is addressed "Dear Miss Jones:" or "Dear Mrs. Jones:"—but when it is not known whether she is married or not, use "Miss." Two or more women are addressed as "Mesdames."

Paragraphs in business letters are not numbered as they are in official correspondence, but items in paragraphs may be lettered and numbered.

The body of the letter includes all necessary information, with well constructed sentences. There must be no errors in spelling, punctuation, or grammar. Avoid stilted or trite phrases; be courteous, and not annoying. Whenever possible, write a one-page letter. The second page is usually indicated by "—2—" at the center top.

The *complimentary close* is the polite phrase or word (adverb) with which you end your letter. Business letters are customarily closed by the "yours" phrase, with "Very truly yours" the most formal. "Sincerely yours" or "Cordially yours" is used for a more personal-business letter and "Very respectfully yours" when writing to a superior. The complimentary close is typed *two-lines* below the preceding line of typing.

Your *signature* is typed or stamped *four lines* below the complimentary close, and hand-signed above the typed signature. For an officer, the order of signature is:

(1.) Name in capitals
(2.) Rank, if any, or
(3.) Functional title
(4.) Authority line, if any.

The signature for a business man usually is:

(1.) Name, not capitalized throughout
(2.) Functional title
(3.) The company name (usually not used, since it is in the letterhead).

Signatures on the official service letter vary from the business-form letter in the following respects: (1) the rank, if any, is included; (2) the functional title is added; and (3) the authority line, if any, is expanded to include the title of the command at whose direction the letter is prepared. Examples:

J. B. JONES
Administrative Officer
Department of the Army

J. B. JONES
Brigadier General, U.S. Air Force
Director of Telecommunications

JANE B. JONES
Lieutenant, U.S. Army
Defense Advisory Committee
on Women in the Services

J. B. JONES
Rear Admiral, U.S. Navy
Head, Division of Administration
By Direction of the Chief
of Naval Operations

J. B. JONES
Captain, U.S. Coast Guard
Commandant of Cadets

JOSEPHINE B. JONES
Colonel, U.S. Marine Corps
Director of Women Marines

In signatures it is incorrect to use titles such as "Mr.," "Mrs.," "Capt.," "Dr.," "Prof." Men and women in business usually use the company's writing paper for all business correspondence, but important executives often have specially engraved or printed paper. Under the company's letterhead, at the left-hand margin, the full name is engraved with the title of office directly underneath. For example:

James Wilson Brown
Editor-in-Chief

An example of a business-form letter is

(name of command and address)

In reply refer to:
3397   110
27 April 1968

Superior Insurance Company
214 North Tenth Street
Jersey City, New Jersey

Attention: Mr. Johnson Henry, Office Manager

Gentlemen:

The business form of letter is used for correspondence addressed to persons or agencies outside the Department of the Navy. If, however, the outside addressee is familiar with the naval letter, it may be used instead of the business-form letter.

The first page of a business letter is typed on letterhead paper, If printed letterhead is not available, the name and address of the activity are typed on plain bond paper. Continuation pages are typed on plain bond paper. In the absence of the "From" line on a business-form letter, letterhead tissue, printed, typed, or stamped, is used for all copies going outside the originating office. Further instructions regarding stationery and copies are given on page 25 of the Navy Correspondence Manual, a copy of which is sent to you under separate cover.

A business letter of less than one page in length is centered on the page so that it presents a well-balanced appearance. A short letter may be double-spaced and it may be typed with the left and right margins as wide as two inches. Full-page and multiple-page letters are typed with one inch margins.

The signature information, placed below the complimentary close, is typed or stamped in block style or in balanced lines.

Very truly yours,

JOHN E. DOE
(appropriate title)

Encl:
(1)

ENVELOPES

Business envelopes usually match the paper and are in sizes ranging from $3\frac{7}{8}$ by $8\frac{7}{8}$ inches to $4\frac{1}{2}$ by $10\frac{3}{8}$ inches. They are usually imprinted with the title of an official or company, or the name of the command, with return address in the upper left-hand corner.

Envelopes are addressed in the same manner as inside addresses, and are single spaced and frequently indented. The letter is folded in horizontal thirds and inserted in the long envelope, or folded first in half and then in thirds for the shorter envelopes.

In business, the address may be from two to five lines. Titles are used in the address: "Mr.," "Dr.," "Prof.," "Capt.," etc.

Mr. John Doe
Executive Vice President
Supreme Book Stores
115 East 53rd Street
New York, New York 10022

The address could begin with the last three lines and the notation: "Attention Mr. Doe" written in the lower left-hand corner. When necessary to signify PERSONAL that word is capitalized above the address.

PERSONAL CORRESPONDENCE

Medium weight paper approximately 6 by 7 inches is customarily used for personal correspondence. A service crest or insignia, monogram, initials, or name and address may be engraved or printed at the top center or upper left-hand corner of the paper. The conventional colors of white or cream, blue, gray, blue-gray, or light tan are most frequently used, with matching envelopes.

Initials may be engraved, or die-stamped in color or in simple block form, at the top center or left of the sheet. Initials are usually $\frac{3}{16}$ of an inch high, and are spaced to take up no more than $\frac{3}{4}$ of an inch over-all. On large sheets of paper, initials may be $\frac{1}{4}$ inch high, and may cover about the same amount of space. Initials are preferable to a monogram, but an address is better than either, in dark blue or black.

When your full name and address are used on the writing paper or on postcards, printing is more frequently used than engraving—owing to the cost. The best printing is black or dark blue, in plain block letters. The name and address are usually printed at the top center of the page, or they may be printed in a straight line across the top—a form used most often on postcards. A printed address, with no name, is used on single sheets for formal as well as for business correspondence, and is placed in the top center of the page.

Men's correspondence cards do not fold over and usually are about 4 by 5 inches, or larger. Your rank, name, and address, if retired, are engraved on the card which usually has an embossed insignia or seal at the top. Such cards may be used for invitations to stag luncheons, dinners, cocktails, etc.

Certain types of informal letters may be typed, *but others must be written by hand*, in a legible manner. It is obligatory to handwrite "bread and butter" and "thank you" letters, as well as letters of congratulation, condolence, invitations to small weddings (or their reply), engagements, birth announcements, or letters to prospective sons- or daughters-in-law. *All* formal letters or cards of invitation are handwritten. Answers to engraved invitations are always handwritten.

SOCIAL OR PERSONAL LETTERS

A social or personal letter will follow basic rules. A long letter, or a social-personal letter, will have the date written at the upper right-hand corner of the page. The date may also be written on the last page, or at the bottom of the first page, near the left-hand margin but slightly below the signature. Only very informal letters have abbreviated dates: the more formal the letter, the fewer the abbreviations.

The basic steps are:

1. *Date:*
   Near the top right: "June 15th" (very informal)
   or Near the top right: "June 15, 1969" (civilian form)
   or Near the top right: "15 June 1969" (Service form)
   or Near the lower left: (same form)
   or Near the lower left: "Saturday" (very formal or very brief).
2. *Salutation:* No inside address, flush with left margin. For example: "Dear Mary,"

or   "My dear Mary,"
or   "Dear Mrs. Jones," etc.

3. *Body of letter:* Indented paragraphs, or a paragraph, brief note. Avoid over-use of the pronoun "I."

4. *Complimentary close:* Start at center of page; occasionally, start at right even with date line. For example:
"Sincerely,"
or   "Sincerely yours,"

5. *Signature:* Directly under, or under and slightly at right, of complimentary close. No title or rank, and with first name for close friends —or when the body of the letter gives no clue to the identity of the signer, then write full name, "John Jones." Otherwise, write your name in full.

The conventional salutations and closings for informal or personal correspondence are:

June 15th

(To a woman)
Dear Mary,
....
....

As ever, (or "Yours ever,")
John (or "John Jones")

(To a man)
Dear George,
....
....
....

Sincerely, (or "As ever,")
John Jones

In letters to a relative or intimate friend, the closing would probably be "Affectionately," "With love," "Devotedly," etc., with the last name of the person writing omitted from the signature. Last names are added to the signature in informal letters when the body of the letter does not give a clue to the identity of the writer.

The date is usually written at the upper right-hand corner of the paper, with no address. On a short note, the day instead of the date may be written at the bottom left of the page, two spaces lower than the signature. On an informal note, the month is sometimes abbreviated; otherwise, it is written out.

BREAD-AND-BUTTER LETTERS

"Bread-and-butter" letters are written within 48 hours after you have spent a night or more in someone's house, and are addressed to the hostess.

THANK-YOU LETTERS

"Thank-you" letters should be written within a week after you have received a gift or a favor. Such a letter is also written following a bereavement, in reply to letters of condolence. Although the envelope is addressed to the hostess, there is no inside address and mention must be made of the host. (See Chapter 18, *Invitations and Replies.*)

A basic form to follow in both the "bread-and-butter" letter and the "thank-you" letter is printed herewith, with parts as indicated:

May 15, 1963

Dear Mrs. Doe,

(A) "Thank you for . . . (the gift or occasion, etc.)"
(B) A sincere comment concerning the occasion or gift; an expression of appreciation; a comment concerning something of mutual interest.
(C) A looking-forward-to-seeing-you-again (soon) sentence.
(D) A "thanks again," and a request to be remembered to the host and/or to any other members of the family.

Sincerely,
John Jones

"MAD" OR "LOVE" LETTERS

It is a wise man or woman who will observe certain rules in writing very personal letters:

• Never state anything that can be used against you.
• Be careful of making direct promises or of stating familiarities.
• Never write anything which might damage another's reputation or harm him in any way—for the person who might eventually be harmed most might be yourself.

You should guard against writing angry or abusive letters. If you must write a letter of complaint, wait several hours or overnight, and then re-read the letter before mailing it.

Letters of apology are sometimes required of even the best of us. Brief and sincere notes of explanation are always advisable when you are unable to keep a certain appointment, or when there has been some other misunderstanding.

RESERVATIONS

When you write a hotel or motel for a reservation, give brief but full information.

For example:

Quarters M
Fort Sam Houston
San Antonio, Texas
April 23, 1969

The Manager
U.S. Hotel Thayer
West Point, New York

Dear Sir:

Will you please reserve a room with bath for my wife and myself, from June first for one week?

If such accommodations are not available at present, please let me know the earliest date you can take us.

Yours truly,
James Smith
Major, U.S. Army

A telegram to a hotel would include the title or rank in the signature:

PLEASE RESERVE SINGLE ROOM WITH BATH FOR ONE WEEK STARTING SATURDAY 8 JUNE. WIRE CONFIRMATION COLLECT.

LIEUTENANT MARY ANN BROWN, USAF
14 NAVAJO PLACE
COLORADO SPRINGS, COLORADO

A man or wife may wire reservations ahead to a bus, plane, or train terminal, in this form:

UNITED AIR LINES
DULLES INTERNATIONAL AIRPORT
CHANTILLY VA.

PLEASE RESERVE TWO SEATS TO STOCKHOLM WIFE AND SELF FIRST AVAILABLE JUNE, REPLY COLLECT.

MAJOR JAMES SMITH (address)

For reasons of clarity, other than in telegrams, use the term "my wife and myself." Upon arrival at the hotel or motel, however, you will register, "Major and Mrs. James Smith," *not* "Major James Smith and wife."

LETTERS OF CONDOLENCE

One of the most difficult letters to write is a letter of condolence—but no letter is more appreciated than the one expressing sympathy at a time of sorrow. Respect and obligation, affection and friendship are the grounds for writing such letters. They should be addressed to the most bereaved, with reference to other members of the family in the body of the letter.

The *brief* letter of condolence has a traditional form, with parts as follows:

1. An expression of sympathy.
2. A kind comment or observation concerning the deceased person.
3. A last word of affection and sympathy.
4. The complimentary close and your signature.

You will always be careful of your choice of words in sending a message following a death which resulted from an accident, suicide, or any catastrophe.

The essentials in writing a letter of condolence are the expressions of sympathy, encouragement, and a desire to help. An example of a letter written to the mother of a classmate killed in an accident, is:

Dear Mrs. Ledbetter,

I have just heard of Larry's fatal accident, and I want you to know that you have my deepest sympathy. Our friendship, which began when we roomed together at the Academy, has always been a solid reality on which I have leaned many times.

Since I am being transferred to Washington next month, I plan to stop over in Memphis en route. At that time, I want to call on you and, if possible, be of some service.

Sincerely,
John Jones

Telegrams are frequently sent, and follow this form:

OUR DEEPEST SYMPATHY.

MARY AND JOHN JONES

or

DEEPLY SHOCKED AT YOUR LOSS, ALL MY SYMPATHY. SINCERELY.

JOHN JONES

(OR MARY AND JOHN, for very close friends.)

REPLIES TO MESSAGES OF CONDOLENCE

Letters, telegrams, and other messages of condolence, as well as floral tributes, should be personally acknowledged by the individual to whom they were addressed. This brief reply of thanks should be handwritten and should be sent within six weeks after the message (or floral tribute) has been received, and preferably earlier.

A sentence or two will be enough, particularly in cases of ill health or extreme age. In cases of illness, extreme age, or shock, a member of the family may write the note of thanks.

All-white paper is used more frequently for correspondence in connection with bereavement than the traditional black-bordered paper of former years. Mourning paper for men is usually all white, or white with an address or initials engraved in black. Women may use all white, or white with a black or gray border about $\frac{1}{16}$ of an inch wide, or with a black monogram or address. A light gray paper is also used.

A reply to a message of condolence may be very brief:

Dear Mrs. Smith,

Thank you so much for your very kind expression of sympathy.

Sincerely,
John Jones

Or, to a long-time friend, you would write a more personal note:

Dear Mary,

Your very kind letter gave me great comfort. Thank you so much for the roses, and for writing. I will call you and Bill as soon as I can.

Very sincerely,
John Jones

In order for the bereaved to acknowledge accurately the messages of condolence, flowers, contributions to charity, etc., an accurate list must be kept by a close friend or a member of the bereaved family when the funeral is held at home. When the funeral takes place at a funeral home, a member of the staff will collect the cards and make a list for the family.

Although social letters of condolence are always handwritten, a letter of condolence may be dictated and typed from a business office to someone related to a person the writer has known mainly in official or business life.

MOURNING CARDS

In case of bereavement, it is correct to send engraved cards of acknowledgment in response to calls, cards of condolence, or floral tributes, where many of the messages of condolence and sympathy are comparatively impersonal but are in the hundreds or thousands. For example:

GENERAL AND MRS. JOHN DOE
ACKNOWLEDGE WITH GRATEFUL APPRECIATION
YOUR KIND EXPRESSION OF SYMPATHY

CHRISTMAS CARDS

Christmas cards are sent to close friends and acquaintances, and these may be limited to those you cannot greet personally. Frequently, in the services, cards are not sent within an activity or base.

Envelopes of Christmas cards are always addressed to *both husband and wife,* even if you know only one or the other. A printed or engraved card without your name carries the signature at the bottom of the greeting, and the rule for signatures is: the person who is signing writes the other person's name first. When cards are engraved or printed, the husband's name may come first, but either way is correct. Or you may sign for both, as: "The John Jones." When the names of several members of a family are listed on the card, the father's name should be written first. It is wise to place your return address in the upper left-hand corner of the envelope when you are unsure of the mailing address. In addressing the envelope to a family, write "The John Jones" rather than "Mr. and Mrs. John Jones and family."

From the strictly rabbinical point of view, Jewish people should not celebrate Christmas or send Christmas cards. However, many Jewish people observe Christmas as a national rather than a religious holiday and send out nonreligious cards as well as receive them.

LETTERS OF REFERENCE

When you are asked to write a letter of reference—for example, for someone leaving the service or your place of employment, you will want to write an honest, straightforward account of that person's ability and character. It is important that the letter be fair both to the future employer and to the employee. The letter should always be dated.

A letter of reference, or any letter written to an unknown reader, needs neither salutation nor closing. The letter is a statement of fact, and is attested to by the signature. The outmoded phrase "To Whom It May Concern" is infrequently used. When you know to whom the letter will be addressed, you of course may use that person's name.

Letters of reference can be typewritten or written by hand. The general points covered in the typical letter of reference are:

- The name of the person or employee.
- The length of his service or employment.
- The nature of his service or work—and *his competence.*
- His honesty and character; his loyalty to the service or business.
- His sobriety.
- His ability to get along with others.
- The reasons for his leaving the service or business; an expression of your regret at losing him, if such is the case.
- Your willingness to answer any further questions concerning him, and an expression of your confidence in him in his new field.

When a person has been unsatisfactory in his work, or when he has a questionable reputation, omissions in your reference are the best way of indicating it. However, you are under no obligation to give him any reference at all.

FORMAL PAPER

Note paper for formal use is about 6 by 7, or 5 by 8, inches in size, and is a fine quality paper in a glazed or kid (velvety) finish. The crest or insignia (if used) is engraved, and the paper is always white or cream color, with matching envelopes.

A double sheet with no crest is often used in answering formal invitations, such as weddings, dinners, dances, receptions, etc. You will write your reply on the first page only.

WEDDING INVITATIONS

A heavy white or cream-colored paper (vellum) is best for an engraved invitation. The crest or coat of arms should be embossed in the paper without color. The customary size is about 5 by $7\frac{1}{2}$ inches or $5\frac{1}{2}$ by 7 inches, and it is folded in half before being placed in the inner envelope.

A favorite size that does not need to be folded is about $4\frac{1}{2}$ by 6 inches, and is slipped sideways in the envelope. The black lettering on engraved invitations may be the conservative Script or the popular Shaded Antique Roman. Among other letterings are Shaded Modified Roman, London Script.

ENVELOPES

WEDDING INVITATION ENVELOPES

Engraved wedding invitations are customarily enclosed in two envelopes. The inner envelope is addressed, "Captain and Mrs. Jackson," and is not gummed, therefore it is unsealed. The outer envelope is fully addressed for weddings or other formal occasions, and the address is always handwritten:

> Mrs. John Smith Jackson (Name written in full, no initials)
> 39 College Avenue (Avenue or street written in full)
> Indianapolis (No comma)
> Indiana (State not abbreviated)

(For additional information, see Chapter 19, *Wedding Invitations and Announcements*.)

SOCIAL CORRESPONDENCE ENVELOPES

Addresses on social correspondence envelopes are handwritten or typewritten, according to the form of the enclosed letter. Abbreviations are not used and commas are omitted at the end of each line.

When addressing a letter to a boy of 12 or under, use "Master." From 13 to 18 he is "John Doe"; after 18 he is "Mr." A girl of all ages is addressed "Miss." "Messrs." is used to address brothers, not a father and son. A man uses "Jr." after his name as long as his father is living.

A confidential letter may have the word *Personal* written in the lower left-hand corner of the envelope. When you are uncertain of an address, *Please Forward* may be written in the lower left-hand corner.

Before you place any letter in an envelope, check it for corrections, signature, and enclosures. When writing more than one letter, re-check to make sure that the right letter is in the right envelope.

INVITATION CARDS

For formal invitations, fine quality cards are customarily used, about 3½ by 5½ inches, or 4 by 6 inches in size with matching envelopes. The card may be plain or partially engraved with a crest.

The popular *fill-in* cards are white or ivory, with the crest or insignia engraved in dark blue or black at the top center. Your name (or administrative position) is directly under the crest, followed by the line: "request the pleasure of the company of." A few key words complete the engraving. For example:

THE SUPERINTENDENT OF THE
UNITED STATES COAST GUARD ACADEMY
AND
MRS. DOE
REQUEST THE PLEASURE OF THE COMPANY OF

AT

ON

AT   O'CLOCK

R.s.v.p.

The name of the guest and other information is written by hand in blue or black ink. The cards are used for almost any occasion, formal or informal dinners, receptions, luncheons, etc.

When an officer's station will not change for some time and many cards are used, or when a retired officer has a permanent address, the address is engraved in the center of the card directly under the "at . . . o'clock" line.

The address is frequently engraved under the R.s.v.p., and the place of entertainment is written by hand under the "at . . . o'clock" line.

Fold-over cards are about 3 by 4 inches in size, and are frequently used for invitations to luncheons, cocktail parties, buffet suppers, etc. These cards are called "informals" and are of smooth heavy paper in white or cream color, with matching envelopes.

Your name is centered on the outside of the card and may be engraved from the same plate used for personal cards. (A name reading "Captain and Mrs. John Jackson Jones" may have the "Captain and" waxed out for a woman's card.) The invitation is usually written on the lower half of the inside of the card.

An informal flat *message* or invitation card is frequently used in place of the *fold-over* card. This card is about 3½ by 4½ inches in size, and is of heavy white or cream-colored paper.

Your name is engraved in the center—or slightly above the center—of the card, with the address in the upper right-hand corner. If desired, a telephone number is engraved at the top left-hand corner of the card.

The message or invitation is written below the name, and an *R.s.v.p.* or *Regrets only* would be written in the lower left-hand corner. They are never used for calling cards. When required, replies to informals and message card invitations are addressed to the hostess only.

REGRETS ONLY

It is customary today for a host and/or hostess, or aides and secretaries, to write or have printed or engraved, *Regrets only* under the R.s.v.p. on invitations (other than wedding and very formal invitations). This means that only those who cannot attend the party or occasion, need reply. (See *illustration*, page 209, 211.)

Frequently, a telephone number is listed under the *R.s.v.p.* or *Regrets only* on the invitation, for the convenience of the guest in replying—usually to an aide or social secretary who firms the guest list.

Telephone numbers are never placed on wedding or very formal social invitations but are used on very important official or less formal invitations.

ENVELOPES

Matching envelopes should be ordered with all informals (fold-over) and fill-in cards, and with some calling cards.

Postal regulations require that envelopes be at least 3 by $4\frac{1}{4}$ inches. When your calling card envelopes are smaller, it is proper to write only the name on this envelope and to enclose it in a larger envelope addressed for mailing. You will remember never to enclose a calling card in an envelope when making a social or official call.

CHAPTER 18

Invitations and Replies

The issuance of invitations, as well as the acknowledgment of them, follows definite social rules which should be observed. These rules may be considered a framework in which you can extend or answer invitations with maximum advantage and minimum effort for both the guest and the host. In general, the types of invitations that you will receive are:

- Informal—These may be issued in person, over the telephone, by handwritten note, informal card, or on a calling card enclosed in a matching envelope.
- *Formal*—These may be fully engraved, partially engraved, telephoned, or handwritten in the same form as the fully engraved invitation.

Although most invitations are informal during the early years of the career of a midshipman, cadet, or young officer, formal invitations are issued by the superintendent or commandant at the various Academies or by college presidents at ROTC units, OCS, OTS, etc. Junior officers, as well as midshipmen and cadets, will often receive formal invitations to debutante dinners and dances; official occasions as well as informal parties are encountered during the annual summer cruises to foreign countries. Senior officers will receive many invitations to state, official, and social occasions throughout their service careers.

When the invitations are extended in person you must be alert and be prepared to accept or refuse without advance notice. When the invitation is one that you will enjoy accepting, there is no difficulty in expressing pleasure. But when you do not care to accept the invitation, your feelings must be concealed.

When you refuse any invitation, your answer should be plausible. Do not fumble with generalities, such as, "Well, I may have the duty that night so I don't know whether I can come or not. . . ." Instead, you may say, "I'm sorry, I'm not free that evening—but thank you."

When you are not sure if you are free to accept the invitation, be frank with the person extending the invitation and say why you cannot commit yourself at the moment; for example, you can truthfully say that you believe you have the watch, etc. You may ask if a delayed reply will be inconvenient, and that if not, you will check your schedule immediately and let the hostess know as soon as you can. If a delay is inconvenient, you should refuse at once, but graciously.

Telephone invitations follow the same pattern as those given face-to-face. The information concerning the time, date, and place, should be repeated in order that no mistake will be made. It is wise to write the information immediately in an engagement book or on a pad; it will be embarrassing later if you forget and arrive at the wrong hour or day.

Oral invitations usually are issued for smaller occasions, including luncheons, dinners, cocktails, teas, children's parties, christenings, informal dances, picnics, morning coffees, etc. Invitations by card—either calling card or the folded informals or larger message cards—are used for large informal parties such as cocktails and receptions, including both afternoon and evening occasions, buffet suppers, teas, children's parties, dances, at-homes, etc.

You will remember to order matching envelopes with the cards. Calling cards used for invitations should have outer envelopes at least 3 inches by $4\frac{1}{4}$ inches in size, in accordance with Postal Regulations. (Of course, you never enclose a calling card in an envelope when making a social call.)

Written invitations are also extended to those who cannot be reached by telephone, or when the location of the house or place of entertainment is difficult to find. Pertinent information concerning the location of the party is sometimes illustrated by charts or clever sketches either drawn or imprinted on the card.

When you receive an informal invitation for a time when a friend will be visiting you, you may state in your answer that you are sorry that you cannot accept the invitation because a classmate or houseguest will be with you at that time. Common sense will dictate whether you should do this, however, since you do not want to place the hostess in the position of *having* to invite your guest.

When it is convenient to your hosts, the hostess probably will invite you to bring your classmate or houseguest with you. Otherwise, she may say something like "I'm sorry; we're only having ten guests, and the dinner isn't buffet—but perhaps another time?" Because, as anyone will realize, when mixed guests are to be seated at the dining table, an extra guest would upset the table arrangement.

INFORMAL INVITATIONS, REPLIES

An invitation given by a married couple is customarily extended by the hostess. An oral invitation, given in person or by telephone, may be stated in a simple manner: "John and I are having a few friends in for supper on Saturday at seven; we do hope that you and Bill can join us. It will be informal."

An invitation to an older couple might be extended in this form: "This is Mary Jones. I wonder if you and Colonel King could have supper with us next Saturday, at seven?"

When the host extends the invitation, it is given in the name of the hostess: "Mary would like you to have supper with us on Saturday at seven."

An invitation written on personal note paper is usually brief, but will give full information. For example:*

Quarters 15
Fort McNair
Washington, D.C.

Dear Mr. Jones,
Captain Swanson and I are having as our houseguests during Christmas leave, Miss Betty Hallam, the daughter of an old friend, and several of her friends from Mary Baldwin College.
We are asking several Mishipmen and Cadets for dinner and and dancing at our quarters on Saturday, the twenty-ninth, at seven o'clock. We sincerely hope that you can join us. Dress is informal.
I am sure that you will find Betsy and her friends most attractive.

Cordially,

Mary Swanson

Monday

Your *reply* should be written on personal stationery, by hand, and must be mailed within a day or two, or as soon as possible. Replies are addressed to the hostess only. For example:

Room 2045, Bancroft Hall
17 December 1968

Dear Mrs. Swanson,
I am delighted to accept your kind invitation for dinner at your quarters on Saturday, the twenty-ninth, at seven o'clock.
The occasion will be of added pleasure since I met Miss Hallam at the Thanksgiving Hop a few weeks ago. Thank you for including me.

Sincerely,

John Jones†

---

* In this chapter, *italics* are used to indicate handwriting when used in invitations, acceptances, and refusals.

† Sign your full name only; it is not proper to add your title or any other information.

When your reply is a *regret*, you should explain the refusal:

> *Room 2634, East Barracks*
> *17 December 1968*

Dear Mrs. Swanson,

　I appreciate your invitation to dinner on Saturday, the twenty-ninth, but unfortunately I am not able to accept since I will be in Montreal during the holidays.

　It was very kind of you and Captain Swanson to include me, and I regret very much that I will not have the opportunity to meet Miss Hallam and her friends.

> *Very sincerely,*
>
> *James Smith*

"THANK YOU" LETTER

After you have been entertained in a home, it is customary that you write—or sometimes you may telephone—your hostess and thank her for the occasion. A "thank you" note is brief, but must be genuine in expressing appreciation. The reply is addressed to the hostess, but will take note of any member of the family:

> *Room 3A20, Vandenberg Hall*
> *2 January 1968*

Dear Mrs. Swanson,

　Thank you very much for a wonderful evening at your quarters on Saturday night. Without a doubt your houseguests were as attractive a group of girls as I have ever met. It was a pleasure to meet Miss Hallam and her friends.

　Your dinner was superb, and the memory of the ice cream pie will last a long time, while I am eating Air Force chow. All of us enjoyed seeing the film which Captain Swanson took in Hawaii. Thank you again for having me.

> *Sincerely,*
>
> *William Brown*

Invitations for luncheons and dinners may be sent on *calling cards*, *informals*, or the larger flat *message cards* with your engraved name. When an *R.s.v.p.* or *Regrets only* is written on the cards, an answer is mandatory. Your acceptance or refusal of the invitation may be made on your calling card, by brief note, or by telephone. An officer's invitation to a stag luncheon could be written on his personal card, as follows:

Lunch
Saturday, 7 May, 1 p.m.

Captain Stephen Sidney Preble

Officer's Club   **United States Navy**

An invitation to a dinner could be written on the hostess's calling card, as follows:

Dinner
Saturday, March 2, 8 p.m.

Major Mary Jane Dickinson

R.S.V.P.   *11 Ridge Road*

The joint calling card, which is about $3\frac{1}{2}$ by $2\frac{1}{2}$ inches in size, is used for various types of invitations. For example:

To meet
Captain and Mrs. Henry Roy Smith

Lieutenant and Mrs. John Doe
At home

Fri. May 18
6-8

420 East
Douglas Valley

You may write your acceptance or refusal on your personal card, with or without a line drawn through the engraved name:

Will be happy to come Saturday at eight

William Orrmond Paul

Bill

**Lieutenant
United States Air Force**

The *fold-over informal* has the name of the host and hostess fully engraved on the outside, with invitations or replies handwritten on the inside. These cards are about 3 by 4¼ inches in size. (See Chapter 17, *Correspondence.*)

Example (1). Invitation.

(Outside)

Colonel and Mrs. Lee Adam Smith

3700 Connecticut Avenue

(Inside)

Cocktails		*Cocktails-Buffet*
Wednesday, June 9th	*or:*	*Wednesday, June 9th*
5–7 P.M.		*6:30–8:30 P.M.*
Regrets Only		*Regrets Only*

Example (2). A reply to the invitation is also written on the informal card.

> *Sorry I cannot join you on the ninth, for I will*
> *be on the West Coast. Thanks for thinking of me.*
> *Jack**

The larger flat informal, or *message* card, has more space for the writing of invitations, replies, notes, etc. In the case of married couples the full names of both may be engraved higher than on the informal, and the address is at the upper right-hand corner of the card. The title and surname of a very senior officer may be used, but a rear admiral, brigadier general, and officers of less rank customarily use their full names.

---

34 Upshur Road

Captain and Mrs. John Henry Jones

Cocktails

Wednesday, October tenth

after Brigade Parade

(If no parade - five o'clock)

AFTERNOON RECEPTIONS

Informal invitations to an official afternoon reception are usually issued on the semi-engraved cards, with the word "informal" or the uniform of the day written by hand at the lower right-hand corner. An admiral's or general's flag, or other insignia customarily centers the top of the card.

The reply to any engraved invitation should be written in the third person. Personal note paper may be used.

Invitations to receptions, garden parties, teas, and at-homes do not require an answer unless a response is requested. Replies to an at-home follow

---

* Since the name of the writer is printed or engraved on the outside of the informal card, it is not necessary to sign one's name. However, a more personal touch is added in signing a first name.

The Class of 1969

at the

United States Naval Academy

cordially invites

to their informal hop

on Sunday, November fourth

at three-thirty o'clock   Dahlgren Hall

R.S.V.P.
(Regrets only)
Hostess Office

the general form for an afternoon reception, but the words "at-home" are not used in the reply.

FORMAL INVITATIONS, REPLIES

Invitations to formal occasions may be fully engraved or partially engraved, or they may be handwritten on the first page of folded white or cream-colored note paper, in the third person. Invitations to formal occasions may also be telephoned. Invitations are issued between two and three weeks in advance of the occasion, but wedding invitations and other invitations, where an advance notice is necessary, may be sent out four weeks in advance.

Invitations to very important functions usually are fully engraved and carry the phrase "request the honor (or pleasure) of your company." Popular letterings are Script and Shaded Antique Roman. An admission card to be shown at the door is frequently enclosed.

Although it is not in accordance with the best social usage, invitations to very large general receptions and parties (but never wedding invitations) are sometimes printed rather than engraved, owing to the great expense of engraving.

An admiral's or general's flag may be used on his invitations, and official seals and insignia in gold or color are often used on invitations for such occasions as inaugurations, dedications, ship christenings and commissionings, and graduation exercises. The family crest or coat of arms may be embossed without color at the top of wedding or other important invitations.

SEMI-ENGRAVED CARDS

The most favored form of invitation is the semi-engraved card which is much less expensive and is adaptable to any date or occasion. It is used mainly for large functions, such as dinners, receptions, luncheons, dances, change of command and other ceremonies, parades, and many others.

The following example is an invitation to the Marine Corps' famous Moonlight Parade:

The Commandant of the Marine Corps and Mrs. _____

request the pleasure of your company

at a Reception and Parade
Tuesday, the twenty-fifth of July
at seven forty-five o'clock
Service Dress White

R.s.v.p.   *Commandant's House*

Oxford 4-1872   *Marine Barracks*
Parade begins nine o'clock

WORDING OF FORMAL INVITATIONS

The following general rules should be followed:

1. Abbreviations and initials are to be avoided, but there are some established exceptions: "Mr.," "Mrs.," "Dr.," "R.s.v.p." (or R.S.V.P.), etc. When an initial is always used in place of a first or middle name, that initial may be used: "Lieutenant J. Marshall Jones."

2. Ranks, titles, and names are written in full: "Lieutenant, junior grade," "Lieutenant Commander," "Major General," "Lieutenant Colonel," "Rear Admiral," etc. The exception is that of "Second" and "First Lieutenant"; both are designated "Lieutenant" in the Army.

3. The date and hour are always spelled out, but only the day and month are capitalized: "Thursday, the seventh of January." "Half after eight o'clock" is preferable to "eight-thirty," although the latter is correct.

4. The person or persons issuing or acknowledging invitations refer to themselves by their full names: "Lieutenant and Mrs. John Jones, junior."

(When your name is very long, "Jr." is correct.) But their guests or hosts are designated by their last names only: "Captain and Mrs. Brown."

5. Honor guests are designated by the phrases: "In honor of . . . ," which is used mainly for prominent persons, and "To meet . . . ," which is usually used for new arrivals and houseguests.

6. "White Tie" written or engraved in the lower right-hand corner of the invitation indicates a very formal function and means full evening dress, military or civilian.

7. "Black Tie" denotes the less formal occasion, and means the dinner dress uniform or tuxedo. (See Chapter 2, *Service and Civilian Dress*.)

8. *R.s.v.p.* means a reply is mandatory.

9. *Regrets only* on less formal invitations, but never on wedding or very formal invitations, means that only those who cannot attend the function need reply. When a telephone number is added, you may answer in kind.

REPLIES TO FORMAL INVITATIONS

1. Answers should be written within 48 hours, preferably 24 hours, after you receive dinner or luncheon invitations. Then a hostess will have time to invite another guest without his feeling like a "fill in."

2. Replies are handwritten, in the third person, on the first page of folded white or cream-colored note paper.

3. An *acceptance* will include your own full title and name, the title and surname of the host and hostess, and the date and time; also the place, if not the host's address. The reason for this repetition is that the hostess may make corrections if the prospective guest has made a mistake.

4. A *regret* includes the same information, except that it makes no reference to the time or place.

5. Envelopes are addressed to the host and hostess, or to an aide or social secretary if so indicated in the *R.s.v.p.* In civilian life it is customary to address the envelope to the hostess (or social secretary) even when the invitation was issued jointly with her husband.

6. A formal dinner or luncheon invitation to a married couple must be refused when either one or the other cannot accept. The rule here is: both or neither.

After accepting a formal invitation, you are committed to the occasion over all other occasions (other than duty), with the exception of your receiving a White House invitation, which takes precedence over any other invitation. In such a case, you will withdraw the previous acceptance. An invitation from the Chief of Mission takes precedence over all other invitations for service attachés, etc.

REPLIES AT THE SERVICE ACADEMIES

If you are a midshipman or cadet at the Service Academies, you will reply to a formal invitation according to the general rules listed elsewhere.

You will remember to write by hand on the first page of folded note paper (white or cream-colored), in the third person. You will answer promptly and include these steps in your *acceptance:*

1. Your title and full name, without abbreviations.
2. The title and last name of your host and/or hostess.
3. The occasion.
4. The date.
5. The time.
6. The place—if other than the host's address.

> *Midshipman John Ray Jones*
> *accepts with pleasure*
> *the kind invitation of*
> *Admiral and Mrs. Lee*
> *to dinner*
> *on Saturday, the seventh of April*
> *at seven-thirty o'clock*

If you are requested to give the name of the young lady you will be escorting to the dinner, her name would be added as follows:

> *Midshipman John Ray Jones*
> *Miss Mary Jane Smith*
> *accept with pleasure*
> *etc.*

If you are requested to furnish her address as well as her name, you will write your formal acceptance without adding her name. Instead, you will write her name and address on the aide's or Flag Lieutenant's *reply card* which is enclosed with the invitation. A *regret* would be as follows:

> *Cadet William Paul Smith*
> *regrets that because of official duties**
> *he will be unable to accept*
> *the kind invitation of*
> *General and Mrs. Williams*
> *for Saturday, the twelfth of May*

ADDRESSING THE ENVELOPE

After writing your reply, you will address the envelope to the person (or office) indicated in the lower left-hand corner of the invitation, or to the person (or office) whose name appears on the *reply card* enclosed in the invitation. For example:

> *Flag Lieutenant*
> *Office of the Superintendent*
> *United States Naval Academy*
> *Annapolis, Maryland*

* Or—*because of illness, a previous engagement, etc.*

When you are replying to a formal invitation issued by an officer and his wife, such as a dinner to be held in their quarters, you would address the envelope to both the officer and his wife. For a less formal or an informal dinner, you would address the envelope to the hostess (the officer's wife). For example:

>Mrs. John Levis Doe
>Quarters 9
>United States Military Academy
>West Point, New York

REMINDER CARDS

To confirm invitations, particularly those sent to a guest of honor, to VIPs or those issued verbally, reminder cards are frequently sent out a short time before the occasion to those who have accepted.

The regular invitation may be used again, with a line drawn through the telephone number and/or the *R.s.v.p.*, with the words, "To Remind," written underneath. Such cards are not acknowledged.

A smaller, partially engraved card may be used, with specific information written by hand. For informal occasions, a calling or joint card may be used with pertinent information written in the upper left-hand corner.

An example of the formal invitation used as a reminder card follows:

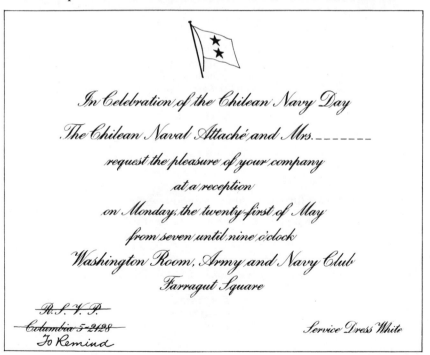

In Celebration of the Chilean Navy Day

The Chilean Naval Attaché and Mrs. _ _ _ _ _ _ _

request the pleasure of your company

at a reception

on Monday, the twenty-first of May

from seven until nine o'clock

Washington Room, Army and Navy Club

Farragut Square

~~R.S.V.P.~~
~~Columbia 5-2128~~
To Remind

Service Dress White

REPLY CARDS

Reply cards are usually enclosed with invitations to large official functions, such as a retirement ceremony, the luncheons following graduation exercises at the Service Academies and Colleges, a ship's commissioning, etc. The purpose of the cards is to facilitate the check-off guest list.

The cards, with self-addressed envelopes, usually are the small fill-in type with specific information to be written by hand. (See facing page.)

HANDWRITTEN INVITATIONS

The formal invitation does not have to be engraved but may be written by hand, on white or cream-colored note paper, in the third person. The wording and spacing follow the engraved form. The address or place of entertainment is usually centered underneath the line indicating the time, but may be written at the lower right-hand side.

Colonel and Mrs. John Smith
request the pleasure of the company of
Lieutenant Jones
at dinner
on Saturday, the ninth of January
at eight o'clock
Quarters 4311D

R.s.v.p.   *Black Tie*

A sample acceptance would be:

Lieutenant Elizabeth Jones
accepts with pleasure
the kind invitation of
Colonel and Mrs. Smith
to dinner on Saturday, the ninth of January
at eight o'clock

A regret would say "... regrets that she will be unable to accept," or "... regrets that because of a previous engagement ..." etc.

FORMAL EVENING RECEPTION

An invitation to a formal evening reception would be:

IN HONOR OF THE PRIME MINISTER OF PATRIA
AND
MRS. CAESAR
THE AMBASSADOR OF PATRIA AND MRS. LEGATE
REQUEST THE HONOR OF THE COMPANY OF

AT A RECEPTION
ON SATURDAY, THE FIFTH OF MAY
AT TEN O'CLOCK

R.S.V.P.   WHITE TIE
2698 CALIFORNIA STREET, N.W.   GRAND BALL ROOM, MAYFLOWER HOTEL

I ☐   WE ☐   ACCEPT ☐   REGRET ☐

THE SUPERINTENDENT'S INVITATION TO THE GRADUATION
EXERCISES AND LUNCHEON ON WEDNESDAY, 4 JUNE 1969

. . . .
NAME

. . . .
ADDRESS

THE FAVOR OF AN EARLY
REPLY IS REQUESTED

(OVER)

(OVER)

UPON RECEIPT OF YOUR ACCEPTANCE, CARDS OF ADMISSION
AND A SPECIAL PARKING PERMIT FOR THE GRADUATION
EXERCISES WILL BE FORWARDED; THEY WILL BE MAILED
THE LATTER PART OF MAY.

The acceptance would be something like this:

Major General and Mrs. James Smith
have the honor to accept
the kind invitation of
The Ambassador of Patria and Mrs. Legate
for Saturday, the fifth of May
at ten o'clock
Grand Ball Room, Mayflower Hotel

The regret would be somewhat as follows:

Major General and Mrs. James Smith
regret that because of their absence from the city
they will be unable to have the honor of accepting
the kind invitation of
The Ambassador of Patria and Mrs. Legate
for Saturday, the fifth of May

SHIP COMMISSIONING INVITATION AND RECEPTION CARD

THE COMMANDANT, FIRST NAVAL DISTRICT,
THE PROSPECTIVE COMMANDING OFFICER AND SHIP'S COMPANY
REQUEST THE HONOR OF YOUR PRESENCE
AT THE COMMISSIONING OF THE
USS JOHN SIDNEY MC CAIN (DL-3)
AT THE BOSTON NAVAL SHIPYARD, BOSTON, MASSACHUSETTS
ON MONDAY AFTERNOON, THE TWELFTH OF OCTOBER
NINETEEN HUNDRED AND FIFTY-THREE
AT TWO-THIRTY O'CLOCK

PLEASE PRESENT THIS CARD
AT THE HENLEY STREET GATE   CAMERAS NOT PERMITTED

THE COMMANDING OFFICER AND WARDROOM OFFICERS
OF THE USS JOHN SIDNEY MC CAIN (DL-3)
REQUEST THE PLEASURE OF YOUR COMPANY
AT A RECEPTION AT THE
COMMISSIONED OFFICERS' MESS
BUILDING 5, BOSTON NAVAL SHIPYARD
IMMEDIATELY FOLLOWING THE COMMISSIONING

R.S.V.P.
COMMANDER, BOSTON NAVAL SHIPYARD

UNIFORM CARD

A small card, stating the prescribed uniform, may be enclosed with an official reception invitation. For example:

```
UNIFORM

White Dress
```

DANCE INVITATIONS

A formal, fully engraved invitation to a debutante dance would follow the form below:

COLONEL AND MRS. JOHN SMITH, JUNIOR
REQUEST THE PLEASURE OF
THE COMPANY OF
Midshipman Jones
AT A DANCE IN HONOR OF THEIR DAUGHTER
MISS MARY MARTHA SMITH
ON SATURDAY, THE FIFTEENTH OF FEBRUARY
AT ELEVEN O'CLOCK
ARMY AND NAVY CLUB

R.S.V.P.
300 FIRST STREET

An afternoon debutante reception would be stated:

COLONEL AND MRS. JOHN SMITH, JUNIOR
MISS MARY MARTHA SMITH
AT HOME
SATURDAY, FEBRUARY FIFTEENTH
AT FIVE O'CLOCK
DOGWOOD HILLS

R.S.V.P.
DOGWOOD HILLS
ARLINGTON

The acceptance would be in the following form:

Midshipman John Fork Jones
accepts with pleasure
the kind invitation of
Colonel and Mrs. Smith
Miss Smith
for Saturday, the fifteenth of February
at five o'clock
Dogwood Hills

Your refusal would be somewhat as follows:

Cadet William Paul Smith
regrets that because of orderly duty
he will be unable to accept
the kind invitation of
Colonel and Mrs. Smith
Miss Smith
for Saturday, the fifteenth of February

A semi-engraved form frequently used for formal dances:

THE COMMITTEE OF
THE KNICKERBOCKER COTILLION
REQUEST THE HONOR OF THE PRESENCE OF
Cadet Robert Paul Doe
AT THE CHRISTMAS BALL
ON *Wednesday, the twenty-sixth of December*
AT *half after ten o'clock*
THE PARK LANE HOTEL

R.S.V.P.
404 PARK AVENUE   WHITE TIE

A less formal invitation may omit the name of the guest:

COLONEL AND MRS. JOHN SMITH, JUNIOR
MISS MARY MARTHA SMITH
REQUEST THE PLEASURE OF YOUR COMPANY
at a small dance
on Saturday, the fifteenth of February
at ten o'clock
Dogwood Hills

R.S.V.P.
DOGWOOD HILLS
ARLINGTON

In replying to invitations that carry the names of several persons on the invitation—such as co-hosts at a dinner or reception, or the names of the parents with that of their daughter written directly underneath, or the names of the sponsors of the event—these names also appear in your reply.

In answering an invitation to a "small dance," your reply omits the word "small."

TELEPHONE INVITATIONS

At large commands where many invitations are issued, the Autovon or Tie-line are frequently used to verify a guest list and to immediately replace someone who cannot accept an invitation.

It is customary to place a telephone number under the *R.s.v.p.* or *Regrets only* on the invitation for the convenience of the guest in contacting the aide or social secretary who confirms the guest list. Such numbers are never placed on wedding or very formal social invitations, when handwritten replies are mandatory, but they are used on very important official and less formal invitations.

Telephone invitations are correct for formal functions, mainly for smaller affairs when the hostess makes the calls herself. The guest may accept at the moment, or if absent when the message was received, may reply by note or telephone.

An aide will call for his chief, or a secretary for a man or woman. In quarters, a steward or maid may call for the hostess.

When the steward or maid receives the call, the conversation may be somewhat as follows:

"Commander Smith's quarters."

"I'd like to speak to Mrs. Smith, please."

"May I ask who is calling, please?"

"I am calling for General and Mrs. Jones."

"I'm sorry, but Madam is not at home. May I take a message?"

"Would you please say that Mrs. Jones would like to know if Commander and Mrs. Smith could dine on Saturday, the fifth of March, at eight o'clock, at quarters 'M'?"

"To dine with General and Mrs. Jones on Saturday, the fifth of March at eight o'clock at quarters 'M' . . . very good. Thank you."

"Thank you."

Your reply is made in the same way: "Will you please tell General and Mrs. Jones that Commander and Mrs. Smith are happy to accept. . . ."

INVITATIONS BY TELEGRAM

A formal invitation sent by telegram might read:

GENERAL AND MRS. JAMES SMITH REQUEST THE PLEASURE OF COLONEL AND MRS. RICHARD JONES COMPANY AT DINNER MAY FOURTH AT ARMY NAVY CLUB EIGHT O'CLOCK

The reply could be stated thus:

COLONEL AND MRS. RICHARD JONES ACCEPT WITH PLEASURE GENERAL AND MRS SMITHS KIND INVITATION FOR FRIDAY MAY FOURTH ARMY NAVY CLUB EIGHT O'CLOCK

POSTPONING OR ADVANCING INVITATIONS

If Colonel and Mrs. Smith must postpone the dance, the announcement to that effect would follow the same form as the invitation:

COLONEL AND MRS. JOHN SMITH, JUNIOR
WISH TO ANNOUNCE
THAT THE DANCE IN HONOR OF THEIR DAUGHTER
MUST BE POSTPONED UNTIL
SATURDAY, THE TWENTY-SECOND OF FEBRUARY

PLEASE RESPOND TO
300 FIRST STREET

When it is necessary to postpone or advance the date of a formal invitation, and engraved notice (or printed notice, when time is short) is sent out similar to the original invitation, with this information:

BECAUSE OF THE
IMMINENT DEPARTURE OF
THE CHIEF OF STAFF OF THE AIR FORCE
THE RECEPTION IN HONOR OF
GENERAL AND MRS. WARD
WILL BE ADVANCED FROM
THURSDAY EVENING, THE TWENTIETH OF JUNE
TO
FRIDAY EVENING, THE FOURTEENTH OF JUNE
AT NINE O'CLOCK
GRAND BALL ROOM, MAYFLOWER HOTEL

R.S.V.P.

WITHDRAWING AN ACCEPTANCE

There are a few valid reasons for withdrawing the acceptance of an invitation: serious illness, a death in the family, prospective absence occasioned by a transfer of duty, official duty, or very important business elsewhere.

As mentioned earlier, an invitation from the White House or Chief of Mission takes precedence over all other invitations. In such cases, if you have already accepted an earlier invitation to a conflicting occasion, you would have to cancel your previous acceptance. For example:

Rear Admiral and Mrs. John Smith Hampton
regret that because of an invitation
to the White House
they must withdraw from
Captain and Mrs. Jones' dinner
on the third of May

RECALLING AN INVITATION

It is better to postpone than to cancel an invitation, once you have extended it, but when unavoidable circumstances warrant, a formal invitation must be recalled. When the occasion was small and the guests would know the reason for the withdrawing of the invitations—such as a bereavement or a serious accident—none need be stated for the withdrawing of the invitations:

THE INVITATIONS OF
CAPTAIN AND MRS. JOHN SMITH
FOR SATURDAY, THE FIFTEENTH OF MAY
ARE RECALLED

But when it is an official occasion involving guests who might not know the circumstances, the reason for recalling the invitation would be stated on printed forms, since engraving takes too long:

CAPTAIN AND MRS. JOHN SMITH
REGRET EXCEEDINGLY
THAT BECAUSE OF THE RECENT DEATH OF
FLEET ADMIRAL OWENS
THE INVITATIONS TO THE RECEPTION IN HONOR OF
THE SECRETARY OF DEFENSE
AND
MRS. WINGATE
MUST BE RECALLED

GUEST OF HONOR

It is contrary to custom to invite guests of higher rank than the honor guest at an official dinner or luncheon. However, when this is unavoidable, the following rules may be employed:

- Ask the ranking guest to waive his right for the occasion in favor of the guest of honor.
- Seat the guests according to precedence, even if it places the guest of honor well down the table. When ambassadors and very high ranking guests are present, this plan must be followed.
- Make the senior guest the co-host if it is a stag party, and if he and the host are of the same nationality.

When the party or dinner is informal, you may have a guest of honor of lower rank than other guests—but not at official or formal affairs. In extending the invitation to someone to be a guest of honor, you may say, "I would like so much to give a dinner for you,"—and when the person is married, ". . . for you and your wife (or husband)," for the invitation must include both. A letter may be written in this form:

Dear Mrs. Jones,
   Will you and Captain Jones dine with us on either Thursday, the third of October, or Saturday, the twelfth at eight o'clock?
   We want to ask some friends to meet you, and hope very much that we may be fortunate enough to find you free on one of those evenings.
                              Very sincerely,
                                          Mary Smith
September seventeen

When invitations to guests are issued over the telephone, you do not use the phrase "in honor of" as this phrase is used only on engraved invitations. The hostess may say instead, "We are giving a dinner next Saturday, the tenth, for Senator and Mrs. Jones . . ." etc.

When invitation cards have been issued, reminder cards may be sent to the guest or guests of honor shortly before the occasion. (See page 215.)

CHAPTER 19

Wedding Invitations and Announcements

The traditional wedding invitation is engraved on white or cream-colored vellum or kid finish paper. The size most customarily used is a double sheet, 5 by 7½ inches, that is folded across its length and then enclosed in the inner of one of two envelopes. If a smaller invitation (usually 4½ by 6 inches) is used, it is not folded but is placed sideways in a single matching envelope.

In case of invitations using the double envelopes, the inner one will have the guest's rank or title and last name written on it in black or dark blue ink. The tissue protecting the engraving on the invitation is not removed before placing in the envelope. The inside envelope is faced toward the back of the outside envelope when inserted, in order that the names will be face up when the envelope is opened.

As a general rule, abbreviations, initials, numerals, are to be avoided. whenever possible, in wedding invitations. The hour is always written out in full. However, Roman numerals may denote a second or third generation: John Paul Truxtun, "II" or "III." The designation "Junior" applies to the next in direct line of descent. The numbers "II," etc., indicate the sequence in the use of the name. A man does not continue to add "Junior" or "Jr." after his name following the death of his father.

SERVICE RANK

Commissioned officers of the rank of commander and up in the Navy and Coast Guard, and of captain and up in the Army, Air Force, and Marine Corps, should use their titles before their names on the invitation. The ranks of junior officers are placed beneath their names. The grades of second and first lieutenant, U.S. Army, are designated lieutenant.

Retired officers of the ranks of commander and lieutenant colonel up, usually keep their titles in civilian life and use their titles on wedding invitations. When issuing a wedding invitation with his wife a retired officer's status need not be mentioned; if he is a widower and issues the invitation in his own name, or if he is the bridegroom, this is designated in two lines: *Commander John Doe*, and underneath *United States Navy, Retired.*

Reserve officers *on active duty only* use their titles on wedding invitations and announcements. High ranking officers who are retired but who keep their titles in civilian life do use their titles.

Noncommissioned officers and enlisted men frequently use only their names with the branch of service immediately below.

GUEST LIST

The groom sends a list of his friends' names and addresses to his mother, who in turn will send the list of names and addresses of friends and relatives of the family to the mother of the bride. If his mother is dead, he will send the list to the bride's mother. If all guests are not to be invited to the reception or breakfast following the wedding, this should be designated on the list by an R for reception, and C for ceremony.

ISSUING INVITATIONS

Invitations are mailed by the bride's mother between three and four weeks before the event. She will also send an invitation to the bridegroom's parents; this is considered a treasured memento. If the parents of the bride are deceased, the invitations would be issued by a close or older relative, a brother or grandparents, etc. In the case of divorced parents, they would be issued in the name of the one with whom she has been living.

Invitations to church weddings do not carry the "R.s.v.p.," therefore they do not require an answer. When a card is included in the invitation, inviting you to the reception or breakfast following the ceremony, the card customarily has an "R.s.v.p." and must be answered. A "Regrets only" is not used.

The home address of the bride's family is usually engraved on the reception or wedding breakfast card, so that replies will be sent to that address and *not* to the place of the wedding.

It is not socially acceptable to include stamped and self-addressed reply cards with wedding invitations, no matter how practical this seems to be. You should know how to reply to a formal wedding invitation in the third person, and examples are to be found on pages 234 and 235.

ADDRESSING INVITATIONS

A formal engraved wedding invitation or announcement has two envelopes: the outside, gummed, which bears the full name and address of the guest or guests, and the inside non-gummed envelope which has only the surname and encloses the invitation or announcement.

The outside envelope will be fully addressed without abbreviations. For example:

Major and Mrs. James Paul Doe
7618 Van Noy Court
Argonne Hills
Fort George G. Meade
Maryland

The inner envelope is addressed: *Major and Mrs. Doe.*

Other adult members of the family, such as a grandmother, daughter, or mother-in-law, etc., should receive separate invitations. For a close relative, you may write *Grandmother*, etc., on the inner envelope.

When there are several adult members of the family living at one address, do not write *and family* on the envelope, but write their names on a separate envelope as follows: *The Misses Jane and Susan Doe* or *The Messrs. John and James Doe*, or when they are of both sexes, address the inner envelope thusly (no "and" between the names):

The Misses Doe
The Messrs. Doe

Or you may write the name or names of teen-age children of the family directly under the parents' names on the outer envelope, and *Miss* or *Misses Doe* on the inner envelope. The outer envelope would be:

Major and Mrs. James Paul Doe
Miss Susan Doe
(address)

Or, when the children are under age, simply write: *Susan, Mary, and John* on the inside envelope under the parents' names.

When members of a family are over 18 and not living at the same address, they each receive an invitation. You will remember that *Messrs.* is used only on envelopes addressed to brothers, not a father and son. An envelope addressed to a girl of any age is always *Miss*.

A return address may be placed on invitations and announcements, handwritten in the upper left-hand corner of the envelope. This may, however, be embossed on the flap (not engraved or printed); or printed stickers (black on white) may be placed in the upper left-hand corner of the envelope or on the flap.

All envelopes are addressed by hand, in black or dark blue ink. It is wise to order extra envelopes to allow for mistakes.

VARIATIONS OF WORDING

There are many variations in the wording of parts of the invitation:

1. When the bride's parents are deceased and a relative is sending the invitations:

MR. GEORGE OLIVER SMITH
REQUESTS THE HONOR OF YOUR PRESENCE
AT THE MARRIAGE OF HIS SISTER
MARY MARTHA
etc.

2. When the bride's parents are divorced and the mother has not remarried, she will use her maiden surname with her former husband's name: Mrs. Brown Smith. When the divorce is "friendly," the wording could be:

MRS. BROWN SMITH
COMMANDER JOHN JAMES SMITH
UNITED STATES NAVY, RETIRED
REQUEST THE HONOR OF YOUR PRESENCE
AT THE MARRIAGE OF THEIR DAUGHTER
ETC.

3. When the bride's father is dead, or her parents are divorced, and her mother has remarried:

MR. AND MRS. PAUL LEWIS DORN
REQUEST THE HONOR OF YOUR PRESENCE
AT THE MARRIAGE OF HER* DAUGHTER
MARY MARTHA SMITH
etc.

4. Or the invitations may be issued in the mother's name only:

MRS. PAUL LEWIS DORN
REQUESTS THE HONOR OF YOUR PRESENCE
AT THE MARRIAGE OF HER DAUGHTER
MARY MARTHA SMITH
etc.

5. If the bride's mother is dead and the father has married again, the form usually is:

COMMANDER AND MRS. JOHN JAMES SMITH
REQUEST THE HONOR OF YOUR PRESENCE
AT THE MARRIAGE OF HIS* DAUGHTER
MARY MARTHA
etc.

This form applies to the bride's mother when she is a widow, or the bride's father when he is a widower, with the exception of the use of their single names and of the word "her" or "his," as appropriate, before the word "daughter."

6. When a young widow is married, the married name of the widow is given, and the form is:

BRIGADIER GENERAL AND MRS. JOHN JAMES SMITH
REQUEST THE HONOR OF YOUR PRESENCE
AT THE MARRIAGE OF THEIR DAUGHTER
MARY MARTHA ADAMS
TO
JOHN DOE BLANK
SECOND LIEUTENANT, UNITED STATES AIR FORCE
ON SATURDAY, THE FIRST OF JUNE
AT SEVEN O'CLOCK
RANDOLPH AIR FORCE BASE CHAPEL
TEXAS

* When the relationship is close, "their" would be used instead of "his" or "her" which would be inclusive of the stepmother or stepfather.

Commander and Mrs. John James Smith

request the honor of your presence

at the marriage of their daughter

Mary Martha

to

Donald James Adams

Lieutenant, United States Navy

on Monday, the first of May

at four o'clock

The Navy Chapel, 3801 Nebraska Avenue, Northwest

Washington, District of Columbia

The traditional wording of a formal wedding invitation. The word "honor"
may be spelled "honour."

Or, when an older widow gives her own wedding, it is usually informal and handwritten invitations are sent. But when engraved invitations are used, the form (in part) is:

THE HONOR OF YOUR PRESENCE
IS REQUESTED AT THE MARRIAGE OF
MRS. DONALD JAMES ADAMS
TO
JOHN DOE BLANK
etc.

7. Engraved invitations are rarely sent to the wedding of a divorcée. A divorcée's wedding is usually a small ceremony to which guests are invited by informal notes. But when invitations are sent, the above forms may be used with the divorcée's given name used with the last name of her former husband: "Martha Smith Adams," or for an older woman, "Mrs. Smith Adams."

8. When there are no close relatives or friends, the bride may send out her own invitations, with the wording (in part) as follows:

THE HONOR OF YOUR PRESENCE
IS REQUESTED AT THE MARRIAGE OF
MISS MARY MARTHA SMITH
TO
DONALD JAMES ADAMS
etc.

9. When sisters are married at a double wedding, the name of the older sister is given first:

COMMANDER AND MRS. JOHN JAMES SMITH
REQUEST THE HONOR OF YOUR PRESENCE
AT THE MARRIAGE OF THEIR DAUGHTERS
MARY MARTHA
TO
CAPTAIN DONALD JAMES ADAMS
UNITED STATES MARINE CORPS
AND
SARAH JANE
TO
FRED PERRY HAAS
ENSIGN, UNITED STATES COAST GUARD
ON MONDAY, THE FIRST OF JUNE
AT FOUR O'CLOCK
CHRIST EPISCOPAL CHURCH, GEORGETOWN
WASHINGTON, DISTRICT OF COLUMBIA

10. At a double wedding, when the brides and bridegrooms are very close friends, but are not related, the invitation may be written according to the rank of the fathers or bridegrooms, or in alphabetical order.

11. When the bride's parents are separated but not divorced, the fact of the separation is frequently ignored, and the invitations are engraved in the customary form.

Brigadier General and Mrs. John Henry Doe

request the honour of your presence

at the marriage of their daughter

Ann Carol

to

James Paul Smith

Lieutenant, United States Army*

on Thursday, the seventh of June

at half after four o'clock

Cadet Chapel

West Point, New York

Wording for a June Week wedding invitation.
* "Second" or "First" Lieutenant is designated in the Air Force and Marine Corps.

12. When the bride is a member of the Armed Forces, she uses her title with the branch of service. For example:

MAJOR GENERAL AND MRS. WILFRED JOHN DOE
REQUEST THE HONOR OF YOUR PRESENCE
AT THE MARRIAGE OF THEIR DAUGHTER
CAPTAIN ELIZABETH ANNE DOE
UNITED STATES MARINE CORPS
TO
etc.

INFORMAL WEDDINGS

A small, informal wedding does not require engraved invitations. The mother of the bride may write short notes of invitation, or may telegraph or telephone the relatives and friends who are to be invited to the ceremony or to the reception, or to both.

The notes are written on conservative paper, usually white or cream color, giving the time and place of the ceremony. If the invitation is only for the reception, the time and place are all that is necessary. Informal invitations may be sent on short notice, but the usual two weeks in advance is customary.

The typical informal note would read something like this:

59 Southgate Avenue

Dear Mary,

Janet is being married here at home to Ensign John Jones, USN, who was graduated from the Naval Academy last week. The wedding will take place Monday, the eleventh of June, at four-thirty. We do hope you will be with us and will stay for a very small reception, afterwards.

As ever,
Bess Smith

Answers to invitations to small weddings (even answers to invitations received by telegram) are made by letter—if you have time. A brief, sincere note on your personal paper would be correct.

RECEPTION INVITATIONS

There are several ways of sending an invitation for a wedding reception. If the wedding takes place in the morning or early afternoon, a wedding breakfast card is enclosed long with the invitation itself.

1. A small card about 3 by 4 inches, engraved on the same type paper as the wedding invitation, in included *inside* the invitation. There is no crest or coat of arms on the card, and the protecting tissue (when provided) is not removed before mailing. The phrase "pleasure of your company," is used, since this is now a social occasion:

COLONEL AND MRS. JOHN JAMES SMITH
REQUEST THE PLEASURE OF YOUR COMPANY
AT THE WEDDING BREAKFAST
FOLLOWING THE CEREMONY
AT
DOGWOOD HILLS
ARLINGTON

R.S.V.P.

2. The reception invitation card is enclosed within the wedding invitation:

Reception

immediately following the ceremony

Officers' Club, Bolling Air Force Base

The favour of a reply is requested
3903 Connecticut Avenue, Northwest
Washington, District of Columbia

3. When a wedding is very small, with *no* wedding invitations to be issued, but with a large reception planned afterwards, the *reception invitations* are engraved on paper about the same size as the traditional wedding invitation:

COLONEL AND MRS. JOHN JAMES SMITH
REQUEST THE PLEASURE OF YOUR COMPANY
AT THE WEDDING RECEPTION OF THEIR DAUGHTER
MARY MARTHA
AND
DONALD JAMES ADAMS
LIEUTENANT, UNITED STATES NAVAL RESERVE
ON MONDAY, THE FIRST OF JUNE
AT FOUR O'CLOCK
DOGWOOD HILLS
ARLINGTON, VIRGINIA

R.S.V.P.

4. The invitation to the reception may be included in the wedding invitation when all guests are invited to *both* the wedding and reception. The following information is added to the bottom of the wedding invitation, following the name and address of the church:

AND AFTERWARDS AT
DOGWOOD HILLS
ARLINGTON, VIRGINIA

R.S.V.P.

5. Do *not* enclose a reply card with the invitation—this is very poor taste.

ACCEPTANCE AND REFUSALS

When you are invited to the ceremony and to the reception, or to the reception alone, the R.s.v.p. is usually requested and *must* be answered. Your reply will follow the form of the engraved invitation, or of the informal letter. You will write in longhand, on cream-colored or white note paper, and the form for the acceptance or regret is similar, except for the lines of acceptance or regret.

Your reply is addressed to the mother of the bride-elect—unless she is deceased; then you address it to the person who issued the invitation.

A simple but desirable form of answering the invitation to the wedding, to both the wedding and the reception, or to the reception only, is:

Lieutenant and Mrs. William Blank
accept with pleasure
the kind invitation of
Colonel and Mrs. Smith
for
Monday, the first of June
at four o'clock

The same general form is used to regret as to accept an invitation. You will remember that in all refusals of invitations, the hour of the occasion and the address are always omitted. When the refusal is for an invitation from a close friend, the reason why is frequently added in the second and third lines, such as: "regret that their absence from the city prevents their accepting."

A more detailed form for answering the invitation is shown in the following regret for a reception only:

Lieutenant and Mrs. William Blank
regret that they are unable to accept
the very kind invitation of
Colonel and Mrs. Smith
to the wedding reception of their daughter
Mary Martha
and
Donald James Adams
on Monday, the first of June

When either the husband or wife cannot accept the invitation, the person accepting may write the reply as follows:

Mrs. William Blank
accepts with pleasure
the kind invitation of
Colonel and Mrs. Smith
for
Monday, the first of June
at four o'clock
Lieutenant William Blank
regrets exceedingly
that he will be unable to accept

A reply to a small or informal wedding invitation is usually sent in the same form in which it was received. If by telephone or telegram, the answer may be sent in the same way to the sender of the invitation. If time is not short, it is preferable that your reply be a handwritten note. An acceptance could read:

Monday

Dear Mrs. Smith,

I am very happy about your daughter's forthcoming marriage to my class-mate, Dick Brown, and am pleased to be included. I'll fly in and will be staying with friends.

Sincerely,
John Jones

MARRIAGE ANNOUNCEMENT

Engraved marriage announcements are issued on the same type paper used for wedding invitations, and are sent out *after* the marriage has been performed. The announcements are sent by the bride's parents or by a person designated to do this.

Wedding announcements are sent to less intimate friends and acquaintances who were not invited to the wedding, or to all friends and acquaintances following a ceremony when no guests were invited. The year is customarily written out in the announcements:

CAPTAIN AND MRS. JOHN JONES SMITH
HAVE THE HONOR OF ANNOUNCING
THE MARRIAGE OF THEIR DAUGHTER
MARY ANN
TO
MR. GEORGE CARL WILSON
ON SATURDAY, THE SEVENTH OF JUNE
NINETEEN HUNDRED AND SIXTY-EIGHT*
TREASURE ISLAND CHAPEL†
SAN FRANCISCO, CALIFORNIA

---

* A departure from the conventional wording of the wedding invitation is the use of the year, written out, in wedding announcements. In some cases, the year is not specified.

† The name of the church may, or may not, be added. The hour of the wedding is not specified.

RECALLING WEDDING INVITATIONS

Because of illness, change of orders—or a change of mind!—wedding invitations may have to be recalled, or postponed, after they have already been issued. Notices must then be sent to all those who had received invitations. The best form for recalling a wedding invitation is:

DR. AND MRS. WILLIAM SMITH
ANNOUNCE THAT THE MARRIAGE OF THEIR DAUGHTER
MARY ELLEN
TO
ENSIGN JOHN LEE JONES
WILL NOT TAKE PLACE

When the wedding invitation is recalled because of a bereavement in the family, the engraved or printed card may state the reason:

DR. AND MRS. WILLIAM SMITH
REGRET EXCEEDINGLY
THAT BECAUSE OF THE RECENT DEATH OF
THE FATHER OF ENSIGN JONES
THE INVITATIONS TO THE MARRIAGE OF THEIR DAUGHTER
MARY ELLEN
TO
ENSIGN JOHN LEE JONES
MUST BE RECALLED

Or:

MRS. WILLIAM SMITH
REGRETS THAT THE DEATH OF
DR. SMITH
OBLIGES HER TO RECALL THE INVITATIONS
TO THE WEDDING OF HER DAUGHTER

The recalling of the invitations in case of a death in the immediate families does not always mean that the wedding may not take place on the scheduled day. If the families agree, a very quiet ceremony may be held on the original day of the wedding, with perhaps only one attendant each for the bride and groom.

When members of the bridal party have already arrived, and some have come from a distance, or when the bridegroom is in the service and has only a few days' leave, or has new duty that will take him some distance, the wedding may be held as scheduled, but with no guests other than members of the families and the bridal party.

POSTPONING INVITATIONS

When it is necessary to postpone a wedding, a form similar to this may be followed:

CAPTAIN AND MRS. JOHN JONES SMITH
ANNOUNCE THAT THE MARRIAGE OF THEIR DAUGHTER
MARY ANN
TO
MR. GEORGE CARL WILSON
HAS BEEN POSTPONED FROM
SATURDAY, THE FIRST OF JUNE
UNTIL
SATURDAY, THE TWENTY-SECOND OF JUNE
AT FOUR O'CLOCK
TREASURE ISLAND CHAPEL
SAN FRANCISCO, CALIFORNIA

"AT HOME" CARDS

When you want friends to know your new address, and when you know where you will be living long enough to make the cards worth while, "at home" cards are often enclosed in the same envelope with the wedding announcement.

The cards are similar to a large calling card—about 3 by 4 inches—and are the same color as the wedding announcement. One form is:

LIEUTENANT AND MRS. JOHN CARL SMITH

9 COLUMBINE VISTA
AFTER THE FIRST OF JUNE   COLORADO SPRINGS, COLORADO

Or a smaller card, about the size of the usual calling card, may be used:

AFTER JUNE 1ST
9 COLUMBINE VISTA
COLORADO SPRINGS, COLORADO

WEDDING ANNIVERSARIES

For announcements of wedding anniversaries, the year of the wedding and the year in which the invitation is issued are customarily stamped or engraved at the top of the anniversary invitation or announcement. The couple's initials or monogram, coat of arms, or a seal, may be engraved in gold or silver, or in black or dark blue ink. Such invitations may be sent out by the couple (or by their children). An example in the first case would be:

1918   1968
MAJOR GENERAL AND MRS. JOHN JAMES SMITH
REQUEST THE PLEASURE OF
Colonel and Mrs. George Ballou's
COMPANY ON THE FIFTIETH ANNIVERSARY
OF THEIR MARRIAGE
ON FRIDAY EVENING, MAY THE THIRD
FROM SEVEN UNTIL NINE O'CLOCK
THE BROADMOOR HOTEL
COLORADO SPRINGS, COLORADO

Or:

1918–1968

MAJOR GENERAL AND MRS. JOHN JAMES SMITH

AT HOME

FRIDAY, THE THIRD OF MAY

FROM FIVE UNTIL SEVEN O'CLOCK

237 MOUNTAIN VIEW ROAD

COLORADO SPRINGS, COLORADO

EASY CONVERSATION

CHAPTER 20

Introductions and Farewells

It is fortunate that the mechanics of making introductions are simple and natural, because you probably will be introducing people to each other for the rest of your life. In the majority of cases, the purpose of introductions is that two or more persons may know each other. The simplest form of introduction is illustrated by a young child who introduces a hero-worshiped older child by announcing, "Mommy, this is Johnny!"

Brevity and accuracy are the two requirements that must be kept in mind when introducing people. The person making the introduction is completely in charge of the situation for the length of time that it takes to effect it. When you are that person, you are momentarily the ringmaster who must be sure not only of what you are going to say but how you are going to say it.

INTRODUCTIONS

When making introductions, all names must be clearly and correctly stated. You must know instantly whose name is stated first. There are a few simple rules you should remember:

A man is always presented *to* a woman—with the exception of the President of any country, a King, or a dignitary of the Church, or when a junior woman officer is officially presented to a senior male officer.

The honored or higher ranking person's name is stated first, then the name of the person being presented.

Young people are presented *to* older people of the same sex.

A single person is introduced *to* a group.

To illustrate these rules, you should introduce these persons in this manner:

241

"Mr. President, may I present Mrs. Jones?"

or: "Mrs. Jones, may I present Admiral Smith?" or, "May I present Admiral Smith . . . Mrs. Jones."

"General Smith, may I present Lieutenant White . . . Miss White is a Navy nurse."

"General Smith, may I present Colonel Jones?"

"Mrs. Jones, this is my daughter Ann," or "Mrs. Jones, Miss White."

"Miss White (or, This is Miss White—)—Ensign Fields, Miss Lewis, Midshipman Brown, Miss Smith, Cadet Long," and so on, irrespective of rank or sex. In this case, when you wish to indicate individuals in the services, junior rank is stated.

SERVICE INTRODUCTIONS

In the Navy, junior officers are those of the rank of lieutenant commander and below, including midshipmen and Coast Guard cadets. They are introduced and addressed as "Mister" at both social and official occasions—with the exceptions of certain military, state, official, or social occasions when the designation of title is necessary. Commanders and up are introduced by rank.

In all other services, company grade officers—second and first lieutenants and captains—and up are introduced by rank. Officers of both grades of lieutenant are introduced and addressed as "Lieutenant."

Cadets at the U. S. Military Academy are introduced and addressed as "Mister," except at certain occasions when the designation is necessary. Cadets at the U. S. Air Force Academy are introduced as "Cadet—" and addressed thereafter as "Mister." (See page 251.)

Servicewomen are officially introduced in the same way as are servicemen. A junior woman officer is presented to a senior male officer.

WHAT TO SAY

In making introductions, the easiest way is simply to state the names of the two persons concerned: "Miss White, Mr. Jones," or "Commander Brown, Mr. Smith." The phrase, "May I present," is more formal, but it is always correct to say, "Miss White, may I present Mr. Jones?" You may then add, "Jack is a Second Classman."

Midshipmen and cadets may introduce fellow classmates in this manner: "Mary, this is my roommate, John Jones—Miss White." If the friendships are less intimate, the introduction may be "Miss White, Mr. Jones." When you introduce your sister or your best girl friend (or your fiancée) to your roommate who knows her name well, you may say, "Mary, this is John Jones." However, this form is reserved for intimate friends only.

Although it is proper to use first names in introductions, it is important that those being introduced are contemporaries or are on equal footing.

When a very close friend or relative is introduced to a stranger, the last name must be worked into the introduction: "Mary, may I present Midshipman John Jones . . ."; then turning to Midshipman Jones, you add, "—Miss White." Otherwise he will have no idea who "Mary" may be.

You should be careful about making personal comments when introducing people. Biographical data or human interest stories that are too long may cause embarrassment rather than establishing the topic of conversation for which they were intended. However, a brief comment can be very helpful in breaking the ice between strangers, and can be the start of a lasting friendship. "Mrs. Wilson, may I present Mrs. Smith? Her husband, as you know, served with General Wilson at Iwo Jima."

To introduce a newcomer to a group, the easiest way is to announce to all present, "This is Miss Brown." Then the names of those present are stated in rotation around the room. Should part of the group be actively engaged in a game or conversation at the time of your arrival, introductions should be made only to those closest to you and the newcomer.

When you yourself are being introduced to a large group of people, you do not need to make the rounds and shake hands with everyone present. A man may shake hands with each man near him—and with any woman who offers her hand first. When a woman is introduced to such a group, she is not always taken around the room. If the group is small and the room not crowded, however, the host or hostess may take the newcomer around and introduce him or her personally to everyone.

FAMILY INTRODUCTIONS

When introducing a member of your family, usually you omit the last name of the person you are introducing. A midshipman or cadet may say, "Mother, this is my roommate, James Smith." If your father is dead and your mother has remarried, you would say, "Mother, this is my roommate, James Smith";—then turning to Midshipman (or Cadet) Smith, you would say, "—Mrs. Northrop."

When the person to whom you wish to introduce your relative may be vague concerning your own name, then you add the last name of your relative. For example: "Colonel Wilson, this is Roger Doe, my brother." After the customary courtesies are exchanged, you might add: "Colonel Wilson is my regimental commander, Roger. Sir, my brother is going to Exeter and hopes to be a plebe next year."

A married man refers to his wife as "my wife" to people who do not know her, and by her first name to people who do know her. You would introduce your wife in this manner: "Mrs. Smith, may I present my wife?" If you want to encourage the friendship, you may add your wife's first name: "Mrs. Smith, may I present my wife, Ruth?"

A man would introduce his wife to a man in this manner: "Ruth, this is Captain Jones . . . my wife." You *never* refer to your wife as "Mrs." at a social occasion, except when you are going through a receiving line at a reception when you present your wife as "Mrs. Brown."

When speaking with very junior officers, enlisted personnel, tradespeople, servants, etc., however, you do refer to your wife as "Mrs.——."

When a wife introduces her husband, she says, "Mrs. Smith, this is my husband," and refers to him as "husband"—not as "Mr."—or "The lieutenant." She will only refer to him as "Mr. Brown" with tradespeople, servants, etc.

When introducing or referring to your wife, you should never use humorous forms such as: "Jim, I want you to meet the missus," or, "Meet the greatest little wife in the world."

When introducing your mother- or father-in-law, you may use the term "My mother-in-law" or "father-in-law," but it is preferable that you say, "Mother (or whatever she is called), may I present Lieutenant John Smith?" Then turning to Lieutenant Smith you add, "Mrs. Woods is Mary's mother" —Mary being the name of your wife. A stepparent would be introduced, "My stepfather, Mr. White," but the relationship need not be mentioned unless you care to.

Half-brothers or sisters are usually introduced as brothers and sisters even though their last name is different from your own. You must give their names, however, when these are different from your own. "Mary, this is Cadet Smith—my sister, Miss White." Relatives, such as cousins, uncles, etc., are so designated at the end of the introduction, rather than in the body of the introduction.

FORGOTTEN INTRODUCTIONS

When you are presented to someone you have met previously but who apparently has forgotten that introduction, you may say: "I believe that I met Miss Lewis at the ring dance last year," or make other reference to the place of introduction. But do not blurt out, "Oh, I've met Miss Lewis— don't you remember?" It is obvious that she does not remember, and such a remark only causes embarrassment.

The fact that a junior officer, midshipman or cadet is not remembered by a senior officer does not imply that the senior officer is rude, or that you, the junior, did not make a good impression. A senior officer meets many people in his career, at many places, and the person who "never forgets a name or face" is a rarity in this accelerated world of today. Introductions made at large social functions, or made long ago, are easily forgotten.

When someone momentarily forgets your name when introducing you, help him out by giving your name, "John Jones." This momentary lapse of memory sometimes happens to even your best friends, and, in reverse, to you. When someone seems to have forgotten you, you may say, "How do you do, Mrs. Smith—I'm John Jones. We met at the station Christmas party."

If a person appears deliberately to forget you were introduced previously, you should not mention having met before. But do not be too quick to take offense at a forgotten introduction.

When a person joins a group and his last name is unknown—or you have forgotten it—it is best to say, "I'm sorry, but I have momentarily forgotten your last name," before attempting introductions.

ACKNOWLEDGMENTS

The customary answer to an introduction for both persons concerned is, "How do you do?" You may add, "So nice to see you." If you want to be certain that you understand the name correctly, say "How do you do, Mrs. Smith.)' You are *not* expected to answer, "I'm fine, how are you?"

—It is good training to listen carefully when introductions are made so that it will not be necessary to have the name repeated. To acknowledge an introduction with a flip remark or with an attitude of indifference is not only improper, but insulting. Introductions should always be treated with the respect that they deserve; they invariably constitute first impressions, and first impressions should be good ones.

Young people frequently say "Hello," to each other, following an introduction. Although the expression "How are you?" is frowned on, it is correct and is used in certain sections of the country. The temptation is to answer the query, which makes for an awkward situation.

Some men acknowledge another man's introduction by saying, "It is nice to know you," which phrase the other man may repeat, or he may merely say, "Thank you."

You should always avoid such acknowledgments as, "I am pleased to make your acquaintance," or, "Pleased to meet you." But—a hostess will cordially greet a guest's friend who is a stranger by saying, "I am so pleased you could come." And when you are introduced to someone who is an intimate friend of a friend of yours, you will probably say that you are pleased to know him!

Never use such trite phrases as, "Cadet Jones, shake hands with Jim Brown," or, ". . . I want you to make the acquaintance of . . . ." Embellishments on introductions can be confusing; it is best to keep introductions as simple and as direct as possible.

SELF-INTRODUCTIONS

Self-introductions are sometimes necessary, but they should be treated with care. Too often, the self-introduction has been used by presumptuous persons, with the result that others are wary of the custom.

There are occasions, however, when self-introductions cannot be avoided. For instance, when you are a stranger at a large reception or cocktail party and the host and hostess are busy elsewhere and cannot introduce you into a new group—then you may introduce yourself.

However, when two persons are of the opposite sex, it is preferable that the lady speak first to the gentleman. If she does not, extreme care must be exercised by the man and he should talk about something impersonal —the decor of the room or a floral arrangement or even the weather— and then introduce himself.

When you introduce yourself at a social or non-official occasion, you do *not use your rank or title.* Say, "My name is John Jones" or, "I am John Jones." When your name is mispronounced and it seems advisable to correct it, say "Excuse me, my name is Jones (or John Jones)." You do not say, "Lieutenant Jones" or "Mr. Jones."

When you are telephoning someone who is your senior, you should introduce yourself "Colonel Brown, this John Jones." If it is an official conversation, you would state your rank or title. A woman would say to the Colonel's wife, "Mrs. Brown, this is Mary Jones. My husband is Lieutenant John Jones, who is serving under Colonel Brown. . . ."

At an occasion when a junior officer is not in uniform but wishes to identify himself to a senior officer, you might say something like this: "Colonel, I'm Lieutenant Hawkins. I was the forward observer in your battalion in the Alaskan maneuver in October of 1960."

INTRODUCTIONS IN GROUPS

Introductions made in large groups must be handled in an efficient way, with the person or persons presented *to* the group. It is impossible to introduce everyone at a large function, but do introduce all guests at small gatherings of a dozen or so. A host and hostess should introduce a guest into a small group upon his arrival, and to the others later, when it is convenient. Otherwise, after the first introduction, the guest is on his own.

WHAT TO DO

When introduced to a man or woman, a man, of course, rises if he is seated. He shakes hands with another man when being introduced—but he will wait for a woman to extend her hand before offering his. If he should forget and extend his hand first, it is no breach of etiquette since he is showing friendliness; however, he will feel more comfortable if he remembers to wait. He may bow slightly when presented to a woman, but he does not bob his head.

When you are at an inconvenient distance from a person to whom you are being introduced, you may nod or bow slightly. At a crowded table in a restaurant, a man may half-rise when a person stops at his table and introductions are made. But if you are the one *making* the introductions, you always stand.

Outdoors, in uniform, the hand salute is customary when a man is introduced to a man or woman; in the Naval Service you do not remove your cap; in the other services, you may salute or remove your cap. In civilian dress, he removes his hat and leaves it off, weather permitting. However, if you should be the only man in uniform in a mixed group, you may feel more comfortable by deferring to civilian practice, and accordingly remove you hat when introduced to a woman.

Usually, a man does not lift his hat to and among men when women are not present. It is awkward to attempt to lift your hat, and then shake hands. But if you are presented to a dignitary or very high ranking man outdoors, when you are in civilian dress, you may as a matter of courtesy remove your hat with your left hand before shaking hands.

If a man is wearing gloves when introduced to a man or woman, he removes his right glove—that is, if he has time. But do not keep a person waiting while you peel it off. When ushering at a wedding or funeral, or when attending a formal dance where white gloves are worn, do *not* remove your glove when introductions are in order. At no time do you need to apologize for leaving gloves on.

In Europe, a man will shake hands with anyone presented to him. The gallant custom of kissing the hand of a Continental woman is not expected of American men visiting in a country where this custom prevails—or when the woman is visting here.

A woman does not rise when introduced to another woman of about her own age, but she will stand when introduced to an elderly woman or the wife of a senior officer. A junior woman officer will stand when introduced to a senior officer (man or woman). She will remain standing until the elderly or senior woman is seated. A woman may shake hands with another woman, when convenient. But the younger or junior woman usually waits for the elderly woman, senior officer, or senior officer's wife to offer her hand first.

A woman does not rise when introduced to a man—unless he is the President, a King, or a dignitary of the Church, or when a junior woman officer is introduced to a senior male officer. When a young woman is in the presence of a very high ranking officer or dignitary, she may rise. A woman customarily extends her hand first to a man of *any* age or rank except to heads of State or members of royal families. Children and teen-agers should stand when introduced to an adult, man or woman.

THE PRESIDENT OF THE UNITED STATES

If you should have the good fortune to present someone to the President of the United States, you would stand straight, look directly at the President, and probably say, "Mr. President, may I present Admiral Brown?"

If you—a man—should be the person being presented, you would wait for the President to offer his hand, and you will bow as you shake hands. A woman being presented to the President also waits for him to offer his hand first. But most men—regardless of rank or title—usually prefer the customary form of a woman offering her hand first.

If you are called upon to make a formal presentation of the President at a banquet, you will give his full title: "Ladies and gentlemen—the President of the United States." In conversation, you address him as "Mr. President."

The Vice President is addressed and introduced in the same way as the President. The wives of Presidents and of Vice Presidents are introduced and addressed as "Mrs." When introduced and when in conversation, a former President is called "Mr." Although he is never so called while in office, an ex-President is given the courtesy title of "The Honorable."

FAREWELLS

After an introduction, the first person to move away might say, "I hope that I see you again soon." The other person will probably answer, "Thank you." He may wish to add such a comment as, "I hope so, too," but this tends to cause a slight awkwardness.

In taking leave of a group of strangers, it makes very little difference whether a person has been introduced all around or merely included in certain conversations. The most courteous action is to bow "good-bye" to anyone who happens to be looking at you. No attempt should be made to attract the attention to those who are apparently unaware that you are leaving. When saying good-bye to an acquaintance, you may say, "Good-bye, it was so nice to meet you," or "I hope we can meet again soon."

It is impossible to say good-bye to all guests at a large party, but you can do so to those with whom you were most recently talking. You will say good-bye to all guests at a very small party, such as a dinner, and you *always* say good-bye to your host and hostess.

When saying "good-bye," both men and women stand. A hostess rises to her feet when she sees that a guest is ready to leave. A woman guest makes the first move to leave, and her husband or escort immediately rises and joins her. The hostess and host shake hands with their guests on departure the same as on arrival.

A departing guest should make some appreciative comment to the hostess: then to the host: "It's been a very pleasant evening, thank you so much." The hostess might answer, "Goodnight, I'm so glad you could be with us."

At a formal dinner, the hostess would remain standing inside the living room when saying good-bye to guests, and the host would walk to the door of the living room or into the hall with a high ranking guest. The high ranking guest is always the first to leave. A steward or butler would open the door for guests and say, "Goodnight, Sir (or Madam)." A guest would answer, "Thank you, goodnight."

At informal parties, or when the host lives in the country, the host usually walks with guests to their cars—and always makes certain that everyone has a way to get home.

CHAPTER 21

American Forms of Address

WRITTEN ADDRESS	SPOKEN ADDRESS	INTRODUCTIONS

A. *NAVAL SERVICE:* Full rank *precedes* the name of commissioned officers; customarily, rank may be abbreviated in official correspondence, but is *written out* in social correspondence. Likewise, the names of the services are often abbreviated in official correspondence, but are written out in business or social correspondence. The rank also precedes the names of warrant officers, midshipmen, Coast Guard cadets, and Merchant Marine cadet-midshipmen. Although the rating *follows* the name of noncommissioned officers in official correspondence, it precedes the name in business or social correspondence. When in civilian dress, a captain and a lieutenant are introduced as "of the Navy" to distinguish the rank from the Army, Marine Corps, and Air Force. In conversation, all admirals are "Admiral."

WRITTEN ADDRESS	SPOKEN ADDRESS	INTRODUCTIONS
Rear Admiral John Jones, U. S. Navy Superintendent United States Naval Academy Annapolis, Maryland	Admiral Jones	Admiral Jones *Or formal:* Rear Admiral John Jones, Superintendent of the United States Naval Academy
Social: Rear Admiral and Mrs. John Jones Superintendent's House Annapolis Maryland		
Lieutenant Commander John Jones, U. S. Navy Gunnery Officer USS *Los Angeles* c/o Fleet Post Office San Francisco, California	Mr. Jones	Mr. Jones (Commissioned officers of the rank of lieutenant commander, and down, are addressed and introduced as "Mister," except for official or social occasions when designation of rank is necessary.)

American Forms of Address—continued

WRITTEN ADDRESS	SPOKEN ADDRESS	INTRODUCTIONS
Social: Lieutenant Commander and Mrs. John Jones 7100 Atherton Drive Long Beach California		
Chief Warrant Officer John Jones, U. S. Coast Guard USCGC *Eastwind* c/o Fleet Post Office New York, New York	Mr. Jones	Mr. Jones
Social: Chief Warrant Officer and Mrs. John Jones 1125 Ocean Drive New London Connecticut		
Midshipman John Jones, U. S. Navy Room 3654, Bancroft Hall United States Naval Academy Annapolis, Maryland	Mr. Jones	Mr. Jones (Upon certain occasions, midshipmen are addressed and introduced as "Mid- shipman" for purposes of designation.)

B. *ARMY, AIR FORCE AND MARINE CORPS:* Although the Marine Corps is an integral part of the Naval Service, the rank is similar to that of the Army and Air Force, and therefore is included with these services. In written correspondence, both official and social, full rank and ratings precede the name and are written out. In conversation, all generals are "General"; all colonels are "Colonel"; and all privates and sergeants are "Private" and "Sergeant."

Brigadier General John Doe, U. S. Army Commandant of Cadets United States Military Academy West Point, New York	General Doe	General Doe *Or formal:* Brigadier General John Doe, the Commandant of Cadets at the United States Mili- tary Academy
Social: Brigadier General and Mrs. John Doe Quarters 101 United States Military Academy West Point New York		

American Forms of Address—continued

WRITTEN ADDRESS	SPOKEN ADDRESS	INTRODUCTIONS
Lieutenant Colonel John Doe, U. S. Air Force 335th Bomber Squadron Langley Air Force Base Virginia	Colonel Doe	Colonel Doe *Or formal:* Lieutenant Colonel Doe, of the 335th Bomber Squadron
Social: Lieutenant Colonel and Mrs. John Doe Quarters M Langley Air Force Base Virginia		
First Lieutenant John Doe, U. S. Marine Corps Marine Corps Base Camp Lejeune, North Carolina	Lieutenant Doe	Lieutenant Doe *Or formal:* First Lieutenant Doe, of the Marine Corps Base, etc. (In the Army, first and second lieutenant are designated "Lieutenant.")
Social: First Lieutenant and Mrs. John Doe 1073 East Peleliu Drive Tarawa Terrace 1 Camp Lejeune North Carolina		
Cadet John Doe, U. S. Army Company C, Corps of Cadets United States Military Academy West Point, New York	Mr. Doe	Mr. Doe (For purposes of identification or designation, the title "Cadet Doe" is used upon certain official or social occasions.)
Cadet John Doe, U. S. Air Force Room 3A20, Vandenberg Hall United States Air Force Academy Colorado	Mr. Doe	Cadet Doe (A cadet at the Air Force Academy is introduced as "Cadet Doe" and addressed thereafter as "Mr. Doe.")
Lance Corporal Jane Doe, U. S. Marine Corps Marine Corps Schools Quantico, Virginia	Corporal Doe	Corporal Doe *Or formal:* Lance Corporal Doe, etc.

American Forms of Address—continued

C. *SERVICE ABBREVIATIONS:* In official correspondence, rank and ratings are abbreviated and fully capitalized in the Naval Service, and are partially capitalized in the other services. The abbreviations for the relative ranks of commissioned officers of the U.S. Armed Forces, according to the Abbreviation Manual of each service, are as follows:

NAVY AND COAST GUARD		ARMY	
Fleet Admiral (Navy only)	FADM	General of the Army	(No abbr.)
Admiral	ADM	General	GEN
Vice Admiral	VADM	Lieutenant General	LTG
Rear Admiral	RADM	Major General	MG
Commodore	COMO	Brigadier General	BG
Captain	CAPT	Colonel	COL
Commander	CDR	Lieutenant Colonel	LTC
Lieutenant Commander	LCDR	Major	MAJ
Lieutenant	LT	Captain	CPT
Lieutenant, junior grade	LTJG	First Lieutenant	1 LT
Ensign	ENS	Second Lieutenant	2 LT

MARINE CORPS		AIR FORCE	
General	Gen	General of the Air Force	(No abbr.)
Lieutenant General	LtGen	General	Gen
Major General	MajGen	Lieutenant General	Lt Gen
Brigadier General	BGen	Major General	Maj Gen
Colonel	Col	Brigadier General	Brig Gen
Lieutenant Colonel	LtCol	Colonel	Col
Major	Maj	Lieutenant Colonel	Lt Col
Captain	Capt	Major	Maj
First Lieutenant	1stLt	Captain	Capt
Second Lieutenant	2ndLt	First Lieutenant	1st Lt
		Second Lieutenant	2d Lt

WARRANT OFFICERS—ALL SERVICES EXCEPT ARMY		BRANCH OF SERVICE	
Chief Warrant Officer (W-4)	CWO	United States Army	USA
Chief Warrant Officer (W-3)	CWO	United States Navy	USN
Chief Warrant Officer (W-2)	CWO	United States Marine Corps	USMC
Warrant Officer (W-1)	WO	United States Coast Guard	USCG
Army: WO4, WO3, WO2, WO1		United States Air Force	USAF
		National Guard	NG

RESERVE OFFICERS

Reserve officers of all the services add the letter "R" after the branch. For example: USAR, USCGR, etc.

Reserve and National Guard officers use their titles only when on active duty.

Note: For the insignia of rank of all commissioned and warrant officers, see pages 40 and 41.

American Forms of Address—continued

WRITTEN ADDRESS	SPOKEN ADDRESS	INTRODUCTIONS

D. *UNITED STATES—Federal, State, and Local Dignitaries:* "The Honorable" is the preferred form for addressing most American officials in office or retired, and is always written out in full on the line above and to the left of the name. The phrase is always used with the full name—and *never* with any other title such as "The Honorable Admiral Jones," or "The Honorable Mr. Jones." In the salutation and close of a letter to the President, you would write, officially or in business, "Dear Mr. President:"; and socially, "My dear Mr. President:"; and, officially and in business, "Respectfully yours," or socially, "Very respectfully,". In writing to all other American officials, the official or business closing is, "Very truly yours," or socially, "Sincerely yours,". Wives of American officials are addressed and introduced as "Mrs.—."

WRITTEN ADDRESS	SPOKEN ADDRESS	INTRODUCTIONS
The President The President The White House Washington, D.C.	Mr. President	The President *Or formal:* The President of the United States *Abroad, add:* . . . of America
Social: The President and Mrs. Doe The White House Washington, D.C.*		
The President's Wife Mrs. John Doe The White House Washington, D.C.	Mrs. Doe	Mrs. Doe
The Vice President The Vice President United States Senate Washington, D.C.	Mr. Vice President or Mr. Doe**	The Vice President *Or formal:* The Vice President of the United States *Abroad, add:* . . . of America
Social: The Vice President and Mrs. Doe (home address)		
The Vice President's Wife (home address)	Mrs. Doe	Mrs. Doe

* Formally written "District of Columbia," although the abbreviation "D.C." is generally used.

** In continued conversation, "Mister—" is used.

American Forms of Address—continued

WRITTEN ADDRESS	SPOKEN ADDRESS	INTRODUCTIONS
The Chief Justice of the Su- *preme Court* The Chief Justice of the Supreme Court Washington, D.C.	Mr. Chief Justice or Mr. Doe	The Chief Justice *Or formal:* The Honorable John Doe, Chief Justice of the Supreme Court of the United States *Abroad, add:* . . . of America
Social: The Chief Justice and Mrs. Doe (home address)		
Associate Justices Mr. Justice Doe The Supreme Court Washington, D. C.	Mr. Justice Doe or Mr. Doe	Mr. Justice Doe *Or formal:* The Honorable John Doe, Associate Justice of the Su- preme Court of the United States *Abroad, add:*
Social: Mr. Justice Doe and Mrs. Doe (home address)		. . . of America
A Cabinet Officer (man)* The Honorable John Doe Secretary of State Washington, D.C.	Mr. Secretary or Mr. Doe	The Secretary of State, Mr. Doe *Or formal:* The Honorable John Doe Secretary of State
Social: The Secretary of State and Mrs. Doe (home address)		
A Cabinet Officer (woman) The Honorable Jane Doe Secretary of Labor Washington, D.C.	Madam Secretary or Miss or Mrs. Doe	The Secretary of Labor, Miss (or Mrs.) Doe *Or formal:* The Honorable Jane Doe, Secretary of Labor

* All Cabinet Officers except the Attorney General and the Postmaster General use the title of Secretary. Although the Service secretaries do not have Cabinet rank, they may be addressed and introduced as "Mr. Secretary," or "The Secretary of the Navy," etc. The Secretary of Defense has cabinet rank.

American Forms of Address—continued

WRITTEN ADDRESS	SPOKEN ADDRESS	INTRODUCTIONS
Social, when married: The Secretary of Labor and Mr. Doe (home address)		
The Attorney General The Honorable John Doe Attorney General Washington, D.C.	Mr. Attorney General or Mr. Doe	The Attorney General, Mr. Doe *Or formal:* The Honorable John Doe, Attorney General

*Secretaries of Defense, and of
  the Army, Navy, and Air
  Force (Under Secretaries
  and Assistant Secretaries)*
The Honorable
John Doe
Secretary of
  the Air Force
Washington, D.C.
	Mr. Secretary
	or
	Mr. Doe
		The Secretary of the
		Air Force, Mr. Doe
		Or formal:
		The Honorable John Doe,
		Secretary of the Air Force

Social: The Secretary of the Air Force and Mrs. Doe (home address)		
Former Presidents of the United States The Honorable John Doe San Francisco, California	Mr. Doe (Or any title, such as military)	The Honorable John Doe, the former President of the United States
The Assistant to the President———— The Honorable John Doe Assistant to the President The White House Washington, D.C.	Mr. Doe	The Assistant to the Presi- dent, Mr. John Doe *Or formal:* The Honorable John Doe, Assistant to the President of the United States
Social: The Honorable John Doe and Mrs. Doe (home address)		

American Forms of Address—continued

WRITTEN ADDRESS	SPOKEN ADDRESS	INTRODUCTIONS
The Special Assistant to the President with Military Rank Major General John Doe, U. S. Army Special Assistant to the President The White House Washington, D.C.	General Doe	The Special Assistant to the President, General John Doe, United States Army
Social: Major General and Mrs. John Doe (home address)		
The Speaker of the House of Representatives The Honorable John Doe Speaker of the House of Representatives The Capitol Washington, D.C.	Mr. Speaker or Mr. Doe	The Speaker, Mr. Doe *Or formal:* The Honorable John Doe, Speaker of the House of Representatives
Social: The Speaker of the House of Representatives and Mrs. Doe (home address)		
American Ambassador (man)* The Honorable John Doe American Ambassador London, England	Mr. Ambassador *Or on leave:* Mr. Doe *Or with military rank:* General Doe	The Honorable John Doe, the American Ambassador (When he is not at his post, the name of the country to which he is accredited must be added: "to—.")
Social: The American Ambassador and Mrs. Doe American Embassy London England or		

* When a woman is a United States Ambassador, or a United States Minister, the word "Madam" is substituted for "Mr." in the spoken address.

American Forms of Address—continued

WRITTEN ADDRESS	SPOKEN ADDRESS	INTRODUCTIONS
His Excellency The American Ambassador and Mrs. Doe London England England	Your Excellency or Mr. Ambassador	His Excellency the American Ambassador
American Ministers (men) The Honorable John Doe American Minister Dublin, Ireland	Mr. Minister or Mr. Doe	The American Minister *Or formal:* The Honorable John Doe, the American Minister *Or not at his post:* . . . to—" (name of country)
Social: The American Minister and Mrs. Doe American Legation Dublin Ireland		
American Chargé d'Affaires and *Consular Officers* John Doe, Esquire American Chargé d'Affaires (or Consul General, or Vice Consul) Paris, France	Mr. Doe	Mr. Doe *Or formal:* Mr. John Doe, the American Chargé d'Affaires
Social: The American Chargé d'Affaires and Mrs. John Doe (home address)		
United States Senator (or State Senator, with ap- propriate State address) The Honorable John Doe United States Senate Washington, D.C.	Senator Doe or Senator	Senator Doe *Or formal:* The Honorable John Doe, Senator from Oklahoma
Social: Senator and Mrs. Doe (home address)		

American Forms of Address—continued

WRITTEN ADDRESS	SPOKEN ADDRESS	INTRODUCTIONS
United States Congressman		
The Honorable	Congressman	Congressman Doe†
John Doe	Doe	*Or formal:*
House of Representatives	or	The Honorable John Doe,
Washington, D.C.	Mr. Doe	Representative from South Carolina
Social:		
The Honorable and Mrs. Doe		
(home address)		
Governors*		
The Honorable	Governor Doe	Governor Doe or
John Doe	or	The Governor
Governor of Maryland	Governor	*Or formal:*
Annapolis, Maryland		The Honorable John Doe, Governor of Maryland or . . . of the State of Maryland
Social:		
The Governor and Mrs. Doe		
Or outside the State:		
The Governor of Maryland		
and Mrs. Doe		
or		
His Excellency the Governor		
and Mrs. Doe		
Mayors		
The Honorable	Mayor Doe	Mayor Doe
John Doe	or	*Or formal:*
Mayor of Boston	Mr. Mayor	The Honorable John Doe,
Boston, Massachusetts		Mayor of Boston or . . . Mayor of the City of Boston
Social:		
Mayor and Mrs. Doe		
or		
The Honorable and Mrs.		
John Doe		
(home address)		

† The title "Congressman" seems to be widely used in informal introductions by the Representatives themselves and by others when introducing them. It is not incorrect to call a Congresswoman "Congressman." The prefix "Representative" is never used in correspondence.

* The Governor is given the title "Excellency" in many states, but the title *Governor* is the one used by the Department of State.

American Forms of Address—continued

WRITTEN ADDRESS	SPOKEN ADDRESS	INTRODUCTIONS
Judges		
The Honorable	Judge Doe	Judge Doe
John Doe		*Or formal:*
Judge of District Court		The Honorable John Doe,
(or whatever court)		Judge of the District Court
Wheeling, West Virginia		
Social:		
Judge and Mrs. Doe		
or		
The Honorable and Mrs. Doe		
(home address)		
Head of a Federal Agency		
The Honorable	Mr. Doe	Mr. Doe
John Doe	*Or formal:*	*Or formal:*
Administrator (name of		The Honorable John Doe,
agency)		Administrator of (name of
Washington, D. C.		agency)
Social:		
Mr. and Mrs. John Doe		
or		
The Honorable and Mrs. John		
Doe		
(home address)		
Head of a Division or Bureau		
of a Department		
Mr. John Doe	Mr. Doe	Mr. Doe
Chief, Federal Bureau of In-		or
vestigation		Mr. John Doe, Chief of the
Washington, D.C.		Federal Bureau of Investiga-
		tion
Social:		
Mr. and Mrs. John Doe		
(home address)		

E. *AMERICAN CLERGY AND CHURCH DIGNITARIES*

WRITTEN ADDRESS	SPOKEN ADDRESS	INTRODUCTIONS
The Presiding Bishop of the		
Protestant Episcopal Church		
in America		
The Most Reverend John Doe,	Bishop Doe	Bishop Doe
D.D., LL.D.		or

American Forms of Address—continued

WRITTEN ADDRESS	SPOKEN ADDRESS	INTRODUCTIONS
Presiding Bishop of the Protestant Episcopal Church in America (local address)		The Most Reverend John Doe, Presiding Bishop of the Protestant Episcopal Church in America
Protestant Episcopal Bishops The Right Reverend John Doe, D.D., LL.D. Bishop of— (local address)	Bishop Doe	Bishop Doe or The Right Reverend John Doe, Bishop of—
Roman Catholic Cardinal His Eminence John Cardinal Doe Archbishop of New York New York, New York	Your Eminence	His Eminence or Cardinal Doe or His Eminence, Cardinal Doe
Roman Catholic Archbishop (or *Bishop*) His Excellency, The Most Reverend John Doe, S.T.D. Archbishop (or Bishop) of Chicago Chicago, Illinois	Archbishop (or Bishop) Doe	Archbishop (or Bishop) Doe or His Excellency, The Most Reverend John Doe, Archbishop of Chicago or His Excellency, The Archbishop of Chicago
Methodist Bishop* The Very Reverend John Doe, D.D., LL.D. Bishop of Denver Denver, Colorado	Bishop Doe	Bishop Doe or The Very Reverend Bishop Doe, Methodist Bishop of Denver
Roman Catholic Monsignor The Right Reverend Monsignor John Doe, S.J. (local address)	Monsignor Doe	The Very Reverend (or Right Reverend) Monsignor John Doe or Monsignor Doe

* All Protestant clergymen with Doctor's Degree may be addressed and introduced as "Dr. Doe," and "The Reverend Dr. Doe," respectively. Without such a degree, they are addressed and introduced as "Sir," and "The Reverend Doe," respectively. In conversation, say "Dr. Doe" or "Mr. Doe."

American Forms of Address—continued

WRITTEN ADDRESS	SPOKEN ADDRESS	INTRODUCTIONS
Protestant Episcopal Archdeacon		
The Venerable John Doe, D.D.*	Archdeacon Doe or	Archdeacon Doe or
Archdeacon of—	Dr. Doe	Dr. Doe
Diocese of Virginia		or
		The Venerable John Doe, Archdeacon of— in the Diocese of Virginia
Deans and Canons		
The Very Reverend John Doe, D.D.	Dean (or Canon) Doe	The Very Reverend John Doe, Dean (or Canon) of
Dean (or Canon) of Washington Cathedral	or Dr. Doe	Washington Cathedral
Washington, D.C.		
Priests, who are Addressed as "Father"		
The Reverend John Doe, S.J.	Father Doe	Father Doe
St. Mary's Church		or
Washington, D.C.		The Reverend John Doe
Mormon		
Mr. John Doe	Mr. Doe	Mr. John Doe,
President of Manti Temple		President of Manti
Manti, Utah		Temple
Rabbi		
Rabbi John Doe	Rabbi Doe	Rabbi Doe
Kneseth Israel Congregation	or	*Or with scholastic degree:*
Annapolis, Maryland	Rabbi *Or with scholastic degree:* Dr. Doe	Dr. Doe
Mother Superior		
The Reverend Mother Mary (and the initials of her order)	Reverend Mother	Reverend Mother
The Convent of—		
(address)		
Sisters		
Sister Mary (and initials of her order	Sister Mary	Sister Mary
(local address)		

American Forms of Address—continued

WRITTEN ADDRESS	SPOKEN ADDRESS	INTRODUCTIONS
Brothers		
The Reverend Brother John Doe	Brother John or	Brother John
Fordham University	Brother	
Bronx, New York		
Cantors		
Cantor John Doe	Cantor Doe	Cantor Doe
Kneseth Israel Congregation		
Annapolis, Maryland		
F. *INDIVIDUALS*		
Professors and Doctors		
Professor (or Assoc. Professor or Asst. Professor) John Doe	Mr. Doe or Professor Doe	Professor Doe
Or with		
Doctor's Degree:		
Dr. John Doe	Dr. Doe	Dr. Doe
Columbia University		
New York, New York		
Divorcées		
Mrs. Smith Doe (the maiden surname is followed by the ex-husband's name)	Mrs. Doe	Mrs. Doe
(local address)		
Widow		
Mrs. John Doe (the same as when her husband was alive)	Mrs. Doe	Mrs. Doe
(local address)		

RÉSUMÉ OF DIFFERENCES IN THE FORMS OF ADDRESS

In the Naval Service:

- All grades of admiral are addressed and introduced as "Admiral"— with the exception of a formal presentation when the full grade would be stated.
- All chaplains are addressed and introduced as "Chaplain Jones."

- Medical and dental officers are addressed and introduced by rank including and above the grade of commander; including and below the rank of lieutenant commander they are called "Doctor."
- In a mixed group it is customary to introduce a captain in the Navy as "Captain, United States Navy," since the rank of captain in the Navy corresponds to the rank of colonel in the Army, Air Force, and Marine Corps—and the rank of captain in these services corresponds to the rank of lieutenant in the Navy.
- A woman officer in the Navy is addressed and introduced in the same way as a male officer in the Navy. For example, a lieutenant commander in the WAVES is "Miss Jones"; a commander is "Commander Jones," etc.
- Navy enlisted women are also addressed in the same manner as the men, excepting a warrant officer is "Miss."
- Marine servicewomen, officers and enlisted, are addressed and introduced by rank or rating.
- Aboard ship, the captain of the ship is *always* "Captain"—regardless of his rank.

In the Army, Air Force, and Marine Corps:

- All officers are addressed and introduced by rank.
- It is not correct in a spoken address to use the title by itself, such as "Colonel." It is correct to say, "Colonel Doe," etc.
- At a social occasion, the various ranks are not necessary to mention (for example, all generals are "General," and first and second lieutenants are "Lieutenant"), but at a formal presentation the full title is stated: "Brigadier General," "First Lieutenant," etc.
- Warrant officers are addressed and introduced as "Mister" or "Miss" (except for formal occasions, or reasons of designation when the full rating is stated).
- Non-commissioned officers are addressed and introduced by their rating, such as "Private Doe," etc., not "Doe" or "John."
- Servicewomen, both officers and enlisted, are addressed and introduced by rank or rating.

In civilian life:

- "The Honorable" is the preferred form for addressing most American officials, in office or retired. The phrase is always used with the full name—and never with any other title.
- "His Excellency" is used in addressing an ambassador but his wife is *not* called "Her Excellency."
- Some of the American officials addressed as "The Honorable" are

American ambassadors and ministers, governors of States and Territories, cabinet officers, senators and congressmen, the assistant to the President, assistant secretaries of executive departments, judges (except judges of the Supreme Court), commissioners of the District of Columbia, American representatives on international organizations, heads of independent federal agencies, and mayors of cities.

- High officials such as presidents, ambassadors, and cabinet members are addressed by their titles only, never by name.
- In addition to the above-mentioned persons addressed as "The Honorable," you should remember that "Once an Honorable, always an Honorable," and that a person out of office may be addressed in writing as "The Honorable."
- The word "Honorable" is never used by the person who holds this distinction in issuing or answering invitations, or on personal or calling cards—or in any other way.

In foreign countries:

American service attachés and other officials serving in foreign countries should consult the Protocol Section of the American Embassy. In Washington, the Foreign Liaison Section of the Office of your Service will advise you on problems of customs and protocol.

CHAPTER 22

The Art of Conversation

For many people, the art of conversation is of little importance. In some walks of life this may be true—but not for you as an officer in the service, or for anyone who chooses to become a professional leader of men.

The general public considers an officer in the services to be a man of position and so renders judgment upon this basis. You must, therefore, devote significant thought and effort to the development of proficiency in general conversation, since you are, so to speak, "on the spot."

The first thing you must do in order to be a good conversationalist is to *have something to say;* second, you *must be able to say it well.*

MANNER OF CONVERSATION

Poor grammar, rude or vulgar talk, and the persistent use of improper and uncouth phraseology are representative of careless personal habits that can be corrected if you take sufficient interest. There are officers who perform their duties acceptably—occasionally, excellently—despite their inability to express themselves clearly and in good taste. But this is the exception rather than the rule.

Errors of a gross nature in conversation are particularly noticed by those officers junior to the speaker—and, paradoxically enough, even by those juniors who themselves use poor grammar.

Juniors, despite shortcomings of their own, expect high standards in their superiors, and justly so. Such use of careless speech will inevitably result in the loss of prestige. The juniors are likely to suspect that a senior who tolerates carelessness in his own speech may well tolerate carelessness in other phases of his official behavior. Such a suspicion is something that every officer wishes to avoid, so it is well that a cadet or midshipman,

ROTC or OCS student, recognize this fact early and cultivate the habit of proper speech in everyday conversation.

OFFICIAL AND SOCIAL CONVERSATION

"The tongue is but three inches long, yet it can kill a man six feet high." This old Japanese proverb can, too often, be only too true.

In the services, the essential difference between official and social conversation is one of situation. Conversation in an *official situation* requires that the conversationalists recognize differences in rank even while carrying on their conversation, Regardless of how pleasant and congenial such conversation may be, the speaker should always remember that such congeniality is never any excuse for not giving due deference for rates.

Social conversation means general talk between persons during which no conscious recognition of rank, as such, is made. Social conversation is more informal and is made up of considerable "small talk." This is pleasant talk that is not important—and not at all harmful. But small talk that is fitting and proper at a dinner party is not carried on during an official conversation.

In both types of conversations, the objectives are the same: to create a personal relationship without tension in which thoughts and ideas may be exchanged. The tone of official conversation is generally more serious, but not necessarily so. Senior admirals and generals are only midshipmen and cadets grown older, and they, like anyone else, often enjoy a light conversation that does not concern career or business problems. Official business, of course, should never be discussed at social gatherings.

When talking with a senior or very high ranking officer, a junior officer shows deference and allows the senior to take the lead in the conversation—but should never freeze up while desperately trying to think of something brilliant to say. At a social occasion, the service officer should be attentive—but not "at attention."

FAMILIARITY

There is an old military maxim that you should always remember: in the relations between seniors and juniors, the senior will never think of the difference in rank—but the junior will never forget it. This adage is true in both social and official relations. Adherence to it will lead to ease and harmony, but violation of it often leads to unpleasantness and, sometimes, to downright embarrassment.

Official conversations between seniors and juniors follow a basic principle: seniors may call you, the junior, by your first name, but this does not grant you similar privileges. It is a gesture of friendly consideration on the part of the senior to call a junior by his first name, and this should be accepted as approbation by the junior.

Upon occasion, a senior will ask a junior to call him by his first name—but such informality must be handled with care on your part, and it must be clearly understood that the familiarity of the first name is *not* to be used in official conversations. Neither does the privilege of calling a senior by his first name automatically carry with it a "back slapping" familiarity—in fact, quite the opposite. The senior must have expected you to exercise the utmost propriety, or he would not have lowered the bars in the first place.

In talking with your contemporaries in the mess, or anywhere else—you must be on guard against telling your personal affairs. Your mess mates and station friends will become very good friends in time, but they are not the same as your parents or your immediate family. When you talk "just a little" with others about your personal affairs, a "little" quickly becomes "too much," and you will find that constraint and unease begin to develop in your formerly easy relationship.

When on duty, conversations between seniors and juniors, and between commissioned and non-commissioned officers, should always be kept on the official and impersonal level. This does not mean that you should resemble Captain Hornblower when talking with those of junior rank, but it does mean that you should avoid undue familiarity either afloat or ashore.

Enlisted personnel appreciate your consideration for their welfare and your interest in their interests, but they do not appreciate—or—want—familiarity. They know that familiarity in manner tends to cause an officer to forfeit his status as an officer; they distrust an officer who talks as though he wants to "join the gang" one moment, and the shortly thereafter issues even a minor reprimand in his official capacity. Any such occurrences hurt the sensibilities of the junior who is reprimanded.

The necessity for reprimands is not frequent, but the same situation will hold when you must make even minor criticisms: their significance is clouded over by the personal element. In positions of command, "Familiarity breeds contempt."

DISSENSIONS

Be careful of dissensions! You will find that you can disagree in your mind completely, and furthermore, can express that disagreement in conversation with a group without "leaving the sea strewn with burning wrecks." It merely takes tact. But there are those who cannot disagree with any expressed opinion without seeming to launch a personal attack on the person who stated the opinion. A good rule to follow is, "Never talk about a senior unless you have something nice to say about him."

An effective way to disagree with an expressed conversational opinion is to make no return comment at all—or, to make a rather roundabout comment which tends to veer the conversation away from the offensive statement without being obvious about it.

When you feel it necessary, however, to go on record as disagreeing with something that has been said, you may do so in a number of polite ways. For example, you may say, with a pleasant smile, "I'm afraid that I do not agree with that," or "I have given the matter considerable thought and have come to an entirely different conclusion." A light but disarming remark could be, "I'm from too far South to agree with such a Yankee idea." In brief, learn how to disagree without being disagreeable.

You may politely, but with firmness, express disagreement by obviously changing the subject. Since this maneuver is not in the best social taste, it should be reserved for situations which require drastic treatment—as when a person enters upon a tirade concerning a religious sect, and you know there is a member of that sect present. In such cases you are within the safest grounds of propriety to change the subject swiftly and decisively in order to avoid an unfortunate situation.

There may come a time, however, when a senior officer states an opinion which is radically against your own convictions. Unless some action on your part is imperatively called for, you naturally avoid comment, out of deference for your senior's greater age and experience. But if your senior then asks you to give an opinion, you may say "I have not entirely made up my mind, Sir," or "I'm not too well versed in that subject, Sir."

When the senior officer persists in an answer, you must state your honest opinion, or you will not be true to your own convictions and risk being labeled as a "yes man." With due respect, you may say "Sir, that is a matter of opinion, but my experience has been to the contrary."

IMPORTANCE OF REMEMBERING

Names are important to remember. You do not like your own name forgotten or mispronounced—so do not forget or fumble another's. Some people have excellent memories for names and faces, others must work at remembering. Most memory courses depend upon associating the name with an object, or repeating a name over and over in your mind after an introduction. If you miss the name on first being introduced, you can quite properly ask to have the name repeated.

When you cannot remember a person's name, and yet it is your duty to make the introduction to a conversational group, it is better to admit your lapse and say, "I'm sorry, but I will have to ask you your name," or "Please tell me your name again." The question should be asked with poise and no embarrassment.

In conversations, it is complimentary to remember another's personal concerns: a birthday or wedding anniversary, or an accomplishment by a member of the family. Any pleasant occurrence—an award, or the recent promotion in grade—that has happened to an individual, often serves to provide a background for conversation.

TABOOS

Controversial subjects—such as religion, race, and frequently, politics—are to be strictly avoided. Unpleasant subjects are not discussed at social functions, and are treated carefully at any time. Examples of such topics to be shunned are death, disasters, accidents, battle losses, serious illness, etc.

Off-color stories and the subject of sex should never be discussed in mixed groups—and the discreet lady or gentleman avoids them as topics at anytime.

Never discuss a person's age in his or her presence. Elderly people do not enjoy being considered decrepit, neither do young people want to feel immature and inadequate. Both the very young and the very old are frequently sensitive about their ages.

EASY CONVERSATION

An essential part of your everyday living is the art of simple, easy conversation. A good conversationalist always has something interesting to talk about, is not overbearing in his attitude, and never irritates his listeners.

In general, plain words are preferable to ponderous phrases, and trite expressions are tiresome. The topics for conversations are endless: newspapers, books, magazines; television personalities and news analysts can always be discussed, and art, music, and concerts appeal to the artistic. Any sport event in season is of interest to most men.

A topic of conversation may be discussed as long as the listeners find it of interest, then new ones must be introduced. When you are talking, look at your listeners and observe their reactions. No monologue is of interest—except possibly to yourself. When you are the listener, pay attention to what is being said. It is extremely discourteous to openly show obvious disinterest—such as allowing your glance to wander off to other people or things.

A good conversationalist does not interrupt or contradict another. He learns to draw out the shy person by finding out his interests, then adroitly asks leading questions concerning that hobby or interest. When talking with a horticulturist, you could ask him about a rose spray; an author would be interested in a new book.

When you want to start a lively conversation, ask a question which presents a challenge: "I hear the Army is strong—who do you think will win the Army-Navy game?" or, "Would it be better to return to the Three R's than to continue with progressive education?"

When you desire a certain subject to be discussed without directly asking about it, you should bring up a related subject or experience that will open the door to the desired subject of conversation. For example, if you wish to hear a man who wears the Congressional Medal of Honor talk about his experiences, you might pave the way by saying, "Sir, how many patrols did you make during World War II?"

In order to talk intelligently on a certain subject to a person of authority, it is well to brief yourself on that subject beforehand. In this way you can converse easily with the personage about his work or accomplishment and at the same time increase your own store of knowledge.

In your desire to make a good accounting of yourself, however, do not be so obvious in expressing your interest that you are considered "greasy." It is an insult to your seniors, or to anyone else, to express more interest than common courtesy allows.

POISE AND GOOD MANNERS

When you talk, do you keep your hands and feet quiet, or do you gesture widely and shuffle your feet? Do you drum on a table with your fingers, or tap your feet on the floor? If you do—stop it. To shift from one foot to the other, when standing, makes you appear ill at ease and detracts not only from your appearance, but also from what you are saying. Finger or foot tapping draws attention to what you are *doing*, rather than what you are saying.

A good conversationalist is always a considerate one; he will reflect upon a new thought before blurting out a remark which may be regretted later. He is tolerant of other's ideas, and does not ridicule or laugh at an unfortunate remark, or tell an amusing story to the discredit of anyone.

Poise in conversation includes the ability to time a conversation—to know when to talk and when to be silent. Relaxation is an essential ingredient for a poised conversationalist; an incessant chatterer will soon exhaust his listeners.

Sometimes, without anyone intending it, two people start talking simultaneously. Such a situation generally happens when there has been a lull in a conversation and both persons attempt at once to relieve the situation. In such cases, if you are one of the two, you should give way amiably and quickly. To fail to do so makes you seem rude and domineering.

A skilled conversationalist can be compared to a ship's captain; he can steer thoughts and ideas into interesting conversational channels, but when necessary, he can chart the course of an unfortunate subject away from the reefs to the safety of calmer seas.

TONE OF VOICE

A well-modulated voice is an asset to anyone. Words should be enunciated clearly, in a pleasant tone which is pitched neither too high nor too low. There are over eight tones in the average voice range, and with practice you can develop a tone best suited to your personality or to the occasion.

If you aren't aware of how your voice sounds to others, try speaking naturally or reading a news item into a recording machine; then play it back. Do your words run together? Do you bark them out? Are you too loud? The range of your voice is always important; speaking in a monotone makes any topic dull and monotonous.

With some effort on your part, you can control your voice by breathing from your diaphragm and developing a range in tone which will improve both your voice and your conversational appeal.

NAMES AND TITLES

Sometimes it's hard to know just what to call a person when he is very junior or senior to you. A senior officer and his wife may call a junior officer and his wife by their first names in an informal and friendly manner—but they are still "Colonel and Mrs. Smith" to you, the junior officer, unless you are requested to call them by their first names.

Officially, senior rank is always observed when speaking with or referring to an officer, regardless of how well you know him. Socially, close friends call each other by their first names regardless of age or rank.

A man does not call a woman by her first name until she takes the initiative, such as calling you by your first name or asking that you call her by hers. Then, you are free to use her first name.

ASKING FOR FIRST DATES

Although the majority of young men attending the Service Academies and in ROTC units are experienced in asking girls for dates, there are some who have had little time or inclination to date before entering these institutions.

Upon first meeting a girl, a rather shy young man usually "talks around" the problem of asking her to drag for the first time. If you are that young man you might say something like, "Do you like sports?" If she replies in the affirmative, you might mention the Army-Navy game or any specific occasion when you can drag. She will usually give you some kind of a lead indicating whether or not she has been asked to the occasion, and in her manner or answer will be a clue to tell you whether or not she would like you to ask her.

If she seems favorably interested, then you can say, "How would you like to meet me after the game and go on to the Brigade hop?"—or to the movies, or whatever the occasion might be. In the case of a fourth classman, you would ask the girl to meet you at the place or occasion limited to your opportunities of meeting young ladies.

Some young men are afraid that a girl will turn them down, thus hesitate to ask for a date. In turn, the girl may be afraid to seem over-eager when you show interest, and what appears to be coolness on her part may be a bit of stage fright. So *ask*.

If a girl, however, refuses you twice, then you should hesitate to continue the pursuit. But do learn to take an occasional refusal with poise—she may have a very sound reason why she cannot accept your invitation.

RULES TO REMEMBER

Do:

- Have something to say—and say it well. Brief amusing stories, a news item, unusual incidents, a TV personality—all are conversation starters.
- Be a good listener.
- Develop the art of small talk; this is pleasant talk about nothing in particular, but does *not* include official or harmful subjects.
- Learn to remember names and faces; nothing will make you more popular.
- Put a shy person at his ease by getting him to talk about his hobbies, pets, children, or known interests.
- Put yourself at ease—by thinking of the *other* person.
- As a host, act as moderator and intervene in a monologue, a "dead" group, or a controversial discussion, by changing the subject.
- Talk in a moderate tone of voice.
- Keep your eyes and ears open—and, occasionally, your mouth *shut*.

Do not:

- Gossip. Say nothing about a person that you would not want him to hear.
- Talk business at a social gathering.
- Substitute sarcasm or ridicule for wit.
- Interrupt or contradict others.
- Monopolize any conversation.
- Talk over anyone's head, or "talk down" to anyone.
- Be "greasy"; insincere flattery is unwelcome.
- Talk endlessly; silence, at times, *is* golden.
- Allow a guest to be stranded with a conversational bore.
- "Clam up"; a shy guest is a burden to a host, who thereupon must force conversation.
- Exclude anyone from a conversational group.
- Give the state of your health when someone says, "How are you?" This is simply a polite expression, generally used in greetings or "small talk."
- Talk about a party you have been invited to—when others have not been invited.

CHAPTER 23

Good Manners Before
an Audience

Any officer in the services must be able to speak effectively in any situation. At the Naval Academy, the need for public speaking is considered so important that midshipmen receive formal classroom instruction in speech, and after-dinner speaking is required of the First Class. In this course, small formal dinners are held at the Academy, with each First Classman delivering a certain number of brief speeches during the year. The dinners are complete with toastmaster, guest of honor, and an instructor who gives helpful criticism. The dinners are prepared under conditions approximating those which can be expected later.

After graduation from the Academies, Officer Training School, or Officer Candidate Schools, an officer will find that one of the most important aptitudes which he (or she) can possess is skill in addressing a group. From the very beginning of his career, he will find himself called upon to address a division aboard ship—or a company ashore—to enter into general meetings in the wardroom or barracks—and to discuss professional matters before groups of other officers at critiques, etc.

Later on he will find himself drawn into the public life of his community. He will be called upon to deliver speeches upon patriotic occasions, to present proposals in public meetings, and to be an active member of service clubs and civic organizations.

Preparedness for such a role is one of the responsibilities which you will assume as a person in public life, where the general public expects experienced leadership from officers in the services. The responsibility for group leadership may not be something that you desire—but it may be something that you must assume.

When you are asked to be president of a PTA or chairman of service

273

night at Rotary, you cannot plead inability to speak in public, or ignorance of parliamentary procedure. The public knows better. They know that you had the opportunity to learn these things, and they expect to find you, if not an expert, at least well grounded in the fundamentals. The best grounding that any officer can have is a clear understanding of the proprieties of public speaking, and the forms of courtesy to be followed when addressing a group.

In effect, public speaking is based upon one's ability to win the interest of the audience, to "get over" to the group, and to treat every man with courtesy and consideration.

It is an axiom in public speaking that your first important objective is to create a favorable relationship between your audience and yourself before attempting to deliver your message. The impression which you leave with an audience is almost as important as the message which you have delivered.

Dale Carnegie recognized the relative importance of this relationship of a speaker to his message in the title of his book on public speaking: *How to Win Friends and Influence People*. You will note that "friendship" ranks ahead of "influence."

APPEARANCE

The *appearance* of the speaker is the first thing an audience notes; then his *mannerisms*, and next his *voice*. A speaker in uniform should be at his or her best—your uniform immaculate, your posture relaxed perfection. A man in civilian dress should be conservatively dressed, tie in order, suit pressed, and hands out of pockets. A speaker should not stand or sit ramrod-stiff; neither should his hands or feet be in constant motion.

An audience expects the speaker to recognize and address properly the leader or chairman of the meeting. It also expects him to use correct forms of address when speaking to the group as a whole, or to an individual member. A speaker can be as polite—or as impolite—to a group of people as he can be to a single person.

PERSONAL CONDUCT IN SPEAKING

You should always avoid "talking down" to a group, or "over their heads." It is insulting to an audience to address them as though you are the only one who knows anything about a given subject—even when you are an expert in that particular field. You should avoid the over-use of the first person pronoun: "*I* think—," "*I* know—," or "*I* did—." Simplicity and ease of speech are as important as your subject matter.

Your yardstick in speaking (or writing) is: Can people understand what I mean? A familiar word is better than a "show off" word or phrase; a short word is preferable to a long one.

No audience likes to hear a speaker apologize for himself or for what he has to say. Any apology puts the speaker on the defensive. Apologetic and self-conscious gestures such as clearing the throat, jutting the chin up and down, straightening a tie, rebuttoning your coat, shifting from one foot to another—all such gestures make an audience as uneasy as the speaker.

Although most words spoken in private conversation are just words, some of these same words may set up a chain reaction against you when used in a speech or before an audience. Experience will teach you what these words and expressions are—either yours or another's—and they should be mentally catalogued "fighting words" and not used again.

From various viewpoints, such *fighting words* could be; "We of the intelligentsia—," or, "You military dictators—," or, "You civilians couldn't understand our service."

To the listener, such words and expressions indicate a disregard for his personal feelings—regardless of whether he is only one of hundreds in the audience and has never seen you before. The listener may merely consider you highhanded for some expression—but you will still be unpopular. A joke which seemed so amusing to one may seem like ridicule to another— if the shoe fits, so to say.

You should be respectful of others' opinions at a meeting, and should attempt to look at various viewpoints from all sides before making up your own mind on a subject. You must always be fair—but firm.

Always give credit whenever credit is due, but be careful of the timing in expressing a compliment made in public. An ill-timed compliment may embarrass the recipient as well as give an impression of "fawning" upon him.

THE FUNNY STORY

A brief amusing story of reminiscence, a good joke, or a good quotation are all ice-breakers at the opening of a meeting. Such stories must be *good*, however, or the speaker will lose his audience and will have to try harder than ever to win them over.

The first rule in telling a story is that it must be amusing to you, the speaker, or you cannot expect it to be funny to your audience—unless you presume them to be of lower intelligence than yourself. In this case, you have played down to your audience.

The second rule is that a joke sparkles best in brevity.

You must, of course, be fully aware of the type of audience you will address when speaking before a club or organization: large or small, mixed or stag, rural or cosmopolitan. You should take into careful consideration the racial, religious, political, and age groups involved. The type of club or organization will determine the tone of your talk, and you must make certain that your material is in keeping with the spirit of the occasion.

An off-color story is a dangerous story to tell before an audience at any time. Such a story told in a locker room or in a foursome may seem to be hilarious to those few—but when the same story is brought out at a public or private gathering, particularly before a mixed group, the one telling the story may be marked as a crude, vulgar, or uncouth oaf.

Lastly, at no time and place must you ever allow your sense of humor to desert you. A good sense of humor will protect you from the barbs of others— intentional or otherwise—and you will also be protected from becoming "too full of yourself."

PARLIAMENTARY PROCEDURE

It is essential that everyone have some knowledge of parliamentary procedure, whether you are the presiding officer at a meeting or the member of an organization who usually prefers to sit in the back row and just listen. You can never tell when you might be moved to "rise to a point of order."

The nationally recognized book on parliamentary procedure is *Robert's Rules of Order Revised.* Incidentally, this book was written by a West Pointer, Class of 1857—Brigadier General Henry Martyn Robert—who became Chief of Engineers, U.S. Army.

ON YOUR OWN

CHAPTER 24

Places of Entertainment

MOVIES AND THEATERS

Without taking a poll, it is safe to say that just about everybody has attended a movie. Yet, in general, there is a lack of common everyday courtesy among many movie-goers—including the peanut and popcorn eater, the paper rattler, the loud whisperer, and the big hat wearer. There is always the person who passes back and forth in front of you; then there is the character who lolls in his seat and overflows on the arms of your seat.

Your manners at a movie or theater ought to be the same whether you go alone, in a group, or escort a woman of any age. Common courtesy should be observed at all times.

A man of any age escorting a woman should take her past the first doors into the lobby where she may wait while you buy the tickets. If the line is long and the weather pleasant, she may prefer to stand outside in line and talk with you.

After you have bought your tickets and have given them to the doorman, you take off your overcoat, when wearing one, in the lobby. Your guest may also take off her coat, but women usually prefer to leave their coats on until after they sit down, when they lay them back over their chair backs.

Before going down the aisle, you should ask your guest where she would like to sit—in front, near the center, etc.—then you will tell the usher so that he can seat you accordingly. She will follow the usher to the seats, ahead of you, and enter the row first.

When there is no usher, or when he is busy elsewhere, you may walk *ahead* of your guest and look for suitable seats. After you have found them, you should step aside and allow your companion to precede you into the row. You should take the aisle seat, so that when you need to go after something you will not have to step in front of your guest. Also, if any question should arise, you will be in a better position to discuss it with the usher.

You always want to be certain that your guest is comfortable, and that she can see the screen or stage. When a hat worn by a woman sitting in front of you blocks your visibility, it is your responsibility to ask the person to please remove her hat—but this must be done with courtesy. When those around you are talking so loudly that you cannot hear well, then you must quietly speak to those persons. If anyone will not comply after a polite request, you may ask the usher to take care of the situation.

However, in looking after the comfort of your guest, you must remember that there are others to consider, and any inquiries concerning her welfare must be made quietly in order that you also are not being a nuisance.

On your way to your seats, particularly if these are in the center of a section, you must be careful of the people you are passing. You should pass facing the screen, as quickly as possible, and you may say "Excuse me" or "Thank you" in a low tone. Watch out for the coat you are carrying, for it often sweeps the heads of people in the row in front of you. And, needless to add, you should be careful not to step on anyone's toes. The persons already seated usually draw their feet well under their chairs and out of harm's way.

Once you are in your seats, you should assist your guest with her coat, and will manage to do this without blocking the view of those seated behind you. The best place for your own coat and hat is in your lap, or your coat may be placed over the back of your seat and your hat balanced on your knees or placed in the rack under your seat, when such is provided.

There is little reason for conversation at the movies or theater, but if you *must* talk, then by all means whisper softly. If you are also one who cannot get through a movie without a little snack (which is banned at many movies as well as theaters), then get something that doesn't crackle when the wrapper is removed or when you are eating it.

Fortunately, smoking is forbidden in most American theaters; however, in some European theaters, particularly in London, it is permissible to smoke during the performance and most seats have ashtrays built into their backs.

Although a darkened movie or theater may have romantic music and a sentimental plot in the picture or play, and the over-all feeling is one of accelerated emotion, do not engage in demonstrations of affection. If for no other reason, remember that you paid good money to *see* the show—not *give* it.

After the movie is over, you precede your guest to the aisle, where she will walk ahead of you to the lobby. Do not assist her with her coat until you reach the lobby; there you can also put on your own coat as well.

When you attend a movie in a large group, or when you are the host to such a group, you will tell the usher how many seats you need and ask if it is possible to get them together. You will precede your guests to the seats, following the usher, and see that guests will be seated in mixed order. When you are host, you do not permit anyone else to help pay for the tickets; when you are guest, you do not insist on paying, or helping pay for them.

If the group decided to attend the movie on the spur of the moment, then couples will go "Dutch treat," with the men paying for their drags or guests.

When a lady gives the movie or theater party and asks you to buy the tickets (usually in advance) and gives you the money for the tickets, you should *not* offer to pay or feel any hesitancy in taking the money.

At the regular theater, you are expected to be on time, with curtain time usually 8:30 P.M. for an evening performance. You may check your hat and coat for a quarter, or you may place them in racks under your seat. But a bulky overcoat is always a problem, and checking it is convenient—unless you are in a hurry after the performance. You may buy a program before taking your seats, but this is not necessary, since the theater management issues a plain but sufficient program. If you want a more detailed program, one is enough for two or more persons.

There are always ushers at theaters, and you should wait for an usher to show you to your seats, with your guest preceding you. During intermission, you may want to go to the lobby for a smoke. If your guest does not care to join you, you may excuse yourself and go ahead. If she cares for a smoke and you don't, you accompany her to the lobby and wait for her.

When the lights in the lobby are dimmed, or when a bell rings, the management is signaling that the next act is about to begin and you must return to your seats immediately. Don't linger over the last drag on your cigarette, and then be forced to stumble over someone's feet in a darkened theater.

If for some very good reason you are late at curtain time, you should stand in the back of the theater until the first intermission.

After a particularly well-enacted scene, you may want to applaud the actor—but if your timing is wrong, this can destroy the effect that the actors are trying to achieve. You remain in your seat until the curtain has been lowered for the last time, then you leave.

OPERAS AND CONCERTS

Operas and concerts are other forms of entertainment that you will encounter through the years. If you are a music lover, you will attend such entertainments at an early age. Frequently, you will be invited to attend either function as a guest. Although the opera once was a full dress affair, you will see a few men in "white tie" and some in "black tie"—and quite a few males in dark business suits. Your hostess will indicate what you should wear; otherwise you should ask her.

If your hostess is a patron of the arts, she may have a box. Each box concontains chairs which are arranged in pairs from the front of the box—where the most desirable seats are—to the rear. It is customary for the hostess to sit in the first row, on the chair farthest from the stage, with the ranking woman guest seated by the hostess in the seat closest to the stage. The ranking man will be seated directly behind the hostess, with the host seated behind the ranking woman. Unless your hostess especially assigns you a seat, you should take the rear seat farthest from the stage.

At concerts, the conductor of a symphony orchestra will turn around and face the audience at the end of a number—and you should not begin applauding until he does so. At a piano recital, you do not applaud between the movements of a sonata, or a similar piece of work, even though the pianist momentarily stops playing.

If you should have the misfortune to develop a coughing or sneezing fit, you should leave the room or auditorium, since any noise is disturbing to an artist.

Intermissions are plainly marked on the program, and this is the only time that you should leave the auditorium, other than for necessity.

Encore numbers are played or sung after the artist has received a number of curtain calls, or after much applause. He will indicate that there will be an encore, and this cue stops further applause.

If the music at an opera or concert is too classical for your uneducated ear, never fidget or show signs of boredom. Most of the other people there will be enjoying the music, and you should not interfere with their enjoyment.

PRIVATE CLUBS

Private clubs, in one form or another, exist all over the country. The types most familiar are the country clubs, the fraternities and sororities at colleges and universities, and the officers' clubs at military installations.

Civic organizations and service clubs, such as Rotary, the Chamber of Commerce, and the Military Order of World Wars have large memberships, and their goal is civic improvement and national and international good will.

Most young men have belonged to a club of some type in high school or preparatory school, where membership was based upon similar tastes and qualifications. Such clubs may have been the 4-H Clubs, Greek letter fraternities, DeMolay, Boy Scouts, athletic organizations, square dancing groups—and many more. The principles of working together are first learned at such clubs, then in colleges and universities where the activities are more advanced but where the principles of working together are the same.

A country club is more of a luxury club than other type clubs. There is usually a club house, golf course, swimming pool, tennis courts, etc. The membership is by invitation, and there probably will be a large initiation fee and sizable monthly club dues.

When you are invited to be a guest at such a club, you should look upon the invitation in somewhat the same manner as being asked into a home.

You will take part in the current activities (customarily, there is a Saturday night dinner dance). On the golf course, you are not expected to pay for anything other than your caddy fee although if you are invited by the same member more than once, you should offer to pay your greens fee. And it is always a mark of politeness to offer to pay your host's caddy fee as well as your own.

Most country clubs have the chit system of signing for services—food, drink, cigarettes, etc.—so that a guest cannot pay for anything. If you are a frequent guest, however, you should suggest some arrangement with your host for sharing expenses; and if he refuses—which he probably will—you should try to repay his hospitality in some way of your own.

The country club may be a very large one, but large or small, you must not take liberties. You should not be careless with cigarette ashes and sprinkle them on the floor, and you do not shove furniture around or roll back the rug when you want to dance. If you must clear a space, you should ask your host or the club manager first; there usually are club rules to this effect.

As a guest, you must remember that your host has accepted the responsibility of introducing you into his club and to his friends, and you naturally do not want to turn this responsibility into a liability. In brief, do not embarrass your host. You will not barge up to a good looking young lady and introduce yourself and say you are Bill Jones's guest—because Bill Jones may not know her either! And if he does know her, he will make the proper introduction—just as he would at home.

Sometimes, when you are stationed in an area where friends of your family or friends of your own are members of a private club, you may be given a guest card for a limited time. The card will be given to you by your friend, or it may be mailed to you by the club. This card must be handled with discretion.

A guest card means that you enjoy the privileges of the club, and that you pay for these privileges—such as food, drinks, and any small fee that accompany the use of the swimming pool or golf course. Sometimes these fees are printed on the card, but, if not, you should inquire at the club's business office concerning such fees. You should realize that there is usually a moderate charge to the member for each guest card which he requests.

When you accept the guest membership, you take the card to the office, where your name is placed on the guest list. You will leave your address where bills are to be sent, and, upon your receiving the bill, you must pay it *immediately*. When you do not pay, your bill is placed on the account of your sponsor—and you may lose a friend. Guest cards do not give you the right to nominate *anyone else* for guest cards in the club. Customarily, a guest card does not give you the privilege of taking guests to the club for meals, etc.

Many private clubs in metropolitan areas have restricted memberships.

Some of these clubs have rooms where members live, or rooms where out-of-town members may stay briefly. The atmosphere of such clubs is more home-like than at a country club, and there will be fewer members.

Private clubs are usually located in the city proper, and generally have rooms for entertaining. There will be a dining room, a library, lounge, and bar, besides bedrooms. Members of these clubs are usually friends of long standing. As a guest, your behavior must be circumspect.

The problem of money is the same here as at the country club—you cannot pay for privileges. If you are given guest privileges for a limited period of time, you are charged with these privileges as at the country club. Although the private town club is more intimate, you yourself must not presume to intimacy with the members.

Many older members of private clubs have many little privileges: certain chairs in certain parts of a room may be "theirs." A table by a window at one side of the dining room may always be occupied by a certain man or group at a given hour. It is well to respect such desires of austere members.

Before or just after leaving a tour of duty, you should write notes of appreciation to all clubs, officials, and individuals that have shown you special courtesies. Such a note should be written to the president of the club.

Most private clubs—including country clubs—do not permit tipping. However, the locker room attendant at the country club may be tipped when he has done some special service for you. You may ask your host what is the usual tip for such services in his club.

COLLEGE FRATERNITIES AND SORORITIES

Men's social fraternities and women's sororities will have their own houses on or near the campus of colleges and universities throughout the country. Anywhere from 40 to 100 members make these houses their homes during the academic year, and a housemother is assigned to each.

Membership is by invitation, and the houses are governed by strict rules of manners and conduct. Infractions of rules cause the members to be fined, and a serious infraction may result in the failure of a candidate to be accepted or the expulsion of one who is already a member.

As a guest, you must observe the fraternity's house rules—particularly those concerning drinking and gambling. At most colleges and universities. drinking and gambling may have as heavy a penalty as at a Service Academy.

A national social fraternity is a closed organization, with private weekly meetings, and a guest should not ask questions concerning these meetings. Any questions concerning the history or membership of a fraternity are in order, but not its business.

Lastly, a guest should endeavor to follow any custom of the fraternity or sorority, such as singing the fraternity song at the table, and standing while singing it.

At a sorority house, the housemother is more in evidence than at a fraternity house and respect is always shown her. As with "drag houses" in Service Academy communities, you are not allowed above the first floor in a sorority house. Most sororities have a curfew, also, and you must be careful to get your date back to her house on time. You will not be permitted to stay on at the house after curfew, so don't try. As a rule, most sorority houses do not have male guests for casual meals, but you will probably be invited for more formal dinners.

Although the interest in fraternities and sororities is mainly confined to college days, many national alumni chapters are formed in cities throughout the nation, with active membership participation.

OFFICERS' CLUBS

Officers' clubs will become the most familiar type of club life which you will experience in your own professional life. Most major stations and posts, both in the United States and overseas, have an officers' club to which you will automatically be extended the privilege of joining. Some of these clubs have monthly dues and others do not, but every officer should join the club of his station and give it wholehearted support.

The majority of these clubs are located on the station or post proper, and have a dining room, several lounges, and a bar. Each club has its own house rules, and you should be quick to discover what they are. You should always take pride in your club, and treat it with the same respect and thoughtfulness that you would your own home.

Some clubs use the chit system, whereby all services must be paid for with chits from a coupon book that you buy from the office. Others are on a cash basis only, and still others have members sign their orders on chits provided for that purpose. When the club is on the latter system, you will be billed at the end of the month, and, as with all other bills, you should pay your club bill promptly. If you do not—and the last date for payment is usually made known to you by the house rules—you may be placed in the unfortunate position of having your name posted in some prominent place as a delinquent member.

As a member, you may have as many guests as you wish—but a young officer must remember that on the chit system the bill is *yours*. If you are with a group whose male members are not in the service, you may settle the bill between yourselves later—but do not do this in front of women guests.

Your conduct in any officers' club must be beyond reproach. There may be many senior officers present, who, though not in your party, may be visiting the club, and loud, boisterous behavior may attract unwanted attention your way. Remember, this is an officers' club, not a boys' or girls' club.

Although the question of rank does not assert itself as such at an officers' club, you should show the same courtesies to senior officers there that you would anywhere else. Respect to age and rank will prompt you into the correct approach when greeting and speaking with seniors; you should neither hold back nor forge ahead.

Dress in all clubs is prescribed by the house rules; some clubs permit sport shirts without ties until 6 P.M., other clubs are more formal. When you visit a club at another station—or a club of a different service—it is wise to find out in advance if there are any big differences in club regulations.

You will find through the years that your officers' club life is an integral part of your service life, and as a member, it is up to you to help keep the club standards high.

CHAPTER 25

Good Sportsmanship

Good manners at sports contests are synonymous with good sportsmanship. Every officer has taken part in athletics at some time in his past, either as a player in the game or as an observer on the sidelines, and undoubtedly will take part in many future games.

The impression of a lady or gentleman is frequently gleaned from behavior at sports events. In the world of sports, there is a saying to the effect that, "If you want to find out what kind of a man he is, play golf with him when he is off his game, or go fishing with him when they aren't biting."

Good sportsmanship embodies the ideals of fairness, self-control, support of the team, and performing to the best of one's ability and honor. Qualities of this nature are expected of anyone, anywhere.

It is good sportsmanship for midshipmen and cadets to cheer when it is announced that another Service Academy is winning a game. You want the other Academy to win every game—except, of course, the one with your own Academy!

Although no one likes to lose, a good loser will compliment the winner on his skill, and a good winner will commiserate with the loser's ill luck.

OFFICIALS

The spectator is always very much a part of any game. The player reacts to the roar of the crowd as much as the fan thrills to the exploits of the player. The officials of the contest are also aware of the spectators and must always be on the lookout for the person who attempts to interfere with the rules of the game, or who tries to intimidate the official by heckling him.

An official is empowered to eject from the stands anyone who abuses the rules of the game and he may stop the contest when discourteous actions continue after due warnings. Thus a penalty may be invoked on a team, or, when the action is serious, the game may be forfeited—which means that one or more spectators can be responsible for the loss of the game by their favorite team.

Officials of amateur or professional contests are selected after passing rigid examinations in a particular sport. The rules of the contest which they enforce have been adopted after intensive study by national sports associations, and the spell out the conduct of play that will ensure fair play for all concerned.

The decisions of officials are matters of judgment made according to vantage point and interpretation of rules. When a spectator becomes enraged over a ruling, he should realize that officials are calling the rule as they see it. Whether you agree or not, you must abide by the decisions of the official in charge of the contest.

BOOING

The American baseball fan is a peculiar brand of individual of intense loyalty to the home team and at the same time its most severe critic. He knows better than the manager when to bunt, hit, and run. The "bum" of the previous inning may become the hero of the day by a timely hit. The fan seems to be a maze of contradictions, and is consistent only in his inconsistencies.

The baiting of umpires at baseball games may be a trend of the times—but it is very poor manners. And throwing debris on the field or at the players and umpires, running onto the field of play, or using abusive or profane language, are most flagrant displays of bad manners.

While enthusiastic cheering for your favorite athlete or team is expected, booing a decision or play which goes against your team is not only childish, but also unsportsmanlike.

SPORTS ETIQUETTE

The most common breaches of good manners at sports events are excessive noises made by spectators or players in an effort to divert the opponent. This interference includes shouting, whistling, clapping of hands, dropping of objects, sudden movements of the arms or legs, or any other distraction.

The sports program at the Service Academies covers the proper behavior of midshipmen and cadets at all sports events, from both the participant and spectator viewpoint. Almost twenty sports are covered. Among the rules of courtesy discussed are those of keeping quiet when an opponent or a member of your own team is attempting a free throw in basketball, a putt in golf, a strike in bowling, or a rally in tennis. Any game of skill demands concentration by the player.

Displays of temper, such as obscene language or fighting, defeat the purpose of the game. Spectators should conduct themselves in such a manner that they do not reflect discredit upon their Academy or college. This includes conduct during liberty periods following the game as well as at the game itself, and is particularly important for uniformed personnel, as the entire service may be judged as rowdy by the isolated indiscretions of a few individuals.

Since many football games are played during inclement weather, there is a problem of personal comfort versus good manners. An umbrella may keep the rain from your head—but it may also block the view of someone behind you. Also jumping up with an umbrella during an exciting play is not without its hazards for those sitting nearby.

Football games are frequently played in weather that is uncomfortably cold for the spectator. A number of persons use this is as an excuse for consuming alcoholic beverages in the stands. This is not only illegal in many stadia, but is a reflection upon the individual. The uniformed member of the Armed Forces has a special responsibility to conduct himself in a gentlemanly fashion.

In golf matches, no one should move, talk, or stand close to or directly behind the ball or hole when a player is making a stroke. Attention should be paid to the casting of shadows between the hole and a ball about to be played. Players should leave the putting green immediately upon determining the result of a hole.

When a ball is lost, or when your twosome or foursome is taking excessive time to play, you should signal other players behind you to go through you and should wait until this second group has played past you and is out of range before continuing play.

When a woman is in your group, you need not carry her golf bag—this is her responsibility. Presumably, she is in good health and able to carry her own bag or she wouldn't be on the course.

The fast-moving game of tennis requires good manners by the spectators in that players are distracted by moving objects in their range of vision. A tennis ball in flight moves with great speed and any unexpected movement in the neighborhood can throw a player off his game. Any movement at the opposite end of the court, especially, should be held to an absolute minimum.

If you should be sitting in a stand that faces more than one court, you should not move from one match to another until play is over. You do not applaud during a rally, but you may when the point has been played out. Errors such as a shot that goes out of court or into the net should not be applauded even if it gives the point to your favorite player. You only express approval for *good* strokes.

A number of specific sports have not been mentioned—not because they are less important, but because the good manners at other sports are similar to those already discussed. The basis of the rules in any sport is the creation of a spirit of fair play. The line between the rules and good manners is a fine one. The distinction might be set in this manner: the rules prescribe penalties to be invoked when there is a violation, whereas there generally is no penalty for a breach of etiquette *except* the censure of your neighbors or the public.

YOUR ALMA MATER

Every service or college man is proud to hear the song of his Alma Mater played or sung. Midshipmen and cadets stand at attention when their own Alma Mater is played or sung, therefore it is good manners that you stand when the song of your opponent's Academy or college is played or sung.

PAYING YOUR WAY

When you are invited as a guest to play on the golf course at a country club, you will want to pay your own way whenever you can. Usually, your invitation is a privilege extended to you by a member, and you should be prepared to pay all other costs—or as many as your host will permit. Such expenses include greens fees, caddies, food, drink, etc.

In making sure that you do the proper thing without embarrassing your host, you must be alert to size up the situation correctly. First, you should find out if the club runs on a cash or a chit basis. Where everything is paid for in cash, the guest has no problem. In such cases, when the member host signs you in, you will have your greens fee ready. If your host *insists* that he takes care of the fees, you will accept and thank him. When he pays for the greens fee, however, you should pay for both caddies.

In some clubs, the greens fee of members and their guests is billed to the member at the end of the month. In this case, you cannot pay your fee, and you should be careful about offering money to your host—unless he is a good friend, and you have made arrangements ahead of time.

When everything is by chit service, you can pay for nothing, and it is useless to insist. Then, you should return your host's hospitality by inviting him to your ship or station, or to some other function of comparable degree.

Sometimes you will be entirely upon your own by virtue of having been introduced by letter or by telephone by your host. In this case you will pay for whatever you can, and make certain of keeping a record of any charges that you have signed on your host's bill, so that you can send him a check promptly. Since you have signed chits in his name, you will generally know how much the charges are.

It is a custom at some clubs for everyone to go no-host or "Dutch treat." When a guest of yours is not aware of this custom, you may make a comment about "chipping in" or "going Dutch treat." And when you yourself have been the recipient of considerable hospitality in which you have not financially participated to your full share, you should unobtrusively press upon the main provider of the group a bill large enough to cover any expense incurred in your behalf.

Certain customs often prevail at clubs, and everyone should be aware of them. For example, the winner of the money at golf is often expected to stand the group to a round of drinks. As a guest of the club, you may wonder how to go about this. The best way is to step forward promptly and say that you want to buy this round—or you may ask your host what is customary at his club. But in any case, you should *make the offer*.

As an officer (sometimes as a VIP) you may run into occasions when you are not expected to pay for anything, and where offering to do so might be in very poor taste. In such cases you usually are the guest of a man who is wealthy or someone who has known your family for a long time—or, perhaps, the host is an older man who desires to extend full hospitality to you as a young officer.

When you go on a boating trip with friends, you may volunteer to split the expenses or to bring a carton of drinks and some food. There must be an understanding beforehand, however, otherwise you may show up with a lot of provisions that merely duplicate your host's preparations. On the other hand, you may find yourself an empty-handed co-host.

When fishing with friends, the host always offers to divide the catch regardless of who caught the fish. In the case of an accident, you replace any lost tackle as soon as possible.

In game fishing, the no-host kind of situation is customary, with a group chartering a boat and splitting expenses. Game fishing is luxury fishing at its best, and is expensive. Prices vary for chartered boats at different ports, the standard price for a charter with three or four persons is $75 to $100 a day.

In party boat fishing, when many people go out, the standard price is $6 for each person for a half-day.

The problems encountered with a skiing party are slightly akin to those of a safari—you usually travel a distance to get to your destination, and you stay a weekend or overnight at least. When unmarried women are in the group, dormitory-style lodging is customary, and the ladies usually pay for their own lodging. Tipping is similar to that in any hotel.

On a hunting trip, guests are expected to bring their own clothing, gun, and ammunition—unless the host has specifically said that he has equipment for all hands.

When you are a guest at a private game preserve or hunting camp, you may be assigned a guide. You should tip the guide anywhere from $2 to $5, depending upon the length of your stay and the services you received. This tip, of course, is in addition to the share of the guide's wages which courtesy or custom would assign to you.

PAYING A WOMAN'S WAY

It was once considered gentlemanly for a man to offer to pay for a woman's expenses, no matter what. When accompanying a woman on a train or subway, or while on a casual shopping trip, a man offered to pay for the transportation, meals, magazines, or whatever she fancied—within reason.

Today, a well-mannered woman who may only be a casual acquaintance will refuse to permit you to pay for such items. She will not object if you buy a magazine or a soft drink, and perhaps even pay a taxi fare—but usually, when the taxi fare is high, she will offer to pay for her own share.

When young people find themselves traveling together to the same destination, by chance or by pre-arrangement, there is no need for a man to pay a woman's expenses, other than for small trifles.

CHAPTER 26

The Overnight Guest

As the host or as the guest, you will frequently extend or receive an invitation to stay overnight. As the guest, you may be invited to stay with a friend when you are passing through his city. A midshipman or cadet will be asked to spend the holidays with a roommate, for example, or to attend a house party. Usually, your friends are in about the same moderate circumstances as yourself, and you will act in their home as you would in your own. As the host, you expect a houseguest to be congenial and courteous.

THE WEEKEND GUEST

The weekend guest is probably the most frequent type of overnight guest. The invitation to stay for a limited number of days is extended in person, by telephone, letter, telegram, or any convenient way. The guest should answer immediately, and his reply must be definite.

When accepting the invitation, the guest must make it clear when he expects to arrive and how—whether by car, plane, or train. In the latter cases, the guest may need to be met by his host, thus the time of arrival is important. When refusing the invitation, the guest must always say *why*.

The host will give advance information concerning the weekend so that a guest will know what to bring with him. When something special is planned —a formal dance, a boating trip, golf, tennis, etc.—the host should suggest the necessary clothes or sports equipment needed. If the hosts do not mention anything in particular, the guest may take for granted that the weekend is informal—but it is better to *ask* than to be caught unprepared.

A guest is always concerned about what luggage to take—what is necessary, what he can get along without. Most guests bring too much luggage, rather than too little, which is cumbersome to all hands. The proper amount is frequently decided by the method of travel—plane, train, or car—but a "two-suiter" with perhaps a small bag, and a shaving kit, takes care of an average weekend. As the name implies, a "two-suiter" bag is just large enough for two suits and the necessary changes of clothing for a few days.

It is a good investment for any officer to have presentable luggage. Although good luggage is expensive, you will need it for the rest of your life, since you are a traveling man or woman. It is wise to invest in good quality luggage as soon as you can afford it.

THE HOUSEGUEST

A houseguest is a guest who stays a longer length of time than an overnight or weekend guest. When you are the houseguest, you may have a suite of rooms and a private bath, or you may fall heir to a small room and share the bathroom with members of the family. But as long as you are a guest in the house, you *must not* complain.

HOUSE PARTIES

As a member of a house party, a man can expect to room with other male guests—but this dormitory-style life should be no problem for you. You must be pleasant with all other guests, many of whom you may never have met before. It is important that you get all names straight at the beginning of the visit—it is a compliment to a stranger that you remember his name. On any house party, the hosts always try to have guests who will be congenial company for each other.

WHAT TO TAKE

In this day of "drip-dry" shirts, pajamas, slacks, and "stretchie" socks, you can take less clothing—which packs easier—than ever before. What you will need depends upon where you will visit—the climate, type of community (a summer colony or a city apartment), etc.—but no matter where you go, travel as light as possible.

Usually, a man needs a dark or conservative suit, shoes, a sport jacket, and slacks—which you will probably wear on the trip—and an extra pair of slacks; one pair of pajamas, two changes of shirts a day, socks, changes of underwear, and house slippers (soft and crushable ones that will take little room in a bag).

For an informal weekend, you will need more sport shirts, a sweater, Bermuda shorts, extra pair of slacks, and swimming trunks, rather than dress clothes. If you are driving, you may take your golf clubs and shoes, tennis racket, or anything else. When your hosts plan a special occasion—such as deep sea fishing, you need not worry about fishing gear, since your hosts will undoubtedly have all necessary equipment or they would not plan such an occasion.

When formal entertaining is planned, you will need your dinner jacket. If you do not own one, take your blue uniform (or service equivalent) with black bow tie, or your summer whites or blues.

After you have packed everything you need, recheck your luggage—particularly your shaving kit—or for women in the Services, your cosmetic kit. Persons who travel on short notice should have a check-off list taped on the inside of the shaving or cosmetic kit, or some other convenient spot. You should include in your list such items as toothpaste, aspirin, cigarettes or cigars, etc.

DUTIES OF GUESTS

The duty of any guest is to be congenial at all times. If you are the guest, then you will not want to be hard to please, a person who contributes little to the pleasure of others. When you take part in a game, try to join in the fun, whether you happen to prefer tennis, quoits, or charades. When you truly can't participate in the activity, then you must give a valid reason.

In a servantless household, a guest will not make himself a burden to his hosts. It is important that you be on time for meals. Your hostess usually tells you at what time meals will be served—so be there. The matter of being on time holds for any activity in which you may engage—a boat trip, a golf game, or any planned event. If anything, be a little ahead of time.

The hour for breakfast may be a minor problem in a household: the host may go to work early, the family may be early or late risers, the children may get off to school in the usual early morning confusion. A hostess may find it easier to send a tray to a guest's room when a guest needs to sleep late. If you do not care for breakfast, or eat lightly, say so and relieve your hostess of extra work.

A considerate guest will be alert to the household routine, particularly in small quarters. If you sleep on the sofa in the living room, then remember that that part of the house cannot be occupied until you are dressed. If you are adept at making beds—and you *do* know how—then it is helpful for you to make your own bed.

When a bathroom is shared by the family and guest, you should be careful not to overstay your fair time or use all the hot water. Try to leave the bathroom as neat as when you entered it. Do not leave damp towels on the floor, or a razor in the wash basin. Always hang up your clothes in your room, and do not leave your hat or gloves on the living room furniture.

You will want to offer to help your hosts when there are no servants, but do not insist if your hostess says "no." Try to be helpful, but don't get in the way.

A thoughtful guest will take a small gift to his or her hostess. Nowadays the old standby of a box of candy is *not* appreciated by a diet-conscious hostess. A small inexpensive gift that is always acceptable is a little bottle of good perfume such as many foresighted officers buy when on foreign cruises. It is a wise officer who buys many small and inexpensive gifts while in foreign countries—gifts that cost only a dollar or two there, but much more in this country.

A guest may choose to take a small gift to each of the children of the family he is visiting, rather than taking a gift to the hostess. In this case, candy or an inexpensive toy is a good choice. When a guest does not take gifts to his hostess or the children in the family, he may send something after his departure. Upon any occasion, flowers are always in good taste.

The rule of thumb concerning gifts is; they should never be expensive, but must always be of *good quality*.

OVERSTEPPING HOSPITALITY

When a guest is visiting in a town or community where he has other friends, he must be careful of using the house where he is staying as a springboard for renewing these other acquaintances.

When you are the guest, you must also remember not to talk endlessly on the house telephone. Your hosts may urge you to have your friends visit you in their home, and you are free do do so, but you must guard against overstepping your host's hospitality.

And if your friends are strangers to your hosts, you must make certain that such a visit would not inconvenience the household where you are visiting. It is better to visit or telephone your friends at times when your hosts have other obligations—or, better still, to save such visits until your own stay in your host's home is over.

ACCIDENTS IN HOMES

When something unexpected happens—such as your breaking a valuable object, or becoming suddenly ill—common sense will tell you what to do. In case you broke something which you can replace, you should replace it at your earliest convenience. If you cannot do so, you may send a gift which you feel your hostess will enjoy, such as flowers or a nice potted plant which can give pleasure for some time.

You will say how sorry you are for such a mishap at the time of the accident, and after your departure you will briefly state on your personal card, enclosed with the replacement or flowers, that you are sorry concerning the incident.

If you should become ill while on your visit, you will let your hosts know—and call a doctor. Any host would be distressed to learn that his guest was ill, but foolishly said nothing about it. Of course, the guest pays for all doctor fees or medicines especially bought for him.

DEPARTURE

When you leave the house—or any place—after a visit, be sure that you have not forgotten anything. A check-off list is handy to avert forgetting. It is a bother for your host to wrap and mail your razor or any other object, so don't forget it.

When you have said that you plan to leave at a given time—do so. Don't be persuaded to take a later bus; your hosts may be sincere in their invitation that you stay longer, but usually a family has other plans or obligations. Anyway, it's *time to leave!*

On the other hand, don't forget to let your hosts know well ahead of time when you expect to leave. It is not good manners to bring your packed bag into the living room and say *thanks* and *good-bye*, then leave. This is inconsiderate, because your hosts will probably wonder if you are hurt or angry, to leave so suddenly.

When there is a servant in a household, you will want to tip her or him something. In the South, many homes have the family cook who is an integral part of the family and whom you undoubtedly met during your visit. Before you leave, stop in the kitchen and give her a dollar or so, depending on the length of your stay. You do not hand the money to your hostess and ask her to give it to the cook—*you* hand it to the cook in person. And you should add something complimentary, such as, "Yours is the best spoonbread I've ever eaten!"

In a large home, unless your hostess asks that you do not give the servants a tip, you should give something to the valet or butler if they performed any services for you. Usually a dollar or so is sufficient, but this is determined by the length of your stay. (See Chapter 10, *Tipping*.)

As soon as you arrive home, or at your station, you will write a note of thanks to both your host and hostess (but addressed to the hostess). (See Chapter 17, *Correspondence*.) You should express your sincere appreciation for their hospitality, and mention some incident or party of note. Your letter should be on its way within two days after you have been entertained.

UNEXPECTED GUESTS

Service people are in a constant state of change, due to new duty stations; therefore they frequently are "on the road." Although it is a pleasant and convenient habit for longtime friends to stay overnight or a few days with classmates while en route to new stations, do not take advantage of being a classmate or descend on near strangers at your own convenience.

You should always telephone a would-be host, either at his office or home, before going to his home—regardless of how long you have known him. Then, you will know if it is convenient for you to stop by, either for a meal or overnight. There may be illness in the family, they may have other guests, or they may have made other plans for the very time you would be stopping there.

VISITS TO CIVILIAN COLLEGES

In visiting a civilian college, a midshipman or cadet should not be too surprised at the differences he will find—particularly the lack of regimentation of the students. Every college campus has its rules, regulations, and conventions, however, and you will discover that these actually differ but little in spirit from those to which you are accustomed.

Informality of dress is the rule at colleges, just as formality of dress is stressed at the Academies. You will further find that there are a few special rules by which the college community lives, and by learning them, you will establish yourself in a congenial friendship with people whose purposes in life are surprisingly similar to your own.

You may be a guest on a college campus, either as a member of an athletic team or as a social guest for the weekend. In either case, your Academy will be judged by your actions. A midshipman or cadet member of an athletic squad should follow the special instructions of the officer representative and coach during his stay on the campus.

As a social guest, the normal rules for a weekend guest apply here. You must be alert to observe the local ground rules, and follow them conscientiously. At all times, you must be congenial.

The rules for visiting a girl's college are necessarily more strict, but the weekends have been planned for the entertainment of men like yourself, and you will have a good time if you are a good sport and observe certain regulations—such as:

- Do not violate rules concerning drinking on or off campus.
- Get the arrangements straight concerning the time of your arrival, departure, transportation, clothes, etc. (You will be facing the same problem every "drag" faces when she comes to your Service Academy.)
- Remember that you have a hostess—and do not play wolf to the entire campus.
- Your hostess may reserve and pay for your room during your stay —and sometimes your meals and tips. But you will pay for taxis, flowers, refreshments, snacks, and all other such supplementary expenses.

CHAPTER 27

Hotel and Motel Manners

Unless you are an experienced traveler, there may be a moment of unease when you step up to the desk clerk in a hotel or motel to register. If you are newly married, a man may wonder about the best way to sign his name—and his wife's—and how much, and whom, he should tip.

Before you started your trip, however, you may have wondered where you could obtain the best information concerning hotels and motels in general. There are a number of reliable sources of information concerning places to stay in each state; such as the AAA, Tour Aids, and books and pamphlets put out by various organizations, individuals, and motel chains.

When you know where you will be at a certain date, and approximately what hour, you should write or wire the selected hotel or motel for a reservation, and if time permits you should ask that the reservation be confirmed. In your letter or wire, you should specify the price of the room that you want, the number of people who will be occupying the room or rooms, what type of accommodations you need (a single room with bath, for example), and the expected length of your stay and the approximate time of your arrival. (See Chapter 17, *Correspondence*.)

Should your request be confirmed, be sure that you do not lose the confirmation; this little piece of paper can be very important when a busy clerk has bungled your reservation.

Any good hotel in any city in the country has a doorman who greets guests upon their arrival. When you are a guest and are arriving by car, you will tell the doorman that you would like a porter to come for your bags—unless you are smart enough to travel light and can carry your bag yourself.

If you plan to use the hotel's garage, tell the doorman and he will arrange to have your car taken to the garage. If you are not using the hotel garage, you may ask the doorman where you can park your car. Unless he does some special service for you, it is not necessary to tip him at this time. If you should arrive at the hotel by taxi, the doorman will open the taxi door, but no tip is required.

When you do not travel light and the porter has taken your bags to the lobby, he will direct you to the desk. If you have a reservation, you tell the desk clerk your name and say that you have a reservation. When you do not have a reservation, tell the clerk that you would like a room with bath—or whatever you want—and ask if such a room is available.

You will undoubtedly want to know what the price of the room will be, so ask. Say, "What is the price of the room?" If the price is more than you can pay, ask the clerk if he has something less expensive. When there is nothing else—you stay or you leave.

REGISTERING

If the price of the room is satisfactory, you will sign the register. It is necessary in all states and in all countries that you sign the hotel or motel register, writing your name and your home town, or your ship or station. Usually, the desk clerk asks for a street address, and at a motel, your car license number.

When you sign the register, you may write, "Lieutenant John Smith, Washington, D.C." In the case of married couples, you sign the register, "Lieutenant and Mrs. John Smith, Washington, D.C."; never "Lieutenant John Smith and wife."

After you have registered, the bell boy will precede you to your room with the keys. After he has deposited your luggage, turned on the lights, and asked you if there is anything else that you will need, you are expected to tip him. If you have one or two bags, 25 to 50 cents is adequate—provided that the luggage is not extremely heavy and that the bell boy has not done some service other than carrying your luggage. When there are several pieces of luggage, your tip should be increased, about 10 or 15 cents per bag, or more at an expensive hotel.

SPECIAL SERVICES

All hotels offer many personal services, and these services are usually spelled out somewhere in the room, along with the prices. In a big hotel, it is often perplexing to know to whom you should make your request. The easiest way is to pick up the phone and ask for "Room Service," telling whoever answers what it is that you want. Sometimes you will be referred to the "valet" (pronounced "val-lay"), in which case you ask for "Valet Service." Large hotels will have a central clearing house for service and "Room Service," and will tell you whom to call, or else will take your order directly.

For any special services, you can pay at the time they are received, or you can have the charge put on your bill by signing the check that accompanied the service. Should you need extra towels or blankets, call the "House-keeper." She will have a maid bring you the necessary items, but you must be specific in what you need. If you need one blanket and three towels, say so. In most hotels, the housekeeper also is in charge of lost and found articles.

Should the luxury of having breakfast in bed appeal to you, remember that food served in the room is always subject to a substantial extra service charge. If you must be economical, the coffee shop to be found in most hotels will have the fastest service at about half the cost.

ROOMS WITH—OR WITHOUT MEALS

European plan means that the price of the room does not include any meals. *American plan* means that the price of the room does include all, or some, meals. The latter plan is usually found in resort hotels, and has one disadvantage: You must take all your meals at the hotel or else you will be losing money. If you want to take your meals when and where the fancy strikes you, it is best that you select a hotel that does not operate under the American plan.

When you prefer the American plan, you will find that you are given a specific table in the hotel dining room which you will occupy at each meal— if the table meets with your approval—during your entire stay. In Europe, this same system is practiced at some hotels under the title of *pension*. When you register at a resort hotel, it is well that you inquire into the practice of serving meals.

HOTEL MANNERS

As a guest, you must be considerate of employees in a hotel, but you should always be impersonal. An important rule to follow in addressing service people in a hotel is to look at them, know what you are going to say, and speak distinctly.

When a guest appears uncertain or ill at ease, some hotel employees become careless with that guest's requests. A guest should be calm but firm when making requests—and, equally, should make no requests that are not reasonable.

You should tip in accordance with your income, the hotel's reputation— and the service rendered. If the service has been poor, you will tip accordingly. While you may not want to under-tip, it is just as bad taste to over-tip —particularly when you cannot afford it.

MOTELS

Motels are a boon to the traveling man or family. The average motel differs basically from a hotel in that there are almost no services provided, no garage problems, and almost no tipping. There is little fuss and bother; you arrive and leave without delay.

At the more expensive motels, you will tip the boy who carries your luggage a quarter for each bag and for bringing ice to your room.

Before you register or pay out any money at a motel, you should ask the motel operator to show you the room that you expect to occupy. This first-hand inspection gives you the opportunity to make sure that the room is clean, in order, and that it meets your standards. If not, you may ask to see another room—or not accept it at all, and go on your way.

Accredited motels are approved by various qualified organizations and they are inspected at regular intervals. You will soon learn to recognize these organizations, for all motels are anxious to advertise the fact that they are approved courts.

Motels require that you pay in advance of your occupancy in order to facilitate early morning checkouts, so be ready to pay promptly upon registering. When you are driving cross-country and know where you will be the following day or night, it is advisable to make advance reservations. In the summer months and in resort areas, motels are generally full by late afternoon. When you find a motel chain that you like, it is well to stay with it on your whole trip. The various managers will assist in solving the advance reservation problem free of charge.

MOTEL MANNERS

Although you are paying for the motel room, you are to treat it with the same respect that you would the belongings of another person. Before taking ashtrays and towels as souvenirs, stop and consider how much it would cost you if guests in *your* home carried off ashtrays and towels.

STRICTLY SERVICE

CHAPTER 28

Salutes

Various customs concerning salutes are covered in the regulations of each service, as well as in specific regulations of the Service Academies, and the reserve and officer training programs.

All servicemen and servicewomen should know the regulations not only of his or her own service, but of all services. The rules for military etiquette are founded on custom and tradition, and their strict observance forms an important factor in the maintenance of discipline which must be observed equally by all officers and enlisted personnel. The responsibility is a mutual one in which the junior accepts the role of initiating the act of courtesy.

ORIGIN OF THE SALUTE

These are various schools of thought on the origin of the salute, one tracing the custom to the days of chivalry when knights in mail raised their visors to friends for the purpose of identification. The junior was required to make the first gesture, in keeping with gradations of rank.

Another possible origin of the salute goes back to the days of the Borgia, when assassinations by dagger were not uncommon, and it was customary for men to approach each other with raised hand, palm to the front, to prove that no dagger was concealed.

However, from the earliest days of military organization, the junior uncovered when meeting or addressing a senior; gradually, the act of uncovering was simplified into touching the cap and, finally, into the present-day salute which means: "I greet you."

THE HAND SALUTE

The hand salute is required on naval and military installations both on and off duty. At other places and times, it may be suspended by regulations or local order.

You will always salute the commanding officer (or any flag or general officer) any time you meet him during the day. You should salute your other seniors the first time you meet them each day. Remember "Precept and Example"; those of less rank than you will imitate you, for better or for worse.

MANNER OF SALUTING

The hand salute is executed by raising your right hand smartly until the tip of your forefinger touches the lower part of your headgear, slightly to the right of your right eye.

The upper arm is parallel to the ground, thumb and fingers are extended and joined, the palm is down, and there is a straight line from the tip of the middle finger to the elbow.

The salute is concluded by dropping your hand down to your side in one clean motion. Avoid slapping your leg as you do so.

In the Army and Air Force, when uncovered you touch your right eyebrow instead of your hat or cap brim.

It is important that you keep your head and eyes turned toward the saluted person.

SALUTING DISTANCE

Saluting distance is that distance at which recognition is easy. Usually it does not exceed *thirty paces*. The first position of the hand salute is rendered when the person to be saluted is *six paces* distant, or at the nearest point of approach if it is apparent that he is not going to approach to within six paces. Twenty-five paces is not considered excessive. Hold the first position of the salute until the person saluted has passed or the salute is returned, then you execute the second movement of the hand salute.

A salute is rendered only at a halt or a walk. If running, a person comes to a walk before saluting.

When overtaking a senior, and the junior must pass him, the salute shall be given when the junior is abreast of the senior and the junior should ask, "By your leave, Sir?"

It is customary in the Air Force that, when a senior officer on foot approaches a junior, the junior render the salute *at or within twelve paces*. Should the junior be at double-time when he encounters the senior, the junior slows his pace to quick-time, renders the salute, then resumes double-time. Should the senior wish to speak to the junior, the junior salutes as the senior approaches and again when the conversation is terminated.

Salutes are usually accompanied by an exchange of greetings, depending upon the time of day, such as: "Good morning, Sir," or "Good evening, Colonel Blank." The customary greetings are:

- From early morning until noon: "Good morning—."
- From noon to evening meal: "Good afternoon—."
- From evening meal until turning in: "Good evening—."

COVERED—AND UNCOVERED

In the *Army* and *Air Force*, you salute when covered or uncovered.

Navy and *Marine Corps* protocol does not call for saluting when uncovered except for the return of uncovered salutes rendered first by Army or Air Force personnel. The exception in this case follows the general rule that "*Social customs or military courtesy should always be interpreted so as to prevent awkward situations.*" Therefore, the Navy establishes an exception whereby any uncovered salute may be returned.

Individuals *under arms* uncover only when:

- Seated as a member of or in attendance on a court or board
- Entering places of divine worship
- Indoors and not on duty
- In attendance at an official reception
- Entering messing facilities during meal hours.

In certain public places, such as a church, theater, or hotel dining room, servicewomen wear their hats or caps when men do not. In such instances, women are technically "uncovered" and do not salute.

WHEN TO SALUTE

The salute is rendered but *once* if the senior remains in the immediate vicinity and no conversation takes place. If a conversation does take place, the junior again salutes the senior on departing or when the senior leaves.

In making reports, the person making the report salutes first, regardless of rank. An example of this is the case of a regimental commander making a report to the brigade adjutant during a ceremony or a commander head of department making a report to a lieutenant officer of the deck.

When men and/or women officers are of the same rank, they salute simultaneously.

The saluting requirement varies upon certain occasions, such as:

- If you, the senior, are in the company of a junior or company grade officer and a field grade officer approaches, the salute will be initiated by the field grade officer who salutes you, the ranking officer. When you return the salute, the junior or company grade officer will salute simultaneously with you.
- If you are in the company of a senior officer and a junior approaches, you salute at the same time as the senior, and you hold your salute until after both officers have dropped theirs. If the senior is unaware

of the junior's salute, do not interrupt him by rendering your salute to the junior.

• Customarily, you will salute with your right hand. If an injury prevents your doing so, render a left-hand salute.

REPORTING TO AN OFFICER

The salute is always rendered by the junior on reporting to a senior. Juniors are expected to rise and stand at attention whenever a senior officer enters their room or an office in which they are present, and remain standing until the senior gives permission to *carry on* or *at ease*.

A junior shall stand at attention when formally addressed or when being addressed by a senior. If covered, the junior shall salute when first addressed and again upon the conclusion of the conversation. If uncovered, the junior stands at attention throughout the conversation unless otherwise directed.

Midshipmen, cadets, and other officer candidates are subject to local regulations which generally require that when addressing an officer, during the salute and before entering upon any conversation, they give their names —as, for instance, "Midshipman Doe, Sir," or "Sir, Cadet Thomas reports to Captain Brown." The salute is held throughout the report and until it is returned by the officer.

It is customary to relax this procedure as officer candidates approach graduation and as they become known to their senior officers. This is a matter for the officer candidate's own good judgment. The word "Sir" shall always be added to statements by the very junior; thus, "I report for duty, Sir." The "Sir" or "Ma'am" is a military expression which is always used in connection with "yes" or "no," whenever conversing with senior men and women officers.

Reporting indoors unarmed: When reporting to an officer in his office, a junior not wearing arms removes his hat or cap (and any outer garments such as an overcoat, raincoat, or overshoes), knocks, and enters when told to do so. Upon entering he should approach to within about two paces from the officer and stand at attention. While standing, a salutation such as "Good morning, Sir, I wish to make the daily magazine report," should be spoken. When the business has been terminated, he leaves promptly.

On shipboard, the salutation and the manner of conducting the following business will ordinarily follow prescribed lines of official informality as befits working shipboard life. Too rigid formality must be avoided. The respect due the senior officer is a most important factor of the situation and as long as this is shown in a sincere manner, proper shipboard procedure will not be a problem.

Reporting indoors, under arms: Ordinarily, in the services reports are not made indoors under arms except in rare cases. In carrying a rifle, a junior enters with the rifle at the trail, halts, and renders the rifle salute at *order arms.* When wearing sidearms or duty belt, the hand salute is given and the hat is kept on.

Reporting outdoors: The procedure outdoors is the same as described in the foregoing two paragraphs. The hat is never removed outdoors, and the junior armed with the rifle may, in approaching the senior, carry it at the trail or at right shoulder arms. He executes the rifle salute at the order or at right shoulder arms.

It is improper to change the rifle position when addressing or being addressed by a senior except during a formal inspection. For example, if at right shoulder arms upon approaching or being approached by a senior, you render the salute at the position held. This avoids awkwardness which would result if the junior approached the senior at right shoulder arms, then came to the order—and then rendered the salute.

The term "outdoors" is construed to include such buildings as armories, gymnasiums, and other huge-roofed enclosures used for drills. Theater canopies, covered walks, and other shelters open on the sides to the weather, are also considered outdoors.

"Indoors" includes offices, corridors, etc. The expression "under arms" means carrying the arms, or having them attached to the person by sling, holster, or other means. In the absence of arms it refers to the equipment pertaining directly to the arms, such as cartridge belt, pistol holder, or automatic rifle belt.

SALUTING IN GROUPS

In formation: Individuals in formation do not salute or return salutes except at the command, "PRESENT ARMS." The individual in charge will salute and acknowledge salutes for the whole formation. Commanders of organizations or detachments which are not a part of a larger formation salute officers of higher grades by bringing the organization or detachment to attention before saluting.

An individual in formation *at ease* or *at rest* comes to attention when addressed by a person superior to him in rank. The group will remain at attention until directed by the senior, "CARRY ON," at which time it is proper for the group to resume normal activity. The group will continue to be aware of the senior's presence during the time he is in conversation with members of the group, or whatever his business may be.

Not in formation: On the approach of an officer of higher rank, a group of individuals not in formation is called to attention by the first person noticing the senior officer, and all in the group come to attention and salute. Individuals participating in games, and members of details at work, do not salute. The individual in charge of a work detail—if not actively engaged—salutes or acknowledges salutes for the whole detail. A unit resting alongside a road does not come to attention upon the approach of an officer.

However, if the officer addresses an individual or group, they come to attention and remain at attention (unless otherwise ordered) until the termination of the conversation, at which time they salute the officer.

SALUTING IN AUTOMOBILES

A senior officer passing in an automobile is entitled to a salute, which will be returned when conditions permit. If driving, he will not return a salute when safety is involved. An official car will carry a plate with stars appropriate to the flag or general officer's rank. Juniors should salute and have no concern whether or not the salute is returned.

In some cases, it may be awkward (due to the presence of ladies or civilians in the car) for the senior officer to return the salute properly. He may then make recognition by a modified salute or a slight nod of the head.

Salutes are not exchanged between persons in different moving automobiles, or between persons in moving automobiles and pedestrians, except:

- When an automobile is clearly marked to indicate the presence of a flag or general officer.
- When required as part of a ceremony.

In case a detail is riding in an automobile, the individual in charge will render the hand salute for the entire detail.

Juniors must be alert to notice the passing of automobiles from which the flag of a high ranking dignitary is displayed and, when such is observed, be punctilious in saluting the occupant of the car. These salutes shall be rendered at all times, day or night, on all occasions when meeting or passing near a senior officer, whether he be covered or not, except upon occasions of such informality that saluting might become continuous or awkward. In circumstances where local regulations prescribe special procedure, those regulations take precedence.

You should remember that officers of high rank, civilian leaders of the state and federal governments, and foreign dignitaries will have the insignia of the highest ranking passenger displayed on the automobile in either flag or plate form.

COURTESIES TO INDIVIDUALS

When an officer enters a room, midshipmen, cadets and other juniors present will uncover (if unarmed) and stand at attention until the officer directs otherwise or leaves the room. When more than one person is present, the first to see the officer commands "Attention!" in a sufficiently loud and clear tone.

When an officer enters a room used as an office, workshop or recreation room, those at work or play therein are not required to come to attention unless addressed by him. A junior, when addressed by a senior, comes to attention—except in the transaction of routine business between individuals at work.

A junior shall always answer "Sir" or "Here, Sir," when his name is called by an officer. However, it is preferable for the junior to call the senior by his title and name, such as "Captain Jones," rather than by the impersonal "Sir." Women officers are addressed as "Ma'am" or by rank, and are accorded the same courtesies as for men.

Juniors escorting young ladies will, on meeting their senior officers, render the customary salute. If seated, you should rise and salute. It is customary for the lady being escorted to remain seated. However, on both occasions, it is considered good form for her to look at the officer being saluted, during the period of the salute, and to that extent she will join in the recognition by her escort of the senior officer.

Civilians may be saluted by persons in uniform, but the uniform hat or cap is not raised as a form of salutation. In turn, the civilian gentleman will tip or raise his hat.

Midshipmen or cadets are expected to salute their contemporaries on duty when addressed by or addressing them officially, and they salute the professors at the various Academies and Colleges.

All officers must remember that personal likes and dislikes having nothing to do with salutes. Therefore, you salute those whom you like and those whom you do not like, without discrimination.

WHOM TO SALUTE

As a member of the services, you will salute all individuals who are senior to you in rank in any of the Armed Forces of the United States or of friendly foreign governments, and also officers of the Coast and Geodetic Survey and of the Public Health Service who are serving with the Armed Forces of the United States.

In addition, there are certain appointed or elected civilian members of both our National and State governments who are so honored. Among the individuals of the United States you customarily salute are the following:

- President of the United States
- Vice President of the United States
- State Governors
- Secretary of Defense
- Senators and Congressmen of the United States
- Deputy Secretary of Defense
- Secretaries of the Army, Navy, and Air Force.
- Assistant Secretaries of Defense
- Under Secretaries of the Army, Navy, and Air Force.
- Assistant Secretaries of the Army, Navy, and Air Force.
- Officers, male and female, in any of the U. S. Armed Forces.

Among the members of the friendly foreign governments whom you salute are:

- Heads of State
- Ambassadors
- Ministers of Defense or other civilian leaders of Defense Establishments and their assistants at or above the level of the Assistant Secretary of the Army, Navy, and Air Force.
- Officers, male or female, in any of the Armed Forces.

WHEN NOT TO SALUTE

In some situations, the salute is not appropriate. In general, you do *not* salute when:

- Engaged in routine work if the salute would interfere.
- Indoors, except when reporting to a senior or when on duty as a sentinel or guard.
- Carrying articles with both hands or being otherwise so occupied as to make saluting impracticable.
- The rendition of the salute is obviously inappropriate.
- A prisoner (the guard does the saluting for the prisoner).
- Working as a member of a detail, or engaged in sports or social functions.
- You are the driver of a moving automobile. However, whenever practicable, you should return the salutes of others.
- In places of public assemblage such as theaters or churches, and in public conveyances.
- You are in the ranks of a formation. However, if at ease in a formation, you come to attention when addressed by a senior.

CHAPTER 29

Flag Etiquette

A military man is expected to be something of an expert upon the national flag, including its history, its etiquette, and the customs and conventions which govern its display and handling. But regardless of whether one is in military or civilian life, every loyal American citizen should know the history of his country's flag.

HISTORY

With the onset of the American Revolution each of the thirteen colonies created its own flag, frequently several of them. They were symbolic of the country and the struggle, carrying a tree, anchor, rattlesnake, or beaver and a motto such as "HOPE," "LIBERTY," or "AN APPEAL TO HEAVEN." A noted one bore a coiled rattlesnake and the motto "DON'T TREAD ON ME." Each regiment raised had its own colors, and the naval vessels and privateers fitted out by each colony flew distinctive flags.

Clearly some standardization became necessary as the colonies drew closer together and the Revolution grew. On December 2, 1775, the Continental Congress approved the design of a flag to be flown by the ships departing to intercept British supply vessels. This flag was first hoisted the following day aboard the *Alfred*, at Philadelphia, by Lieutenant John Paul Jones. It consisted of thirteen red and white stripes and, on a canton, the British Union Jack with its crosses of St. George and St. Andrew.

On January 1, 1776, identical flags were displayed in the lines of the colonial forces besieging Boston, the same day that the new Continental Army came into being. This famous flag has been called the Continental flag and, later, the Grand Union flag. After the Declaration of Independence,

313

continued use of the British Union Jack became inappropriate, and a new flag was created. The first Act of Congress establishing the Stars and Stripes, June 14, 1777, ordained the present arrangement of stripes but merely stated that the thirteen white stars would represent "a new constellation" on a union of blue.

It is not surprising that different arrangements should appear. The Continental Army adopted a design in which the thirteen stars were arranged in a circle so that no colony should take precedence. The first Navy version of the Stars and Stripes had the stars arranged in a staggered formation in alternate lines and rows of threes and twos, on a blue field. Even variations in the stripes continued, and privateers continued to use the superseded flag with its British Union Jack. But eventually order emerged from what must have been a chaotic condition.

Both stars and stripes continued to be added: after the admission of Kentucky and Vermont, a resolution was adopted by Congress on May 1, 1795, making the flag one of fifteen stars and fifteen stripes. This flag flew over Fort McHenry on the occasion of its bombardment by a British fleet and inspired Francis Scott Key to write "The Star-Spangled Banner," later to become our National Anthem. This resolution provided for the addition of a stripe and a star for each new state.

Realizing that the flag would soon become unwieldy, Captain Samuel C. Reid, U.S. Navy, who commanded the *General Armstrong* during the War of 1812, suggested to Congress that the stripes be fixed at thirteen in number to represent the original thirteen colonies that had struggled to found the nation and became its first states, and that a star be added to the blue field for every state coming into the Union. This suggestion became the text of a resolution by Congress, effective April 18, 1818, whereby the flag should contain thirteen alternate red and white stripes representing the thirteen original states, with a new star being added for each new state on the July 4th following its admission. The flag next ordered had twenty stars.

During the Mexican War the Stars and Stripes had twenty-eight and twenty-nine stars; during the Civil War it had from thirty-three to thirty-five, no stars being removed because of the states which had seceded. In the Spanish-American War it had forty-five stars. During the first and second World Wars and the Korean conflict it had the familiar forty-eight stars. With the admission of Alaska as a state on January 3, 1959, and Hawaii on August 21, 1959, the forty-ninth and fiftieth stars were added.

The *jack*, a nautical device, corresponds in design to the blue field and its stars. It is flown from the jackstaff (in the bow) from government vessels while at anchor, provided that the National flag is being displayed. Another American flag frequently seen is the yachting ensign, displayed by privately owned craft, which consists of the thirteen red and white stripes and a blue field with thirteen stars and arranged in a circle about a white foul anchor.

HOW TO DISPLAY THE FLAG

The National flag should be raised and lowered by hand. It should be displayed only from sunrise to sunset, or between such hours as may be designated by proper authority. You do not raise the flag while it is furled. Unfurl it, then hoist it quickly to the top of the staff. In lowering it, however, lower it slowly and with dignity. Place no objects on or over the flag. For instance, various articles are sometimes placed on a speaker's table covered with the flag. This practice should be avoided.

When displayed in the chancel or on a platform in a church, the flag should be placed on a staff at the clergyman's right, and all other flags at his left. If displayed in the body of the church, the flag should be at the congregation's right as they face the clergyman.

Do not use the flag as a portion of a costume or athletic uniform. Do not embroider it upon cushions or handkerchiefs, or print it on paper napkins or boxes.

Other miscellaneous rules are:

- When displayed over the middle of the street, the flag should be suspended vertically, with the union to the north in an east-and-west street, or the east in a north-and-south street.
- When displayed with another flag, from crossed staffs, the flag of the United States of America should be on the right (the flag's own right) and its staff should be in front of the staff of the other flag.
- When the flag is to be flown at half-mast, it should be hoisted to the peak for an instant, and then lowered to the half-mast position; but before being lowered for the day, it should again be raised to the peak. By "half-mast" is meant hauling down the flag to one-half the distance between the top and the bottom of the staff. On Memorial Day the flag is displayed at half-mast until noon only, then it is hoisted to the top of the staff for the rest of the day.
- When flags of States or cities or pennants of societies are displayed on separate halyards, but from the same pole on which the flag of United States of America is being flown, the latter should always be hoisted first and lowered last.
- When the flag is suspended over a sidewalk from a rope, extending from house to pole at the edge of the sidewalk, the flag should be hoisted out from the building, toward the pole, union first.
- When the flag is displayed from a staff projecting horizontally or at any angle from the window sill, balcony, or front of a building, the union of the flag should go clear to the peak of the staff (unless the flag is to be displayed at half-mast).
- When the flag is used to cover a casket at funerals or ceremonies honoring a person deceased, it should be so placed that the union is

at the head and over the left shoulder. The flag should not be lowered into the grave or allowed to touch the ground.

- When the flag is displayed in a manner other than by being flown from a staff, it should be displayed flat, whether indoors or out. When displayed either horizontally or vertically against a wall, the union should be uppermost and to the flag's own right; that is, to the observer's left. When displayed in a window, it should be displayed in the same manner; that is, with the union or blue field to the left of the observer in the street. When festoons, rosettes, or drapings in the National Colors are desired, bunting of blue, white, and red should be used, but never the flag itself.
- In this country or in any parade of U. S. troops, when carried in a procession with another flag or flags, the Stars and Stripes should have the place of honor at the right; or, when there is a line of other flags, our National flag may be *in front* of the center of that line.
- International usage forbids the display of the flag of one nation above that of another nation in time of peace.
- When the flags of two or more nations are displayed, they should be flown from separate staffs of the same height, and the flags should be of approximately equal size.
- A federal law provides that a trademark cannot be registered which consists of, or comprises, among other things, "the flag, coat-of-arms, or other insignia of the United States, or any simulation thereof."
- At all times, every precaution should be taken to prevent the flag from becoming soiled. It should not be allowed to touch the ground or floor, or to brush against objects.
- When the flag is used at the unveiling of a statue or monument, it should not be used as a covering of the object to be unveiled. If it is displayed on such occasions, it should not be allowed to fall to the ground, but should be carried aloft to form a feature of the ceremony.
- The pledge to the flag is as follows: "I pledge allegiance to the flag of the United States of America and to the Republic for which it stands, one Nation, under God, indivisible, with Liberty and Justice for all."

APPROVED FLAG CUSTOMS

Laws have been written to govern the use of the flag and to ensure a proper respect for the Stars and Stripes. Custom has decreed certain other observances in regard to its use.

All services have precise regulations regarding the display of the National flag—when, where, and how it shall be hoisted or lowered.

In the *Naval Service*, when naval vessels are at anchor, the National

Ensign and the Union Jack are flown from the flagstaff and the jackstaff, respectively, from 8 A.M. to sunset. When other vessels are entering or leaving port, the flag is flown prior to 8 A.M. and after sunset.

When the ship is getting under way or coming to anchor, cruising near land, falling in with other ships, or engaged in battle, the National Ensign is flown during daylight from the gaff, or as directed.

It is the custom at all bases, posts, and stations to raise the flag every morning at 8 o'clock, and it remains flying until sunset or retreat (about 5 P.M.).

Only one flag may be flown above the Stars and Stripes, and that is the Church Pennant, a dark blue cross on a white background. Code Signal Books of the Navy, which date back to the early 1860's, state: "The Church Pennant will be hoisted immediately above the ensign (National flag) at the peak or flagstaff at the time of commencing and kept hoisted during the continuance of divine service on board all vessels of the Navy."

A chaplain's flag may be displayed at the place of divine worship or in his office, and it may be flown from the chaplain's car.

Civilian dignitaries of the federal and state governments, as well as flag and general officers, are entitled to individual flags which indicate their title or grade. They also have automobile flags which are attached to a staff on official cars.

The National flag may be displayed on all days when the weather permits, but it should especially be displayed on New Year's Day, January 1; Inauguration Day, January 20; Lincoln's Birthday, February 12; Washington's Birthday, February 22; Armed Forces Day, third Saturday in May; Memorial Day (half-staff until noon), May 30; Flag Day, June 14; Independence Day, July 4; Labor Day, first Monday in September; Constitution Day, September 17; Columbus Day, October 12; Veterans Day, November 11; Thanksgiving Day, third or fourth Thursday in November; Christmas Day, December 25; and such other days as may be proclaimed by the President of the United States, as well as on the birthdays of States (the dates of their admission into the Union), and on State holidays.

If a serviceman or servicewoman dies while on active duty, the flag for the funeral ceremonies is provided by the Service to which he or she belonged. However, if he—or she—dies as an honorably discharged veteran, the flag is provided by the Veterans Administration, Washington, D.C., and may be procured from the nearest post office.

In filling out the application, the person signing for the flag must state whether he is the next of kin or, if of other kinship, he must state his relation. The flag must be presented to the next of kin at the proper time during the burial service. If there is no relative of the deceased or, if one cannot be located, the flag must be returned to the Veterans Administration in the franked container provided for that purpose.

Postmasters require proof of honorable discharge of a deceased service member before issuing the flag for use at funeral ceremonies, but flags are issued promptly upon proper evidence being presented.

When the National flag is worn out, it should be disposed of with due reverence. According to an approved custom, the union is first cut from the flag; and then the two pieces, which now no longer form a flag, are cremated.

UNITED NATIONS FLAG REGULATIONS

The United Nations flag code prescribes that the United Nations flag may be displayed as follows:

- With one or more other flags, all flags should be displayed on the same level and be of approximately equal size.
- On no occasion may any flag so displayed be larger than the UN flag.
- On either side of any flag without being considered to be subordinated to any other flag.
- Normally only on buildings and on stationary flagstaffs from sunrise to sunset.
- The UN flag should not be displayed on days when the weather is inclement.
- The UN flag should never be carried flat or horizontal, but always aloft and free. It should never be used as a drapery of any sort, festooned, drawn back, nor up in folds, but always allowed to fall free.

The United Nations flag may be displayed on the following occasions:

- On all national and official holidays.
- On United Nations Day, October 24.
- On the occasion of any official event honoring the United Nations.

HONORS TO THE NATIONAL ANTHEM

Outdoors: The following rules are customarily observed whenever and wherever the National Anthem or "To the Colors" is played (not in formation):

- At the first note, all dismounted personnel present will face the music, stand at attention, and render the prescribed salute—except at the "Escort of the Colors" or at "Retreat" you face toward the color or flag. The position of salute will be retained until the last note of the music is sounded.
- Vehicles in motion will be brought to a halt. Persons riding in a passenger car or on a motorcycle will dismount and salute as directed above. Occupants of other types of military vehicles remain seated at

attention in the vehicle, the individual in charge of each vehicle dismounting and rendering the hand salute. Tank or armored car commanders salute from the vehicle.

* During *colors*, a Navy boat under way within sight or hearing of the ceremony either lies to or proceeds at the slowest safe speed. The boat officer (or in his absence, the coxswain) stands and salutes—except when dangerous to do so. All other persons in the boat remain seated or standing, and do not salute.
* The above marks of respect are shown the National Anthem of any friendly country when played upon official occasions.

Indoors: When the National Anthem is played indoors at a formal gathering, individuals will stand at attention and face the flag (if one is present), otherwise, face the music. You do not salute, unless covered or under arms.

Morning Colors is the daily ceremony of raising the National flag. *Evening Colors* or *Retreat* is the ceremony of lowering the flag and putting it away for safekeeping.

Retreat is a daily ceremony at Army and Air Force posts and bases, and is held at a definite time in the late afternoon, usually 5 P.M. During bad weather or when a band is not present for the ceremony, a bugle call, "To the Colors," is played instead of the National Anthem.

The *Retreat Parade* is the ceremonial parade in the Army and Air Force; the *Dress Parade* is the ceremonial parade in the Navy.

At posts and bases where there is a saluting cannon, the evening gun is fired—and this symbolizes the closing of the official day's routine duties.

IN CIVILIAN DRESS

Outdoors: All men in civilian dress remove their hats or caps and hold them with their right hand over their left breast. Ladies will stand quietly.

Indoors: All men and women stand quietly, facing the flag/or music, with their hands free at their sides.

OTHER HONORS

To colors: Military personnel passing an uncased color (standard) salute at a distance of six paces and hold the salute until they have passed six paces beyond it. Similarly, when an uncased color (standard) passes by, you salute when it is six paces away and hold the salute until it has passed six paces beyond you. Small flags carried by individuals are not saluted.

Personal honors: When personal honors are rendered, military personnel present salute at the first note of the music and hold the salute until the completion of the ruffles, flourishes, and march.

When a gun salute is rendered, military personnel being saluted, and other persons in the ceremonial party, will render the hand salute throughout the firing of the gun salute. Other persons in the vicinity of the ceremonial party will stand at attention.

Acknowledgment by persons in civilian dress may be made by standing at attention. A gun salute to the National flag requires no individual action. Other than standing at attention during dress parades—say, on the parade field at a Service Academy—all officers under the canopy are considered to be in the ceremonial party.

Military funerals: Military personnel will salute during the passing of a caisson or hearse in a funeral procession. You will salute whenever honors are rendered: when the body is removed from the hearse to the chapel, from the chapel to the hearse or caisson, and from the hearse or caisson to the grave. You salute when the volleys are fired and when "Taps" is sounded. In civilian dress, men will stand at attention, uncovered, and hold their headdress over the left breast. (See Chapter 36, *The Military Funeral.*)

MOURNING FLAG

The colors are hoisted to the peak of the flagpole or staff, and then they are lowered halfway. When the flag is removed, it is again raised to the peak before being lowered. Where flags cannot be flown at half-staff, they should have a black streamer from the spearhead halfway down the flag. Flags hung horizontally or perpendicularly should bear a black bunting border of appropriate width.

INCLEMENT WEATHER

Flags are not flown at night or in inclement weather. A code of display adopted by Congress on 22 June 1942 states: "It is the universal custom to display on the flag only from sunrise to sunset on buildings and on stationary flagstaffs in the open. However, the flag may be displayed at night upon special occasions when it is desired to produce a patriotic effect."

CHAPTER 30

Aboard Ship

WARDROOM LIFE

Wardroom country aboard ship is the naval officer's seagoing home—a home in which he should be proud to entertain his relatives and friends. It is also his club where he may gather with his fellow officers for moments of relaxation, such as a discussion of the daily problems, enjoying a movie, radio, musical or TV program, or just a game of acey deucey, or bridge over a cup of coffee. Whatever the event, it is a place where members should conduct themselves within the ordinary rules of propriety, common sense, and good manners.

All members of the wardroom mess have a collective responsibility for the wardroom's appearance, the service of food, and the cleanliness of officers' rooms and the wardroom country in general. Punctilious performance of duty by the stewardsmen can only be assured by the close attention of all officers and the exaction of high standards of service at all times.

The stowage, cleanliness, preservation, and appearance of the wardroom, galley, pantry, staterooms, and heads and showers set the pattern for the ship. In the Navy the expression is so often heard: "The standards set in wardroom country are the standards found throughout the ship."

Officers' country (the wardroom, staterooms, washrooms, and heads assigned to officers) is out of bounds for enlisted personnel unless these are on official duty. The wardoom is normally not to be used as an office by any member, so contacts with enlisted personnel should be confined to their part of the ship or to the departmental office. On a small ship, this may be your stateroom.

321

UNIFORM

The uniform of the day is the uniform in the wardroom, and it is also the uniform for dinner except on formal occasions. When khaki is the uniform of the day, the requirements for the wearing of the coat for meals is relaxed on some ships, depending upon the informality of the occasion and the desires of the commanding officer. When special guests or ladies are present, however, it is generally considered that the formality of the occasion demands that the coat be worn. Except when at sea, the tie should be worn with the khaki uniform. When at sea, the wearing of the tie, particularly for meals, is considered to be subject to the desires of the commanding officer. Short-sleeved shirts are worn with some uniforms.

Officers should not loiter or remain in the wardroom in civilian attire. An exception to this is when you are waiting temporarily for a liberty boat, or because of some similarly sound reason. Whenever civilian clothing is worn, it is expected to be in keeping with the dignity of the officer as well as of the occasion.

STATEROOM

An officer's stateroom should be orderly and clean at all times so that it presents an exemplary appearance to anyone who might enter. This involves an orderly manner of living by the officer himself as well as an adequate performance by the stewardsman assigned.

The stewardsman is responsible for cleaning the room, making the bunk, tending to the uniforms and belongings, and placing the stateroom in order at least once each day—and normally as soon after breakfast as practicable. It should be remembered, however, that stewardsmen have other staterooms assigned and wardroom duties to perform, and your co-operation is necessary to maintain your stateroom in shipshape order. The requirement for a neat stateroom is obligatory for all ranks.

Officers normally stow their own clothes and put out what must be cleaned. Slovenly habits of not stowing clothes are a frequent source of complaint against junior officers. If an officer improperly insists on doing some chores—such as tending to his laundry, carrying his chair to the movies, and jumping up from the table to help himself—you can rest assured that the stewardsman will not stop him.

RELATIONS WITH STEWARDSMEN

Every officer must always be civil and just in all his relations with stewardsmen. If you have a complaint, make it to the mess caterer or mess treasurer who has charge of the stewards.

The stewardsman is usually interested in his job of keeping your room shipshape—but don't expect him to take any greater interest in its appearance than you do.

In any financial dealings—such as asking the stewardsman to pick up your dry cleaning—be sure to give him the money for the payment, with the request that he return the change. He should never furnish his own money for your service.

In general, one word of praise is worth ten of censure in dealing with stewardsmen, and you accomplish most by keeping your tones cheerful. But remember—tipping of stewards is forbidden.

WARDROOM HABITS

You always remove your cap upon entering the wardroom. Never be boisterous or noisy in the wardroom; it is the home of all officers, and their rights and privileges should be respected. You should also show consideration for your fellow officers by moderating the volume when using the radio, phonograph, or television.

When playing cards, you should choose a table location that will not interfere with others.

Don't abuse the use of the duty stewardsman by sending him on long errands—other members are also entitled to a share of his services.

There is no objection to your dropping into the wardroom for coffee, but don't make a practice of lingering there during working hours. Such a practice may mark an officer as being the indolent type.

When you have finished with your coffee, set the cup and saucer on the pantry shelf or sideboard if there is no stewardsman immediately available. Remember that mess tables must be cleared at least 30 minutes before meals, in order to permit the stewardsmen to set up on time.

Wardroom magazines and newspapers should be carefully handled, not left adrift; neither should they be damaged, hoarded, or removed from the wardroom where they have been placed for availability to all members.

When smoking, you will ensure that an ash tray is available before lighting up. If ventilation is a problem, you should accordingly reduce smoking or else stop it completely.

Obscene, vulgar, and off-color tales do not belong in an officer's general conversation at any time—and are out of place especially in the wardroom. The junior officer pursues the correct course by being the best listener in the mess, the senior officer by setting the example of dress, manners, consideration, and intelligent conversation.

Unkind and unfavorable comments about other officers, and critical opinions about seniors, are not appropriate *at any time.*

When guests are present—especially when they are seated alongside you —engage them in conversation when the opportunity arises. Ship talk—a subject likely to be unfamiliar to some guests—should not be discussed in detail. Guests in any walk of life—teen-age youth or oldster—should never be "talked down to" nor treated condescendingly just because they are unfamiliar with service customs or matters.

MEALS

The hours for wardroom meals are designated by the president of the mess, subject to the approval of the commanding officer. (On small ships—destroyers and smaller— the president of the mess is usually the commanding officer.) Breakfast hours may be shifted from time to time to conform to daily routine. In any event, except for Sundays and holidays, the wardroom should be cleared by 0800.

Lunch is usually served at 1130 under way and 1200 in port. Dinner normally will be served at 1730 under way, 1800 in port or 1830 when in foreign ports. The custom of serving dinner at 1830 provides for time to make calls during prescribed calling hours, and the more leisurely dinner hour also permits the unhurried arrival of invited guests and allows sufficient time for officers returning from shore to shift into the uniform of the day prior to dinner. Punctilious arrival at meals is expected.

When troops or other officers not attached to the ship are embarked, it may be necessary to adjust meal hours in order to ensure maximum convenience and service for all concerned. On small ships, when the establishment of a wardroom mess is not possible because of the lack of personnel and facilities, officers may be subsisted from the general mess in accordance with the pertinent article from the *Manual of the Bureau of Supplies and Accounts*. In such cases, consideration should be given to adjusting the officers' meal hours to those of the general mess.

SEATING

Seating arrangements in the wardroom depend upon Navy tradition and custom, and are usually set up by the mess treasurer and approved by the executive officer. If there is any chance for confusion, a seating diagram should be posted on the wardroom bulletin board. The president sits at the head of the senior table with the mess treasurer at the opposite end. Members are seated at the right and left of the president in order of seniority. This system is also followed in seating officers who are aboard for temporary duty or for transportation.

Guests of senior officers usually sit at the senior table, with the honored lady on the right of the presiding officer, the host officer second, and other guests taking precedence over regular mess members. In large ships with a number of mess tables, the guests are seated next to their officer hosts and as close to the place of honor as possible. The space next to a guest should never be left unoccupied. At formal dinners, the use of place cards is desirable.

COURTESIES AT THE TABLE

The senior officer should be punctual in seating himself by the time the meal is scheduled to begin. In the event he is delayed, he should inform the next senior officer whether or not to proceed with the serving of the meal. Other members of the mess should arrive in the wardroom from three to five minutes prior to meals, in order to be present for introductions and to be seated at the same time that the senior officer sits down.

You never sit down to meals before the senior officer takes his seat. If you are *late* for the meal, you make apologies to the senior member at your table. If business *unduly detains* you, notify the senior officer present and ask the steward to save a ration for you; then eat later with the officers coming off watch. When you are to be *absent*, notify the chief steward in advance. This not only will permit him to arrange the seating but will enable him to do better planning and thereby reduce the mess bill.

During the serving of the meal, demands upon the stewardsmen for personal service should be kept to a minimum. However, you may ask the steward for a second helping if you desire it.

The senior officer present usually makes any announcements. If you have something you wish to bring before the members, request his permission and brief him on your subject. Officers going on watch should eat before regular meal hours and be clear of the wardroom prior to the regular meal.

All officers should promote a cheerful atmosphere at the table. A good rule to follow is: "Don't talk shop during mealtime, but save it until after dessert and coffee." The practice of smoking throughout the meal has never been sanctioned by Navy custom. You should wait until coffee is served before you light up.

You should never discuss religion or women in the mess. It is wise to avoid unfavorable comment about the food. If you have constructive criticism to make, privately advise the mess treasurer or mess caterer, who wants to do a good job.

Only under unusual circumstances should an officer be disturbed by professional matters during a meal. If the business is urgent, the officer should excuse himself from the table and conduct the business outside the wardroom.

If two seatings at the table are required, you must avoid unnecessary loitering at the table that may delay the second service. And you should never ask for meals to be served in your stateroom except in case of sickness or when especially authorized by the commanding officer.

All officers will remember to remove their caps when passing through *any* messing compartment at mealtimes and in sick bay.

GUESTS

The mess should have a written policy in regard to guests—which will ensure coverage of the following items: (a) How guests of any individual are to be distinguished from guests of the mess; (b) What charge, if any, is to be made for guests; and (c) What proportionate charge should be made for children as compared to adults.

Officers should be encouraged to bring their guests aboard ship for dinner, but not repeatedly. Each guest should be treated as the guest of the entire mess, and it is the duty and privilege of each member to carry out his social obligations as co-host.

An officer bringing guests into the wardroom will comply with the following procedure:

- Inform the mess president beforehand of any plan to have guests.
- Give the mess president advance background facts about guests.
- Notify the mess treasurer and steward of the number and names of the guests in order that place cards and seating may be arranged.
- Make certain that the guests understand, beforehand, the time the meal is to be served. This will permit them to arrive on time so as not to be embarrassed by either late or early arrival. If the ship is at anchor, the host should be sure that his guests are well informed as to the weather and the boat schedule.
- Ensure by advance arrangements that the guests will not be unduly delayed at the naval base gate because of identification.
- Be available on the quarterdeck to welcome guests aboard.
- Take the guests to his stateroom for removal of their coats and hats, if practicable, before mealtime.
- Designate a certain room for the use of women guests.
- Introduce all members present to his guests (each member should come forward to meet them).
- Arrange for the guests to depart at a reasonable hour. Generally, dinner guests leave within an hour after the movie, smoker or party.
- Notify the officer of the deck well in advance as to the boat in which the guests are to depart.
- If possible, accompany the women guests home, or have them accompanied by a fellow officer; otherwise, arrange for the women guests to return to their homes in groups.

EXCHANGE OF MEAL COURTESIES

It is courteous for the wardroom occasionally to invite the commanding officer—if he messes separately—to have a meal in the wardroom. The same courtesy is normally extended to the unit commander by the ship's mess president. The unit commander will appreciate an occasional invitation to a meal in the wardroom of the ships of his command—particularly the flagship. Included with the unit commander in all such invitations is generally the chief of staff (chief staff officer). In some cases, as appropriate and desired, the senior officers of the unit commander's staff are also invited.

It is customary for unit commanders and commanding officers, if maintaining a separate mess, to return such meals as opportunity permits. The difficulty of an all-inclusive return of such courtesies to each individual in a mess, should, however, be appreciated.

PAYMENT OF MESS BILL

Every officer attached to a ship belongs to one of the officers' messes in that ship, and he is required to pay to the mess treasurer the full amount of his mess bill monthly, and in advance. No officer is excused from such payment except as provided in Navy Regulations.

An officer ordered to detached duty, or sent to a hospital, is entitled to a rebate of the full amount of his mess bill for the period of his absence or as prescribed by his mess by-laws. An officer ordered temporarily to duty away from the ship to which he is attached, so that he does not avail himself of the privileges of the mess during such absence, is "ordered on detached duty" within the meaning of this paragraph, even though such duty is merely in addition to his duty aboard his regular ship.

An officer granted leave of absence for more than six days (including travel time) is normally entitled to a rebate of the amount of his mess bill for the period of his actual absence in excess of six days, but no rebate shall be allowed for the first six days of leave.

Officers and others in a transient or temporary duty status, who are not entitled to reimbursement for meals, shall be charged at a rate prescribed by the president of the mess. Officers in such status may become temporary members of the mess if their temporary duty becomes of an extended nature.

All of these above special cases are normally covered in the by-laws of each mess. Also, on small ships, and when the officer complement is too small to maintain a wardroom mess, the *Manual of the Bureau of Supplies and Accounts* provides for officers subsisting from the ship's general mess on a cost-per-meal basis. This provision is also applicable when ships are in the shipyard for overhaul and it is necessary to disband the organized mess.

During time of war, however, wardroom life cannot follow the pattern just described. Prolonged general quarters, additional watches, the disadvantages of concentrating officers in a single compartment of the ship— are all factors which modify peacetime conditions. The importance of the wardroom should not, however, decline; it is merely that each ship must alter her routine to fit the particular circumstances encountered.

SOCIAL ACTIVITY

There are many pleasurable ways that ship's spirit can be nurtured, all of which require the interest and participation of all hands and the example and direction of seniors. Included among these are:

- Mess nights—scheduled evenings when the mess members and their ladies and other guests gather aboard ship for dinner and/or entertainment (movies or smokers). Family night may similarly be held.
- Parties, picnics, and dances ashore at beaches and service clubs.
- Group participation in recreational and athletic opportunities.
- Various kinds and types of tournaments such as golf, tennis, bridge, chess, and cribbage.

It is one of the Navy's better customs to have a night (or more) each month designated aboard ship as "Guest Night," when the officers wear dress uniform and the "number one" dinner is served. Mess members know that in bringing aboard their wives, their dates, or guests to whom they wish to pay special honor, the guests will receive the most favorable impression of the mess, the ship, and the Navy.

Every wardroom mess should tender a formal dinner to the commanding officer at some convenient time soon after his assuming command. This should be a formal dinner with ladies attending, and with all hands present.

In similar fashion, a farewell dinner should be held in honor of the commanding officer prior to his being detached. These two dinners may be held separately, or a combined "Hail and Farewell" party is appropriate.

Informal farewell dinners and welcome aboard dinners for new members are generally not feasible in large messes. Additions and detachments of officers in large messes are best cared for at the regular monthly formal mess dinners when the president makes a brief speech of introduction or farewell for members—and their wives—who are leaving or "coming aboard." These officers then make suitable short responses.

In small messes of a dozen members or less, the number of arriving and departing members is generally such that each occasion may well call for separate observance. Outside entertainments by the mess need not follow any set rule but are governed by the individual circumstances, and the collective desires of the mess members, and personal desires to do things as a group.

VISITS AND CALLS ABOARD SHIP

You are expected to make an official call on your commanding officer in his cabin within 48 hours after reporting in. Beforehand, ask the executive officer when it will be convenient for you to do so.

When making the call in the prescribed uniform, be sure that your linen is clean and your uniform well pressed, and that you look your best. Before entering the CO's cabin, you would say, "Orderly, please tell the captain that Ensign Brown wishes to pay his respects."

Official courtesy calls should last no longer than *ten minutes*, unless the caller is specifically requested to remain longer. It is important that you learn to make a quick but courteous exit, and you should not stand in extended comments or long conversations after it becomes evident that departure is imminent.

During these initial calls, seniors closely observe their juniors, and modesty in demeanor and restraint in conversation are recommended for the junior.

In years past, a senior in sending an oral communication to a junior, would use this form: "Rear Admiral Jones presents his compliments to Captain Smith and says, etc., etc.," Such a message was delivered by an orderly. Today a less formal address may be used, according to the desires of the officer, but it is still perfectly acceptable to use the more formal greeting which includes "presents his compliments, etc., etc." A junior, however, *never* presents his compliments to a senior.

CALLS ON FOREIGN SHIPS IN FOREIGN PORTS

When an American warship calls at a foreign naval activity, the visited country's senior officer present will probably send a liaison officer to call upon the visiting ship's commander to offer courtesies and to exchange information as appropriate. This liaison officer is usually invited to the wardroom after his visit with the commanding officer. He gives pertinent information and assistance to wardroom members who are planning excursions ashore as well as to those who wish information in general about the port of call. If security clearance and official approval for such an act are obtained, it is proper to make the liaison officer an honorary member of the mess, with an invitation to live aboard during the visit. It is also courteous to include his family in an invitation to be guests of the wardroom for a visit.

After the prescribed exchange of official calls by senior officers, it is appropriate and courteous for committees of the visiting ship's officers to make calls on the wardrooms of the other foreign ships in port, in the same order in which the respective commanding officers have exchanged visits.

For this purpose the wardroom should have calling cards which are suitable for use in extending formal invitations for a meal, for movies in the mess, or for receptions.

The liaison officer may deliver to the wardroom guest cards or invitations to honorary membership in the port's officers' club, or country club, as well as invitations to social functions, such as cocktail parties or dances, etc. These invitations should be answered promptly, in handwritten replies. If visiting officers are made honorary members of any club, they should be sure to visit the club and sign the guest register there.

When your ship is in a foreign port for several days, it is desirable that members of the mess give a dinner to their foreign hosts to repay the hospitality and kindnesses that have been extended to the ship. A buffet supper usually is the most practicable method of entertaining.

Thank-you notes for all courtesies received during a visit should be written promptly by the visiting ship's officers upon its departure from the port.

CALLS ON FOREIGN SHIPS IN U.S. PORTS

When a foreign ship visits your home port, special rules of good manners and courtesy apply. A committee is customarily sent to the visiting ship to ask if there is anything you can do to make their visit more pleasant—especially if you have recently visited the home country of the ship, or when your own ship is close aboard the visitor. In some ports, when foreign ships arrive, the nearest ship of the home navy may be designated as the "host ship." It is then the host ship's specific responsibility to assist the visitor in any way possible. This usually includes— in addition to exchanges of visits and meals —a standing invitation for the movies and/or appropriate athletic and recreational events.

Generally, when more than one U.S. ship is present, the senior officer present designates a ship to send a committee; this action precludes too many visits.

ETIQUETTE OF THE QUARTERDECK

PIPING IMPORTANT OFFICIAL VISITORS ALONGSIDE

Piping a boat alongside—following a gun salute, if any—commences at the discretion of the boatswain's mate, lasts about 20 seconds, and ends as the official visitor steps onto the lower gangway platform. Those on deck cannot see this but may ascertain the progress of the honored visitor by observing the boatswain's mate, who stands where he has a full view of the visitor's movements. Those on deck stand at attention but do not salute during this pipe, and you will observe that the boatswain's mate does not salute. The visitor coming aboard takes no outward note of this pipe, but proceeds smartly from boat to gangway and ascends to the upper platform.

PIPING ABOARD

As the "piping alongside" ends, there is a pause, during which time the boatswain's mate steps back one pace and waits for the honored guest to ascend the ladder until his head reaches the level of the deck. At this point the boatswain's mate salutes with his left hand and commences piping the visitor aboard. All hands in the quarterdeck area salute—and hold the salute for the full duration of this pipe, plus the ruffles and flourishes or music, whichever shall be the last rendered.

As this "piping aboard" commences, the visitor ascends to the upper gangway platform, pauses, faces aft, and salutes the colors. He then turns, salutes again, holds his salute, and proceeds through to the end of the line of sideboys; then he halts, holding his salute until the end of the music. If there is no music, he holds his salute until he reaches the end of the line of sideboys. Still holding the salute he looks at the officer of the deck or senior welcoming officer, and says, "Sir, may I have (or, Sir, I request) permission to come aboard?" He then completes the salute, the boatswain ends his piping, and all hands on the quarterdeck area complete their salute.

Senior officers and ranking dignitaries have personal variations of this salutation when coming aboard, since in most cases they are acquainted with the senior officer greeting them and naturally make their salutation a personal one.

All hands stand at attention during the greeting ceremonies, which will frequently involve inspection of the guard, to be followed by introduction of the distinguished guest to certain principal officers on deck. During this personal greeting ceremony only those personally involved will salute, shake hands if appropriate, and be prepared for suitable short rejoiner if addressed. All others stand at attention until the visitor has left the quarterdeck and "carry-on" has been sounded.

Upon departure, notice is sent to the quarterdeck by the flag lieutenant, the sideboys are paraded, and all hands in the quarterdeck area act as follows:

Attention is sounded just prior to the arrival of the visitor on the quarterdeck. The visitor steps into the quarterdeck area, takes leave of the principal officers, turns, addresses the officer of the deck, and says, "Sir, may I have (or, Sir, I request) permission to leave the ship?" The visitor, holding his salute, proceeds through the line of sideboys, faces the national colors and pauses to terminate his salute, then proceeds down the gangway.

The boatswain's mate terminates his piping as the visitor's head passes below the level of the deck. All hands in the quarterdeck area terminate their salute and remain at attention when this pipe ends.

The boatswain's mate observes the visitor going down the gangway, and as the visitor steps into the boat, commences piping the boat away from the side. During this ceremony all hands in the quarterdeck area remain at attention but do not salute.

The gun salute is fired just before the boat comes alongside upon arrival, and as soon as the boat is clear upon departure. The visitor's boat lies to during the gun salute. All hands on deck stand at attention and salute during the gun salute.

The officer receiving the gun salute stands in his boat, faces the quarterdeck, and renders the hand salute from the first to the last gun.

It will be a high point in the junior officer's life when he receives side honors aboard ship. Therefore he should memorize the correct procedure so that he will not embarrass himself, his ship, or his country—because it might happen—that the first time he receives side honors might be aboard a foreign ship.

SALUTING ON THE QUARTERDECK

As already stated, all officers and men, whenever reaching the quarterdeck of a man-of-war, whether from a boat, a gangway, or from shore, shall salute the national ensign. And, as stated, in leaving the ship the same salutes shall be rendered in inverse order.

It was formerly customary for all hands to salute when coming into the quarterdeck area from any part of the ship. This custom is no longer strictly followed in some of the smaller ships, but is a custom that should be recognized.

In man-of-war routine today it is generally customary for all hands having no official business on the quarterdeck to keep clear. Those having official business approach the officer of the deck smartly and salute him and carry out their official conversation. Those having official reason to come on the quarterdeck, and whose business does not require that they address the officer of the deck, will generally approach the quarterdeck area in an alert manner, salute the officer of the deck if he is in the vicinity, and then speak to the quartermaster, or any other person with whom they have official business.

A person having entered the quarterdeck area while the officer of the deck is at the other gangway need not make a point of this initial salute until the officer of the deck has occasion to come near, at which time he should come to attention and render the salute.

The situation to bear in mind is that the quarterdeck is an official area, with very official responsibilities calling for a precise routine. This routine is governed by the officer of the deck, who is responsible. All strangers coming into this area, whether from off the ship or another part of the ship, should do so only for official reasons and should stay as short a time as possible and conduct themselves officially while in the prescribed quarterdeck area. Loitering in the area of the quarterdeck is never condoned.

LADY GUESTS ABOARD

When you bring a lady guest aboard, she will precede you. If this is her first such visit, it may be well to explain to her the proper procedure. Upon reaching the quarterdeck she should step quickly aboard—and then step out of the way so that you (her officer escort) will be clear as you execute the ritual of saluting the colors aft, and then turning and saluting the officer of the deck. It is well for her to be careful *not* to stand between you and the officer of the deck as you exchange salutes. You will then introduce her to the officer of the deck. If she wishes to make some recognition of the flag when coming aboard or leaving a ship, she should hesitate at the top of the gangway and glance up for a moment at the flag. When women are not military personnel, they are not privileged to honor the flag with a salute.

A woman member of the Armed Forces renders the same salute and honors as her male counterparts.

VISITORS

Strangers to the Navy way of life should be told—tactfully—in advance of a visit that liquor and pets are not brought aboard ship. There are various rules about bringing cameras on board, and these should be determined beforehand.

SHIP LAUNCHING

After a ship is authorized by Congress there are three ceremonial occasions during her construction and fitting out: the keel laying, the launch and christening, and the commissioning.

The construction of a large warship usually requires about three years from keel laying to launching. The name of the ship and its sponsors are chosen by the Secretary of the Navy upon the recommendation of the Chief of Naval Operations. There are over 125 types of ships whose name sources are not set by law but which have been standardized by tradition and approved by the Navy.

Although a ship is assigned a name long before she is launched, the ship does not receive her name until she is christened. Since mariners facing the unknown perils of the sea place their faith not only in a stout ship but in an unseen guiding spirit, the religious part of the christening ceremony is important.

Carriers are usually named for famous men, ships of the Old Navy, or historic battles; *cruisers* for cities; *submarines* for fish and other creatures of the sea; and *destroyers* for American heroes and Secretaries of the Navy.

Aircraft carriers are usually sponsored by the wives of naval personnel associated with aviation, and submarines are sponsored by wives of personnel in that service. Sponsors for vessels named in honor of particular persons are usually the nearest female relative of the honored person. Although women are sponsors nowadays, in early years men performed this honor. The first recorded christening of a U.S. ship is that of the frigate

Constitution on 21 October 1797 by Captain James Sever, USN. One person usually christens a ship, but a co-sponsor may be named.

The mayor of a city is usually invited to nominate a sponsor for a cruiser named in honor of the city. The commandants of Naval Districts are authorized to designate sponsors for some of the smaller vessels built within their districts.

At the time of the launching, the sponsor, ship officers, officials of the shipbuilding company, and the commandant of the Naval District in which the vessel has been built (or his representative), will assemble on a flag-decorated platform erected for the occasion at the bow of the ship.

The chaplain of the naval shipyard or district will offer a prayer for the officers and men of the Navy and the ship. The band will play the National Anthem, and as the ship begins to move down the ways, the sponsor will break a bottle of wine or water—usually champagne—across the ship's bow and say, "In the name of the United States I christen thee. . . . "

SHIP COMMISSIONING

The commissioning ceremony marks the initiation of a ship into the operating forces of the U.S. Navy. Until then, the ship has been the responsibility of the commandant of the Naval District or of the naval shipyard where she has been built. Therefore, no ensign, jack, or commission pennant flies beforehand.

Guests are invited by card to the commissioning ceremony, and the invitation usually includes a reception or lunch following the ceremony, as well as an inspection of the ship. A printed program will give the ship's background, sponsors, officers, and crew. Officers will wear dress uniform and ladies will wear suits, or appropriate daytime dresses, with hats and gloves. The ceremony will last about an hour.

The crew will be assembled on the quarterdeck or other open area, usually in two ranks facing inboard. Officers will be assembled in two ranks athwartships facing aft, and there will be a band and Marine or seaman guard. Distinguished guests and speakers, and other guests, will be seated nearby.

The first watch will be on the quarterdeck and quartermasters will be stationed at the National Ensign, Union Jack, and Commission Pennant. When "Attention" is sounded, the National Anthem is played and the flags and pennant are hoisted simultaneously.

The commandant will formally turn the ship over to the prospective commanding officer, who will read his orders from the Navy Department. His first order is, "Set the watch." The presentation of a plaque or gift to the ship by a state, city, or sponsor, will then take place, followed by the benediction.

CHAPTER 31

Service Organization

As a serviceman or servicewoman, you will know well the organization and traditions of your own service, but you should be equally aware of those of the other services. Each has its definite mission, its own regulations, and its important differences in customs and traditions.

THE ARMED FORCES

The President of the United States is the Commander in Chief of the Armed Forces of the United States. He is assisted in national security affairs by such agencies as the National Security Council, the Central Intelligence Agency, the Office of Emergency Planning, and the Bureau of the Budget.

The National Security Council was established by the National Security Act of 1947, as amended, and has as members the President, Vice President, Secretary of State, Secretary of Defense, and Director of the Office of Emergency Planning. The Secretaries and Under Secretaries of other executive departments and of the military departments serve as members of the Council when appointed by the President and with consent of the Senate.

The Council administers the Central Intelligence Agency whose Director is appointed by the President with consent of the Senate. The Agency coordinates all intelligence activities of the government relating to national security.

The mission of the Armed Forces is to deter aggression and to ensure the security of the United States. The Secretary of Defense is the principal assistant to the President in all matters relating to the Department of Defense.

Within the Department of Defense there are three military departments: the Department of the Army, the Department of the Navy, and the Department of the Air Force. The services within these departments are the Army, Navy, Marine Corps and the Air Force. The Coast Guard is normally under the jurisdiction of the Department of Transportation, but in time of war, or at other times when the President so directs, it will become a part of the Navy and be subject to the orders of the Secretary of the Navy. Each military department is separately organized under its own Secretary and functions under the direction, authority, and control of the Secretary of Defense.

The Department of Defense is headed by a civilian Secretary of Cabinet rank appointed by the President. He is chairman of the Armed Forces Policy Council which includes the Deputy Secretary of Defense, the Secretaries of the Army, Navy and Air Force, and the Service Chiefs. His main assistants are the Deputy Secretary; Assistant Secretaries for Administration, Installations and Logistics, International Security Affairs, Manpower, Public Affairs, Systems Analysis; a Director of Defense Research and Engineering; a Comptroller; and Assistants for Atomic Energy and Legislative Affairs and General Counsel of the Department.

The Joint Chiefs of Staff are the principal military advisers to the President, the National Security Council, and the Secretary of Defense. They constitute the immediate military staff of the Secretary, serving in the chain of command that extends from the President to the Secretary, and through the Joint Chiefs to the commanders of unified and specified commands: the Alaskan, Atlantic, Continental Air Defense, Pacific, U.S. European, U.S. Southern, U.S. Strike, and Strategic Air Commands.

The Joint Chiefs of Staff consist of the Chairman; the Chief of Staff, U.S. Army; the Chief of Naval Operations; the Chief of Staff, U.S. Air Force; and the Commandant of the Marine Corps, who has coequal status with members of the Joint Chiefs of Staff when they are considering matters of concern to the Marine Corps. The Chairman is normally on a rotating basis among the services and is appointed by the President on the recommendation of the Secretary of Defense.

THE FOUNDING OF THE SERVICES

The American Revolution brought about the forming of Continental land and sea forces which evolved into the Army, Navy, and Marine Corps. Although the U.S. Coast Guard was not founded until 1970, it is the oldest service in point of continuous service. The U.S. Air Force, the youngest of the services, was established in 1947.

Even before the Colonists declared themselves an independent nation, the Second Continental Congress voted on June 14, 1775, to raise companies of infantry and appointed a committee to prepare regulations for an army.

On June 15, 1775, the Continental Congress appointed George Washington as Commander in Chief of the Continental Army. On July 3, he took command of the American forces at Boston; they were composed mainly of militia and minutemen. Thus, when the Declaration of Independence was adopted on July 4, 1776, the Army was already one year old.

The Navy and Marine Corps have always been closely correlated. The birthday of the U.S. Navy is October 13, 1775, when Congress created a Naval Committee of three members, with four more members added shortly thereafter.

The Continental Congress first referred to "Marines" on October 5, 1775. On November 10, 1775—the official birthday of the Marine Corps—Congress authorized the Naval Committee to form two battalions of Marines. The first recruiting station was at Tun Tavern in Philadelphia.

After The Revolutionary War was won in 1783, there was a general military decline. The Continental Navy was disbanded; only a handful of Army privates was left to guard the stores at Fort Pitt and West Point. There was no sea force for the protection of the maritime interests of the new United States until the organization of the Revenue Cutter Service by Alexander Hamilton, the first Secretary of the Treasury, in 1790. From 1790 until the re-establishment of the Navy in 1798, the Revenue Cutter fleet served as the only Armed Force afloat. The Navy Department was established in 1798. Benjamin Stoddert was appointed as the first Secretary of the Navy. In July 1798, Congress re-created the Marine Corps as a military service. The Marine Band, formed that year, has performed at White House functions for every President except George Washington. In 1800, the Marine Headquarters were moved from Philadelphia to Washington, D.C.

In 1915, the Revenue Cutter Service was combined with the Lifesaving Service under the name of United States Coast Guard. Then, in 1939, the Lighthouse Service was incorporated into the Coast Guard. Three years later, in 1942, the Bureau of Marine Inspection and Navigation was transferred from the Commerce Department to the Coast Guard.

The U.S. Air Force was a major component of the U.S. Army until July 26, 1947, when the President signed the Armed Forces National Security Act which created a Department of the Air Force.

WOMEN IN THE ARMED FORCES

Congress recognized the need for women in the services by creating the Army Nurse Corps in the Medical Department of the Army in 1901 and the Navy Nurse Corps in 1908—but they did not have full officers' rank, pay, or other benefits.

During World War I, the Navy Department enlisted 11,275 "Yeomanettes" and 305 "Marinettes." Army and Navy nurses numbered 1,000 at the beginning of the war and over 20,000 by the war's end. In 1920, members of the Army Nurse Corps were given "relative" military rank and authorized to wear officer's insignia of grade from second lieutenant through major.

PERMANENT STATUS

In 1942, Congress established the Women's Army Auxiliary Corps

(WAAC), which was renamed the Women's Army Corps (WAC) the following year; the Women Accepted for Volunteer Emergency Service (WAVES); and the Women's Reserve of the Coast Guard (SPARS, for the motto, *Semper Paratus*). In 1943, the Marine Corps Women's Reserve was established.

The Army and Navy Nurse Corps and the Women's Medical Specialist Corps were given permanent status in 1947, and in 1948 the Air-Wacs were separated from the Army and renamed the Women in the Air Force (WAF) in the newly created U.S. Air Force.

In June 1948, permanent status in the Regular and Reserve Services was given to each of the women's components, with the exception of the SPARS who have a wartime mission. Over 266,000 servicewomen, officers and enlisted, served during World War II.

RANK STRUCTURE

Women in the services are an integrated component of the military establishment; they are appointed, recruited, assigned, trained, disciplined, promoted, and discharged as are men, and are entitled to the same benefits.

Servicewomen have the same rank through the grade of colonel in the Army, Marine Corps, and Air Force, each of which has a director; and through the rank of Commander in the Navy and Coast Guard (in wartime), each of which has a director. The Nurse and Medical Specialist Corps have a limited number of women who hold the permanent rank of colonel or captain.

DACOWITS

The Defense Advisory Committee on Women in the Services (DACOWITS) was created in 1951. Its chairman and members are appointed by the Secretary of Defense from among civilian women who are professional and civic leaders throughout the United States.

The Secretariat is headed by an executive officer with the rank of lieutenant colonel in the Army, Air Force, or Marine Corps, or of commander in the Navy, on a rotating basis. She is responsible to the Assistant Secretary of Defense for Manpower. The staff is composed of representatives of the women's components.

ORGANIZATION OF THE SERVICES

In order that you may have a general knowledge of the operating plan of the Services, their organizations, and their officer education programs, a brief resume of each Service follows.

THE DEPARTMENT OF THE ARMY

The Secretary of the Army is responsible for the affairs of the Army Establishment. Command flows down from the Chief of Staff and his assistants, through the General, Special, and Technical Staffs, to Army units and installations throughout the world.

The Secretary is assisted by the Under Secretary of the Army; Assistant Secretaries for Financial Management, Research and Development, Manpower and Reserve Forces, Installations and Logistics; a Director of Civil Defense; Administrative Assistant; General Counsel; Chiefs of Information and Legislative Liaison; the Judge Advocate General and the Inspector General.

The Chief of Staff has a Vice Chief and Assistant Vice Chief of Staff; a Sentinel System Manager; and Assistant Chiefs for Intelligence, Force Development, Communications-Electronics; Deputy Chiefs for Military Operations, Personnel, Logistics; Chiefs of Research and Development, Office of Reserve Components, Army Audit Agency, Military History, Engineers, Support Services, National Guard Bureau, Army Reserve, Personnel Operations, Chaplains; the Adjutant General, Provost Marshal General and the Surgeon General.

The Secretary of the General Staff has Deputy Secretaries for Staff Services, Staff Action Control, Coordination and Reports; Directors of Studies, Management Information Systems, Force Planning Analysis and a Sentinel System Office.

PRINCIPAL COMMANDS

The key U.S. Army commands include the Army Materiel Command (AMC), the Army Combat Development Command (ACDC), the Continental Army Command (CONARC), the Army Strategic Communications Command (ASCC), and the Army Air Defense Command (ARADCOM).

U.S. CONTINENTAL ARMY COMMAND (CONARC)

The Continental Army Command, with headquarters at Fort Monroe, Virginia, controls the Continental United States (CONUS) Army areas and co-ordinates the general training, organization, and equipment of the Army in the field, as well as the training of the Army National Guard and AROTC. Its mission is to provide for the defense of the United States and, in the event of an enemy invasion, to regain control of the invaded area, and to preserve peace and security.

The Commanding General CONARC, commands the six CONUS armies and the Military District of Washington, D.C. The armies, and their headquarters, are:

First U.S. Army, Fort George G. Meade, Maryland
Third U.S. Army, Fort McPherson, Georgia
Fourth U.S. Army, Fort Sam Houston, Texas
Fifth U.S. Army, Fort Sheridan, Illinois
Sixth U.S. Army, Presidio of San Francisco, California

U.S. ARMY AIR DEFENSE COMMAND (ARADCOM)

ARADCOM is a major command organized to carry out the Army's responsibilities for the air defense of the North American continent.

The Command is responsible to the Commander in Chief of the North American Air Defense Command at Ent Air Force Base, Colorado.

U.S. STRATEGIC ARMY CORPS (STRAC)

STRAC is a major component of the United States Strike Force, with headquarters at Fort Bragg, North Carolina. It is a balanced, combined arm strategic force, held in a constant state of readiness to meet with appropriate tailored force the requirements of cold, limited, or general war.

STRAC is composed of two Corps, each containing four divisions, plus supporting elements. (See *Tactical Air Command* page 351.)

OVERSEAS HEADQUARTERS

The U.S. Army maintains the following overseas headquarters:

Seventh U.S. Army, Heidelberg, Germany
Eighth U.S. Army, Seoul, Korea
U.S. Army, Alaska, Fort Richardson, Alaska
U.S. Army, Caribbean, Fort Amador, Canal Zone
U.S. Army, Europe, Heidelberg, Germany
U.S. Army, Pacific, Fort Shafter, Hawaii
U.S. Army, Ryukyu, Okinawa

THE UNITED STATES ARMY

The U.S. Army provides for the security of the United States, particularly within the Zone of the Interior. Its components are:

1. The *Regular Army:* The permanent Army maintained in times of peace as well as in war; garrisons the United States and its overseas possessions and bases; helps train the National Guard, Army Reserve, and AROTC.

2. The *Army Reserve:* An organized force which can be activated into a war component of the Army Establishment to meet emergency requirements. The structure is: the *Ready Reserve*, the *Standby Reserve*, and the *Retired Reserve*.

3. The *National Guard:* Augments the Regular Army and has been a major source of manpower in past wartime mobilization. This is the civilian militia of the country.

DIVISIONS OF THE ARMY

The Army is divided in the field into *Corps* and *Divisions.* The *Company*, the smallest unit, is usually commanded by a captain and is composed of squads and platoons. Other units are *Troop* and *Battery, Battalion, Regiment, Battle Group, Division, Corps*, and *Army.*

The Army has the following combat branches: Infantry, Armor, Artillery, Corps of Engineers, and Signal Corps.

The Technical and Service branches are: Adjutant General's Corps, Quartermaster Corps, and Finance, Ordnance, Chemical, Military Police, Transportation, Judge Advocate General's Corps, Chaplains, and Women's Army Corps.

Under the Surgeon General of the Army are the Medical, Dental, Veterinary, Army Nurse, Army Medical Specialist, and Medical Service Corps.

OFFICER EDUCATION PROGRAM

There are three main areas of educational training which lead to commissions in the Army:

1. The *U.S. Military Academy*, at West Point, New York, the oldest of the Service Academies, was established by Congress on March 16, 1802. The *Corps of Cadets* will ultimately be composed of over 4,000 young men. The motto is *Duty, Honor, Country.* The colors are black, gold, and gray. The mascot is the Army mule. The official song is "Alma Mater." Upon completion of the four-year course, graduates receive Bachelor of Science degrees and commissions as second lieutenants in the U.S. Army.

2. *Officer Candidate Schools* (OCS), for men, are located at Ft. Sill, Oklahoma, Fort Belvoir, Virginia, and Ft. Benning, Georgia. Candidates are enlisted men from the Regular Army, the Reserve, or the National Guard, who have a high school diploma or equivalent. OCS graduates are commissioned second lieutenants in the Army Reserve. Women candidates are trained at the U.S. WAC School at Fort McClellan, Alabama.

3. *Army Reserve Officers Training Corps* (AROTC), has over 250 units in various colleges, universities throughout the nation. The first unit was established in a civilian institution at Northfield, Vermont, in 1819, and the AROTC has proved a major source of officers for the Army. The program is also administered in high schools, military institutions, and junior colleges.

WOMEN'S ARMY CORPS (WAC)

During World War II, approximately 150,000 WACs served in the United States, Europe, Africa, the Southwest Pacific, China, India, Hawaii, and Alaska. There are about 12,000 WAC officers and enlisted women now on active duty. Approximately 500 are in the Reserve.

The direct commission program constitutes the major source of WAC officers. Unmarried candidates must have a college degree. All basic enlisted and officer training is conducted at the U.S. WAC Center, Fort McClellan, Alabama.

ARMY NURSE CORPS (ANC)

Members of the Army Nurse Corps are all commissioned officers and registered professional nurses. Direct commissions are available to qualified professional nurses who are between the ages of 20 and 35. Student nurses may, as officer candidates, participate in the Army Student Nurse Program while completing their education and then be commissioned as officers in the ANC.

During World War II, the ANC reached a peak strength of some 57,000 Army nurses who provided nursing care. Today there are about 5,000 Army nurses, both women and men, serving as staff nurses, supervisors, teachers, and administrators in Army hospitals throughout the world.

ARMY MEDICAL SPECIALIST CORPS (AMSC)

The AMSC, an all-officer corps established in 1947 as the Women's Medical Specialist Corps, is composed of dietitians, physical therapists, and occupational therapists.

Members of these three professions served as civilians with the Army at home and abroad from 1917 to 1943 when they were given relative rank. Army United States status followed in 1944.

Direct commissions are available to applicants who meet the professional education requirements and are otherwise qualified. Most of the approximately 560 members of the Corps are assigned to Army hospitals, with a few officers assigned to Research and Developments Units, to Army Headquarters, and to the Medical Field Service School.

Students in training at approved colleges may participate, as officer candidates, in the Army Student Dietitian or Student Occupational Therapist Program while completing the final 12 to 24 months of their undergraduate education as enlisted members of the Women's Army Corps. They are then commissioned as second lieutenants, AMSC, for the final year of their education and enrolled in the Army Dietetic Internship or Occupational Therapy Clinical Affiliation. These two advanced programs are also open to men and women college graduates. A 12-month Physical Therapy Course is also offered to women college graduates.

THE DEPARTMENT OF THE NAVY

The Secretary of the Navy (SECNAV) is responsible for the affairs of the Naval Establishment. In his immediate office are the Under Secretary, the Special Assistant, and Assistant Secretaries for Manpower Reserve, Installations and Logistics, Financial Management, Research and Development; a number of Chiefs and Directors of administrative Staff Offices. Command flows down from the Chief of Naval Operations (CNO), through the Fleet Commanders and the Naval Technical Assistants, to all bases and ships of the fleet, and from the Commandant of the Marine Corps and the Commandant of the Coast Guard (in wartime) to their respective forces.

The Chief of Naval Operations is the principal naval adviser to the President, the Secretary of Defense, and the Secretary of the Navy. The Office of the CNO includes the Vice Chief and the Assistant Vice Chief of Naval Operations; Deputy CNOs for Manpower and Naval Reserve, Fleet Operations and Readiness, Logistics, Air, Plans and Policy, and Development; Assistant CNOs for Intelligence and Safety; the Inspector General; the Judge Advocate General; the Comptroller; the Chiefs of Information; and of the Bureaus of Naval Personnel and Medicine and Surgery; Marine Corps Liaison: Directors of Offices of Antisubmarine Warfare Programs, Strategic Offensive and Defensive Systems, Naval Communications, Program Planning, and Oceanographer of the Navy.

The Commanders or Chiefs of Headquarters Commands are for Naval Material, Naval Air Systems, Naval Electronic Systems, Naval Facilities Engineering, Naval Ordnance Systems, Naval Ship Systems, Naval Ship Engineering Center, Naval Supply Systems, Weather Service, and Military Sea Transportation Service.

The Department of the Navy has three main parts:

1. The *Operating Forces* composed of the several fleets, the Sea Frontiers and Naval District Forces, the Military Sea Transportation Service, the Fleet Marine Forces, the Coast Guard (in wartime), and other units as may be assigned.

The Chief of Naval Material is responsible for the supplies, facilities, equipment, weapons, maintenance and supporting services for the Operating Forces.

2. The *Navy Department*, the executive headquarters in Washington, D.C. Here are the Offices of the Secretary of the Navy and CNO, and their staffs; the Headquarters of the U.S. Marine Corps and the U.S. Coast Guard, the Naval Material Command, and all the Bureaus, Boards, and Offices.

3. The *Shore Establishment*, composed of more than 1600 activities which supply, maintain, and support the Operating Forces. Some of these activities and their missions are:

a. *Sea Frontiers.* The five commands are Eastern, Western, Caribbean, Hawaiian, and Alaskan. They are part of the Operating Forces and, for limited purposes, are a part of the chain of command to the Shore Establishment. They are responsible for frontier defense, control and protection of shipping, and conduct of antisubmarine warfare within frontier waters. Sea Frontier Commanders have been assigned military command over naval districts for the purpose of logistic support.

b. *Naval Districts.* Ten continental and four extracontinental, with each having a Commandant who is the regional representative of the CNO and Secretary of the Navy.

c. *River Command.* Potomac River Naval Command is headed by a Commandant who is responsible to the CNO and SECNAV.

d. *Naval Bases.* A typical group of shore activities in a given area, includes a shipyard, a naval station and supply depot, and sometimes a naval air station. Naval Bases furnish direct logistic support to the Operating Forces.

e. *Naval Air Base Commands.* Furnish aviation logistic support to the Operating Forces.

Three Naval Training Centers for recruits are located at San Diego, California; Great Lakes, Illinois; and Orlando, Florida.

FORCES AFLOAT

The forces afloat are comprised of the various active and reserve fleets, Sea Frontier Forces, Military Sea Transportation Service (MSTS), the Coast Guard (wartime), and other ships and craft, as required.

The major commands afloat are the *Pacific Fleet*, the *Atlantic Fleet*, the *Naval Forces, Europe*, and *MSTS*. The ships and craft of the fleets are organized into commands by types, such as these Forces: Amphibious, Mine, Submarine, Naval Air, Cruiser, and Destroyer. The type commanders—such as Commander, Cruiser or Destroyer Force, Pacific or Atlantic—report to the Commander in Chief, Pacific or Atlantic Fleet, as appropriate.

The Commander in Chief, Pacific Fleet (CINCPACFLT), has under his command the First and Seventh Fleets; the Commander in Chief, Atlantic Fleet (CINCLANTFLT), has the Second Fleet; and the Commander in Chief, U.S. Naval Forces, Europe, has the Sixth Fleet. The vessels which make up the fleets are provided by the type commands.

SHIP ORGANIZATION

The Commanding Officer (CO) heads the complement of officers and enlisted men aboard any naval vessel. He is called the captain, regardless of rank. The Executive Officer (XO) is next in charge. The Officer of the Deck (OOD) is the officer on watch in charge of the ship. He is subject only to the orders of the CO and XO.

In general, the over-all organization of a ship is as follows:

1. Four major command departments: *operations, navigation, gunnery* (or deck), and *engineering.* Each is headed by officers eligible to exercise command, such as the Operations Officer, who is assisted by the Communication Officer and others, and the First Lieutenant, who is head of the deck department, etc.

2. Three staff departments: *supply, medical,* and *dental,* on large ships.

3. *Air department* in aircraft carriers and seaplane tenders.

4. *Repair department* in repair ships and tenders, and an ordnance repair department in submarine tenders.

COMPONENTS OF THE NAVY

The United States Navy is composed of the *Regular Navy*, whose officers and enlisted personnel make the service a lifetime career, and the *Naval Reserve*, whose men augment the Regulars in time of crisis.

The divisions of the Naval Reserve are: *Ready Reserve, Standby Reserve*, and *Retired Reserve*.

Naval officers are divided among the *unrestricted line*, the only officers who exercise command at sea and aviation pilots; *restricted line*, designated to perform specific duties only, including engineering (EDO), weapons engineering (WEDO), aeronautical engineering (AEDO); special duty officers only (SDO) for cryptology, law, intelligence, photography, public affairs, hydrography; limited duty officers (LDO) for deck, operations, ordnance, administration, bandmaster, engineering, hull, electrician, electronics, cryptology, aviation, air intelligence, photography, meterology, aviation ordnance, avionics, and aviation maintenance; and *staff corps*, which includes Medical, Dental, Nurse, Medical Service, Supply, Chaplain and Civil Engineer.

NAVAL AVIATION SHORE ESTABLISHMENT

The Shore Establishment includes Navy and Marine Corps air base commands, air stations, the Naval Air Training Command, and various offices and depots.

The Naval Air Training Command, with headquarters at Pensacola, Florida, has three distinct programs: *Flight Training*, basic and advanced; *Technical Training*, at Memphis, Tennessee; and *Reserve Training*, with headquarters at Glenview, Illinois.

FLEET AVIATION

Fleet aviation is composed of Naval Air Force, Atlantic Fleet, and Naval Air Force, Pacific Fleet, and their subordinate commands. Each Force is headed by a flag officer.

OFFICER CANDIDATE PROGRAM

Candidates for commissions in the Navy receive their training in five main areas:

1. The *U.S. Naval Academy*, the largest of the Service Academies, was founded as the Naval School at Annapolis, Maryland, on October 10, 1845.

The *Brigade of Midshipmen* is composed of over 4,000 young men. The motto is *Ex Scientia Tridens* (From Knowledge, Sea Power). The colors are Navy blue and gold. The mascot is Bill the Goat. The official song is "Navy Blue and Gold." Upon completion of the four-year course, graduates receive Bachelor of Science degrees and commissions as Ensigns in the U.S. Navy. A limited number are commissioned in the other Services.

2. The *Naval Officer Candidate School,* located at the Naval Base, Newport, Rhode Island, was established to meet the need for officers during the Korean conflict. Eleven classes a year lead to commissions for 5,500 naval officers—which accounts for more than half of the junior officers who enter the Navy each year. Officer candidates are college graduates, with some having prior enlisted service. Since its founding on April 10, 1951, the School has graduated more than 60,000 officers. The *U.S. Naval Schools Command,* at Newport, consists of the following Schools: *Chaplain Indoctrination, Communications, Women Officer School* (WOS), *Electronic Technicians "Class C,"* and *Officer Indoctrination*—for doctors, lawyers, and warrant officers. A commanding officer heads both Commands, which come under the jurisdiction of the Naval Base.

3. The *Naval Reserve Officer Training Corps* (NROTC) was established in 1926, with the first units at Yale University, Harvard University, Georgia Institute of Technology, Northwestern University, the University of California, and the University of Washington. There are 52 units in colleges and universities throughout the nation. Regular NROTC midshipmen wear the same uniforms as USNA midshipmen. Upon graduation, they are commissioned ensigns in the Navy or second lieutenants in the Marine Corps.

4. *Naval Aviation Cadet Training Program* (NAVCAD) is for high school graduates who have two years of college or the equivalent. They take ground instruction at Pensacola and a 14-month flight indoctrination course, after which they become naval aviators with commissions in the Naval Reserve or Marine Corps. Reserve Aviation Officer Candidate Training is open to college graduates serving on active duty as enlisted men in the Regular Navy or Naval Reserve, with a 14-month training course at Pensacola and Corpus Christi, Texas.

5. *Naval Reserve Officer Candidate* (ROC) is for college men who take two 8-week summer training courses at the Naval Officer Candidate School at Newport between the sophomore and junior years, and the junior and senior years. Following graduation from college, they receive commissions as ensigns, USNR in the General Line, the Supply Corps, or the Civil Engineer Corps. Qualified officers or officer candidates may apply for the Naval Aviation Officer Candidate (NAOC) pilot training program, or the Naval Aviation Officer (NAO) program which offers training in non-pilot air crew specialities and non-flying aviation technical fields.

WOMEN IN THE NAVY

On July 30, 1942, Congress authorized the Women's Reserve with the title *Women Accepted for Volunteer Emergency Service*, which was shortened to WAVES.

There are over 3,000 officers and 5,300 enlisted women currently on active duty.

Candidates for commissions are college graduates, who take a 16-week indoctrination course at the Women Officer School (WOS) at Newport, R. I.

College students in their junior year may apply for the officer program and be commissioned ensigns upon graduation the following year. Qualified enlisted women are also appointed to NOS (W). Postgraduate training is available to officers in the various fields at the General Line School, Monterey, California.

NAVY NURSE CORPS; MEDICAL SPECIALISTS CORPS (W)

There are 2,400 nurses on active duty in the Navy Nurse Corps. The Candidate Program permits qualified senior students to take a nursing education program under contract to the Navy. Following graduation, they receive commissions as ensigns, Nurse Corps, USNR.

The Nursing Education Program provides for selected enlisted women in the Navy to be assigned to a collegiate nursing school leading to a degree. Each graduate agrees to serve on active duty as a Nurse Corps officer for a period of one year for each year of schooling.

The Womens' Specialists Section, Navy Medical Service Corps is composed of over 100 dietitians, physical and occupational therapists. They serve in naval hospitals at home and overseas.

THE UNITED STATES MARINE CORPS

The Marine Corps is a service within the Department of the Navy. The Commandant of the Marine Corps (CMC) is the senior officer of the U.S. Marine Corps and is directly responsible to the Secretary of the Navy for its administration and readiness, and for the total performance of the Marine Corps.

The Commandant has an additional responsibility to the Chief of Naval Operations for the readiness and performance of those elements of the Operating Forces of the Marine Corps assigned to the Operating Forces of the Navy.

Headquarters Marine Corps is organized along general staff lines and, in addition to the Commandant, is composed of the Assistant Commandant; Chief of Staff; Deputy Chiefs of Staff for Air, Plans and Programs, Research and Development, Administration and Manpower; Assistant Chiefs of Staff, G-1 (Personnel), G-2 (Intelligence), G-3 (Operations), and G-4

(Logistics); Directors of Management Analysis Group, Marine Corps Reserve, Information, Personnel, Policy Analysis, Women Marines, Administrative and Exchange Service Division, the Command Center; Chaplain; Legislative Assistant; Inspector General, and Quartermaster General. In addition, there are other necessary departments and divisions to help conduct the operations of the Corps. Headquarters Marine Corps is located at Navy Annex, Washington 25, D.C.

THE OPERATING FORCES

The major elements of the Operating Forces of the Marine Corps normally are assigned to the Fleet Marine Forces (FMF), the fighting force of the Corps. However, Security Forces, Forces Afloat, and other unassigned forces are also Operating Forces. The Fleet Marine Forces are integral parts of the fleets, having the status of type commands. There is an FMF Atlantic with Headquarters at Norfolk, Virginia, and an FMF Pacific with Headquarters at Camp H. M. Smith, Hawaii.

A *Fleet Marine Force* consists of a Force Headquarters, Force Troops, one or more Marine Divisions, and one or more Marine Aircraft Wings.

The *Marine Division* is composed of a headquarters battalion, three infantry regiments, a motor transport battalion, pioneer battalion, antitank battalion, service battalion, medical battalion, reconnaissance battalion, and an artillery regiment.

AVIATION

The missions of Marine Corps aviation are closely related to the support of the ground forces.

The *Marine Aircraft Wing* is composed of a headquarters, facilities for air control, operations, aircraft repair and maintenance, and such transport, fighter, helicopter, and attack squadrons as required for the mission assigned.

The mission of the Fleet Marine Force is to provide combined arms, together with supporting air components, for service with the Fleet in the seizure or defense of advanced naval bases and for the conduct of such land operations as may be essential to the prosecution of a naval campaign.

AIR GROUND TEAMS

The Marine Corps is composed of over 300,000 men and women officers and enlisted personnel, and is organized into air-ground teams:

- The *1st and 3d Marine Divisions* are stationed in Vietnam. They are supported by the 1st Marine Aircraft Wing.
- The *2d Marine Division* at Camp Lejeune, North Carolina, is supported by an Aircraft Wing and the Marine Corps Air Station at Cherry Point, North Carolina.

- The *5th Marine Division* is located at Camp Pendleton, California, and is supported by the Marine Corps Air Station at El Toro, California. The *1st Marine Brigade* is stationed in Hawaii.

THE SUPPORTING ESTABLISHMENT

The Marine Corps supporting establishments are those activities which are not part of the Marine Corps operating forces. They include Marine Corps bases and barracks, supply installations, reserve and recruitment districts, clothing depots, air bases and stations, Marine Corps Schools, and the Department of the Pacific.

Two major Recruit Depots are at Parris Island, North Carolina, and San Diego, California, where recruits receive basic training.

MARINE CORPS DEVELOPMENT AND EDUCATION COMMAND

Marine Corps Schools, established at Quantico, Virginia, in 1917, was founded in the District of Columbia in 1891 as a School of Application for second lieutenants. Now called the Marine Corps Development and Education Command, there are two major subordinate commands.

1. The *Marine Corps Educational Center*, composed of the Senior, Junior, Basic, Extension, Ordnance, and Communication Officer Schools. Also, several special courses including the Officer Candidate Course, Platoon Leaders Class, NROTC, Artillery Officer Orientation Course, and Women Officer Candidate Course.

2. The *Marine Corps Development Center*, which develops the tactics and equipment employed by the landing forces in amphibious operations.

Both Commands are supported by Marine Corps Air Station, the Schools Demonstration Troops, a Headquarters Battalion, and a Training and Testing Regiment.

OFFICER CANDIDATE PROGRAM

Commissions in the Marine Corps are received in the following areas:

1. *U.S. Naval Academy.* A quota of each year's graduating class is commissioned as Second Lieutenants in the Marine Corps. Preference is given to those who were enlisted men in the Regular or Reserve Marines, and to sons of career Marines.

2. *Naval Reserve Officer Training Corps* (NROTC). The program is the same for Navy and Marine candidates, with the exception of functional differences, and is available to high school graduates or equivalent. Marine candidates take one summer training course of six weeks at the Marine Corps Schools.

3. *Platoon Leaders Classes* (PLC). This program is for college undergraduates and qualified enlisted Marines who have been screened by the Training and Test Regiment at Quantico. There are PLC (Ground) and PLC

(Aviation) programs. Commissions are in the reserve, with training at Basic School.

4. *Officer Candidate Course* (OCC). This program is for qualified college seniors or graduates who are screened at Training and Test Regiment, and after being commissioned as second lieutenants in the Reserve are trained at Basic School.

5. *Naval Flight Training* (Marine Aviation Cadets). Candidates with two years of college or the equivalent may become Marine Aviation Cadets in the Naval Aviation Flight. Training Program. Upon completion of 18 months of intensive training, the aviation cadet is commissioned a second lieutenant in the USMCR. Second lieutenants commissioned under the Officer Candidate Program are also provided the opportunity to be trained as Naval Aviators.

6. MARCAD. This program supplies the Marine Corps with trained aviators. Members must have at least two years of college, and take 18 months flight training as aviation cadets.

MARINE CORPS RESERVE

The continental United States is divided into six Marine Corps Reserve and Recruitment Districts, with each headed by an officer of the Regular Establishment. The categories of the Reserve are: *Ready Reserve, Standby Reserve*, and *Retired Reserve*.

There are approximately 50,000 Ready Marine Reservists in some 300 Organized Air, Ground and Volunteer Training Units in 35 states.

The 4th Marine Division/Wing Team, USMCR, constitutes the Corps' strategic reserve, not on active duty but prepared to be mobilized in as little as 30 days and deployed overseas in 60 days.

WOMEN MARINES

During World War II, some 19,000 officers and enlisted women served in the Marine Corps Women's Reserve, with 40 per cent assigned to aviation. There are 200 officers and 2600 enlisted women currently on active duty.

Candidates for commissions are unmarried, and must receive a baccalaureate degree prior to commissioning.

An Officer Candidate Course is conducted each summer at Quantico, Virginia, followed by the Officers' Basic Course for newly commissioned second lieutenants.

THE DEPARTMENT OF THE AIR FORCE

The United States Air Force was officially established by the Act of 1947 which placed the Department of the Air Force on coequal status with the Army and Navy.

The Secretary of the Air Force is responsible for the affairs of the Department of the Air Force. His chief assistants are the Under Secretary and the Assistant Secretaries for Research and Development, Installations and Logistics, Financial Management; an Administrative Assistant; General Counsel, and Directors of Information, Legislative Liaison, Space Systems Policies are channeled from the Secretary and his assistants to the Chief of Staff and the Air Staff.

The Chief of Staff has the following Air Staff assistants: the Vice Chief, Assistant Vice Chief, and Secretary; the Director of Administrative Services, the Chief Scientist, and the Secretariat.

The technical assistants are the Assistant Chiefs of Staff for Intelligence, and Studies and Analysis; Chiefs of Air Force Reserve, Chaplains, Operations Analysis; the Inspector General; the Judge Advocate General; the Surgeon General; the Chairman of the Scientific Advisory Board and the Comptroller.

The Deputy Chiefs of Staff, and their assistants, are for Research and Development, Systems and Logistics, Personnel, Plans and Operations, Programs and Resources.

Each Deputy and the Comptroller has a family of directorates under them, with responsibilities for specific phases of their functional area. The directors are delegated authority to work independently and in co-operation with each other.

At division or branch level, this team system eases the formalized channels of communication and facilitates the handling of heavy workloads.

AIR FORCE STRUCTURE

The basic Air Force structure is: Flight (the lowest tactical echelon), Squadron, Group, Wing (the basic unit), Air Division, Numbered Air Force, and Major Command.

MAJOR COMMANDS

The U.S. Air Force has 15 major Air Commands, and five separate operating agencies under Headquarters, USAF. They are:

Strategic Air Command (SAC): Offutt AFB, Omaha, Nebraska. In case of aggression against the United States, SAC could immediately furnish nuclear attacks. The deterrence of war is the primary function.

Air Defense Command (ADC): Ent AFB, Colorado Springs, Colorado. Defends the Continental United States, Canada, and Alaska against air attack. ADC operates all defense equipment, including weapons, ground environment, and the military air defense warning system.

Tactical Air Command (TAC): Langley AFB, Hampton, Virginia. Forces of TAC and STRAC (Strategic Army Corps) make up STRIKE COMMAND, which is a unified command under the operational control of the JCS. Headquarters are at MacDill AFB, Florida.

Air Force Communications Service (AFCS): Scott AFB, Illinois. Operates communications and a world-wide system of terminal and en route navigational aid to include air traffic control services at overseas bases.

Air University (AU): Maxwell AFB, Montgomery, Alabama. Prepares officers for command or staff duties with all types of Air Force organizations; provides education and specialized training in scientific, technological, and other areas; administers the Air Force ROTC and functions as the AF educational, doctrinal, and research center.

Military Airlift Command (MAC): Scott AFB, Illinois. Provides global air transportation for Armed Forces personnel, airlifts, air rescue, air weather, and photographic and charting services.

AF Logistics Command (AFLC): Wright-Patterson AFB, Ohio. Provides global support of combat units and weapons systems with materials and supplies.

Headquarters Command (HQ COMD USAF): Bolling AFB, Washington, D.C. Administrative and logistic support of Headquarters, USAF and nonself-supporting AF units stationed in the Washington area; special services.

Air Training Command (ATC): Randolph AFB, San Antonio, Texas. Procures airmen for the Regular AF, officer candidates, aviation cadets; technical and special training.

AF Systems Command (AFSC): Andrews AFB, Maryland. Responsible for system programs in ballistics, space, aeronautics, and electronics, from development, testing, and production through installation and checkout.

USAF Security Service: Kelly AFB, San Antonio, Texas. Handle communications-electronics intelligence security, and direct security activities of the Air Force.

OVERSEA COMMANDS

U.S. Air Forces in Europe (USAFE): Lindsey AS, Wiesbaden, Germany. Maintains tactical units in constant readiness. Controls USAF operations in the area, in coordination with allied military and civilian agencies. Provides administrative support for all AF units and activities in the European Theater.

USAF Southern Command (USAFSO): Albrook AFB, Canal Zone. Aids Latin-American republics in developing air forces consistent with national requirements, desires, and support capabilities; maintains air traffic control in Panama area; supervises USAF portion of Military Assistance Program for Latin America and provides logistic support; conducts a USAF school in Latin America.

Pacific Air Forces (PACAF): Hickam AFB, Hawaii. Assists in strategic defense of the Pacific and Far East in cooperation with units of other U.S. services and U.S. allies in the area.

Alaskan Air Command (AAC): Elmendorf AFB, Alaska. Gives early warning of attack on the United States and Canada; provides air defenses for Alaska and the Northwest Arctic approaches to North America; supports SAC in Alaska.

Aeronautical Chart and Information Center (ACIC): St. Louis, Missouri.
Office of Aerospace Research (OAR): Washington, D.C.
Air Force Accounting and Finance Center: Denver, Colorado.
U.S. Air Force Academy (USAFA): Colorado Springs, Colorado.
Air Force Reserve (AFRES): Robins AFB, Georgia. Responsible for the Air Force Reserve, Civil Air Patrol, Air Explorer program, selective service liaison, Office of Civil and Defense Mobilization liaison.

OFFICER TRAINING PROGRAM

Candidates for commissions in the U.S. Air Force receive their training in three main areas:

1. The *U.S. Air Force Academy*, at Colorado Springs, Colorado. Established by Congress on July 27, 1954, at Lowry AFB near Denver, moved to its present site in late August 1958. The *Cadet Wing* will ultimately be composed of 4,000 young men. Colors are blue and silver. The official song is "The Air Force Song." The mascot is the falcon. On completing the four-year course graduates receive Bachelor of Science degrees and commissions as second lieutenants in the U.S. Air Force.

2. *Officer Training School*, at Lackland AFB, San Antonio, Texas, is co-educational and was established for precommissioning training of men and women college students. All must be college graduates, but seniors may apply within 135 days prior to graduation. *USAF Pilot Training Program* is divided into the undergraduate and advanced phases. Graduates receive commissions as second lieutenants, USAFR.

U.S. Air Force ROTC: Units are established at various colleges and universities throughout the country. Young men who complete the four-year program of drills and academic work receive, upon graduation, commissions in the Air Force Reserve.

AIR RESERVE FORCES

Half a million officers and men in the *Air National Guard* and the *Air Force Reserve* throughout the 50 states are prepared to bolster the U.S. Air Force's tactical and airlift capability.

In peacetime, the Air National Guard and the Army National Guard form the militia of the individual states. In a national emergency, the Guard becomes part of the Federal forces. The Air Force Reserve is entirely a Federal organization. Their training is by the major air commands which have operational control of the units in an emergency.

WOMEN IN THE AIR FORCE (WAF)

Approximately 40,000 members of the Women's Army Corps served in the Army Air Force as Air-Wacs during World War II. In June 1948, the WAF was established in the newly created U.S. Air Force. There are over 860 officers and 6,000 enlisted women now on active duty.

Officers are secured through Officer Training School (OTS), which is a three-month course designed for college graduates. Upon completion of the course, the trainees receive commissions as second lieutenants. Enlishted women take a basic indoctrination course of eight weeks at Lackland AFB, San Antonio, Texas.

NURSE AND MEDICAL SPECIALIST CORPS

There are over 4,300 men and women nurses on active duty in the Air Force Nurse Corps.

The Medical Specialist Corps is composed of approximately 250 men and women dietitians, occupational therapists, and physical therapists.

THE UNITED STATES COAST GUARD

The U.S. Coast Guard is a part of the Armed Forces of the United States. It is also the principal Federal peacetime agency for maritime safety and law enforcement.

The Coast Guard has a dual role: during peacetime, it functions under the Department of Transportation which was formed in 1967; during times of war or national emergency, it becomes a service in the Naval Establishment. But in war or peace, it remains an Armed Force at all times.

Coast Guard personnel receive the same pay and allowances as the Navy, have the same rank structure, and wear the same uniform—except for identifying insignia.

When operating in the Department of Transportation, the Commandant of the Coast Guard, a full admiral, is responsible to the Secretary of Transportation; when operating with the Navy, he is responsible to the Secretary of the Navy and to the Chief of Naval Operations. The Secretaries of Transportation and Navy are authorized to make available to each other such personnel, vessels, etc., as are advisable.

Coast Guard Headquarters are located in Washington, D.C. The Commandant has an Assistant Commandant, a Planning and Control Staff, and Offices of Engineering, Finance and Supply, Merchant Marine Safety, Operations and Personnel.

PEACETIME MISSION

Law enforcement is one of the chief duties of the Coast Guard. It includes the safeguarding vessels, harbors, ports, and waterfront facilities in the United States and its territories, and a security check of Merchant Marine officers and seamen.

The Coast Guard operates the International Ice Patrol; it maintains ocean stations in the North Atlantic and the North Pacific which provide meteorological data, as well as search and rescue facilities for transoceanic ships and planes. Other SAR facilities include the AMVER reporting system and providing relief and assistance during times of flood or other disasters.

It maintains over 40,000 aids to navigation, including LORAN stations, manned light stations, and lightships. The Coast Guard has also assisted many newly established nations in setting up organizations similar to the Coast Guard.

OFFICER CANDIDATE PROGRAM

Commissions in the Coast Guard are received in the following areas:

1. The *U.S. Coast Guard Academy* has been located at New London, Connecticut, since 1910. A School of Instruction had been established in 1877, which was the forerunner of the Academy. In 1910, the old Army post at New London, Fort Trumbull, became the Coast Guard Academy and remained as such until 1932, when the Academy moved into new buildings along the Thames River. The bark *Eagle* is used for the training of cadets on their summer cruises. The *Corps of Cadets* is composed of approximately 800 men. The Academy motto is *Scientiae Cedit Mare* (The Sea Yields to Knowledge). The colors are royal blue and white. The Alma Mater song is "Coast Guard For'er." Upon completion of the four-year course, graduates receive Bachelor of Science degrees and commissions as ensigns in the U.S. Coast Guard.

2. At the *Coast Guard Reserve Training Center*, Yorktown, Virginia, the Service operates an Officer Candidate School, a school for indoctrination of merchant marine inspectors, and a number of training courses for Coast Guard Reservists.

The Coast Guard offers advanced postgraduate and specialized training to officers at the Naval Postgraduate School, Air Force Institute of Technology, Massachusetts Institute of Technology, Geroge Washington University, and other leading colleges and universities.

WOMEN IN THE COAST GUARD (SPARS)

The name SPARS was coined from the initial letters of the Coast Guard's motto and its English translation: *Semper Paratus*—Always Ready.

There were 15 officers and 153 enlisted WAVES in the first contingent of SPARS, with training at the Coast Guard Academy. By the end of World War II, there were 1,000 SPAR officers and 10,000 enlisted women serving in the United States, Alaska, and Hawaii.

By late 1947, all SPARS had been discharged. Two years later, the Women's Reserve was reactivated and the Coast Guard again numbered women among its personnel.

SPARS served during the Korean conflict on a voluntary basis. There currently are a few SPARS on active duty in the Coast Guard Reserve.

UNITED STATES MERCHANT MARINE

The merchant ships of the United States are an important part of her sea power. In peacetime, they provide the means for the exporting and importing of products throughout the world. During times of war, merchant shipping provides a link between the fighting forces overseas and the production army at home. The Government has subsidized the construction of passenger and cargo merchantmen, with certain requirements of the Navy, in order that the ships might be converted for Navy use in times of war.

MARITIME ADMINISTRATION, U.S. DEPARTMENT OF COMMERCE

The Maritime Commission was established by the Merchant Marine Act of 1936, for the purpose of directing the national aspects of merchant shipping and shipbuilding. Originally an independent agency, in 1950 the Commission came under the U.S. Department of Commerce and was split into the Maritime Administration and the Federal Maritime Board. A later reorganization—in 1961—made the Federal Maritime Board an independent agency, while the Maritime Administration remained with the Department of Commerce.

There are six academies training men for officer commissions:

1. The *U.S. Merchant Marine Academy* at Kings Point, New York, four-year course (second year spent aboard merchant vessels).
2. The *California Maritine Academy* at Vallejo, three-year course.
3. The *Maine Martime Academy* at Castine, four-year course.
4. The *Massachusetts Maritime Academy* at Buzzards Bay, three-year course.
5. The *State University Maritime College* at Fort Schuyler, Bronx, New York, four-year course.
6. The *Texas Maritime Academy* at Galveston, four-year course (a department of the Agricultural & Mechanical College of Texas).

Graduates who qualify may receive a baccalaureate degree in the appropriate field, Merchant Marine licenses as Third Mate or Third Assistant Engineer, and commissions as Ensigns in the Naval Reserve.

U.S. MARITIME SERVICE

The U.S. Maritime Service was established in 1938. Until 1954, the Service operated training stations at Alameda, California and at Sheepshead Bay, New York. It is now a voluntary uniformed service with ranks and ratings similar to those of the Coast Guard.

PERSONAL MATTERS IN EVERYDAY LIFE

CHAPTERS

CHAPTER 32

Your Religion

The religious beliefs of men have very much in common, regardless of formal religious affiliations. Notwithstanding the many different religious denominations and the great variety of individual attitudes toward religion, the student of theology is generally impressed by the similarities, rather than the differences, in the basic teachings of all religions.

When you understand these similarities, it becomes apparent how ill-mannered and foolish it is for any person to make light of another's beliefs, or to make derogatory remarks about the faith of another. A person who does so is violating a basic fundamental of both his own and the other's religion—*to love thy neighbor*.

Religious discussions in dissimilar groups are generally unwise because statements, seemingly innocent to the speaker, may seem offensive to a listener. This does not mean that you should refuse to state an opinion on a religious subject, or to enter into a discussion, but it does mean that you should be careful of the company in which a religious discussion is carried on. Unless the group is composed of men of good will, intelligence, and tolerance, such discussions tend to break down into heated arguments and end in violent wrangles.

It is not enough for an officer simply to understand and respect the beliefs of another. In the social observances of religious ceremonials there are many occasions in which individuals of different religions are brought together in a common participation. It is necessary that you know the proper behavior and procedures to be followed on such occasions, since they will become a part of your everyday living.

As you go about your daily social and official life, you will be called upon to take part in numerous religious ceremonies, in either an active or impassive role. In most cases, you will do no more than stand quietly, uncovered, and with bowed head, until the ceremony is concluded.

There are other occasions when you will take an active part in the ceremony, such as funerals, weddings, baptisms, and services of thanksgiving. Simple benedictions by a chaplain in an outdoor ceremony mean that you will uncover and follow the motions of the chaplain.

Ceremonies in a church or chapel will require specific knowledge of procedure. A member of a wedding party or a funeral cortege will need to learn everything possible about his responsibilities before the ceremony. In some cases, you will find yourself a participant in an unfamiliar church or synagogue, and it is advisable that you find out ahead of time from the chaplain, or clergyman of that particular faith, what you are to do.

CHILD'S BAPTISM

The baptism of an infant is usually held in a chapel or church. A Protestant child should be baptized within the first year of its life, preferably when one or two months old. The baptism frequently follows the regular Sunday morning service.

A Catholic infant is baptized at an age of two weeks to one month, and the ceremony is frequently held at an early hour on Sunday afternoon.

In the denominations of Judaism, a ceremony for male infants is held in a synagogue, home, or hospital eight days after birth. The naming of female infants takes place the week following birth, during services at the synagogue.

The chaplain (rabbi or priest) should be consulted in advance concerning the time and place of the baptism. The parents issue invitations by note or telephone, with a reception, tea, or luncheon following the religious ceremony. The party will be held at the home of the parents, or wherever·they designate, and guests are close friends and relatives of the families.

In Protestant families, a male child may have two godfathers and one godmother, and a female child may have two godmothers and one godfather, or they may have more. A Catholic child usually has one godfather or one godmother. A Jewish infant will have a godfather or a godmother. When godparents cannot attend the ceremony, a proxy may take his or her place.

A white cake and wine—usually champagne—or fruit punch, may be served at the reception. Toasts to the child's health and prosperity will be proposed by a godfather when dessert is served at a luncheon, or later on at the reception or tea.

Officers of the father's immediate service unit usually present the child with a gift, such as a silver christening cup, which may be engraved with the the child's name, date of christening, and the title of the donors.

BLESSINGS AT THE TABLE

As a guest at a meal, you may be called upon to take part in a simple family observance of religious custom. These expressions of thanksgiving may help you:

Catholic: "Bless us, O Lord, and these, Thy gifts, which we are about to receive from Thy bounty. Through Christ our Lord. Amen."

Jewish: "Lift up your hands toward the sanctuary and bless the Lord. Blessed art Thou, O Lord our God, King of the universe, who bringest forth bread from the earth. Amen."

Protestant: "Bless, O Lord, this food to our use, and us to Thy services, and make us ever mindful of the needs of others, in Jesus' name. Amen."

When you are a guest in a home of another religious affiliation, do not attempt to use a blessing of the host's religion unless you are familiar with it. Instead, use your own favorite grace and say it in your own sincere way.

CHAPTER 33

The Military Wedding

Throughout the course of your service career you will be called upon to take part in weddings. You may be an usher or the best man. Perhaps the wedding will be your own. It is difficult, sometimes, for officers at sea or at some remote base, post, or station to obtain the correct and detailed information concerning wedding ceremonies, and what is expected of the groomsmen.

The military wedding is like other weddings—except that the officers in the bridal party are in uniform, and the bride and groom usually leave the chapel or church under the traditional arch of swords. The groom's sword will be used by the bride to cut the first piece of cake at the wedding reception.

The uniform worn will be in accordance with the kind of wedding planned —formal or informal—and with the seasons of the year. Evening dress uniform may be worn at the very formal wedding, and dinner or mess dress uniform at the less formal. Dress blues or whites will be worn at informal weddings. Boutonnieres are never worn with uniforms.

The arch of swords takes place immediately following the ceremony— preferably when the couple leaves the chapel or church, on the steps or walk. The arch may be formed inside the chapel or church, upon leaving the chancel, *but this depends upon the religious convictions of the officiating chaplain or clergyman.* Ushers' swords are unbuckled and left in a side room until after the religious ceremony, when they are buckled on in preparation for the arch of swords.

Since a church is a sanctuary, the arch is formed *with permission* inside chapels and churches. In case of bad weather, the arch may be formed in the vestibule.

CHAPEL WEDDINGS

The chapel is reserved on a first-come, first-served basis. Permission for its use should be obtained as soon as possible, in order to secure the desired date and hour for your wedding. Whenever possible, applications should be made in writing to the chaplain's office in advance of the event—preferably six weeks or more.

There is no charge for the use of the chapel, but a donation to the Chapel Fund is accepted. The fund is for the maintenance of candles, flowers, marriage books, and many other supplies.

Although a chaplain never requests—and therefore does not expect—a couple, or any member of the bride or groom's families, to donate to the fund, it is a considerate gesture for them to do so. For example, the cost of the average wedding decorations in the Naval Academy Chapel is twenty dollars.

Since June is the traditional month of weddings, it is advisable to make wedding dates earlier than usual for that month. June Week weddings are held in the chapels of all the Service Academies at scheduled times—on the hour and the half-hour.

In order to schedule the many June Week weddings, forms are sent early in the year to all First Classmen who plan marriage in the chapel, to be filled out and returned to the chaplain's office. Drawings are made for positions. A mass rehearsal is held for all couples before graduation day.

The first wedding ceremony in the chapel will be performed early on the afternoon of graduation day. Ceremonies are also held in various churches in the Academy communities. Photographers may take pictures after any chapel wedding, but never during the ceremony. Pictures are usually taken when the wedding party leaves the chapel.

Rice and confetti are prohibited *inside* or *outside* the chapels.

THE CHAPLAIN

As in the case of all weddings, it is important that the engaged couple consult their chaplain (clergyman) before the wedding—a month or so, if possible. Where they are of mixed faith, or where the bride has been married previously—these facts must be brought to the attention of the chaplain or clergyman before the couple continue with their wedding plans.

He will advise you concerning such requirements as medical tests, obtaining the marriage license, and the signing of the Marriage Register.

Although most chaplains prefer to officiate at ceremonies held in the chapel to which they are assigned, a clergyman from the couple's home church may assist at the ceremony—if this is acceptable to the chaplain and is so arranged beforehand. The officiating chaplain will be in accordance with the religious preference of the couple. The chaplain, like the clergyman, is bound by his ordination vows to uphold the laws and regulations of his particular church regarding marriage.

Service chaplains are of many faiths, and as commissioned officers, they are subject to transfer. Therefore, customs change in the chapels and what is customary in one may not be carried out in another.

Chaplains on active duty are paid by the service which they represent, and will not accept a fee. However, it is customary to offer a civilian clergyman an honorarium. The bridegroom pays this fee, which is usually placed in an envelope and handed to the clergyman by the best man sometime before the ceremony.

Since the amount varies throughout the country, the prospective bridegroom should contact the office of the chaplain or clergyman to determine such fees, as well as those for an organist and soloist, if used.

During June Week, group counseling is held for couples, with discussions led by a medical doctor and by chaplains of all faiths at each session.

THE MUSIC

Since wedding ceremonies are religious ceremonies, the organist will play traditional wedding music and selections from the library of sacred music available in the chapel or church. The couple selects the music.

In the case of service weddings, when the organist is attached to the station, he will receive no fee for his services. At other chapels, such as the Navy Chapel in Washington, D.C., the organist is a civilian and receives a fee for the wedding, and an additional fee when he attends the rehearsal. If the organist accompanies a soloist, there is an additional fee. Solos, if any, are always sung before the ceremony begins.

It is not necessary that the organist and soloist attend the wedding rehearsal, unless the couple so desires. The fees should be given to the organist and soloist at the rehearsal—or at some convenient time prior to the wedding. The bride's family pays these fees.

It is customary for the bridal chorus from Wagner's *Lohengrin* and the wedding march from Mendelssohn's *Midsummer Night's Dream* to be used in the chapels for the processional and recessional.

FLOWERS AND DECORATIONS

Rules for decorating the chapels vary throughout the nation. At the Naval Academy Chapel, flowers, candelabra, and white hangings are furnished by the Chapel Altar Guild and are the same for all weddings.

At West Point, two vases of flowers are permitted at the altar of the Cadet Chapel, the Old Cadet Chapel, or the Post Chapel. Participants make their own arrangements with florists, except during June Week when First Classmen who are to be married are assessed for altar flowers at nominal expense. White pew markers and palms, furnished by the florists, may also be used.

Other chapels, including the Navy Chapel in Washington, D.C., do not furnish decorations, and if desired, are paid for by the bride's family. Any decorations which require alterations to the chapel or church, or which are to be fastened to the pews, walls, or items of furniture, will not be permitted without the chaplain's (clergyman's) approval.

For chapel weddings held during holiday seasons, such as Christmas and Easter, flowers and decorations are furnished by the chaplain's office.

PLANNING THE WEDDING

The bride's family always announces the engagement and sends out the wedding invitations and announcements—unless the parents cannot do so, or are deceased. In such cases, a close relative of the bride may act in this capacity, and sometimes the groom's family accepts this responsibility. (See Chapter 18, *Invitations and Replies*.)

The parents of the bridegroom-elect should call on the family of the bride-to-be before the engagement is announced. If the family lives in a distant city, a note should be written or a phone call made to them. The bride-elect should, by note or voice, be cordially welcomed into the family.

ENGAGEMENT ANNOUNCEMENT

A formal engagement is announced by the bride-elect's parents, or closest relative, usually between six weeks and six months before the wedding date (the future groom's orders may determine the length of the engagement). Such an announcement is frequently made at a reception, tea, etc.

In order to inform friends in a widespread area of the engagement—particularly service personnel who are in a constant state of transfer and whose new duty stations may not immediately be known—it is helpful to have the announcement published in a newspaper.

When the announcement is sent to a newspaper to be printed by a certain date—but not before that date—then state the date of release at the top left of the announcement, FOR RELEASE MONDAY, MARCH 15. The account should be signed by the mother or closest relative, for purposes of authenticity. For example:

> Capt. John James Smith, USN (Ret.) and Mrs. Smith of Baltimore, Md., announce the engagement of their daughter, Mary Ann, to Ens. Donald James Adams, USN, son of Mr. and Mrs. William Claton Adams of St. Louis, Mo.
>
> Miss Smith was graduated from Wellesley College, and made her debut at the Bachelors Cotillon in Baltimore in 1966. Ensign Adams attended Gilman School and was graduated from the U.S. Naval Academy, class of 1968. He is in flight training at Pensacola, Fla. The wedding will take place in December.

ESSENTIALS OF A WEDDING

The essentials of planning a wedding are: (1) religious ceremoney; (2) a father (brother, uncle, or any male relative of age) to give the bride away; (3) a best man for the groom; (4) an attendant for the bride; (5) a bouquet or corsage for the bride; (6) rings for the bride and groom (when he desires one); (7) a reception—if no more than a wedding cake and punch, tea or coffee; (8) a wedding trip—preferably a week or longer.

The invitations should be ordered by the bride's family *six weeks* in advance of the wedding date, and they should be mailed out by the bride's family *three to four weeks* before the wedding day. Her family sends marriage announcements *after* the wedding takes place to those to whom invitations were not sent.

WEDDING EXPENSES

The bride's family carries out the plans and main expenses of the wedding since they are responsible for their daughter up to the moment of her marriage. *But the groom should help decide the size and style of his wedding.*

EXPENSES OF THE GROOM

The expenses of the groom and his family include the engagement and wedding rings; marriage license; bride's bouquet (which she selects; the center of the bouquet may be removable and used for the going-away corsage); the corsages for both mothers; the ties and gloves for the best man and ushers, and mementoes for each. Also, the clergyman's fee, if any—and, of course, the wedding trip.

If the ushers and best man are in civilian dress, the groom pays for their boutonnieres, as well as boutonnieres for the fathers. But the ushers and best man pay for their own clothes (or rental charges), other than their ties and gloves, and for their transportation to and from the city or place of the wedding. The groom, or members of his or the bride's family, will find places for the groom's attendants to stay, otherwise the groom pays for any hotel bills incurred by his attendants.

The groom gives his bride a gift on, or just before, the wedding day. The gift is something lasting, usually jewelry. He pays for his bachelor dinner, if he has one, and it is held a few days before the wedding, but preferably *not* the night before. His gifts to his attendants are usually of gold or silver, such as cigarette cases or lighters, cuff links; they should all be alike.

A gift of substance will be given by his parents to the couple.

EXPENSES OF THE BRIDE'S FAMILY

The bride's family pays for most of the expenses of the wedding—up to the moment she leaves their care. This includes the wedding invitations and/or announcements; wedding photographs before and during the event (at least one is given to the bridegroom's family; if they want more, they should offer to pay for them); trousseau; flowers for the church and reception and any other decorations not furnished by the chapel or church; fees for the organist, soloist, sexton, if any; bridesmaids' bouquets and present for each (which are presented by the bride and are usually jewelry, such as a bracelet); all reception expenses, and any car expenses to and from the wedding (and, frequently, the reception); also the hotel bills for out-of-town bridal attendants when they cannot be accommodated in the parents' home or the homes of relatives or friends. The bridal gown and all accessories are paid for by the bride's parents (but *not* the gowns of the bridal attendants), and they usually give the bride as nice a gift as possible for the new household.

REHEARSAL DINNER

The rehearsal dinner may be given by the groom's parents, the bride's parents, or an intimate friend or relative of either family. Guests will be the members of the bridal party, the minister and his wife, and the wives and husbands of attendants. Other close relatives and friends of the couple may be invited, if desired.

WEDDING REHEARSAL

In order that a wedding ceremony may proceed smoothly, it is customary that a rehearsal be held in the chapel or church at least a day or so in advance of the wedding.

It is also a violation of good manners to hold such rehearsals immediately after a cocktail party or a dinner.

Although it is a growing custom to schedule the rehearsal the night before the wedding, it is important that the rehearsal be held *before* the dinner for the bridal party.

The hour of rehearsal is set with the chaplain or clergyman, and at the convenience of all members of the bridal party *who are expected to attend*. No words of the ceremony are spoken during the rehearsal, but the chaplain or clergyman will indicate at what point each member takes his role. The actual wedding rings are not used, but the motion of placing the rings on the bride's and groom's fingers is practiced.

During June Week at the Service Academies, group rehearsals are held for all members of the bridal parties who cannot schedule earlier rehearsals.

THE WEDDING RING OR RINGS

When you are the prospective bridegroom, you will go with your fiancee to the jeweler in plenty of time to select and order the wedding ring—or rings, if you also want one.

The modern wedding ring has little space for much engraving, so it is customary to inscribe only the initials and date, with the bride's initials coming first: "A.B.S. and M.W.J. 6 June 1963"; or the man's initials may be used first in this case: "M.W.J. to A.B.S.—"; or they may simply be inscribed: "A.B.S.-M.W.J." When the wedding band is wide and you desire an inscription, any personal phrase may be used.

After the ring is selected, the bride-elect will not see it again until the ring is placed on her finger during the ceremony. You will pay for her ring, and it will be delivered to you.

When you also want a wedding ring (in the double ring ceremony), yours will be a little wider and heavier than woman's wedding ring. You will wear it on the third finger of your left hand, just as the bride will, and not on your little finger. Your ring will be a gift from the bride. She pays for it, and it is engraved in a similar way to her own.

TIME OF THE WEDDING

The date and time of the wedding will be decided by the couple and the bride's mother, but in the services the time is frequently a matter of convenience for the bridegroom. At the Academies, June Week weddings are held according to the time chosen by drawings.

The most favored hour for the wedding differs in various sections of the country, with evening weddings perhaps held more frequently in the southern and southwestern states (probably due to the weather), and afternoon weddings often held at four, half-past four, or five o'clock, in northern and eastern states. High noon or half-past twelve is the favored hour for a morning wedding.

A formal wedding may be held in the daytime or in the evening—frequently at eight or half-past eight o'clock. The most formal wedding is one held in a church or chapel, but a formal wedding may also be held at home. Weddings—formal or informal—are held at almost any convenient hour of the day or evening.

Couples of various religious faiths will always discuss the time, day, and hour of their weddings with their chaplains or clergymen, priests, or rabbis, with particular concern for the Lenten season and holy days.

WHAT TO WEAR

At a service wedding, officers will wear the uniform in accordance with the formality of the wedding. *Evening dress uniform* conforms to civilian *white tie and tails. Dinner* or *mess dress uniform* is in accordance with *black tie. Service blues* or *whites* compare to a dark blue or conservative business suit or a cutaway. Any male member of the bridal party not in uniform will dress accordingly. (See Chapter 2, *Service and Civilian Dress.*)

In service weddings, the uniforms of the groom, best man, and ushers will be alike. In civilian ceremonies, the groom and best man will be dressed alike, but the ushers may be dressed like the groom and best man, or there may be slight differences in their shirts and ties. The fathers usually dress like the groom except that their ties need not match.

At service weddings, formal or informal, the groom and best man do not wear gloves because of the necessity of handling the ring, or rings. The ushers wear white gloves throughout the ceremony. At civilian weddings, the groom and best man carry gloves, if they so desire, but these need not be carried at informal weddings.

When you are a member of a civilian wedding party, you will want to know the general dress for formal, semiformal, and informal, daytime or evening ceremonies:

FORMAL DAYTIME (BEFORE 6 P.M.)

The groom, best man, and ushers will wear cutaways complete with stiff collars and ascots, and boutonnieres.

The groom and best man may wear stiff collars and ascots, with the ushers wearing soft collars and ties. All ushers should be dressed alike.

The bride will wear a long white (ivory or pale pastel) wedding gown with or without a train, with a matching veil attached to a cap or headdress, and white or matching accessories. She will carry a white bridal bouquet or white flowers on a white prayer book and wear white gloves.

The long or short formal gowns of the bridal attendants will be alike in style, of the same or different colors, with matching headdresses and accessories. They will carry bouquets smaller than the bride's.

FORMAL EVENING (AFTER 6 P.M.)

"White tie and tails" will be worn by all men in the very formal bridal party, with different boutonnieres the only distinguishing mark between them.

Summer formal evening weddings call for dinner jackets, usually white, since tails are not customarily worn during summer months.

The bride and bridal attendants wear the same type of gown as at the formal daytime wedding.

SEMIFORMAL DAYTIME (BEFORE 6 P.M.)

Men will wear dark business suits, white shirt, black shoes and socks; at a summer wedding, they may wear navy jackets and white trousers, or white suits.

The bride will wear a long or short formal gown (white or pastel) with no train, matching headdress and accessories; she will carry a bridal bouquet. The bridal attendants will wear gowns of approximately the same length as the bride.

SEMIFORMAL EVENING (AFTER 6 P.M.)

The groom, best man, ushers, and fathers of the bride and groom will wear dinner jackets with black ties and boutonnieres.

The bride and her attendants will wear the same as for a semiformal daytime wedding with the exception that the bride may wear a train of less formal length.

INFORMAL DAYTIME OR EVENING

Dark blue or gray business suits, white shirts, black shoes, boutonnieres for all the men in the bridal party. The bride and her attendants will wear street-length dresses or suits (*never* black), hats or a small headdress, and corsages. The bride will remove her gloves before the ceremony.

For the informal daytime or evening wedding, the men in the wedding party may wear summer white suits, white flannels with a dark coat, or any conservative summer suit.

SECOND MARRIAGES

A second marriage for a man does not affect the ceremony. When his bride has never been married before, the wedding may be as formal as desired.

However, a second marriage for a woman means a small and informal wedding. She does *not* wear the traditional white wedding dress or veil, but usually wears a dress of pastel color (or white), long or short, with a small headdress, corsage or a prayer book with a flower marker. Only the reception may be large.

PARENTS OF THE COUPLE

While the fathers dress similarly to the groom at a civilian wedding, the mothers of the couple will wear street-length dresses for any daytime wedding and usually a dinner dress for an evening wedding. They will wear something on their heads—a small hat or a veiling with flowers, etc.—and long gloves, but *never* a black dress or black gloves. The fathers will wear boutonnieres and the mothers will wear corsages.

GUESTS

Officers will wear service blues or whites at an informal wedding, or a dark blue or gray business suit, or any conservative suit according to the season. The same type of business suit or dress blues or whites are worn at a formal daytime wedding, since cutaways are almost never worn now, except by the men in the wedding party.

For a formal evening wedding, you will wear the dinner or mess dress uniform or a dinner jacket, or evening dress uniform or "tails" at a very formal wedding. Men may wear "Black tie" at the most formal evening wedding, and dark business suits at less formal or semiformal weddings.

Women wear long or short evening dresses, with a small headdress and gloves for the formal evening wedding; for a less formal ceremony, women wear cocktail-style dresses, with headdress and white gloves. An afternoon-style dress or suit (not sports) may be worn to a morning wedding and a "dressy" dress or cocktail suit is worn at an afternoon wedding. Black is suitable, if desired. Children wear their best party clothes, but they do not attend the wedding unless their names have been included on the invitation.

BRIDAL ATTENDANTS

The bride and groom may have only one attendant each; at a chapel or home wedding these would be the best man and maid or matron of honor. Usually, there are a maid or matron of honor and from two to six brides-maids at the average wedding.

The bride will ask a sister or very close relative, or an intimate friend, to be her maid or matron of honor. The bridesmaids are close friends of the bride and usually include a sister or relative of the bridegroom.

Ushers and bridesmaids may be married or single, and they may be in the briday party together. However, it is *not* necessary to ask a husband or wife to be a member of the wedding party when only one or the other is a close friend of the bride or groom. The husband or wife not included in the wedding party would be included in any pre-nuptial parties, but need not be invited to sit at the bridal table at the reception unless the bride and groom so desire.

At a very large wedding, there may be both a maid and matron of honor and as many as eight or ten bridesmaids, as well as junior bridesmaids (10 to 14 years of age), flower, girl (4 to 7), pages, train bearers, and a ring bearer (4 to 5 years old). The ring bearer wears a white or a dark suit and white shirt—never a miniature tux or tails.

Frequently, the bride gives a dinner for her bridesmaids on the night that the groom gives his bachelor dinner. When such a dinner is given, this is the time for the bride to give the bridesmaids their presents.

THE BEST MAN

The groom chooses his best man and ushers from among his closest friends and relatives. His best man may be a brother or intimate friend, and occasionally is his father.

The best man is the bridegroom's aide. It is his duty to carry on, regardless of what arises. In order to instill calmness in members of the bridal party, he must maintain it himself.

Before the ceremony, the best man checks on the groom's uniform, gloves, marriage license, wedding ring, sword—and if the ceremony is held in a church, he takes care of the clergyman's fee (ten dollars and up, furnished by the groom), which is enclosed in a sealed envelope. He checks to see what has to be signed, and if everything is in order. He notifies the ushers to be at the chapel or church at least twenty minutes before the ceremony, and he will arrive with the groom to be sure that the latter is not late and that he is properly dressed. During the ceremony, he will produce the ring at the chaplain's (clergyman's) request.

Following the couple's vows, the best man joins in the recessional, in which he customarily escorts the maid or matron of honor. Afterwards, he may wish to hurry on to the place of reception and check on details—such as stowing the bridal luggage in the going-away car. He does not stand in the the receiving line at the reception, but is near to the groom to be of further help. His is the first toast to the bride and groom at the bridal table.

THE USHERS

The ushers represent not only the groom but the families of the bride and groom as well. They act as unofficial hosts, greeting the guests in a pleasant manner, and are escorts to the bridesmaids. Ushers will give the couple individual gifts, or they may prefer to give a major gift together.

The number of ushers depends on the size of the wedding. An average-sized chapel wedding may be well handled by four to six ushers, with more serving at a large formal wedding. When the wedding is very small, no ushers may be needed. It is not necessary to have an equal number of ushers and bridesmaids. Usually, there are more ushers than bridesmaids since they have definite duties to perform.

The main duty of the ushers is to seat guests in the chapel, church, or home. In accordance with the chaplain's faith, ushers may—or may not—wear swords while ushering. If not, the swords are left at a place convenient for the arch of swords (sabers) ceremony.

It is preferable that six ushers in uniform perform this ceremony, although more or fewer ushers may do it. Ushers may be in the uniform of one or more Services.

When there are ushers who are non-military and who are in civilian suits, they should be paired. During the arch of swords (sabers) ceremony, when held at the chancel area, the non-uniformed ushers may unobtrusively step to the side following the wedding vows, or they may step to the side following the recessional when the arch is held outdoors.

Ushers do not stand in the receiving line at the reception. They will make themselves useful in talking with the guests, and as dancing partners when dancing is held.

USHERING

When guests arrive at the chapel, church, or home , ushers ask if they wish to be seated on the bride's side or on the groom's side, or they may ask, "Are you a relative (or friend) of the birde or groom?" Guests are seated accordingly—on the *left* of the chapel facing the altar for the bride's friends, on the *right* for the groom's. An usher always offers his *right arm* to the lady when escorting her down the aisle.

However, when one side of the church is rapidly filling while the other side remains empty—as may happen when the groom's relatives and friends cannot go a distance to the wedding—then the ushers may ask late-arriving guests to sit on the groom's side of the church.

A woman who arrives with her husband or other male guest will be escorted to the proper pew, with the usher asking the man to follow. Children will follow their parents. A man attending alone walks beside the usher—who does not offer his arm.

Each woman is escorted to a pew separately unless there are many guests waiting to be escorted. Then, the usher may offer the senior woman his right arm and ask the others in the party to follow. He may make appropriate remarks while escorting, but quietly, and in keeping with the dignity and reverence accorded a sanctuary. Guests should not be hurried to their seats, but the seating must be done with a minimum of delay; they are never seated during the rendition of a solo.

Guests who arrive first are given the choice aisle seats, and later arrivals will take the inner seats. In a large wedding, the head usher may be given a typed alphabetical list of guests and the seating arrangement.

The commanding officer of the groom, and his wife, may be invited to sit in the front pew on the right if the parents of the groom are unable to attend. Where the groom's parents are in attendance, the commanding officer and his wife may be accorded courteous recognition by being seated with the groom's immediate family.

Flag and general officers, and other commanding officers, may be seated in accordance with rank just behind the families of the couple, but rigid protocol is not adhered to at weddings.

The head ushers are so designated by the groom. One usher will escort the groom's mother to her pew on the right. Just before the ceremony is to start, the head usher will escort the bride's mother to her pew on the left—and she will be the *last* person to be seated. The chapel doors will then be closed, but if they are not locked the late-comer may seat himself in the back of the chapel. *But guests are not expected to be late.*

SEATING THE GUESTS

It is customary that the members of the bride's family sit at the left side of a center aisle, facing the altar. Relatives and friends of the family will sit behind them. The members of the groom's family, their relatives and friends, will sit at the right side of the aisle.

When there is no central aisle, the bride's family and friends will sit at the left side of the right-hand aisle, and the family of the groom and their friends will sit at the right of the left aisle.

ON TIME!

Everyone is expected to be on time at a wedding. The bride and her party should be in the chapel or church 30 minutes before the designated hour, and should go directly to the dressing room where they make final preparations. *It is inexcusable for the bridal party to be late.*

The groom, best man, and ushers should also arrive at the chapel or church 30 minutes before the time of the ceremony; ushers should have plenty of time to seat early arriving guests.

All guests should be seated before the exact time designated. When there is a soloist, guests should wait quietly at the rear of the chapel or church until the conclusion of the song.

CHAPEL OR CHURCH PEWS

When the center aisle of the chapel or church is banked by candelabra, two ushers will light the candles some 15 minutes before the hour of the ceremony. They will proceed to the front of the chapel or church, with each usher lighting the candles on his side with the aid of tapers. The pews are frequently marked by ribbons or sprays of flowers at the pew ends.

Runners are infrequently used in service chapels. When they are used in a chapel or church, two ushers will march in step to the front of the chapel or church, where they will grasp the runner, face the back, and walk until the runner is stretched as far as it will go.

TWO AISLES

When the chapel or church does not have a single central aisle, but has two aisles, you may select one aisle and plan the wedding as though that were the only one. Or you may use one aisle for the processional, and the other aisle for the recessional. When you use the right aisle for the processional, the bride's section is at the left of the "bride's aisle," as always.

THE WEDDING CEREMONY

THE PROCESSIONAL

A wedding in the Naval Academy Chapel follows the procedure explained here in detail. In general, this same procedure would be used in other service chapels, as well as in other churches.

The procession forms upon the completion of the ushers' duties, with the ushers taking their places at the head of the procession in the vestibule.

The first note of the wedding march is the signal that the ceremony is about to begin. By this time, everything is in order, with everyone in his or her place. The order of procedure is:

A. The chaplain enters from a side door, faces the altar in a quiet moment of prayer, then turns left and advances toward the congregation.

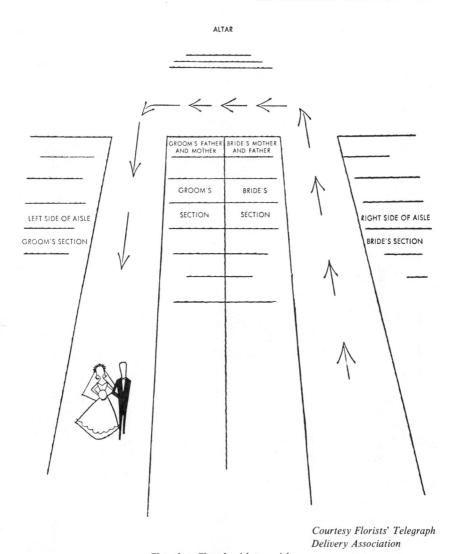

ALTAR

GROOM'S FATHER AND MOTHER | BRIDE'S MOTHER AND FATHER

GROOM'S | BRIDE'S

SECTION | SECTION

LEFT SIDE OF AISLE

GROOM'S SECTION

RIGHT SIDE OF AISLE

BRIDE'S SECTION

*Courtesy Florists' Telegraph
Delivery Association*

Chapel or Church with two aisles.

B. The groom enters, followed at about two paces by the best man, and both are in the same marching step as paced by the chaplain. As they approach the altar area, they pause in a moment of prayer, then turn left and face the congregation and the direction from which the bride will enter.

C. Simultaneously with the appearance of the groom and best man, the first ushers start forward *in pairs*. The pairs of ushers are separated by *six pew spaces*. Ushers are paired so that the shorter ones precede the taller. (In other chapels and churches the ushers may walk singly.)

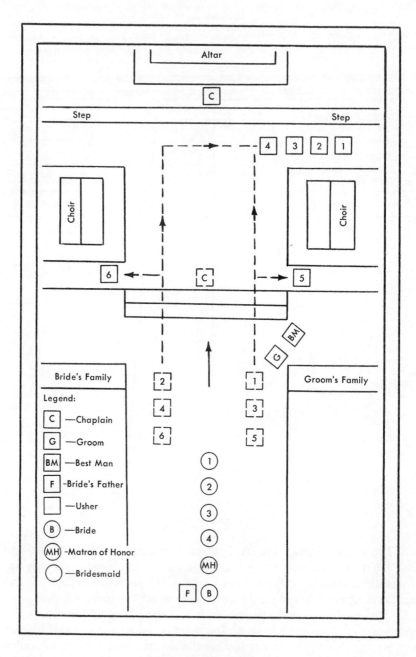

The wedding procession.

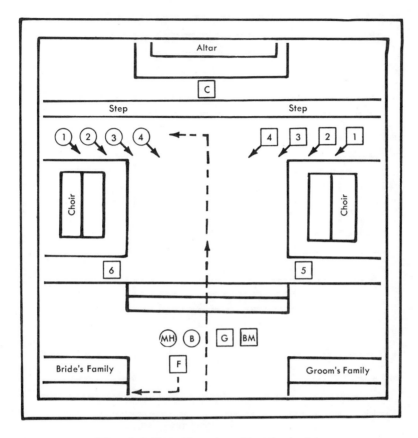

When the bridesmaids are in position, the chaplain
will advance toward the bride and groom.

D. The ushers face the altar until all are in position, then they turn together and face the approaching bride.

E. The bridesmaids follow the ushers, walking *singly* in order that their loveliness may be observed by all guests. They are also *six pew spaces apart*. The bridesmaids face the altar until the arrival of the maid of honor. (The bridesmaids may also walk in pairs.)

F. The maid or matron of honor is *eight pew spaces* behind the bridesmaids. She will also face the altar, then she and the bridesmaids *together turn right* and face the bride.

G. When there are a ring bearer and flower girl (in that order), they will walk *ten pew spaces* between the maid or matron of honor and the bride—or, five pew spaces behind the main or matron of honor, and five pew spaces in front of the bride. (A ring bearer and/or flower girl may walk singly or in pairs. They are not used as frequently as in former years.)

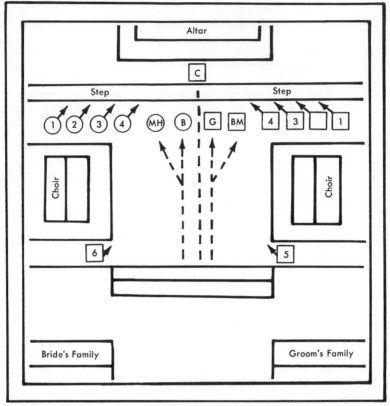

Positions for the ceremony at the altar.

H. The bride approaches on the *right* arm of her father.* The members of the bridal party are now facing toward the chaplain, and the congregation is facing the altar.

I. When the bride reaches a point between the groom and the maid of

* Although the bride customarily enters upon the right arm of her father, it may be advisable that the bride approach the altar on the left arm of her father because; (a) it is less awkward at a certain point in the ceremony. When the father (or whoever gives the bride in marriage) is asked. "Who giveth this woman to be married to this man?" his answer, "I do" or "Her mother and I do," means that the bride is nearer the pew where the mother is seated. (b) At the time when the father places his daughter's right hand in the hand of the groom, if the daughter's right arm is in the father's left arm, this means that the passing of her hand to the hand of her husband-to-be is quite simple. (c) Moreover, when the father is on the left side of his daughter, he then must make a choice of crossing in front of her and taking her right hand and placing it in the groom's, or going around her train and coming up between the bride and groom taking her hand and crossing it over. (d) Since the bride's mother is sitting at the left side of the chapel or church, it is symbolic of the bride's devotion to both parents that she pass between her mother and father on her way to the altar—which she cannot do when she is on the right arm of her father.

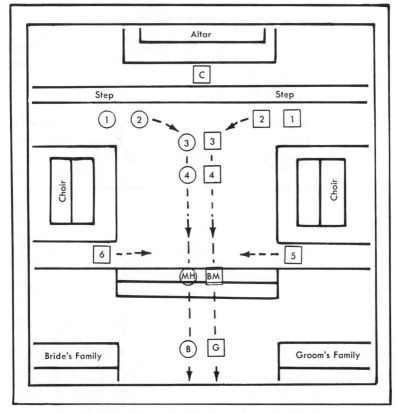

The bride and groom are the first to leave the chancel.

honor, she pauses about three paces from the groom, the groom advances to meet her—at which time her father pauses, and she takes the *groom's* left arm.

J. Before the ceremony, the bride will tell the chaplain whether she would like the guests to be seated or to remain standing throughout the ceremony. When guests are to be seated, the chaplain says, "At the request of the bride, all guests will now be seated." The father of the bride then gives his daughter in marriage, and goes to his seat.

K. The chaplain leads the way to the altar and the wedding ceremony now takes place. Upon reaching the altar steps, the bride hands her bouquet or prayer book to the maid or matron of honor, and at the appropriate time the best man gives the groom the wedding ring. If the groom will also wear a wedding ring, the bride at the same time receives it from the maid or matron of honor.

L. At the conclusion of the ceremony, the bride and groom are con- gratulated by the chaplain, and the groom may now kiss his bride. She receives her bridal bouquet or prayer book from the maid or matron of honor, and holds it in her right arm ready for the recessional.

M. When the arch of swords ceremony takes place inside the chapel, it will be at this time—when the bride and groom rise from their kneeling position after the benediction.

THE RECESSIONAL

The bride and groom are the first to leave the chancel, with the bride on the *right arm* of the groom. The maid or matron of honor and the best man walk out together, followed by the bridesmaids and ushers in pairs.

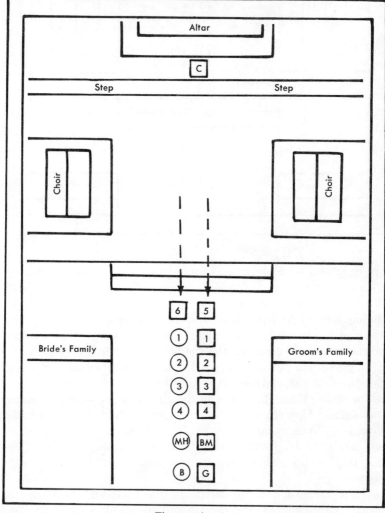

The recessional.

When there are two more ushers than bridesmaids—as shown in the diagrams—the fifth and sixth ushers act as escorts to the bride's and groom's mother, who are the first (in that order) to leave the chapel.

There is no effort made to keep step with the music during the recessional, but everyone walks with a natural, smooth gait—neither hurried nor slow. Following the families' departure, the guests leave in no precedence of departure.

It is important when a wedding reception follows elsewhere, that the bride and groom go immediately to an anteroom, or any secluded area, after they reach the vestibule in order that they are not immediately extended congratulations and best wishes by the guests.

It is the duty of the ushers (in fair weather) to see that all guests go outdoors immediately after the wedding for the arch of swords ceremony. An usher may clearly—and courteously—request that guests "Please proceed to the chapel steps."

Members of the bridal party usually stand at either or both sides of the outer door of the chapel, with guests standing at any convenient place along the steps or walk.

When the ushers have taken their positions on the steps or walk, the best man will notify the bride and groom that the arch of swords ceremony can proceed.

ARCH OF SWORDS (SABERS) CEREMONY

Although the ushers usually act as sword bearers, other officers may be designated as sword bearers—which would accelerate the arch of swords ceremony following the wedding ceremony. It is customary that six or eight ushers (or designated sword bearers) take part in the ceremony. Although the chaplain's office will furnish swords (sabers) for the ceremony, it is customary, such as at West Point, for the cadets to furnish their own white belts, gloves, and breastplates.

If the ushers have removed their swords, they now hook them on. In an outdoor ceremony, they proceed down the steps of the chapel where they form, facing each other in equal numbers.

In the *Naval Service*, the head usher gives the command, "Officers, DRAW SWORDS," which is done in one continuous motion, tips touching. The bride and groom pass under the arch—*and only they may do so*—then they pause for a moment. The head usher gives the command, "Officers, RETURN (swords brought to the position of 'present arms') SWORDS."

Swords are returned to the scabbard for all but about *three or four inches* of their length. The final inches of travel are completed in unison, the swords returning home with a single click.

When the arch of swords ceremony is held indoors, it takes place just as the couple arises after receiving the blessing. All members of the bridal party wait until the ushers' swords are returned to their scabbards before the recessional proceeds.

In the *Army* and *Air Force*, the *Arch of Sabers* is carried out in this way: when the bride and groom rise from their kneeling position after the benediction, the senior saber bearer gives the command, "CENTER FACE." This command moves the saber bearers into position facing each other. The next command is "ARCH SABERS," wherein each saber bearer raises his right arm with the saber, rotating it in a clockwise direction, so that the cutting edge of the saber will be on top, thus forming a true arch with his opposite across the aisle.

After the bride and groom pass under the arched sabers, the command is, "CARRY SABERS," followed almost immediately by "REAR FACE," with the saber bearers facing away from the altar, thus enabling them to march down the side aisle. They form again with arched sabers on the steps of the chapel.

A HOUSE WEDDING

A couple may be married at home if they so desire. A wedding at home can be as large and as elaborate as a church wedding.

The room farthest away from the door is usually the best place for the ceremony. A screen may be placed in front of a fireplace, and vases of white flowers may be effectively used. A long narrow table or altar will be placed in front of the screen, and here is where the bride and groom will stand. The arrangement of the altar should be according to the direction of the chaplain or clergyman. The room should be emptied of as much heavy furniture as possible, with chairs and sofas placed along the walls. Other chairs will be placed in the room to form an aisle.

The immediate families of the bride and groom will sit in the first rows of chairs placed to the left and right, respectively, of the aisle. The first chair at the left side of the aisle is for the bride's father, or whoever gives her away. There will be other chairs, but some—or most—guests will stand. The ushers will not have lists, but they will stand near the front door and tell guests where they should go.

As soon as all guests have arrived, the groom's mother goes up the aisle with her husband. The bride's mother will be the last to be seated; she is escorted by a male relative or the No. 1 usher.

The chaplain or clergyman, the groom and best man, will take their places as they would in church. The groom and best man stand near the altar, at the right side of the aisle, with the best man just behind and at the right of the groom. The bride's mother rises at the first note of the wedding march, and the procession follows the same form as in the chapel or church—except that ushers are *not* included.

The bridesmaids will enter the room first, then the bride and her father. When the ceremony is over, the bride and groom usually stand at the altar, with guests coming up to extend their best wishes and congratulations. The groom will kiss his bride at the altar—since he is always the first to kiss the bride after the ceremony.

The couple will go directly to the place of the reception, with the guests following. There is usually no seated bride's table, and the reception may be as elaborate or simple as desired.

At a very small afternoon wedding at home, with only members of the immediate families and intimate friends attending, the bride may wear a long bridal gown or she may wear a pastel-colored or white afternoon dress or suit, with a corsage.

The parents of the bride and groom, and the couple, will stand a little apart to greet guests. A buffet tea may be served, with a wedding cake centering the table. Punch, tea, and sandwiches would be placed in convenient sequence around the table. Invitations to such a small wedding may be handwritten, with wedding announcements sent out after the ceremony. (See Chapter 18, *Invitations and Replies*.)

At a formal evening wedding (usually held at eight o'clock or half after eight) the members of the bridal party may be in full evening dress, with men in dinner or mess dress or evening dress uniform, or in "Black" or "White tie." The women guests will wear evening dress, with their heads covered somewhat; the mothers of the bride and groom, and older women guests, usually wear long dresses with matching jackets or stoles, with heads and arms partially covered.

At less formal weddings men wear dark business suits, and women wear cocktail-type dresses with heads and arms partially covered.

VARIATIONS IN THE PROCEDURE

There are variations in the traditional wedding procedures—such as when the bride's parents are divorced, when one or the other of the parents has remarried, or when the bride's father or mother is dead. When the bride is a divorcée or a widow, the wedding is small but the reception may be as large and formal as desired.

When the bride's parents are divorced, the mother customarily gives the wedding and the reception. The bride's father may give her in marriage, but he may—or may not—go to the wedding reception. On the day of the wedding, the father will call for the bride just before the ceremony. He usually waits in the car, and sends word to the door that he is there.

Sometimes, the mother gives the wedding and the father gives the wedding reception. In this case, when the father has remarried, his *present* wife will act as hostess; if his *first* wife (the bride's mother) attends, she will attend as an important guest.

If the father has not remarried and he and his former wife are friendly, he may ask her to stand in the receiving line with him at the reception (regardless of whether she has remarried)—but *he* may precede her in the line since this is his home, not hers. If he has not remarried, he may also receive guests by himself.

At the chapel or church, the father will sit in the second pew during the ceremony; if he has remarried, he will sit in the third pew on the left with his present wife—if she attends. If the relationship is truly congenial, the father and his present wife, will attend the reception.

When the bride's mother has remarried, her present husband sits with her during the ceremony in the first pew at the left of the aisle. At the wedding reception, he will act as host. When the relationship with a stepfather has been a happy one, and the father of the bride is at a distance or cannot attend the ceremony, the stepfather may give the bride in marriage.

When the *bride's father is deceased*, a brother, uncle, cousin, or a male relative of suitable age (at least 21 years old) may give the bride away. A classmate of the father, or close friend, may give the bride in marriage. It is not proper for a bride to be given in marriage *by her mother or any other woman.*

When the *bride's mother is deceased*, and the father has remarried, the stepmother may be in charge of the wedding plans. If the bride prefers, an aunt, grandmother, or close friend of the family, may act in this capacity.

When the *bride's parents are deceased*—or when they are living at a considerable distance from the place of the wedding, or when they cannot give the wedding for financial reasons, or will not for reasons of religious differences—the parents of the bridegroom may offer to give the wedding and/or the reception. The couple may prefer to marry quietly in the bride's parish, with members of the families and very close friends attending. When the bridegroom's parents give the reception his mother stands first in line.

At a *double wedding*, when two sisters are being married, the elder takes precedence over the younger throughout the ceremony. The elder sister will walk up the aisle with her father, and the second sister will walk with a brother, uncle, or other male relative or older intimate male friend of the family. The father will give both daughters away—the elder daughter first, then the younger.

The bridegrooms will stand at the head of the aisle, with their best men behind them, the bridegroom of the elder sister nearer the congregation. The elder sister is at the left and the younger at the right during the ceremony, with the vows repeated separately. The elder sister goes down the aisle *first* when the ceremony is over.

Usually, the sisters have the same bridesmaids, half of whom each sister selects. The ushers are also divided in this way, but each bride should have her own maid or matron of honor, and each groom should have his own best man. In the wedding procession, the maid or matron of honor would directly precede each bride, with the ushers, bridesmaids, etc., preceding the entire bridal party.

The family of both grooms may share the first pew at the right of the chapel or church, or the family of the groom of the elder sister will sit in the first pew, and the family of the groom of the second sister will sit in the second pew.

At the wedding reception the elder sister stands before the younger sister, with the traditional order followed thereon. The mother of the brides will stand at the door to greet guests, with the mother of the elder daughter's husband next to her, then the mother of the other groom beyond.

When the brides are not sisters at a double wedding, the older girl, or the highest ranking of the brides' fathers, or the highest ranking bridegroom may decide the question of which bride precedes the other. Sometimes the question is settled by alphabetical order of the brides' names. The same precedence would follow at the reception.

WEDDING RECEPTIONS

The type of reception planned will depend upon the type of wedding—formal or informal—as well as the number of guests to be invited, and the time of day the wedding will take place.

A wedding may be large or small, simple or elaborate, and the reception will be in keeping with these points. A reception may be held at home, in a private or officers' club, at a hotel, or in the church parlors. When not held at home, reservations for the use of the reception room or rooms should be made well in advance of the wedding date.

RECEIVING LINE

At a comparatively large reception, such as one held at an officers' club, the mother of the bride customarily stands just inside the door, with the groom's mother standing next to her. The bride's mother greets the guests and introduces then to the groom's mother, then each guest will move on to greet each member of the bridal party, with the line formed a little apart from the mothers.

The fathers of the bride and groom may stand with the mothers for a time, but usually they prefer to be nearby and to mix with the guests. The best man and ushers never stand in the line; the best man will be near the groom, however, ready to help in any way possible, while the ushers act as unofficial hosts.

If the mother of the bride is not living, her father may receive the guests, or he may wish to ask a close relative, such as a grandmother or aunt, to receive with him. He would stand just inside the door and introduce the guests in this manner, "This is Anne's grandmother, Mrs. Smith . . . Mother, Colonel James."

The bride and groom always stand together, and the bride is always on *the groom's right*. Next in order will be the maid or matron of honor, then the bridesmaids. If a flower girl stands in the line for a while (she usually is

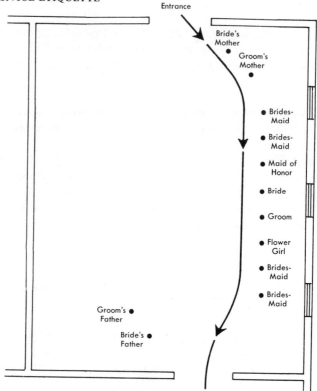

A version of the receiving line.

seven or under), she will stand on the groom's left. When sisters are brides-maids, the older sister will precede the younger. The line will remain intact until all guests have been greeted.

If you are a guest at a reception and there is no one to announce you as you approach the line, you announce yourself. You would say to the bride's mother (who will extend her hand first), "I'm John Jones, Mrs. Smith. Such a lovely wedding." You will shake hands briefly, but you will not linger in the line even though you may be a longtime friend.

When you greet the bridal party, you offer *best wishes to the bride* and *congratulations to the bridegroom*. You *never* congratulate the bride. You may say a few words to the groom about how lovely his bride is, and he may answer, "Thank you so much," and agree that she is lovely as he passes you along. Usually, you have little more time than to say, "How do you do."

The simplest form of reception is one where the bride's mother and father greet the guests and introduce them to the groom's parents, with the guests going over to the bride and groom standing together and wishing them well.

At a small reception, the mothers of the bride and groom may stand in a continuous line with the bride and groom and the maid or matron of honor.

At a large reception, the receiving line may be in this order: half the bridesmaids, the maid or matron of honor, the bride, the groom, the flower girl, and the rest of the bridesmaids. The mothers of the bride and groom will be standing in the customary position near the door to the reception room, and the fathers will be standing nearby and/or mixing with the guests.

Women in the receiving line wear gloves, but take them off as soon as the line is disbanded. However, when the bride's gown has long sleeves, she will remove her gloves. Women guests wear gloves when going through the line; then remove them.

RECEIVING LINE AT THE CHAPEL

When a small reception is planned, to which it is impossible to invite all the guests who may come to the wedding, a receiving line may be held in the foyer of the chapel—for example, the Navy Chapel in Washington, D.C.—immediately after the recessional. Such receiving lines may be formed in other chapels and churches throughout the country, but confirmation must be obtained from the chaplain or clergyman.

This type of receiving line is a friendly and thoughtful way of receiving the congratulations of the congregation. Guests who may have come from a distance and at some personal inconvenience will thus have the opportunity to speak to the bride and groom and to wish them happiness.

When such a receiving line is formed at the chapel, the same procedure is followed as at the reception. The bride stands on the groom's right and the maid or matron of honor at the right of the bride. The bridesmaids usually stand at the right of the maid of honor.

The bride's mother customarily receives alone at the door, but she may be accompanied by the groom's mother. The fathers of the bride and groom stand beside their wives, if they choose, or they may walk about among the guests. The ushers and best man are *not* in the receiving line.

RECEPTION FOOD

There are three main types of food served at wedding receptions: a light buffet tea at small and informal receptions, with more elaborate food at the formal afternoon reception; or a wedding breakfast, which follows morning or noon weddings; or a buffet supper served following evening ceremonies.

At a very small reception, a wedding cake and punch with which to toast the bride are all that need be offered. It is customary at an afternoon reception, however, that a buffet tea include tea and coffee, thin sandwiches, small cakes, and punch or champagne. At any type of reception, however, there is always a wedding cake.

At a late afternoon reception, the menu could be a seafood salad (shrimp, lobster, crab), ice cream molds, tea, coffee, and cakes. The menu could also be cold turkey or chicken, salad, ice cream or sherbet, tea, coffee, and cakes. By adding a hot soup and omitting the tea, either menu could be used for a buffet breakfast.

The menu for the wedding breakfast could be breast of chicken, tomato aspic, biscuits, ice cream or sherbet, wedding cake and champagne or punch. Creamed sweetbreads and peas, or baked ham and salads, little cakes, demitasse, champagne and/or punch are frequently served.

A menu often served to guests who will eat standing up is: creamed chicken and peas, salad, ice cream molds or meringues, cakes, coffee, and champagne or punch. This is good for afternoon or evening receptions.

The buffet menu may be roast turkey, ham, or beef—or all three, if the reception is very large. Any wedding breakfast, luncheon, or supper may be served to guests seated at tables, but customarily is served buffet style, with the food and plates on a long table or tables, and with guests serving themselves and eating standing up.

SEATING ARRANGEMENTS

At a seated wedding breakfast or supper, there are usually two tables, one for the bride and groom and bridal party, the other for the parents and their intimate friends. The bride's table is always covered with a white cloth, and the wedding cake is placed in the center of the table. At a large table white flowers may be placed on either side of the cake.

The bride and groom will sit together at one end or at the center of the table, with the bride on the groom's right. The best man will be at the right of the bride, and the maid or matron of honor will sit at the left of the groom. The bridesmaids and ushers will alternate around the table.

The parents' table is set with a white cloth and bowl of flowers, and the parents of the bride will sit across from each other as they would in their own home.

The father of the groom will sit at the right of the bride's mother, and the chaplain or clergyman will sit at her left. The mother of the groom will sit at the right of the bride's father, and the wife of the chaplain or clergyman will sit at his left. Members of both immediate families, with intimate friends, will sit at the table. All other guests may be seated at small tables for four or six each, or they may not be served at tables but eat standing up.

At smaller weddings, the bride's table and the parents' table are combined. Such an arrangement could be:

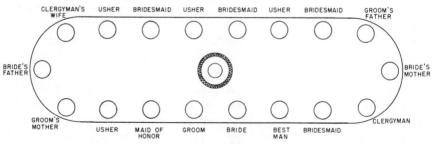

Bride's and parents' table combined.

At a buffet table, the food will be placed in convenient sequence together with stacks of plates, rows of silver, and napkins, with guests serving themselves at the table. The cake will be the centerpiece, or it may be placed on a smaller table, with guests coming to the table for a serving.

Champagne or punch is always placed on a table by itself except at a very small wedding, when it may be set on the main buffet table. There is usually a non-alcoholic drink served in addition to the champagne or punch—hot tea or coffee in winter, and iced tea or fruit juice in summer.

At the bridal table, the groom will unsheath his sword and hand it to the bride, who stands to his right, and she will cut the first piece of cake with his hand over hers. Whether or not there is a seated bride's table, the first toast is always proposed by the best man to the bride and groom. Other toasts may be to the bride's mother, proposed by the groom; then toasts to the bridesmaids, etc. (See Chapter 9, *Toasts*.)

When dancing follows, the bride and groom will have the first dance together, usually a waltz. Then the father of the bride dances with the groom's mother, and the bride's mother with the groom's father. After the first dance, the bride dances with her father-in-law and the groom dances with his mother-in-law; then the bride dances with her father, the best man, and the ushers, while the groom dances with his mother, the maid or matron of honor, and the bridesmaids. When the attendants join in, other guests also participate. The dancing may continue for an hour or so. Music is usually provided by a trio, unless the wedding is very large when more musicians would be needed.

GOING AWAY

It is a tradition that the bride throw her bouquet to her bridesmaids standing in a group, either from the stairs or in the doorway of an apartment or one-floor building. The bride will then change her clothes, and the groom will also change into traveling clothes, while the guests wait to see the couple off.

The parents will tell the bride and groom good-bye, in private, then the couple will go outdoors to a car that is waiting at the door while the guests traditionally throw confetti and rice on the couple. The destination of the wedding trip, and its duration, are strictly up to the couple—and the length of time the groom may have on leave, or between duty stations.

PUBLISHED WEDDING ANNOUNCEMENT

Wedding accounts for publication in metropolitan newspapers should be sent to the society editor of the paper as soon as possible. When pictures are used, either candid or those taken by a professional photographer, glossy prints 8 by 10 inches in size are best.

The account should include all the pertinent information in the engagement announcement, plus accurate information such as: the date and time of the wedding, the name of the officiating chaplain (clergyman), the church or chapel, and the place of the reception. It is of interest to mention the new address of the couple or the duty station of the bridegroom. When either one is from a very old or distinguished family, such a fact may be included in the account.

A home-town paper will include additional information: the names and home-towns of the entire bridal party, as well as descriptions of the bridal gown and bouquet and, usually, that of the bridesmaids' and mothers' gowns and corsages as well.

When space permits, a newspaper will carry a list of distinguished or out-of-town guests and relatives, but a complete list of guests is never published. When you are the groom you may wish to send a brief account to your alumni magazine or Service paper, if such news is published.

WEDDING PRESENTS

When you have been invited to a wedding, you should be aware of the customary rules for giving wedding presents. These are as follows:

- You send presents to friends and relatives when they are close to you—but you are not obligated to send a present to everyone who sends you a wedding invitation or announcement.
- When you receive an invitation to a wedding reception, you send a gift if you accept, but you need not if you regret.
- You do not send more than you can afford—but you should always remember that quality is superior to quantity.
- When you receive many invitations (such as the innumerable June Week weddings at the Service Academies), you send presents only to those classmates or friends close to you, whether you attend the ceremony or not.
- When you are invited to the ceremony, but not the reception, you are not obligated to send a present—but you may, if you so desire.
- When there is no reception, an invitation to the wedding takes its place and you may send a present, depending upon your friendship with the couple.
- When there are no invitations or announcements, you send a present to the couple according to your friendship with them. Every young couple enjoys a wedding present, and will always treasure it. If you prefer, you may take or send the couple a house-warming present.
- In case of a broken engagement, the lady returns the gifts to the senders with a brief but tactful note. There is no need to explain why the engagement was broken, other than saying it was by mutual consent.
- When a marriage is dissolved shortly after it has taken place, presents need not be returned.

Wedding presents are sent to the bride-elect's home before the wedding. After the wedding, presents are sent to the couple at their new address. It is the duty of the bride to write thank-you notes to each person or family sending the gift as soon as possible after a gift is received. (She also writes brief notes of thanks to those who gave her shower presents—even though she thanked them at the party.)

Concerning showers, it is better for friends of the bride-elect to get together and give her one or two showers than five or six which is an imposition (and expense) on friends—and exhausting to the guest of honor. Showers may be given but are not customary for second or subsequent marriages.

Although writing many thank-you notes is a chore, a thoughtful bride will *always* include in each note some mention of the gift itself. Therefore, she must keep a list of each person or family sending a gift and a notation concerning the nature of the gift. It is inexcusable to be neglectful in writing a thank-you note for each gift.

Ushers customarily give individual or joint gifts to the couple before the wedding. It is a growing custom that a joint gift is selected because a handsomer present can be given. Bridesmaids also give individual or joint gifts.

It is always better to give a small but choice gift rather than a larger—but cheaper—present. Most jewelry and large department stores have a bridal list with information as to her choice of silver, china, and glass. One or two cups and saucers, a single piece of silver, or a handsome goblet would be much more appreciated than a dozen inexpensive iced tea glasses. It is proper for a bride to exchange duplicate presents.

A practical and welcome gift to a young couple is money, in cash, checks or bonds. Such a gift can be given in the name of the bride and groom either before the ceremony or reception, or in the name of the bride-elect before the wedding, like any other gift.

MARRIAGE FINANCES

When you are the groom, you should have your financial house in order before marriage—with finances to cover the wedding trip, regardless of how short or extended the trip may be. A wedding trip may be en route to a new duty station, and in this case motel or hotel reservations should be made in advance.

You also must have finances to cover the establishing of your new household, which may be in a town or at a base unfamiliar to you. A classmate or friend stationed there frequently is of assistance in helping you find temporary quarters.

Sometimes the family of the bride or the groom give the young couple a check as a wedding gift, and financial problems are of no immediate concern. But a young couple should work as a team in household finances, fully understanding the limitations of a paycheck.

Since you are an officer and are subject to duty in remote areas, someone must handle your household and other financial obligations while you are gone. A young wife can contribute much to the success of a new marriage by her ability to handle capably these financial obligations. A household budget should be worked out, and thoroughly understood by *both* of you, before the hour of departure.

CHAPTER 34

Hospital Manners

Nothing is more exhausting to a hospital patient than to have a visitor who comes too soon after surgery or a serious illness, or who stays too long, or talks too loudly. If the patient were in good health and feeling fine, he would not be in the hospital. Some visitors, however, seem to regard a hospital room as a fine place for a social hour.

Any visitor in a hospital should observe the following rules:

- Walk quietly in hospital corridors, and talk quietly. Women particularly should guard against high heels clacking on tiled floors.
- The length of time of your visit depends upon the patient's condition, and how he is momentarily feeling. Five minutes may be too long. Fifteen minutes is generally long enough, unless you are a relative or *very* close friend, and even then the patient may not care to see anyone. Twenty minutes to half an hour is plenty of time for any visit.
- There are definite visiting hours in any hospital, and visitors should check them before going there. Make sure in advance that a patient wants visitors, by telephoning to the hospital or the patient's home.
- Visitors should not sit on the patient's bed and should avoid jostling the bed. Do not scrape the floor by moving your feet or chair in a noisy manner. Do not pace restlessly about the room.
- Do not visit anyone in the hospital when you have a cold. Sick persons are apt to be more susceptible to contagious diseases.
- Do not ask embarrassing questions concerning the patient's illness or surgery. He will tell you about it if he cares to.

When you are visiting in a hospital, do remember these *do's* and *don't's:*

- When there are several other visitors ahead of you in the room, you

393

should wait outside until some leave. If the patient has many visitors, he may be getting weary, so cut your own stay—unless he urges you to remain.

- *Don't* smoke in a hospital room unless the patient is smoking, or doesn't mind if you do. But find out about it first.
- *Don't* visit anyone immediately after surgery or a very painful illness, unless the patient is a very dear relative or friend.
- *Do not* visit a new mother too soon after the event—unless it is your wife! You may always see the new baby by looking through the glass door of the nursery.
- When you wish to help the patient in some small way, you may change the water in flower vases, crank a bed up or down when necessary, write or mail letters, or remove unwanted objects cluttering the room.
- When you want to take the patient a small gift, flowers are always nice—but *don't* overdo it: too many flowers remind some persons of funerals. When a patient is to be in the hospital for some time, a potted plant is always nice. You may wish to take a small bottle of perfume to a woman. Men usually like to read books or magazines, and they always want a daily newspaper. Newspapers are usually delivered at most hospitals, but a visitor may care to do this for a friend.
- Don't talk too much. Even simple questions may be tiring for the patient to answer.

When you are the patient in a hospital, there are some *do's* and *don't's* for you:

- *Do* be considerate of your nurse or corpsman—they are there to help you, not to wait on you. A nurse or corpsman is a professional man or woman—not a servant.
- *Do* cooperate with hospital rules, and *don't* make too much of a fuss concerning pills, needles, etc.
- In a private room, you can suit yourself (within reason) concerning the volume of your radio or TV, air conditioner, etc., and you may smoke with the doctor's permission. *But* in a semiprivate room or a ward, you must be considerate of your fellow patient or patients. Smoke can be disagreeable to another patient and your radio may drive him wild.
- *Do not* give orders to your nurse, and *do* call her by name: "Miss Smith," or "Mrs. Lee." Otherwise, call her "Nurse," but never "Miss." When the nurse doesn't tell you her name, you may properly ask her what it is. You *do not* ask her the details of your illness—you ask your doctor.

- Patients *do not* tip a trained nurse or a corpsman. You may give them a gift when you leave. In this case, it is proper to give the floor nurse a box of candy and the head corpsman a carton of cigarettes which may be divided among all the attendants on the floor.
- In a civilian hospital, you may tip the maid who has cleaned your room, or a porter who has served you. Ward patients *do not* tip.
- If you do not want to see a visitor—*don't*. A "no-visitors" sign can be placed on your closed door by your nurse who can also notify the desk that no one is to be admitted to your room. No explanation should be made to the visitor—after all, this is a hospital not an officers' club.

CHAPTER 35

Emergencies

ACCIDENT OR DEATH

When there has been an accident or the death of an officer while on leave or en route to a base, post, or station, such information should be immediately telephoned or wired to the commanding officer of the nearest Armed Forces activity. Any authorized person may send the message. The following information should be given:

- The officer's full name, rank, and service number.
- Where the death or accident (or illness) took place; the extent of the injury and present condition—if living; the name and address of the physician in charge; the name and address of the hospital or place where the patient or deceased is at that time; and the address where the person giving the information can be reached.

The person telephoning or wiring the information should ask for instructions, and then carry them out meticulously. A military officer will be assigned to check on the accident or illness. In case of an automobile accident, for example, it is necessary to have verification that the accident was not the fault of the deceased or injured, and that no negligence or carelessness on the part of the deceased or injured was involved—otherwise the wife or family may not receive all forthcoming benefits.

A member of the deceased or injured officer's or enlisted man's family can always obtain help from the commanding officer of the Armed Forces activity and its chaplain. All services handle funeral arrangements for the widow, and legal advice is available without the services of a private lawyer. Service personnel, whether officer or enlisted, will receive emergency medical treatment at any government hospital or, when none is available, at a civilian hospital.

MESSAGES OF CONDOLENCE

The purpose of the message of condolence is to express your sympathy to the closest member, or members, of the deceased person's family. The brief note, letter, telegram, or telephone call should be taken care of immediately upon your receipt of the news of the death. (See Chapter 17, *Correspondence*.)

You may find a letter of condolence difficult to write—many persons do. But when you realize how important it is for the bereaved person or persons to receive a message of sympathy, then you will immediately write or send it, when necessary.

When writing or sending the message, you may address it to the nearest living relative—whether you know him or her, or not. On the death of a male friend, you send the message to his wife, if he was married, or to his parents, if he was single. If there are no surviving parents, the message should be addressed to a brother or sister, or any near relative.

Letters of condolence are always written by hand, usually on plain white paper of the more formal type. Your letter should be short and simple—but sincere. Since you desire to express comfort to the bereaved, do not dwell on the illness or manner of death.

It is better to avoid Biblical quotations—not only in the interest of brevity, but because such a quotation may prove offensive in cases where the religious faith of the deceased's family is incorrectly judged. Most people prefer to grant to the chaplain or family minister the privilege of interpreting the Bible.

The words *died*, *death*, and *killed* are used only when absolutely necessary. It is frequently difficult to be sincere in expressing your feelings without occasionally using such words, but they should be used as infrequently as possible. However, it is better to use these words than such trite expressions "John's untimely passing," or, "Now that Fred has left us."

FLORAL OFFERING OR CONTRIBUTIONS TO CHARITY

In sending flowers to a funeral, *they are never sent in the name of the deceased*. If the services are to be held in a home, the flowers should be sent to the nearest relative. When services are to be held in a chapel, church, or funeral home, the florist will send them there, addressed to "The funeral of Mr. Smith Jones." You write your full name on the plain white card enclosed with the flowers. If the relationship with the bereaved is a close one, then sign your name "John Doe" or "Ann and John Doe." Do not write "Ann and John." You may sign "Captain and Mrs. John Doe" or enclose your personal card or joint card.

When the obituary notice states "Please omit flowers," then you omit them. If the notice states that contributions may be sent to a charity in lieu of flowers, you may send a check to the charity enclosed with a note stating that the check is in memory of the deceased.

You may send your personal card to the family saying that you have done this, but of course you never mention the amount sent to the charity. The charity should notify the bereaved family upon the receipt of the contribution.

Later, a member of the family (or in case of illness, a close friend) will acknowledge the flowers, contributions to charity, telegrams of condolence, etc., in brief handwritten notes. A note of appreciation should be sent to the chaplain (or officiating clergyman) thanking him for his help. (See Chapter 17, *Correspondence*.)

CALLS ON THE BEREAVED

When you live near the bereaved person or persons, you will want to call on him or her—if they are close friends or relatives. The purpose of such a call is to give comfort and sympathy to the bereaved. When speaking to them, you may say, "I'm so sorry," and briefly but warmly press their hand. You do not ply them with questions; if they want to talk to you, you should listen and answer sympathetically.

Whether you can be of assistance or are invading a family's privacy depends upon how well you know the bereaved. Your own good sense should give you the answer. When you cannot be of assistance, all calls should be brief.

In some cases, a family may urgently need assistance—as well as sympathy—whether you know them well or not. Such a case may follow an accident and death, which are always a shock to a family. Then, you may be able to help out with tact, thoughtfulness, and consideration of others' feelings.

If you are married, you and your wife may care for any children in the bereaved family for a day or two. Perhaps you may best help by wiring or telephoning friends of the family who are at a distance. Someone is usually needed in a bereaved house to answer telephone calls or to do whatever generally is necessary.

You should never take offense if you should call on a bereaved family and whoever answers the door says that the family is not receiving visitors. (Such calls, of course, are never returned.) You may leave your personal card with the phrase, "Deepest sympathy," written across it.

When calls are received at the funeral chapel, a member of the family or its representative should be present during the afternoon or evening when calls are expected to be made.

When signing the register in a funeral home, a married couple will sign on one line, "Lieutenant and Mrs. John Doe." Should they visit the funeral home at different times, they would sign separately as "Mrs. John Doe" and Lieutenant John Doe." A single person would sign his or her name in full, such as "Major James Smith" or "Captain Mary Ann Brown."

When making a call, try not to become over-emotional, for such actions will be adding to the bereaved's distress rather than comfort. Friends less close to the bereaved family may call at the funeral home, rather than at the house.

GENERAL BEHAVIOR

When a death notice states "Funeral Private," you do not attend the funeral—unless you are a close friend and have been notified by the family beforehand. When services are open to the public but the "interment private," you will attend the services but do not go to the cemetery.

Mourners attending the funeral services (other than members of the family) will dress conservatively, but black clothes are not necessary.

IN MOURNING

During the past quarter of a century, there have been many changes made in the conventions of mourning—particularly in the matter of dress. Most people feel that grief is a private thing, and that the public appearance of an individual *after the funeral* is not determined by set rules but by necessity and personal feelings.

Members of the family wear mourning at the funeral, with women customarily dressed in all black or white, according to the season. Navy blue and other dark shades are sometimes worn. Servicemen wear the prescribed uniform, with retired officers and civilian men wearing dark suits and ties. It is no longer customary for men to wear black arm bands, or mourning badges, although you may do so, if desired, or when required by uniform regulations.

It is not necessary to wear mourning clothes for a long length of time following the funeral—unless you so choose.

However, customs vary throughout the nation, and conventional mourning is observed in certain sections. But whatever the length of mourning, the transition from black to bright colors should be gradual for women.

A period of mourning may be observed if the individuals concerned care to do so, or they may not observe a mourning period following the funeral.

How long a person should stay in social seclusion following a bereavement is a personal matter. It is proper that the bereaved attends the theater, concert, movies, and small quiet gatherings not too long after the loss—in many cases it is desirable that a bereaved person does not stay in seclusion.

Wedding invitations may be sent to those in mourning, and it is correct for the bereaved to accept such an invitation if he so chooses. Small weddings for members of the immediate families may continue, after being scheduled, during a time of mourning.

Generally, the gaiety of the occasion will determine whether a bereaved person attends a social function within several months after a death in the immediate family. Men usually do not resume their social life for at least two months afterwards, and a widow usually does not go to large formal functions—such as dances, balls, etc.—for several months. Remarriage may properly take place after a year.

OUTSIDE HELP

In times of trouble, you or members of your family should seek the advice of the legal officer. Such an officer is stationed at almost all bases and stations of the services. He is usually a member of the bar and will advise you, or tell you whom to contact, on such matters as wills, taxes, estates, power of attorney, divorces or separations, medical and dental care, pensions, etc.

Although the legal officer cannot represent service personnel in civilian courts, he can give you names and addresses of reputable civilian counsel, if and when needed. Your problem, no matter how grave, will be held in confidence.

In times of emergency, there are many sources of help, depending upon the nature of your trouble. The base or station chaplain is always ready to talk with you concerning personal problems. The Veterans Administration administers benefits provided by federal laws for veterans and for dependents of deceased veterans who served in the Armed Forces of the United States in war or peacetime.

When a person needs help on problems such as alcoholism or mental disturbances, possibly despondency with threats of suicide, help can be received from various agencies which furnish facts on early symptoms of the diseases.

The names of such agencies can be obtained from your chaplain or medical officer who will put you in touch with the nearest agency.

SERVICE AND SOCIETIES

There are a number of service organizations which give immediate financial assistance to the various components of the services and their dependents. Each organization has auxiliaries, sections, or branches throughout the United States, as well as in other parts of the world. They are not connected with the American Red Cross, but work in co-operation with that organization.

Financial assistance is given for such needs as: non-receipt of pay or family allowances; expenses incidental to emergency leave; medical, dental, and hospital expenses; funeral expenses; emergency food supplies; unpaid rent with eviction notices; the training of dependents in order to make them self-supporting; assistance with educational or vocational training for Service children above the high school level.

The various organizations include: the *Army Emergency Relief* (AER); the *Army Relief Society*, whose main assistance is to the widows and orphans of the Regular Army personnel; the *Navy Relief Society*, which includes the Marine Corps and the Coast Guard; and the *Air Force Aid Society*. All have headquarters in Washington, D.C.

These organizations raise funds by membership dues and fund-raising campaigns conducted by such groups as officers' and NCO clubs and service women's clubs, as well as by the proceeds from balls, special shows, and athletic events.

HOUSING PROBLEMS

The *Armed Forces Hostess Association*, located in the Pentagon, Washington, D.C., has an extensive file on world-wide housing for Service personnel. The office is staffed by volunteer workers who are wives of Army, Navy, Air Force, Marine Corps, and Coast Guard officers stationed in the Washington area.

In addition to the housing files, information is also available on clothing needs, travel tips, schools, churches, commissaries, etc. When you write for information, make certain that your questions are specific. You should give your full name and grade; service; base, post, or station; and include a self-addressed and stamped return envelope.

The *Armed Forces Housing Office* in the Pentagon handles housing requests for Service personnel transferred to the Washington area. Staff members will help you in renting or buying a house, and will advise you on the location of schools, shopping areas, and transportation systems. There is no charge for these services.

CHAPTER 36

The Military Funeral

The military funeral ceremony is based on a few simple customs and traditions that have developed through the years. The ceremony demonstrates the nation's recognition of the debt it owes for the services and sacrifices of the members of the Armed Forces.

The casket is covered with the American flag. It is usually transported to the cemetery on a caisson, and is carried from the caisson to the grave by six military body bearers. In addition to the body bearers, honorary pallbearers are usually designated who march to the cemetery alongside the caisson or ride ahead of the chaplain.

At the cemetery, the casket is placed over the grave and the body bearers hold the flag-pall waist high over the casket. After the committal service is read by the chaplain, a firing party fires three volleys. A bugler sounds "Taps," and the military funeral is completed. The body bearers then fold the flag and it is presented to the next of kin.

These basic elements are the foundation of all military funerals, whether last rites are being conducted for a private or seaman, or final honors are being paid at the grave of an admiral or general.

GENERAL

1. Military funerals are divided into the three following classes:

    - With chapel service, followed by the march to the grave or place of local disposition with the prescribed escort.
    - Without chapel service, the funeral procession forming at the entrance (or at a point within reasonable distance) of the cemetery.
    - With graveside services only.

2. A military funeral with full honors includes the following elements:

- Band
- Escort as appropriate, including firing squad and bugler
- Colors
- Clergy
- Caisson and body bearers
- Honorary pallbearers.

3. The services of a chaplain are provided unless the family of the deceased requests another clergyman to officiate. If a civilian clergyman officiates, he will be expected to follow the same general procedures as the chaplain. The desires of the family are given the fullest consideration possible in the selection of the elements, but the funeral is conducted as prescribed in appropriate Service Regulations.

4. The commanding officer or his representative assists in making the funeral arrangements and supervises the conduct of the funeral.

5. When honorary pallbearers are desired, they are selected by the family of the deceased or its representative, or when so requested, by the commanding officer.

6. All persons attending the military funeral in uniform will face the casket and execute the hand salute at any time the casket is being moved, during the firing of the volley, and while "Taps" is being sounded. Honorary pallbearers in uniform conform to the above rules when not in motion. Military personnel in civilian clothes and civilian men will stand at attention, uncovered, and hold the headdress over the left breast.

7. The word "chapel" is interpreted to include the church, home, or other place where services are held, exclusive of the service at the grave.

8. The word "casket" is interpreted to include a receptacle containing the cremated remains of the deceased.

FUNERAL WITH CHAPEL SERVICE

Before the service begins, the funeral escort is formed in line facing the chapel. The band forms on the flank toward the direction of march.

Members of the immediate family, relatives, and friends of the deceased should be seated in the chapel before the casket is taken in. Chapel ushers should ensure that a sufficient number of front seats on the right side of the chapel facing the altar are reserved for the immediate family. The two front pews on the left are reserved for the honorary pallbearers. If body bearers are used to carry the casket into position inside the chapel, seats are reserved for them in the rear of the chapel.

The conveyance bearing the remains to the chapel should arrive a few moments before the time set for the service. Since the casket normally is covered with the National Colors, the escort is called to attention and the Escort Commander salutes as the conveyance arrives.

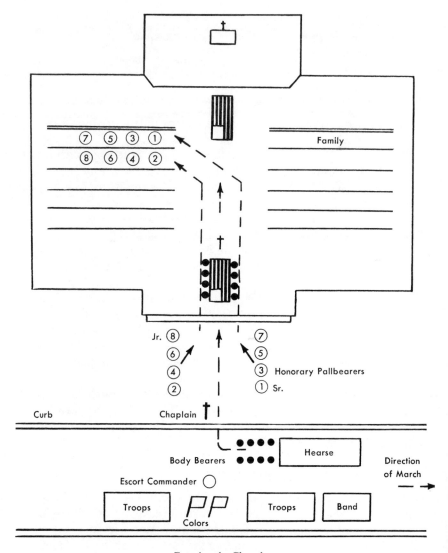

Entering the Chapel

Honorary Pallbearers salute while Honors are being rendered; then they fall in behind the casket to enter the Chapel.

When all is in readiness to move the casket into the chapel, The escort commander brings the escort to present arms. At this command, the band renders honors, if appropriate, followed by a hymn. At the first note of the hymn, the casket is removed from the conveyance by the body bearers and carried between the ranks of the honorary pallbearers, if any, into the chapel. As soon as the casket enters the chapel, the band ceases to play. The escort is then brought to order and given at ease.

When honorary pallbearers are present, they are formed in two ranks facing each other, thus forming an aisle from the conveyance to the entrance

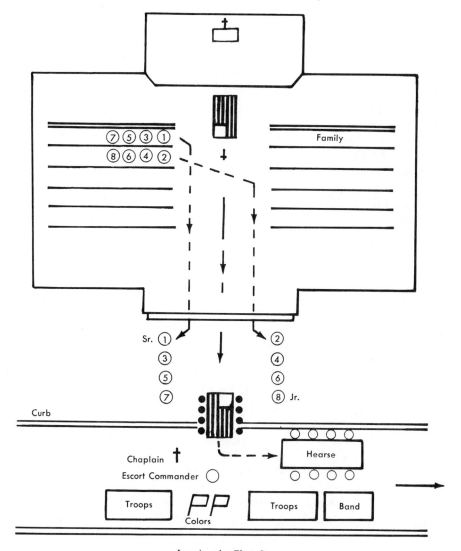

Leaving the Chapel

Honorary Pallbearers precede the casket out of the Chapel and take reverse position, as indicated. They salute while Escort renders Honors and hold the salute until the band ceases playing; then they take positions on either side of the hearse or caisson. (If riding, they proceed to cars ahead of the chaplain's car.)

to the chapel. At the first note of the music, and while the casket is being carried between them, the honorary pallbearers uncover or salute as appropriate. They will then follow the casket in column of twos into the chapel and sit in the pews to the left front.

The funeral director—or in his absence, the chaplain's assistant—moves the bier as previously prescribed by the chaplain. If there is no bier, the body bearers carry the casket as instructed by the chaplain beforehand.

At the conclusion of the chapel service, the body bearers follow the honorary pallbearers, or if there are none, they follow the chaplain in column of twos as the casket is moved to the entrance of the chapel. When honorary pallbearers are present, they form an aisle from the entrance of the chapel to the conveyance (caisson or hearse) and uncover or salute as prescribed.

After the casket has been placed on the caisson or in the hearse, the honorary pallbearers enter their cars, or if marching, form column of files on each side of the caisson or hearse with the leading member of each column even with the front wheels of the conveyance. When they ride, it is the body bearers who form column of files on each side of the conveyance.

The family group follows the casket out of the chapel and will remain at the chapel entrance until the honorary pallbearers have broken ranks to take their position. The ushers will then escort the family to their conveyance, with all other mourners proceeding to their own cars.

When the casket appears at the entrance of the chapel at the conclusion of the service, the funeral escort and band repeat the procedures as prescribed for entering the chapel. The band ceases playing and the escort is brought to order when the casket has been secured to the caisson or in the hearse.

The procession to the grave site is formed in the order of march shown on the facing page.

The escort commander puts the band and escort in march, and the procession marches slowly to solemn music. If there is a considerable distance from the chapel to the grave, the escort—after leaving the chapel area—may march at ease in quick time, with no band music. The escort is brought to attention in the vicinity of the grave.

As the procession nears the grave, the marching elements move to their predesignated positions. The band and military escorts are formed in a line behind and facing the foot of the grave, with other marching elements placed as near as practicable. The firing squad takes position so that it will not fire directly over the mourners.

When the caisson or hearse comes to a halt, the honorary pallbearers again form in two ranks with an aisle extending from the conveyance toward the graveside. If the grave is too near the road to permit this formation, they should take their positions at the graveside before the removal of the casket from the caisson or hearse.

Police Escort

Escort Commander

Band

Troops

Colors

Honorary Pallbearers (when riding)

Chaplain

Personal Flag

Hearse or Caisson (Honorary Pallbearers, when marching)

Body Bearers (alongside hearse or caisson if no pallbearers)

Family

Enlisted Men from Command of Deceased

Officers from Command of Deceased

Delegations

Societies

Citizens

Procession to the Grave Site

The Escort Commander makes all turns at road intersections and he should turn about occasionally to make certain that the escort is in correct formation. A police escort will precede the Escort Commander to keep traffic clear en route to the grave site.

When all is in readiness to remove the casket from the conveyance, the escort commander commands, "Present, ARMS." At this command, the band renders honors if appropriate, followed by a hymn. At the first note of the hymn, the body bearers remove the casket from the caisson or hearse.

Preceded by the chaplain, the body bearers carry the casket between the

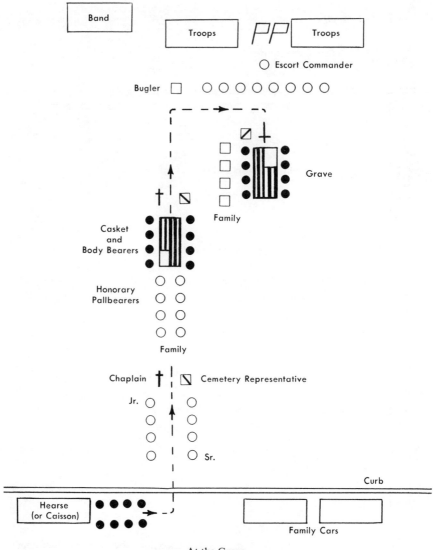

At the Grave

Honorary Pallbearers salute while the casket is being removed from the hearse or caisson and hold the salute until the casket has passed between them. They salute at the grave during volleys and "Taps."

ranks of honorary pallbearers to the grave and place it on the lowering device. They remain in position facing the casket; then, they raise the flag from the casket and hold it in a horizontal position waist high until the conclusion of "Taps."

As soon as the casket has passed between them, the honorary pallbearers face toward the grave and follow the casket in column of twos to their position at the grave. The family will proceed to their designated places.

When the casket has been placed over the grave, the band ceases playing and the escort is brought to the order. The escort commander then commands. "Parade, REST." The graveside service is now conducted by the chaplain. After the benediction, he moves two steps to the side or rear.

Upon the conclusion of the service, the escort commander brings the escort to attention. He commands, "Escort less firing squad, present ARMS: firing squad, FIRE THREE VOLLEYS." The firing squad fires volleys of blank cartridges; then, they assume the position of present arms on the command of the non-commissioned officer or petty officer in charge. They remain in this position until the conclusion of "Taps." which is sounded by the bugler immediately after the last volley. The entire escort is then brought to order.

The body bearers box the flag, with the senior body bearer giving it to the chaplain or commanding officer who will present it to the next of kin or a representative of the family.

After the presentation of the flag, the band and escort are put in march by the escort commander. When retiring from the vicinity of the grave site, care should be exercised not to detract from the solemnity of the occasion.

FUNERAL WITHOUT CHAPEL SERVICE

When the funeral is without chapel service, the escort usually forms at or near the entrance to the cemetery. The officer in charge supervises the transfer of the casket from the hearse to the caisson or makes provision for the hearse to be included in the procession from the point of origin to the grave site.

When honorary pallbearers are present, they are formed in a single line facing the caisson or hearse. Their order of march is the same as already described. While the casket is being transferred, the escort is brought to present arms, the band plays an appropriate air, and the honorary pallbearers uncover or salute as appropriate. The family and friends remain in their cars during the transfer of the casket. The funeral procession then forms and proceeds as prescribed.

GRAVESIDE SERVICE

The military elements (chaplain, body bearers, firing squad, and bugler) participating in a graveside service are in position before the arrival of the remains. The procedure is the same as already described.

The leader of the firing squad gives the appropriate orders for the firing of three volleys and the bugler sounds "Taps" immediately upon completion of the last volley. The senior body bearer gives the order to march off after the flag has been presented to the next of kin.

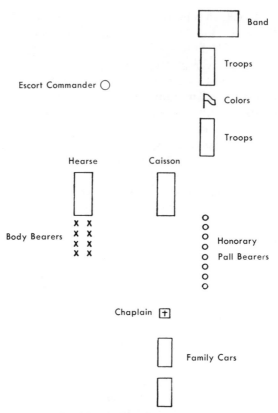

Receiving the Remains at the Gate

CREMATION

For all phases of the funeral where the receptacle containing the cremated remains is carried by hand, one body bearer will be designated to do so. Four men detailed as flagbearers will follow the receptacle when it is carried from the conveyance into the chapel, from the chapel to the conveyance, or from the conveyance to the grave. The flag is folded and is carried by the leading flagbearer on the right.

When the receptacle has been placed on a stand before the chancel of the chapel or in the conveyance, the folded flag is placed beside the receptacle. If the caisson is equipped with a casket container for the receptacle, the open flag is laid upon the container as prescribed for a casket.

In cases where the remains are conducted to a crematory and the ashes are to be interred with military honors at a later time, the ceremony consists only of the escort to the crematory. Arms are presented as the remains are carried inside, and the firing of volleys and the sounding of "Taps" are omitted.

When the ceremony is held at the crematory, with no further military honors, volleys are fired and "Taps" is sounded at the discretion of the commanding officer.

CANNON SALUTE

The funeral of a flag or general officer (active or retired), which takes place at or near a military installation, will be marked with minute guns equal to the number to which the officer was entitled and will be fired at noon on the day of the funeral.

The cannon salute corresponding to the grade of the deceased will be fired immediately after the benediction, followed by three volleys of artillery, guns firing simultaneously, or three volleys of musketry.

AVIATION PARTICIPATION

When there is aviation participation in a military funeral, it is timed so that the airplanes appear over the procession while the remains are being taken to the grave.

When the funeral is that of an aviator, it is customary for the airplanes to fly in a normal tactical formation less one aircraft, indicating the vacancy resulting from the loss of the deceased.

FRATERNAL OR PATRIOTIC ORGANIZATIONS

A fraternal or military organization of which the deceased was a member may take part in the funeral service with the consent of the immediate family of the deceased.

When the ritual is military or semi-military, the rites begin immediately upon the conclusion of the military religious service. If the ritual contains the firing of three volleys and the sounding of "Taps," the military firing bugler are used at the appropriate time.

SPECIAL MILITARY FUNERAL

A special military funeral is held for the following dignitaries:

- Deputy Secretary of Defense.
- Former Secretary of Defense.
- Secretaries of the Army, Navy, and Air Force.
- Chairman, Joint Chiefs of Staff.
- Five-Star Generals and Admirals.
- Chief of Staff, U.S. Army.
- Chief of Staff, U.S. Air Force.
- Chief of Naval Operations.
- Commandant, U.S. Marine Corps.
- Commandant, U.S. Coast Guard.
- Other personages specifically designated by the Secretary of Defense.
- Foreign military personnel when designated by the President.

In each service, the commanding officer of the military or naval command or district in which the death occurs is the designated representative of the Secretary of Defense to make the necessary arrangements for the special funeral plan.

For example, the Commandant, Potomac River Naval Command would be the representative of the Secretary of Defense to make arrangements for the special funeral or a naval personage in hiis Command. Upon the request of the Commandant, the Chief of Naval Personnel would handle the following details:

1. Issue invitations and pertinent information to invited guests.

2. Include with the invitations appropriate parking stickers for automobiles, and seating tickets for the Amphitheater when interment is to be in Arlington National Cemetery.

3. Appoint and notify an officer for liaison with the family of the deceased.

4. Provide press releases and coverage.

5. Notify persons selected as escort commander, honorary pallbearers, and special honor guard (for arrival ceremony).

Upon request, the Commandant, U.S. Marine Corps or the Commandant of the U.S. Coast Guard will perform these functions for deceased personnel of their Services.

When the death of a dignitary occurs in Washington, D.C., the remains will be moved to a selected place of repose where it will be attended by a Guard of Honor composed of members of all the Armed Services. When death occurs outside the immediate area, the remains will be transported to Washington for final honors. The remains will be met at the point of arrival —MATS Terminal, Washington National Airport; Union Station; Andrews Air Force Base, etc.—by a reception party and escorted to the place of repose.

After three days of repose, the remains will then be escorted from the place of repose to the Amphitheater, Washington Cathedral, or church where the funeral service will be held.

When burial is to be outside of Washington, the remains will be escorted from the Capitol to the point of departure where honors will be accorded.

BOXING THE FLAG

The flag that covers the casket symbolizes the service of the deceased in the Armed Forces of the United States. The three volleys that are fired, according to ancient belief, are to scare away evil spirits. The playing of "Taps" over over the grave marks the beginning of the last sleep and expresses confidence in an ultimate reveille to come.

The flag is folded immediately after the sounding of "Taps." The body bearers hold the flag at the pall over the grave and fold the flag in the accustomed manner. The senior body bearer will hand it to the chaplain or the officer in charge, who in turn will present it to the next of kin or a representative of the family.

DUTIES OF PALLBEARERS

Active pallbearers, called body bearers, are six to eight men who carry the casket whenever necessary. At a military funeral, they are service personnel appointed by the command.

Honorary pallbearers are persons who have no duties to perform other than rendering appropriate honors to the deceased. They may be few, or more, in number, but never more than twelve. They are appointed by the family of the deceased, usually from among the close friends or honored acquaintances of the deceased, or at the request of the family, they may be appointed by the commanding officer

The officer in charge of the funeral arrangements will give detailed information to the active and honorary pallbearers in advance of the funeral, including the uniform to be worn, mourning sleeve bands, etc.

CHECK-OFF LIST

The officer in charge of a military funeral must have specific information in order to carry out the arrangements. To ensure accurate information, a check-off list should include the following:

1. *General Information*
   a. The name, grade, and serial number of the deceased.
   b. Religious faith.
   c. Name and address of funeral director.
   d. Name and address of next of kin.

2. *Personnel*
   a. Chaplain of appropriate faith; name, grade, and serial number.
   b. Appropriate escort.
   c. Band, color guard (4 men), body bearers (6 or 8), honorary pallbearers (usually 6 to 10), firing squad (8), bugler.

3. *Equipment*
   a. Aerial escort.
   b. Caisson.
   c. Blank cartridges for funeral volleys.
   d. Interment flag for civilian funeral director.

4. *Next of Kin*
   a. What type of service is desired: time, date, location.
   b. The name, rank, serial number, address of service chaplain, or the name and address of civilian clergyman.

    c. Type of funeral procession, if desired.

    d. Honorary pallbearers, selected by family or command; their names, addresses, telephone numbers.

    e. The type of graveside ceremony: with volleys? "Taps?"

    f. Ceremonies by fraternal or patriotic organizations.

    g. Approximate number of relatives and friends attending services.

    h. Music: any particular compositions?

5. *Civilian Funeral Director*

    a. Name and location of cemetery, exact location of grave site.

    b. Time and date of interment services.

    c. Will he transport flowers from chapel to grave? Collect cards from flowers to be given to next of kin?

6. *Miscellaneous*

    a. Determine routes of march, positions, etc.

    b. Arrange for traffic control.

    c. Make certain equipment is ready at the right time and place.

    d. Ensure that each person taking part in the funeral ceremony knows his duties.

MISCELLANEOUS RULES

1. The casket is always carried foot first, except that of a clergyman which is carried head first.

2. When the flag is draped over the casket, the blue field is over the left shoulder of the deceased.

3. The cap and sword of the deceased are never displayed on the flag-draped casket, but may be placed under it.

4. The bearer of the personal flag of a deceased general or flag officer will march in front of the hearse or caisson.

5. Mourning Flag: The colors are hoisted to the peak of the flagpole or staff, and then they are lowered halfway. When the flag is removed, it is again raised to the peak before being lowered. Where flags cannot be flown at half-staff, they should have a black streamer from the spearhead halfway down the flag. Flags hung horizontally or perpendicularly should bear a black bunting border of appropriate width.

6. The National Ensign is never dipped at a funeral, but a unit or battalion flag is dipped when appropriate.

7. The word "pall" denotes the flag held at the waist level, stretched taut, and kept even at all points while being held.

8. Military funerals are rarely postponed on account of bad weather.

9. The distinction between grave site and graveside is: grave site is the section of the cemetery where the funeral will take place; graveside is the lot in which the burial takes place.

10. At a military funeral, service personnel wear the prescribed uniform with mourning sleeve bands. At a non-military funeral, men wear dark business suits; mourning bands are no longer customary.

11. A chaplain at a military post or base is never given a fee for his services, but a note of appreciation for his help should be written by a member of the family.

12. A fee of ten dollars, or more, is given to a civilian clergyman. The fee may be enclosed in a letter of appreciation or the fee may be included in the bill of the funeral director.

Official Order of Precedence

U.S. ARMY

1. Medal of Honor
2. Dist. Serv. Cross— Army
3. Navy Cross
4. Air Force Cross
5. Dist. Serv. Medal— Army
6. Dist. Serv. Medal— Navy
7. Dist. Serv. Medal—AF
8. Silver Star
9. Legion of Merit
10. Dist. Flying Cross
11. Soldiers Medal
12. Navy-USMC Medal
13. Airman's Medal
14. Bronze Star
15. Air Medal
17. Joint Serv. Comm.
18. Army Comm.
19. Navy Comm.
20. AF Comm.
23. Purple Heart

30. Gold Life Saving
31. Silver Life Saving
33. Army Good Conduct
34. AF Good Conduct
35. Navy Good Conduct
36. Marine Good Conduct
37. USCG Good Conduct
43. WW-I Victory
44. WW-I Occup.
47. American Def.
48. W.A.C.
49. American Camp.
50. Asiatic-Pac. Camp.
51. Euro.-Afr.-Mid. East. Camp.
52. WW-II Vict.
53. WW-II Occup.
54. China Service
55. Humane Action
56. National Def.
57. Korean Service
58. Antarctica Service
59. Armed Forces Exped.

60. Vietnam Service
62. Armed Forces Res.
67. Phil. Defense
68. Phil. Liberation
69. Phil. Independence
73. United Nations
74. U. N. Medal (Observer)
81. Rep. of Vietnam Campaign

------

24. Pres. Unit Cit.
25. Navy Pres. Unit Cit.
26. Valorous Unit Award
27. Meritorious Unit Cit.
29. Navy Unit Comm.
28. AF Outstanding Unit Award
70. Phil. Pres. Unit Cit.
71. Rep. of Korea Pres. Unit Cit.
72. Vietnam Pres. Unit Cit.

NOTE (A)—All Unit Citations (24, 25, 26, 27, 28, 29, 70, 71, 72) will be worn above the pocket on the right breast.
NOTE (B)—WW-II Area Campaign Ribbons (49, 50, 51) will be worn in order earned.
NOTE (C)—Foreign decorations will precede United Nations Ribbon.
NOTE (D)—Rep. of Vietnam Campaign (81) follows all other Ribbons.

AS PER AR 672-5-1, (CHANGES 1 THROUGH 14)

U.S. NAVY-MARINE CORPS AND COAST GUARD

1. Medal of Honor
3. Navy Cross
2. Dist. Serv. Cross— Army
4. Air Force Cross
6. Dist. Serv. Medal— Navy
5. Dist. Serv. Medal— Army

7. Dist. Serv. Medal—AF
8. Silver Star
9. Legion of Merit
10. Dist. Flying Cross
12. Navy USMC Medal
11. Soldiers Medal
13. Airman's Medal
14. Bronze Star
15. Air Medal

17. Joint Serv. Comm.
19. Navy Comm.
21. USCG Comm.
18. Army Comm.
20. AF Comm.
22. Sec. Navy Comm. for Achievement
23. Purple Heart
25. Navy Pres. Unit Cit.

416

29. Navy Unit Comm.
24. Pres. Unit Cit.
28. AF Outstanding Unit Award
30. Gold Life Saving
31. Silver Life Saving
32. Reserve Spec. Comm.
35. Navy Good Conduct
36. Marine Good Conduct
37. USCG Good Conduct
33. Army Good Conduct
34. AF Good Conduct
38. Naval Res. Medal
39. Naval Res. Meritorious
40. Organized USMC Res.
41. Navy Exped.
42. Marine Exped.
43. WW-I Vict.
45. 2nd Nicaraguan

46. Yangtze Service
54. China Service (1937-39)
47. American Def.
49. American Camp.
51. Euro-Afr-Mid. East. Camp.
50. Asiatic-Pac. Camp.
52. WW-II Victory
55. Humane Action
53. WW-II Occup.
54. China Service (1945-57)
56. National Def.
57. Korean Service
58. Antarctica Service
59. Armed Forces Exped.
60. Vietnam Service
62. Armed Forces Res.
66. USMC Reserve
73. United Nations

74. U.N. Medal (Observer)
67. Phil. Defense
68. Phil. Liberation
69. Phil. Independence
70. Phil. Pres. Unit Cit.
71. Rep. of Korea Pres. Unit Cit.
72. Vietnam Pres. Unit Cit.
75. Navy Dist. Marksman
76. Navy Dist. Pistol Shot
77. Navy Expert Rifleman
78. Navy Expert Pistol Shot
79. USCG Expert Rifleman
80. USCG Expert Pistol Shot
81. Rep. of Vietnam Campaign

NOTE (A)—WW-II Area Campaign Ribbons (49, 50, 51) will be worn in order earned.
NOTE (B)—Armed Forces Expd. (59) and Vietnam Service (60) will be worn in order earned.
NOTE (C)—Foreign Decorations precede United Nations Ribbon (No. 73).
NOTE (D)—Frames authorized on Unit Citations will be Regulation Navy Size.
NOTE (E)—Rep. of Vietnam Campaign (81) will follow all other Ribbons.

AS PER NAVY UNIFORM REGULATIONS 1959, CHANGE No. 3

U.S. AIR FORCE

1. Medal of Honor
4. Air Force Cross
2. Dist. Serv. Cross— Army
3. Navy Cross
7. Dist. Serv. Medal—AF
5. Dist. Serv. Medal— Army
6. Dist. Serv. Medal— Navy
8. Silver Star
9. Legion of Merit
10. Dist. Flying Cross
13. Airman's Medal
11. Soldiers Medal
12. Navy USMC Medal
14. Bronze Star
15. Air Medal
*16. AF Combat Readiness
17. Joint Serv. Comm.
20. AF Comm.
18. Army Comm.
19. Navy Comm.

23. Purple Heart
24. Pres. Unit Cit.
25. Navy Pres. Unit Cit.
28. AF Outstanding Unit Award
29. Navy Unit Comm.
34. AF Good Conduct
33. Army Good Conduct
35. Navy Good Conduct
36. Marine Good Conduct
37. USCG Good Conduct
47. American Def.
48. W.A.C.
49. American Camp.
50. Asiatic-Pac. Camp.
51. Euro-Afr-Mid. East. Camp.
52. WW-II Vict.
53. WW-II Occup.
55. Humane Action
56. National Def.
57. Korean Service
58. Antarctica Service

59. Armed Forces Exped.
60. Vietnam Service
61. AF Longevity
62. Armed Forces Res.
63. Air Reserve Forces Meritorious Serv.
64. AF NCO Academy Graduate
65. AF Small Arms Expert Marksmanship
67. Phil. Defense
68. Phil. Liberation
69. Phil. Independence
70. Phil. Pres. Unit Cit.
71. Rep. of Korea Pres. Unit Cit.
72. Vietnam Pres. Unit Cit.
73. United Nations
74. U.N. Medal (Observer)
81. Rep. of Vietnam Campaign

NOTE (A)—WW-II Area Campaign Ribbons (49, 50, 51) will be worn in order earned.
NOTE (B)—Antarctica Service (58), Armed Forces Expeditionary (59), Vietnam Service (60), National Defense (56) (earned after 1 January 1961) to be worn in order earned.
NOTE (C)—Foreign Decorations precede Philippine Pres. Unit Citation (70).
NOTE (D)—Frames on AF Unit Citations will be Regulation AF size.
NOTE (E)—Rep. of Vietnam Campaign will follow all other Ribbons.
* As of 21 Sept. 67 Combat Readiness is worn preceding Good Conduct Med.

BIBLIOGRAPHY

BOOKS

Ageton, Arthur A., with William P. Mack. *The Naval Officer's Guide.* Annapolis: U. S. Naval Institute, seventh edition, 1967.

Air Officer's Guide: 1968–1969. Harrisburg: Stackpole Books.

Banning, Kendall. *Annapolis Today.* Revised by A. Stuart Pitt. Annapolis: U. S. Naval Institute, sixth edition, 1963.

Compere, Tom, and Vogel, William P., Jr. (ed). *The Air Force Blue Book.* New York: The Bobbs-Merrill Company, Inc., 1959.

——. *The Army Blue Book.* New York: The Bobbs-Merrill Company, Inc., 1960.

——. *The Navy Blue Book.* New York: The Bobbs-Merrill Company, Inc., 1960.

Land, Elizabeth, and Glines, Carroll V., Jr. *Complete Guide for the Serviceman's Wife.* Boston: Houghton Mifflin Co., 1956.

Lovette, Leland P. *Naval Customs, Traditions, and Usage.* Annapolis: U. S. Naval Institute, fourth edition, 1959.

Post, Emily. *Emily Post Book of Etiquette for Young People.* New York: Funk & Wagnalls Co., 1967.

Pye, Anne Briscoe, and Shea, Nancy, *The Navy Wife.* New York: Harper and Row, 1966.

Radlovic, I. Monte. *Etiquette and Protocol.* New York: Harcourt, Brace and World, Inc., 1956.

Robert, Henry M. *Robert's Rules of Order Revised.* Chicago: Scott, Foresman & Co., 1956.

Shea, Nancy. *The Air Force Wife*. New York: Harper and Row, second edition, 1966.

——. *The Army Wife*. New York: Harper and Row, 1954.

Thomas, G. C., Heinl, R. D., Jr. and Ageton, A. A. *The Marine Officer's Guide*. Annapolis: U. S. Naval Institute, third edition, 1967.

Vanderbilt, Amy. *Amy Vanderbilt's New Complete Book of Etiquette*. Garden City: Doubleday & Co., Inc., 1963.

SERVICE ACADEMY PUBLICATIONS

Bugle Notes, A Handbook for the Cadets. Department of Tactics, U. S. Military Academy.

Cadetiquette. Department of Tactics, U. S. Military Academy.

Contrails, A Handbook for the Cadets. Air Force Cadet Wing, U. S. Air Force Academy.

Reef Points, The Handbook of the Brigade of Midshipmen. U. S. Naval Academy.

The Running Light, A Handbook for the Corps of Cadets. U. S. Coast Guard Academy.

PERIODICAL

Air Force and Space Digest. Air Force Association, Washington, D.C.

OFFICIAL PUBLICATIONS

Army, Department of the. *The Army Personal Affairs Handbook* (DA Pamphlet 608-2). Washington, 1966.

——. *Drills and Ceremonies* (Field Manual, FM 22-5), 1968.

Navy, Department of the. Office of Chief of Naval Operations. *Landing Party Manual*. Washington: Government Printing Office, 1962.

——. Bureau of Naval Personnel. *Naval Funerals at Arlington National Cemetery* (NavPers 15956). Washington: Navy Supply System, 1966.

——. Bureau of Naval Personnel. *Naval Orientation* (NavPers 16138-E). Washington: Government Printing Office, 1969.

Bureau of Naval Personnel. *The Wardroom* (NavPers 1002). Washington: Government Printing Office, 1963.

Tarrant, Ruth Gibson (comp.). *Social Usage and Protocol*. Foreign Liaison Section, Office of Naval Intelligence. Washington: Navy Supply System, 1958.

INDEX

The text of this book is composed by the George Banta Company,
Menasha, Wisconsin in ten point Monophoto
Times Roman with two points of leading. The titles are
Eusebius display

The book is printed offset on fifty-pound Hammermill Loch Haven offset.
It is bound in Columbia Fictionette.

The book was printed, and bound by
The Maple Press Company, York, Pa.